FERMENTED VEGETABLES

Fermented Vegetables

10th ANNIVERSARY EDITION

CREATIVE RECIPES FOR FERMENTING
72 VEGETABLES, FRUITS & HERBS IN
Brined Pickles, Chutneys, Kimchis,
Krauts, Pastes & Relishes

KIRSTEN K. SHOCKEY &
CHRISTOPHER SHOCKEY

 Storey Publishing

The mission of Storey Publishing is to serve our customers by
publishing practical information that encourages
personal independence in harmony with the environment.

EDITED BY Carleen Madigan and Sarah Guare
Slattery
ART DIRECTION AND BOOK DESIGN BY
Alethea Morrison and Ian O'Neill
TEXT PRODUCTION BY Jennifer Jepson Smith

COVER PHOTOGRAPHY BY © Erin Kunkel,
except for © Carmen Troesser, back, author
INTERIOR PHOTOGRAPHY BY © Erin Kunkel
ADDITIONAL PHOTOGRAPHY BY © Dina Avila,
82–84, 88–89, 97, 110, 188–189, 244–245, 262–
263, 352–353 and © Kirsten K. Shockey, 417, 418
ILLUSTRATIONS BY © Daniel Everett
HAND LETTERING BY Alethea Morrison

Be sure to read all of the instructions
thoroughly before undertaking any of the
techniques or recipes in this book and follow
all of the recommended safety guidelines.

Storey books may be purchased in bulk for business,
educational, or promotional use. Special editions or
book excerpts can also be created to specification.
For details, please contact your local bookseller
or the Hachette Book Group Special Markets
Department at special.markets@hbgusa.com.

Storey Publishing
210 MASS MoCA Way
North Adams, MA 01247
storey.com

Storey Publishing is an imprint of Workman
Publishing, a division of Hachette Book Group, Inc.,
1290 Avenue of the Americas, New York, NY 10104.
The Storey Publishing name and logo are registered
trademarks of Hachette Book Group, Inc.

ISBNs: 978-1-63586-539-4 (paperback);
978-1-63586-540-0 (ebook)

Printed in the United States by Versa Press on
paper from responsible sources
10 9 8 7 6 5 4 3 2

Library of Congress Cataloging-in-Publication Data
on file

"Here, try this," we'd say as we thrust some new creation at our sometimes skeptical children on the other side of the fork. Taste testing became habit for them, just something they did in our house with two fermentistas on the loose. Now and then they'd ask, hopefully, if we were ready to move on to become bakers or chocolatiers. Still, they were always willing to give us their honest assessment and support.

Thank you, Jakob, Kelton, Dmitri, and Ariana.

Love, Mom & Pop

Contents

PART 3

In the Crock

FERMENTING FROM A TO Z

— 132 —

PART 4

On the Plate

INCORPORATING FERMENTED FOODS
INTO YOUR DAILY MEALS

— 352 —

Why We Still Ferment

Every artist was first an amateur.

— RALPH WALDO EMERSON

WE BEGAN WORK ON THE FIRST EDITION OF THIS BOOK in 2011, perhaps one of the last years in which fermented food had not yet attained its now-perennial spot on the top-10 food lists. That year was all about the superpowers of kale and green smoothies, gluten-free every-thing, and the newfound habit of taking pictures of your food to post before eating. Our small fermentation company was taking up every free minute of our lives. We needed a change. We shifted from being producers to educators, with no idea how our book would indeed make that change happen for us.

This second edition represents what we have learned from teaching fermentation in the near-decade since the first edition became a bestseller. We've taught multiday intensives on our farm and led workshops from Barcelona to Santiago. We've done staff training in cramped restaurant kitchens and at outdoor fermentation festivals, and consulted with farmers and new fermentation companies.

We've also written four more books on fermentation. When the COVID-19 pandemic hit, everything changed. Suddenly there were no festivals, no workshops, no restaurants, and no book tours. But by then, we were part of a tight community of fermentation educators, and we were all facing the same challenges. So we did what so many people had to do: We pivoted. We cofounded The Fermentation School, an online school where dozens of fellow fermentation educators around the globe work cooperatively to teach a wide range of fermentation arts to the world. The journey continues as the concentric circles get larger.

We are bringing all that experience to this new edition. We know a lot more about fermentation than we did a decade ago. You probably do, too. Where you are in your fermentation journey has a lot to do with what you can get out of this book. We invite you to think about what fermentation means to you. Or don't—we don't have any hard-and-fast rules around here. Fermentation is what you make of it. Our goal is that you understand the science (or magic, if you prefer) of it so you can do whatever you want with it. And we'd also love to see a fermenting jar in every kitchen!

Health

Fermented foods are good for us for numerous reasons. First, they're filled with "good" bacteria—microbes that predigest the food we eat (so it delivers more nutrients to our bodies) and outcompete "bad" bacteria (the kind that can make us sick or unwell) in our digestive systems. They help us maintain balanced, healthy microbial diversity in our gut, which means that our digestion works better and we are less susceptible to chronic diseases. These good bacteria also produce vitamins that we need to stay healthy, including most of the B vitamins and vitamin K.

Finally, growing research confirms the strong connection between the health of our gut and our mood and food cravings. Having a balanced microbiome, it turns out, is a key contributor to maintaining balance in our feelings and behaviors.

Yes, you can get a good dose of good bacteria in the form of probiotic pills, but if you want to build and maintain that healthy mix in your microbiome, you'll need to manage the right prebiotics, probiotics, and postbiotics. That's a lot of pills and management. Meanwhile, research has shown that when we eat fermented foods, the probiotic microbes in those foods often survive in our digestive tract all the way to our colon, where they do the most good, and they do so better than the probiotic strains taken by themselves, as in a pill form.[1] In other words, a regimen of probiotic pills will be less effective than just eating good, fermented foods we make ourselves. The probiotics are happier that way, and so are we.

Flavor

You're human—often, knowing that something is good for you won't be enough to convince you to eat it. Incorporating fermented foods into your diet is, we believe, all about taste. Fermentation unlocks new, complex, deep flavors. Each batch offers a unique terroir—a taste experience that comes from time and place. You'll come to eat fermented vegetables because you want to, because you enjoy (or crave) them, not because you should. They offer flavors that if not your parents then certainly your grandparents or great-grandparents knew well. This is the way food used to taste—and trust us, it's *amazing*. When you practice at-home fermentation, you will learn how to create these flavors for yourself and your family.

Convenience

Fermentation makes life easier. Hard stop. Fermented foods are one of humankind's first processed convenience foods. Our society (or at least the food industry) would lead us to believe that we don't have the time to prepare food from scratch at home. We know, purchasing a jar of unpasteurized sauerkraut is easy, and we aren't saying that finding some time to chop a cabbage can't be challenging. You may have already started purchasing kraut or kimchi, or you may be just about ready to do so. That is a fantastic place to start. However, we also have learned that it doesn't take as long to prepare a quart or so of fermented vegetables as you might think. Once you chop or shred, salt, and stuff the veggies in a jar, you're done. The microbes do the work of processing your food in a way that makes it more nutritious and fairly shelf stable.

When you make your own, you can choose the vegetables and flavors you like best, and you control the time and salt. In a few hours on a weekend, you can prepare a variety of different flavored jars of live-preserved food that will keep in your fridge for a while, offering up freshness when your fridge feels bare. We like to think of it as having an instant flavor pantry ready to add freshness and nutrition to any quick and easy meal. (You'll meet Soirée-Leone on page 22 for a wonderful example of this in practice.)

Community

We are social creatures. We like to find others who share our interests, who lean in to enjoy the aromas of our latest batch, who want to know how we made it and want to try our creations. We are here to tell you there are a lot of us out here in the world who share your interest or passion for this process and these foods. You will meet some of them in this book.

Environment

Fermentation connects us to our community, local food systems, and the planet we live on. Our food systems play a big role in the environment due to at least three factors: transportation, pesticides, and food waste.

Eating closer to home reduces the carbon needed to get food from field to table. We have all learned to enjoy the ability to buy anything at any time of the year. But much of the food you'll find in grocery stores was harvested, processed, and shipped to your market from regions far distant—sometimes even when an abundant supply of that food grows in your own region. The ability to preserve local food is a big benefit of fermentation, allowing you to enjoy local asparagus in the fall or basil leaves midwinter. Even better, the preserved versions of many types of produce are often more flavorful and healthier than the raw versions.

Preserving your own local food also allows you to maintain quality control and to avoid the pesticide residues found on most nonorganic produce. Organophosphate pesticide residues are a worldwide public health concern, not only for their effects upon our health but also due to their pollution of soil and water systems. Even better, lactic acid bacteria, responsible for the fermentations described in this book, have been shown to degrade pesticides that were present on vegetables before fermentation.[2]

One more plug for the environment: A whole lot of good food is wasted every day—globally, about one-third of food doesn't ever make it to the table. Fermentation is one answer to reducing the food waste in our homes, schools, and restaurants. Small steps, taken by many, lead to big changes for the environment.

Fun

Fermenting is fun. Each batch is a little science experiment that you get to eat. Like a potted plant or garden bed, ferments require some basic care and tending, but appreciate extra love. They do their own thing and you get to be part of it. You nurture them, maybe you talk to them, certainly you watch them change over time, and then you eat them.

In a way, fermentation carries so much potential for transformatively healthful and pleasurable eating that it can feel overwhelming. And it can all start with one vegetable, one recipe, and one jar.

About This Book

In part 1, Dipping into the Brine: Fermentation Fundamentals, you'll learn the scientific nuts and bolts of fermentation. You'll read about what happens during fermentation and how transformation changes the food for good—be it for preservation, flavor, or health. You'll also learn about equipment and salt, which is the only ingredient you'll need other than vegetables.

Part 2, Mastering the Basics: Kraut, Condiments, Tsukemono, Pickles, and Kimchi is a thorough tutorial on the ins and outs of fermentation techniques. We'll guide you through the processes from the traditional—mastering sauerkraut, brine pickling, kimchi, and tsukemono—to more contemporary condiments. This section also provides a troubleshooting guide.

In part 3, In the Crock: Fermenting from A to Z, you'll learn how to ferment a vast range of vegetables, fruits, and herbs. Along with recipes, we'll share suggestions and tips. Throughout, we'll offer ideas to inspire your own creations and to let you in on our sometimes humbling experiences in the kitchen.

Part 4, On the Plate: Incorporating Fermented Foods into Your Daily Meals, gets us to the good stuff: eating. We had fun coming up with these recipes, sometimes just to hear our kids say, often woefully, "You're not going to put a ferment in that, are you?" We aim to rock sauerkraut's rap as a hot dog food and to introduce new flavor profiles that will delight you and your family.

Throughout the book, you'll find stories and recipes highlighting people in the fermentation community who bring this artisanal food to tables across the country.

Whether you're new to fermenting or a lifelong devotee, this book has something for everyone. Let's get started.

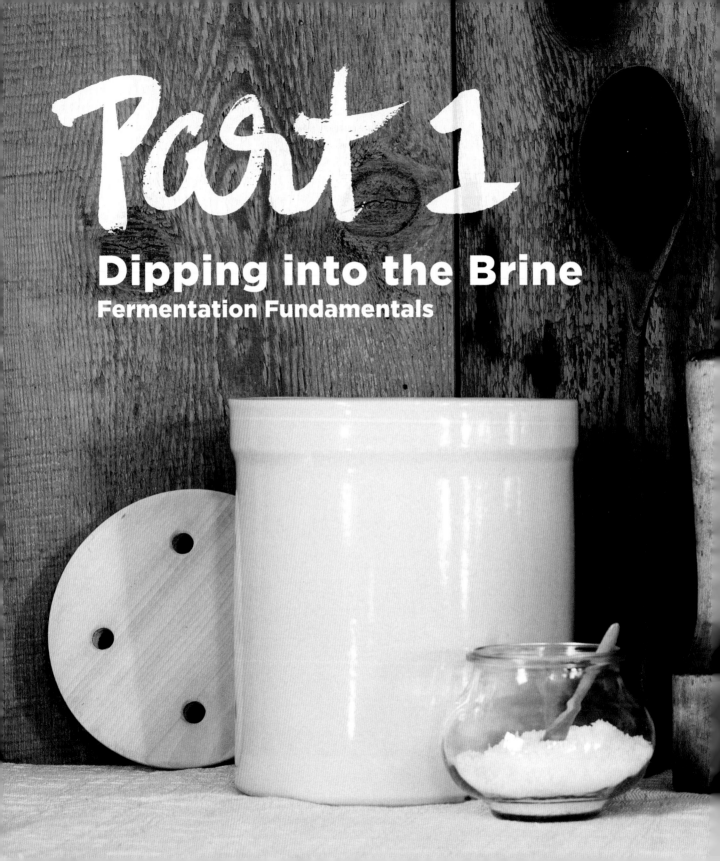

Part 1

Dipping into the Brine
Fermentation Fundamentals

MICROBES ARE EVERYWHERE, from the highest mountaintop to the deepest ocean floor. They are also on and in every living being. Many of the microbes on the food we eat are the same type that live within our digestive systems, where they pull nutrients from the food we eat, thereby making them available to us their host. It doesn't get much more symbiotic than that.

We haven't understood the details of this relationship for most of humanity's time on the planet. Our distant ancestors simply noticed that ripe fruit sometimes became alcoholic, and when given a little more time, it lost its alcoholic punch and became sour. They learned that when they chopped vegetables and herbs, mixed them with salt, and stored them in containers, that mixture also became sour, and it preserved the vegetables and stretched the valuable salt. They found that milk stored in bladders curdled into something tasty. Without the tools to see microbes or the techniques to experiment and isolate, they simply passed down their knowledge, changing the ingredients, processes, and storage methods to match their climate and culture. They knew these fermented foods were essential to their survival. Microbial culture is more or less the same throughout the world. Lactic acid bacteria is doing the same thing with Korean radishes as it is with one's local pickling cucumbers—or whatever else a human has chosen to put in their vessel. Using microbes doesn't require special equipment, just a little knowledge and care. Any vegetable—no matter the quality—becomes incredibly rich and healthy thanks to the work of microbes.

There's a saying, sometimes attributed to Picasso: "Good artists copy; great artists steal." But that concept isn't always interpreted in the best way, we believe. Our human culture is more complicated. Recipes and techniques have been passed down by grandmothers or aunties, traded by travelers, and handed along with meals shared since the beginning of time. This is how we humans connect. It is how food moves and evolves. We believe in respect and acknowledgment. We believe in naming our teachers, whether that is an individual or a whole cuisine that has inspired us. Reading someone's recipe, then making it yourself, then changing it to suit your own taste is how we all cook. Indeed, we hope you take our ideas and recipes and make them your own—our joy is seeing you inspired. Share your creations with the world; you should be proud. We hope you then also appreciate and acknowledge those cultures or humans whose work led you to your creation. When we do this, we build upon others' work positively and supportively, just as we might while sitting around a table, sharing a meal and finding understanding.

The field of fermentation is undergoing a tremendous amount of experimentation and innovation right now—new ingredients, new techniques, new storage methods, and new ways to eat these foods. Fermentation is simple, yet it is powerful in its ability to heal and to help us take control of diet, our participation in our food systems, and the flavors we bring to the table. It is a bold first step. It's time to take that step together.

CHAPTER 1

Back to the Future

VEGETABLE FERMENTATION AS PRESERVATION

Fermenting vegetables is a simple, inexpensive process that's been used reliably to preserve food for a few thousand years. Then, in the early 1900s, technical innovations promised things fermentation just couldn't deliver. Canned jars of food remain stable on a shelf for years. Blanch your veggies, toss them into a bag, and store in the freezer—what could be easier? No heavy crocks to clean, no time spent monitoring and skimming; it was all very modern and clean and safe.

Only in more recent years has science begun to understand what all that sterilizing and freezing did to the vitamins, minerals, and microbes that make vegetables good for us—not to mention the flavor. As that pendulum swings, conversations now also consider the energy required to sustain processing and preservation techniques. From the moment food leaves the field, it is sucking energy. It takes energy to package and transport food to its next stop and then to keep it edible, whether that is through refrigeration, pasteurization, canning, freezing, or other methods.

When we bring produce home, we hope to keep it long enough to enjoy it, but that doesn't always happen. Food waste takes up 22 percent of the space in America's landfills—more space than any other category of waste—fruits and vegetables are the most likely to be thrown out. Once in the landfill, the tossed food degrades and releases methane—a significant contributor to global warming.

Enter fermentation, or, to be accurate, reenter fermentation. Lactic acid fermentation is an ideal way to preserve the bounty while retaining nutrients and deepening the flavor profile. It's also a strategy for saving money and seasonal eating. Fermentation "recipes" don't always have to be complex or ingredient driven. Sometimes you just need a quick way to preserve produce so it won't go bad and have to be tossed. Just ferment it! Later, you'll be glad you did.

Sauerkraut belongs in a barrel, not a can.
Our American mania for sterile packaging
has removed the flavor from most of our foods.
Butter is no longer sold out of a wooden tub, and
a whole generation thinks butter tastes like paper.
There was never a perfume like an old-time gro-
cery store. Now they smell like drugstores, which
don't even smell like drugstores anymore.
—CARY GRANT AS DR. NOAH PRAETORIUS,
IN *PEOPLE WILL TALK* (1951)

Soirée-Leone: Advocating for Multiple Voices

Soirée-Leone is a writer, an educator, a home-steader, and a preservation queen whose larder—stocked with home-canned foods, crocks, jugs, bottles, and cheeses—is located in an agricultural region of Tennessee just south of Nashville.

Gateway to Preservation

A self-described equal-opportunity preserver—fermentation is only one method she uses—Soirée began her journey in preservation in the 1990s when she joined an intentional community that kept milk goats. She learned cheesemaking, which became her gateway into preservation and value-added processing. Soirée found that her cheese was a valuable asset in the barter economy. This led her to bread making and canning, and she soon realized that she could make the same things she would normally buy at a store, just better and cheaper.

A Dedicated Advocate

A passionate community advocate for food accessibility, Soirée sells baked goods at her local farmers' market, working on a scale that makes sense for a home producer within a local foodshed. She views preservation as an opportunity for reframing food and diet while more deeply exploring family connections and foodways. "You don't see many Black voices in food preservation at the national level," she says, adding that she wants to see vibrant conversations that include multiple voices. It's important to have these conversations across all regions, she believes, so that preservation and fermentation become familiar and frequently used techniques, instead of being seen as alternative, hippie, white, or affluent. The context needs to be about putting food on tables everywhere. As an educator, Soirée helps people put strategies in place to maximize their food dollars and to get the most out of what they buy.

Soirée begins to mitigate food waste as soon as she walks into the kitchen from the market, the garden, or a gleaning run. Instead of stuffing everything in the fridge, she begins to process all the fresh items, from making broths or jams to fermenting. She chops ingredients to ferment into a jar or two of what she calls "instant soup" (borscht is a favorite) that will be ready to go when she needs to get a meal on the table fast. "I am incapable of remembering to defrost in advance," she says. These fermented soups are simply poured in the pot and cooked in their brine until the vegetables are tender.

You will find Soirée's recipe for sour corn on page 212.

Soirée-Leone views preservation as an opportunity for reframing food and diet while more deeply exploring family connections and foodways.

Preserving the Harvest

You'll probably consume many batches of your fermented vegetables within a few days or weeks of making them—you won't be able to help yourself—but fermentation is a nutrition-enhancing, long-term preservation method. If you're serious about preserving the harvest from your garden or farmers' market, you might consider a ferment refrigerator, which is simply an old refrigerator tucked in an out-of-the-way corner to be filled with finished ferments. This isn't unprecedented: Modern Koreans, who traditionally buried their *onggi* pots (earthenware fermentation crocks) in soil or under straw for preservation, consider their kimchi refrigerator a basic household appliance. It will allow you to keep your ferments alive, catch flavors just where you like them, and effectively keep them there.

While refrigeration is new, fermentation for preservation is not. Although it's nice to have one, you don't need a separate refrigerator for your ferments. Most will keep well at cooler room temperatures. See Chapter 9 for details.

Ferments can be frozen, but the textural results will vary depending on the vegetables or fruits used. Most of the probiotic bacteria won't survive freezing, as their cell walls expand to the point of rupture.

Ferments can be canned, too, and we will briefly talk about that process (see page 127).

One woman told us that when she was a child in Wisconsin, her grandmother would sometimes give her a bowl and send her down the stairs, through a dark cellar, to get a portion of sauerkraut. She remembered removing the lid of the sauerkraut barrel and then carefully folding back a thick mat of mold. She'd fill the bowl, pat down the remaining kraut, carefully replace the mold mat, and cover with the lid. This mold mat sounds awful, right? But it kept the kraut anaerobic—that is, alive without oxygen—and therefore safe to eat.

Christopher Writes

The questions started coming at our first farmers' market. "So are you guys sauerkraut makers?" people asked. The question stumped us. Technically yes, but we also made kimchi. Later we added a line of crackers made from brine and began serving assorted brines in shot glasses; at that point we were makers of sauerkraut, kimchi, and crackers, as well as bartenders of the brine.

"Traditional food preservationist" sounded like someone who would work in a museum. I've seen "fermentationist," but that's quite a mouthful. A "zymurgologist"? Zymurgy is the branch of chemistry relating to fermentation, and although the word is super cool, it's more appropriate for the brewing arts. "Pickler" is the traditional word for the occupation, but that only confused folks. People assumed this meant we made cucumber pickles, which would mean that for most of the year we were picklers sans pickles.

One frosty day, after we'd set up for the day's market, I headed to Noble Coffee for our morning brew. As Daniel prepared the drinks, he asked what I did. I told him we followed the season, combining the best of the vegetables as they came in from the fields. I rhapsodized about the difference between an early crisp beet and one overwintered and oozing sugars.

"Sounds like a barista to me," he said, handing me two steaming cups.

"You know what we are?" I asked Kirsten when I got back to our stall.

"Hungry?" she guessed, passing me a breakfast burrito.

"Fermentistas," I said proudly.

Preserving Culture

Throughout this book you will hear many voices, a tiny sampling from the millions of people taking part in the traditions of fermentation. In the years since this book first came out, we heard from a lot of you as you rediscovered flavors remembered from childhood—taste memories.

Like so many culinary traditions, fermentation is connected to culture, economics, and the health of ourselves and the environment. At the same time, fermentation is deeply traditional and sacred and always evolving, as it always has and likely always will be.

"Fermentation has always been with and all around us, whether we are aware of it or not. We made these foods for a reason and they are the same basic things in different locations—at its core it is still adding salt to vegetables. The flavors migrate and travel," says Minnie Luong. Minnie owns and operates Chi Kitchen, which produces traditional-style kimchi in Rhode Island. She was drawn to fermentation through her personal history with it. She grew up eating fermented foods, and her father, who was a single dad, inspires her work. She uses family recipes and sources ingredients locally to make her company's Asian slaws and kimchi. "Food is the love language in my family," Minnie shares. Growing vegetables, fishing for squid, and making food was how her family spent time together. Today, Minnie, her father, and the rest of her family give each other ferments as gifts and bring them to family meals, and they have playful competitions to determine the crunchiest, the spiciest, and so on.

Minnie's story is an example of the social benefits attached to fermentation. When we cook with family or friends, from the food preparation to gathering daily at the table, we build bonds. In this way, food keeps us connected, both tangibly and immeasurably.

Consider fermenting vegetables as a group activity. Enlist your family, friends, and guests to chop, slice, grate, salt, massage, pound, and press with you. No experience is necessary, so even the youngest members can participate. As for the I-don't-like-kraut set, they're sure to at least taste a ferment they helped make.

THE PERKS OF FERMENTING VEGETABLES

Fermentation preserves vegetables raw and without heat, so it retains their vitamins, minerals, and enzymes. But did you know it often enhances them? And, as discussed, the organisms that enable fermentation are themselves beneficial. Here's how fermentation helps:

- » Preserves and enhances B and C vitamins
- » Makes nutrients more readily available
- » Aids in digestion
- » Doesn't call for chemical preservatives
- » Supports the immune system

Health and Well-Being

Fermentation does amazing things to raw vegetables. The list of health benefits is truly incredible.

To begin, natural sugars in the vegetables are greatly reduced as the microbes convert them to tangy lactic acid, contributing to the amazing flavors we love. In this process, the vegetables are also broken down at the cell and nutrient level, making more available to our bodies vitamins such as B_9 (folate), B_{12} (cobalamin), and C, and minerals such as iron.[3] Vitamin B_{12} is especially important because it doesn't exist in plants but is produced by the bacterium *Limosilactobacillus reuteri*, both in our colons and in fermented vegetables. Fermentation of vegetables also boosts the amount of antioxidants (molecules that inhibit the oxidation of our cells) they contain.[4] In all these cases and more, we get more from the same vegetable if it is fermented.

Speaking of those microbes, you have by now undoubtedly heard of probiotics—microorganisms that, when consumed, maintain or restore beneficial bacteria in our digestive tracts. Well, fermented foods are their poster child. The microbes that do this fermentation work of consuming sugar, producing lactic acid, and releasing nutrients are the same beneficial microbes that live in our GI tract, doing good work for us from within. So when we eat fermented foods, we eat the good microbes, thereby refreshing their numbers in us, which is crucial for our gut microbiome and therefore our health and well-being.

But that's not the end of the story. There is a third pillar of our microbiome: postbiotics. If probiotics are the beneficial microbes and prebiotics are their food, then postbiotics are the substances the probiotics produce that are beneficial to us. These postbiotics include some very beneficial-to-humans compounds, including short-chain fatty acids, enzymes, peptides, functional proteins, vitamins, and organic acids. Think of sourdough bread. You have a bubbly starter that you allow to ferment. The yeasts and bacteria in the starter process the carbohydrates, producing compounds that remain in the dough. Then you throw that live community into a hot oven and all the microbes die, or become deactivated, to use a nicer term. Those postbiotic compounds are still there in that lovely sourdough slice that you cut off before it's really cooled enough and dip in a nice olive oil. The same goes for your vegetable ferments when they are cooked—their microbial community may be deactivated by the cooking, but they will still provide health benefits thanks to the postbiotics.

Prebiotics are the foods that gut microbes need to eat in order to thrive. They include the plant fibers that our bodies cannot digest, but our resident gut microbe team thrives on. The fermentation process makes these plant fibers easier for us to digest, and when we eat the ferment, some of the plant fibers also enter our gut as prebiotics. It's a beautiful synergy.

A Word about Histamines

Histamine is a chemical that occurs naturally in our bodies as part of our immune response to threats, such as an injury (infection) or allergen. When our immune system is healthy, said threat triggers specialized cells, called mast cells and basophils, to release histamine. Histamine dilates capillaries, helping them to become more permeable, and increases circulation so white blood cells get to where they are needed. This response is designed to help our bodies fight off invaders and to promote healing. Histamine intolerance occurs when our body is unable to break down histamines properly, leading to an excess buildup in our system.

When we eat histamine in our food, an enzyme called diamine oxidase breaks it down.[5] For most people, this process works smoothly and histamines are not a problem, but when things get unbalanced, there can be trouble. This might occur, for instance, if that enzyme isn't working properly, which could result from excessive alcohol intake or as a side effect of a medication. Some people have histamine intolerances that can show up in various symptoms. Or, we could eat too much histamine and overwhelm our body's regulation. In more extreme or acute cases, when a food such as spoiled fish (scombroid poisoning) or wine has produced excessive amounts of histamines, the result is histamine toxication. It might show up as flushing of your face and neck, rashes, swelling, and booming headaches.[6]

To our knowledge, there isn't a reliable test for histamine sensitivity. For most people who have trouble processing histamine, the best course of action is to reduce the amount of high-histamine foods in their diet. There are impressive lists on the internet spanning a wide range of foods, including fermented vegetables.

Our friends lactic acid bacteria (LAB) are responsible for producing histamine and tyramine in fermented foods. In general, plant-based fermented foods contain lower amounts of histamines than animal-based ferments, but the level can vary widely among plant ferments depending upon the following factors:

» The variety of vegetable
» The fermentation conditions (temperature, pH, oxygen levels, amount of salt)
» Whether the fermentation is spontaneous (the kind we recommend in this book) or driven by a commercial starter
» The age of the ferment

In a study of 120 different commercial sauerkrauts, histamine levels varied between 0 and 229 mg per kg of sauerkraut. In another study of 50 commercial pickles, they ranged between 16 and 75 mg per kg. What does this mean? Simply that it is really hard to tell how much histamine is in your ferments. Also, because the level of histamine that triggers symptoms of toxicity varies by person, it means there is no hard-and-fast rule to determine whether a fermented food—or any other food that contains histamines—is generally safe for those suffering from histamine reactions. If you are one of those folks, we recommend talking with your healthcare professional about how you might include fermented vegetables in your diet.

CHAPTER 2

The Inner Life of Pickling

THE SCIENCE BEHIND VEGETABLE FERMENTATION

First and foremost, we want you to have fun with fermentation. We know from teaching thousands of people that it can feel scary and intimidating. But fermenting vegetables is super safe and an easy entry into the art of fermentation. People have been successfully fermenting for thousands of years with very few resources and very little equipment—you got this!

You are working with microbes, so there will be some surprises. Since we wrote the first edition of this book, we received thousands of questions through social media, email, and live events along the lines of "[insert ferment story]—what went wrong?" Sometimes we can help figure it out, and sometimes, who knows? Not enough salt? Too much oxygen? Was it this or that? All told, the real learning takes place in your own practice— in the observations you make, the flavors you taste, and the experiments that excite your curiosity. In short, in trying. You will be met with both success and failure. Sometimes you will forget a particular project and it will thrive. Sometimes you will nurture something every step of the way and it will be a flop. The big takeaway here is that you are working in collaboration with the vegetables and the microbes they bring with them. Fermentation is empowering and humbling. Our goal is to help you build intuition for the process.

There are several slightly different procedures used to produce lacto-fermented vegetables. First is kraut making (also called dry brining, which can seem like a misnomer because it is anything but dry) and a million condiment variations, described in Chapters 4 and 5. Next is brine pickling, covered in Chapter 6, and finally we have variations that combine techniques, such as tsukemono (Chapter 7) and kimchi (Chapter 8). In this chapter, we'll explain how these processes work, what is really going on in your crock, and why it is safe.

Vegetables + Microbes: A Lacto-Fermentation Starter Kit

Let's start with the microbes. The recipes in this book all use the simple process of lacto-fermentation—what many call spontaneous, native, or wild fermentation (not culturing)—to acidify vegetables. Yes, these fermented veggies develop flavor and a healthy population of probiotic goodness—they have culture, for sure. However, semantically speaking, "culturing" implies the addition of a culture, a starter dose of a desired strain of bacteria. Culturing is important in cheesemaking, especially if you are looking to make a specific variety. But in pickling, the microbes you need are right there on the fresh vegetable. In fact, studies show that commercial cultures increase the lactic acid bacteria population in ferments such as sauerkraut for the first few days, but after about 2 weeks, the total good microbe count starts to drop, and by day 80 there are no good microbes left.[1] In contrast, the same sauerkraut made with just the microbes naturally found on the raw produce keeps at least 75 percent of its microbes for months.

All fresh fruits and vegetables, but especially those grown using organic methods, are naturally covered in microorganisms. That is a good thing. These little guys come from plant surfaces, soil, water, and air. Some of them are pathogens. It's not just bacteria, mind you, that are clinging to our future meals. Molds and yeasts are there, too, in larger numbers than the friendly lactic acid bacteria that we want to encourage in our lacto-fermented vegetables. All are held in check while the plant is living. But as soon as it's harvested, it's a race against time because these microorganisms cling to and grow on any spot on the plant that's cut, damaged, or bruised. Rinsing and refrigerating produce retards the growth of microorganisms for a while.

When we bring veggies in from the garden or home from the market, it is our responsibility to

LACTOSE INTOLERANCE AND LACTO-FERMENTATION

"I am lactose intolerant. Can I eat lacto-fermented vegetables?"

The answer is yes. Fermented vegetables contain no lactose or casein. The term *lacto-fermented* is bewildering to people trying to navigate food intolerances. To begin with, the words are similar. But lactose is milk sugar. *Lacto* simply refers to the lactic acid produced by the action of bacteria in the Lactobacillaceae family—the lactic acid bacteria (LAB).

Additional confusion may arise because dairy ferments, such as yogurt and cheese, also rely on the Lactobacillaceae family of bacteria, in this case to turn milk acidic. Many sauerkraut recipes further the confusion by calling for whey as a starter culture because it contains lactic acid. But whey is not necessary for lacto-fermentation, as you'll read on page 63, and no dairy need ever get near a lacto-fermented kraut, kimchi, or pickle.

preserve their nutrients until we eat them. Lactic acid fermentation is a noble way to approach nutrient and flavor preservation. Once vegetables are preserved this way, we can eat them as slowly as we like, and here's why: All those microorganisms clinging to the plant, good and bad, are just waiting for their turn to alter the vegetables. When we ferment vegetables, we are choosing sides; we are electing the "good guys." Through a simple process that hasn't changed in thousands of years, we allow the lactic acid–forming bacteria to take over, permanently outcompeting the pathogens and creating healthy preserved food for us. They aren't outcompeting because we favor them; they're outcompeting for their own survival, but this still works out well for us.

But we are getting ahead of ourselves here. When we set up a ferment, we are setting the table for the lactic acid bacteria (the good guys) to feast. The rest of this section and the next is in many ways about how to be great hosts to the LAB by providing an ideal environment (comfy and good snacks), because when their needs are met our ferments are successful. When veggies are tucked in, the LAB begin to consume the sugars, in a sense predigesting them so the vegetable's nutrition is more bioavailable to us. In doing so they also produce digestive enzymes (for themselves, but they help us, too), acid, and CO_2. Acid is the superpower in preservation, safety, and flavor. The CO_2 is in all those fun bubbles that can cause a bit of low-level mayhem if not managed.

For many ferments, we shred (or micro-thinly slice) the vegetables to break down their cell structure, which helps the salt get in there to do its job more efficiently. Shredding also frees up the plants' sugars, which is what lactic acid bacteria feed on. For brine pickling, we use the vegetables whole or cut in larger pieces.

WHAT ABOUT BACKSLOPPING?

Backslopping is a rather unappetizing word for the technique of using a little bit of a previous ferment to start a new one. This is an important part of sourdough making and maintenance but is unnecessary in vegetable fermentation. We think this is a popular trick mentioned "out there" due to fear that the ferment will be unsafe. Backslopping doesn't bring safety to the table. As we mentioned, everything you need is already on the raw vegetables, so there is no need to add competing microbes from the late stages of fermentation. The microbes that get the party started are different from the ones that keep the party going or stay to the end of the party. When we add the late-succession microbes, they often just languish until the conditions are right for them. Or, anecdotally, we and others have noticed that the flavors can be flat or slightly oxidized when using a fair amount of fermented brine to backslop.

We do use a little bit here and there, because it is a good way to add some quick acidity. Brine also is a great way to add instant pickle flavor to some veggies you want to eat right away.

How Salt Works

Salt helps us, the makers, manage the fermentation. While microbes do the work, we can use the salinity of the ferment, among other factors, to steer the process.

How cool is it that just a little salt can preserve fresh vegetables with vitamins intact for months, even years? In lacto-fermentation, the first purpose of salt is to draw juices out of a vegetable's cells, which is how, in most cases, the all-important brine is created. This brine is crucial because the lactic acid bacteria are anaerobic, meaning they don't need oxygen. Many of their competitors need oxygen, though, and keeping this whole operation under brine is the easiest way to keep oxygen—and all those undesirable microorganisms—out.

Salt enhances the texture of preserved vegetables because it hardens the pectin in the vegetables' cells; this helps retain crispness. And let's face it, a little salt enhances the flavors in ferments, as it does in all food.

The increased salinity gives the bacteria we want the upper hand, as the correct salt content (salinity) in the ferment does not inhibit the LAB but does inhibit the undesirable bacteria or yeasts that cause decay (or possibly make us sick). For example, salt inhibits yeasts, which break down sugars into alcohol instead of lactic acid. A mere 0.8 percent salinity (this is the ratio of weight of the vegetable to salt—0.8 g salt per 100 g vegetables) is considered the minimun for the salt to do its job. This ratio might, but won't necessarily, prevent the "funky" flavors or fizziness that yeast can cause. Ideally the percentage is kept a little higher; otherwise you risk a soft texture. However, too much salt will stop lactic acid bacteria in their tiny tracks, inhibiting fermentation, but you won't go there by accident because that salinity also makes a ferment inedible. Our standard in dry brine fermentation is around 1.5 percent, which for 100 pounds of shredded cabbage (a mountain heaped way above the rim of an 80-quart bowl) means a little more than 2 cups of salt. For flavor comparison, the salinity of seawater is 3.5 percent.

Salt is one of our controls. Studies show that ferments with higher salinity develop fewer histamines. We also use it in regard to temperature. Lactic acid bacteria work faster in warm temperatures and more slowly in cool temperatures. We can use less salt in our ferments in the winter and may need more salt in the summer for a more stable fermentation process and tastier end product.

With salting, as with most things, moderation is the key, and your taste buds are your best guide (see page 34).

SALT IN BRINE PICKLING

Sometimes we want to pickle vegetables whole or cut in larger pieces. Although shredded or thinly sliced veggies will create their own brine when mixed with salt, whole or chunked vegetables will not—the salt won't come into contact with enough of their cells to pull out enough liquid. In these cases, we prepare a salt brine and drop the vegetables in it. The vegetables interact with the salt in the brine in the process of osmosis, which dehydrates the vegetables' own cells, such that the water is replaced by salt water; this begins the lactic acid fermentation.

SALT CONCERNS

While we don't have any specific salt-free recipes, you can read about some innovations in salt-free brines on page 114. There are also many other techniques discussed in online fermentation communities; some require a blender, and others use seaweed or celery seeds in place of salt. With extra care, fermentation can be accomplished without the salt, and people do so successfully. Expect these ferments to be softer and at times mushy.

But why not use salt in your ferments? Our bodies need salt. Salt regulates fluid exchange in our cells, so that nutrients can enter them. Without it, our organs cease to function. A study published in the *American Journal of Medicine* in 2006 reads, "Sodium intake of less than 2,300 mg [the daily recommended allowance] was associated with a 37% increase in cardiovascular disease mortality and a 28% increase of all cause mortality." In other words, without the correct balance of salt and water, the systems in our body stop functioning.

For perspective, those ancestors who didn't use refrigeration also didn't have processed food. One serving of Kentucky Fried Chicken popcorn nuggets has 1,820 mg of sodium. In comparison, a generous 1-cup serving of basic sauerkraut has about 969 mg of sodium, and an entire quart made with 1 tablespoon of Himalayan pink salt contains 3,877 mg. As with most things, when it comes to salt, understanding your own body combined with common sense and balance are key.

WHOLE VEGETABLES IN SALT BRINE

Packing It In: More Salt Is Not Better

You've probably seen descriptions of fermented foods containing the phrase "packed in salt." Older recipes often suggested layering vegetables in salt, but this inevitably leads to a product that is way too salty for modern taste buds. This technique is important for *part* of some recipes, as you will see on page 284, but not for a regular brine or sauerkraut-type ferment. Our forebears made saltier krauts because they had no refrigeration, while at the same time they had very little salt in the rest of their diet.

It's a misconception that more salt creates a safer product. Salt draws out the liquid from what is being preserved. This liquid becomes the brine, and it needs only enough salt to make it more hospitable to the lactic acid bacteria that acidify the vegetables. The acidification is the preservative, not the salt. Too high a salt percentage (say, more than 10 percent) can inhibit proper fermentation.

More than once, folks came to our market stand to confess they'd made a batch of kraut that was too salty to eat, and they were still waiting for it to mellow out. It's always hard to break the news that this kraut isn't going to get any more palatable. It does not get less salty as it ferments and ages. The key to success is to add salt gradually and taste as you go. See Chapter 4 for more details.

Thinking Outside the Crock:
Your Fermenting Environment

Environmental factors that can affect your active ferment (prior to storage) include temperature, light, oxygen, pH, and time. Temperature and light are the external conditions that affect all the magic going on inside your vessel. Within, let's explore the significance of oxygen, pH, and that ever-slippery fish: time.

TEMPERATURE AND LIGHT

Ferments are most comfortable in the same temperatures where we are most comfortable—between 55 and 75°F/13 and 24°C. It's good to keep the temperature relatively consistent, but it's not something to stress about—there is a lot of leeway. We use ambient temperature to guide us, but it is the temperature within the fermentation that matters. For example, where we live, summer temperatures might hit 80°F/27°C or higher in our home during the day and drop to around 60°F/15°C overnight. We never worry that a ferment is overheating because the higher ambient temperature is not sustained long enough to warm up the containers.

The higher the temperature, the quicker the acid develops, resulting in a shorter fermentation time. When the temperature is too high, everything speeds up, which is evident in underdeveloped acidity within the vegetable and possible off-flavors. How high is too high? At around 85°F/29°C, things will simply move much faster. For the most part that is not damaging, but when temperatures climb above 95°F/35°C for extended periods, or you live in a tropical climate, know that your ferment will be finished a day or two faster. Or, you may want to mitigate this by cooling your ferment. This can be as simple as placing the vessel on cool tiles on the floor, in a tub with cool water (making sure no water can seep in), in a cooler with an ice pack, or in the fridge during the hottest part of the day. When the temperature is around 103°F/39°C, the LAB will start to die off.

Conversely, when the ferment is too cold in the early stages, the lactic acid bacteria are sluggish and can't reproduce fast enough to develop the acidity that keeps the rotting organisms out. As the microbes work, they create a small amount of heat, and sometimes this isn't enough. The temperature for the first days of the ferment should be above 60°F/15°C or so for the microbes to get going. Once fermentation has started (generally a few days; you will see bubbles), feel free to move your vessel to a cooler spot.

It is best to keep your vessel out of direct sunlight, which can cause high temperature fluctuations in your ferment. However, you will find that different cultures have different rules for vegetable fermentation. For example, you will read that in Himalayan traditional achar, the sun's UV rays are part of the fermentation. We recommend keeping your ferment on a counter, or nearby, so you can easily keep an eye on it, especially when you're first learning. They say a watched pot doesn't boil, but an unwatched ferment *will* bubble over.

EXHALING: CO_2, OXYGEN, AND YOUR FERMENT

With bubbles and pressure, jars become volcanoes of brine (remember shaking soda cans as a kid?). These volcanoes are visceral and visual results of the CO_2 that is being created during fermentation. You will see signs of CO_2 early on, often in the first few days. The CO_2 will build, becoming quite active for the next week to 3 weeks, and sometimes a little longer. That said, vegetables with low sugar levels may not put on much of a show. That is okay; as long as your ferment acidifies it is successful, whether you saw any bubbling or not. Bubbles are more of an indicator of high sugar content than they are of the action of fermentation.

During fermentation, the most important task is preventing oxygen from moving in, and the best way to do this is by ushering CO_2 out the door. We'll cover how to do this in a bit, but right now let's look at why this is the case. We need to keep our veggies submerged in brine in order to create an oxygen-free environment for the lactobacilli to thrive, unencumbered by the oxygen-loving competing microbes (a.k.a. spoilers). As CO_2 is created throughout the ferment, air pockets develop. Two things happen: The first thing is that air pockets push up the brine to the top of the ferment and right out of the jar. That's not good—we don't want to lose this precious liquid. The second is that all those little CO_2 pockets could be replaced by oxygen. We don't want this. For these reasons, it's best to get CO_2 out of your ferment.

In order to manage CO_2 you may find you need to periodically top up your pickles with fresh brine, or press down your krauts or condiments, sometimes repeatedly, to allow the brine to reenter the spaces and to keep the vegetables submerged. The surface is the weak point—aerobic (air-requiring) microbes will proliferate if given the opportunity. Most of the time any mold and bacteria can be skimmed off, leaving a safe and fresh ferment underneath. If left unattended, the aerobic microbes could lower the brine acidity by eating the lactic acid, resulting in a spoiled ferment.

A TICKING CROCK: TIME AND YOUR FERMENT

Fermenting takes time. Over time, the chemistry silently changes, melding flavors, breaking down starches, and enhancing the food's digestibility. Think about the bread-making process as an instructive analogy to the curing times of your fermentations. In a bread recipe there is the fairly concrete baking time—*45 minutes at 350°F*—but then there is the rise time, when the dough must rise *in a warm, draft-free place until it has doubled in size*. If you bake bread, you know this amount of time depends on the temperature, quality of yeast, quality of water, and other factors. In both cases, you are waiting for a live biological process to work diligently at what it does best—process sugar. So, instead of *until doubled*, you will have *until sour* as your guide. Smaller vessels or warmer temperatures will mean shorter fermentation cycles; larger crocks or cooler temperatures take longer.

We are often asked when optimum probiotic content is achieved. The answer, in part, depends upon what you are fermenting. One study that tracked probiotic microbes in sauerkraut found that after 7 weeks, those microbes began to disappear. During the fermentation, there is a progression of diverse bacterial species as they move through the cycle. Different colonies peak at distinct points during fermentation. There are also seasonal conditions and types of vegetables to consider, and of course what is included in the fermentation. For example, some spices such as ginger, turmeric, and cayenne seem to help protect the probiotics from the acids of our stomach and gastrointestinal tract. Those same spices may alter (speed up or slow down) the development of the probiotic microbes. Ultimately, the thing to understand is that you will get the benefits whenever you choose to eat your fermented vegetables. If they taste great, then you will eat them, and that alone will make them infinitely healthier than anything that the curing time or process can deliver.

Your vegetables are considered properly fermented when they are below a pH of 4.6. Remember from science class that pH is a measure of the acidity and alkalinity of a solution—in our case, the brine—shown by a number on a scale of 0 to 14. The value of 7 represents neutrality; the lower numbers indicate increased acidity, and higher numbers, increased alkalinity. When the pH is closer to neutral, the solution is more welcoming to the growth of many microorganisms, although not always the ones we want; we want only the acid-loving lactic acid bacteria to find the brine hospitable, so we are aiming for numbers below 4.6.

While acidity level can be objectively determined with a pH test, in our experience the proper acid development is clear to the taste buds (incidentally, in all the ferments that we've double-checked with a test, the pH was well below 4.6). That said, we want you to be comfortable and successful, so if it will put you at ease to know the pH level, consider using pH test strips or a pH meter (see page 52).

LET'S HEAD TO THE KITCHEN

You may be new to vegetable fermentation. Maybe you've heard rumors of nasty smells and scum. You know there are bacteria, and you've been told your whole life that bacteria make you sick. Turns out, science tells us, we are the sum of all of our good bacteria, and not having enough of them in our bodies and on our skin is bad for our health. Fermented vegetables are a live food and sometimes behave in ways you may not expect. You may encounter unfamiliar odors, tastes, and textures. Throughout this book, we will present you with information that will give you the opportunity to understand your experiences and to learn the artistry of vegetable fermentation.

CHAPTER 3

Crocks and Rocks

THE TOOLS OF THE TRADE

One of the attractive qualities of vegetable fermentation is its minimalism. Fewer kitchen equipment pieces are required than for most culinary pursuits—no special pots, pans, or kettles, not even a stove. You need only a bowl, a knife, a cutting board, any jar or crock with a lid, and a bit of salt. You can elaborate on this list with artisan crocks, hand-turned hardwood tampers, round glass weights, and various lids and systems that have been "invented" over the past decade, but you should procure only what makes the process accessible and comfortable for you. The things that give you confidence for successful fermentation are not necessarily the same things that give us or your best friend confidence. You do you! This chapter will help you navigate what is out there.

Material Considerations: Preparing, Curing, and Eating Fermented Foods

You often hear *never touch your sauerkraut with metal*. Why? Fermentation works as a preservative by acidifying. As vegetables ferment and become acidic, certain kitchen implements may chemically react with the developing acid. This can cause strange flavors, off-textures, or bad kraut.

METALS

Raw vegetables are not acidic and therefore won't react with your utensils. At this point, it is nice to have a container big enough to toss, mix, massage, or pound the ingredients in, as your initial vegetable volume is often double that of your final product. Go ahead and use your large stainless steel bowl.

Concern begins during fermentation as the acids develop, so from here on out you want to use nonreactive materials: stoneware (the crocks), glassware, wood, hard plastics, silicone, and high-quality stainless steel.

Common reactive metals to avoid with acidified foods are aluminum, copper, cast iron, and low-grade stainless steel. Because stainless steel is an alloy, the quality of metals used in its composition can vary. Much of the stainless steel cookware available will react with the salts and acids in fermenting food. The best type of stainless steel for the fermenting stage is a high-grade surgical quality.

Using pots or implements made of reactive materials will result in metals, such as chromium and nickel, leaching into your ferment. Don't use them during fermentation, for storage, or when cooking this acidic food. We once cooked a potato soup using brine broth in our favorite cast-iron soup pot. The soup turned gray-lavender and tasted like metal; it was inedible.

However, when it's time to eat your creations, there's no need to hunt for wooden forks every time—once your ferment is done, serving and eating with stainless steel cutlery is fine.

> *Some housewives are in the habit of using copper vessels for pickle making because copper gives a good color to pickles. Never use a copper kettle because the copper salts which give this color and which are transferred to the pickles are poisonous. . . . If proper methods are followed, the salt and acids in the brine produce the desired firmness without any additions.*
> —A 1918 TENNESSEE EXTENSION PUBLICATION

PLASTICS

Use plastics consciously. The more malleable a plastic, the more volatile it is. For example, soft flexible plastic wrap exchanges synthetic ions with food more quickly than a #2 plastic jug, and a more rigid plastic bowl is even less reactive. It is the polyvinyl chloride (PVC) typically found in plastics, especially wrap, that leaches toxins, including the hormone-disrupting toxin diethylhexyl adipate (DEHA), into the surface layers of food. Another ingredient in many plastics is bisphenol A (BPA), which has received a lot of press for the damage it can do to our health.

Use plastic sparingly, especially because its manufacture consumes nonrenewable resources. We recognize plastic products can be the simplest choice for a successful ferment—for example, water-filled ziplock bags can act as a weight and keep oxygen off the ferment. Freezer bags don't contain phthalates or BPA (they are an inelastic, not stretchy, plastic) and won't degrade in acid or salt. Heavy-duty freezer bags can be carefully washed and reused.

If you want to get away from plastic altogether, you can ferment without it. For small jar fermenting, the burping method can replace the water-filled bag. For the flexibility of plastic, you might try nonreactive silicone for strainers and other utensils used with acidic krauts and pickles. We have also used parchment paper cut to shape or round silicone mats, which have a long reusable life, directly on top of ferments. Silicone is sold in different shapes and sizes, and you can cut it to fit your crock. Small glass or ceramic disks that fit in jars can replace plastic in smaller ferments.

Fermentation Vessels

Ceramic vessels have proven themselves over time. That said, you might not want to use your grandparents' old stoneware crock that has been holding utensils or dried flower arrangements, at least without testing it for lead first (many older glazes had lead in them). You can take your crock to a local lab for a test or do it yourself with a lead paint test kit, available at hardware stores. Find an area on the outside of the crock, preferably along the bottom, and scratch the surface to take a sample for testing. Also check your crock for hairline cracks, as they can be a source of contamination.

Crocks are available in a variety of sizes at many hardware, garden, and cookware or fermentation stores, as well as directly from artisans' shops and websites including craft marketplaces such as Etsy. Unfortunately, not all of them come with lids or followers, which we will explain in a moment. For big batches, straight-sided crocks are your best bet for a low-cost, large vessel that is not plastic. They are great for achieving excellent flavor, but they are heavy.

One thing to consider when shopping for a crock is how much upper body strength you'll need to move it around. Our 7.5-liter ceramic crock weighs 19 pounds empty; when it's completely full, we are lugging 33 pounds. For larger batches, stainless steel variable volume fermenters (available through winemaking suppliers) are wonderful.

WATER-SEAL CROCKS

These vessels have a deep outer rim with a trough that holds water. When the lid is placed in the trough, the water creates an airlock. The lid nests in the water in such a way that allows carbon dioxide to escape without allowing the outside air into the crock. Many come with heavy split-weight followers (see page 46) that nest into the pot, making these crocks almost foolproof. Compared to simple straight-sided stoneware crocks they can be expensive, but they do eliminate some of the difficulties around controlling the fermentation environment.

However, trough management is required. The seal only works when the trough is full of water. You will need to add new water regularly to counter evaporation. The water trough can also take some finagling when you are removing your fermented goodies, especially if the water has gotten murky. When the trough is clean, it is simpler to remove what is inside without contamination. Here's how:

» As you lift the lid, slip a plate under it to prevent trough water from dripping into the brine.
» Clean out the water. The easiest way to do this is to remove most of it with a turkey baster and use a towel to sop up the rest.
» When there is brine to remove, use a ladle instead of trying to lift the crock to pour it off.

JARS

The advantage of using glass jars is that they are cheap (free even, if you recycle jars that contained products like other pickles), you can see what is happening inside, and you can make small batches. You can also experiment without committing to a large amount. Crocks are beautiful, but jars may be more practical for day-to-day fermentation. We use them when the cucumber plants are producing enough for a jar of pickles every day, but not enough to make a full crock. When a day's worth of cucumbers mature to pickles, they can get sealed and stored in the same jar.

Jars can be used in different ways—without a lid, with their own lid, with an airlock, as the weight in a larger jar—you will learn the options. They may require some babysitting to keep the

Looking into a water-seal crock; water in the rim creates an airlock when the lid is in place.

ferment under the brine and the brine in the jar. Jars can be harder to weight sufficiently to keep the CO_2 from creating air pockets. The tendency is for the gas to push the brine up and out of the jar. In the early stages of an active ferment this may mean either burping your sealed jar (see Burping Method, page 44), or gently pressing on the top to get the brine back down into the vegetables. You always want your vegetables submerged. The advantage of a jar is that you can see whether your ferment needs tending. (In well-packed water-seal or onggi crocks, this constant pressing is not an issue.)

Jars can also present a disadvantage in a large-batch situation. It can be unwieldy and time-consuming to monitor a bunch of individual ferments of the same batch; you are dealing with more variables and more surface area, the latter of which can cause more loss to spoilage. It is more practical and makes for a more consistent product to make one large batch of pickles, kraut, or kimchi and then to transfer the finished ferment into smaller jars for long-term storage in the refrigerator.

ONGGI POTS

The traditional vessel for making kimchi is called an onggi pot. The type of soil used to make the clay, which is worked by hand, leaves small pores. This creates a breathable pot, which is one of the unique characteristics of onggi pottery. The pores allow fermentation gases to leave, taking smell and any bitter taste with them and ensuring the quality of the fermented food inside.

The one drawback is that it's difficult to find a follower for these pots, as the opening is smaller than the surface area you must cover inside. Traditionally rocks are used. This works well when a few are stacked on outer cabbage leaves as followers.

TRADITIONAL ONGGI POTS

Burping Method

We have found that the most efficient way to manage jar ferments is by "burping" the jars to release the pressure that builds up from the production of carbon dioxide. Use a jar with a tight-fitting lid that is the appropriate size for the amount of vegetables. This means enough headspace to allow the ferment to heave a bit and to have a weight if you are using one. We always use some kind of follower: leaves, the butt ends of vegetables, or a weight. This method does require your active participation. If you aren't someone who will remember to interact with your jar (how are you with houseplants?), then you might prefer the ziplock bag method (see page 47) or an airlock lid.

Once your ferment is tucked securely in the jar, tighten the lid. You will be able to see and feel that the lid is bulging when the fermentation activity begins. This might be a few hours later or a few days. Quickly twist open and then tighten the lid to release the pressure (this pushes out any oxygen in the jar). After that first time, CO_2 blankets your ferment, so in future burps, it is key that you don't fully open the lid or take it off, which will reintroduce oxygen. Weck-style jars are designed such that they will self-burp. If you are using bail top jars, pull lightly on the rubber ring to release pressure, then the ring will return to its position.

If the ferment is too active and is fizzing and coming out of the jar when you burp, you may need to remove the lid, press your ferment back down to release any air pockets, and tighten the lid. The activity will once again push out the oxygen as you burp it.

If your ferment is liquid, like pepper paste, shake the jar before burping to remix the separated contents.

After that first burp, burp the jar daily until the fermentation slows, and then you might burp the jar every few days or not at all. Once the activity ceases, your ferment is done.

You can also use this method for room-temperature storage. When the ferment is slowing down, stop burping it. This will leave a little pressure in the jar and keep that CO_2 blanket in place to protect your ferment, which you can store unrefrigerated indefinitely. This is especially handy for hot sauces you may want to age and olives that need a long ferment. For most vegetables, though, flavors will begin to degrade after several months.

One last note: If you forget to burp a jar with an active ferment for a few days, the pressure that builds up inside may make it difficult to open the jar. Put it in the fridge to calm the volcano of brine and bubbles to some extent before you try to open it. If you are thinking *Oh no, what about exploding jars?*, don't worry. In theory this can happen, but it is much more likely with yeast and sugar ferments. In a lacto-fermentation, there is a small chance it could occur with high-sugar vegetables in a weakened jar. However, usually the metal lid will crease, popping the seal and releasing the pressure (and making a mess) before the jar will break.

FOOD-GRADE BUCKETS

While 5-gallon plastic food-grade buckets are a popular and inexpensive choice for larger home-scale batches of kraut or pickles, they are not our first choice as a fermentation vessel. We can taste a subtle difference in krauts fermented in stone or glass versus plastic. When in business, we did, however, store and transport large batches of finished ferments in plastic buckets—sealed lids and handles are not overrated.

VACUUM-SEALED BAGS

Many people use vacuum-sealed plastic bags for fermentation, the kind that use an appliance to remove the air and seal the bag. The vegetables to ferment are put in the bag with the salt, all air is removed, and the bag is sealed. As fermentation commences, the bag puffs up like a balloon as it fills with CO_2. (And who doesn't like that fun visual confirmation of action?)

When the bag is full, the ferment is often ready. It can be stored as is, but once the bag is opened, the contents must be transferred to a jar for further storage. This method has the obvious advantages of requiring very little management during fermentation and allowing you to keep many projects going in a little space. While we have used this method and enjoy the convenience, we don't care for the single-use plastic waste and are always leery of plastic in contact with our food.

Followers and Weights

Because keeping your vegetables submerged in brine is crucial to success, it is essential to find a way to maintain this anaerobic environment. Followers and weights are designed just for this job.

PRIMARY FOLLOWERS

The primary follower goes right on top of your ferment. It acts as a barrier, keeping any small bits of vegetable submerged in the brine. It can be a large cabbage leaf or other edible leaves (see page 64), a piece of parchment paper, some cheesecloth, or a piece of silicone mat or food-grade plastic drying screen from a food dehydrator, cut to the size of your crock to create a blanket. If you are working with a jar, you might find that a squeezed citrus half, the butt of an onion or celery bunch, half an apple or potato, or the like fits nicely over everything in the jar.

Ideally, you'll place the primary follower right on top of the ferment in a vessel or jar filled near to the top. As the heave of the CO_2 pushes this follower, it will press back on the ferment, in this way also doing the job of a weight in keeping all the vegetables submerged.

SECONDARY OR WEIGHTED FOLLOWERS

For straight-sided crocks and other vessels, you will need a secondary follower and weight. Some followers are weighted, like the ceramic ones, but most are not. Often when they are, the weight is not enough to keep the vegetables submerged. When fermentation begins, it produces an abundance of carbon dioxide. It is surprising how much CO_2 can shift a ferment. The more weight your secondary follower has, the better you are able to keep the brine in the vegetables and not flowing over the top of the jar or crock.

Various Followers
Wood, Stone, a Plate

This follower will need to fit the opening of the container and nestle over as much of the top of the ferment as possible. For most straight-sided crocks, a plate can work; for a larger opening, check at thrift stores, where you might find a flat glass plate from a microwave that will do the job.

You can make a follower out of wood by cutting it from a solid piece of hardwood, such as maple, but not aromatic wood like pine or cedar, as this will affect flavor. You'll also need to take into consideration that the wood will soak up brine and expand in the crock. To make a wood follower, mark the dry wood about ½ inch smaller than the diameter of the inside of your crock to allow for that expansion. Drill a small hole in the center of the round to allow brine to flow through and give you something to hold on to when you want to remove it.

Soak a new wooden follower in water for a day or two to gauge expansion before you try it in your crock. We like to condition our wooden followers by periodically rubbing them with an ointment made from a 50:50 mix of olive oil and melted beeswax.

Most water-seal crocks come with a two-piece ceramic follower that fits snugly down into the crock. These are porous, so when not in use they need to be stored upright to allow airflow; otherwise, they can become musty.

WEIGHTS

You can find weighted followers made specifically for jars and other kinds of vessels. For a wide-mouthed pint or quart jar, you could use a water-filled, sealed pint jar over the primary follower to act as a weighted follower. Other options for weights will vary, depending on the size of your crock or jar. Remember not to use reactive materials, for example, a heavy can of tomato sauce.

Some people like to use a beautiful round river stone. Just avoid using one with high lime content. Sanitize it by boiling it for 10 minutes.

The larger the batch, the more weight you will need.

THE ZIPLOCK BAG METHOD

A popular way to make a combination follower and weight is the ziplock bag method. Filled with liquid, marbles, or salt and zipped tight, the bottom of the plastic bag seals like a primary follower and keeps everything in the brine like a weighted follower. While this is still technically an open method it also acts a little like an airlock, as the CO_2 is able to escape along the sides of the jar and the wrinkles in the bag, letting very little to no oxygen back in. This all-in-one solution works extremely well for jars and other small vessels and was our favorite method for concentrates, pastes, chutneys, or any ferment with very little brine. Now, we use a little bit of parchment and the burping method on these types of ferments.

If you like the bag method, you can use it on larger ferments, even 55-gallon barrels—although of course with much larger bags. It's best to use heavier-gauge freezer bags. The quart size works well for half-pint, pint, and quart jars. A gallon jar requires a gallon-size bag. Half-gallon jars can use either size, but if you have enough room, the extra weight provided by a gallon bag is helpful. For larger crocks, use a 2-gallon or larger bag.

To employ, open the bag and place it in the jar on top of the vegetables, pressing it onto the surface and wedging it around the edges. To add weight, fill the bag with water until there are no air pockets, then seal the bag. You can also fill the bag with marbles, salt, or Basic Brine (page 102) so that if the bag leaks, it won't dilute your ferment

as fresh water would (and if you are concerned about leaks, fill the bag over the sink first to test it). We have had a leak only once or twice. If you do experience a leak, the ferment may not be ruined; only the flavor and texture will be affected.

Coverings

A covering lets air escape while keeping out dust, bugs, or other contaminants while you're actively fermenting with an open method (not sealed as with burping or an airlock lid). Use cheesecloth, muslin, a kitchen towel, or another clean cloth, draped over the top of an open jar or straight-sided crock. We have seen lids made from wood, which are beautiful, but the downside is that they cannot cover a weight that might be sticking above the rim of the crock. Our solution: homemade cloth shower caps!

Christopher Writes

My mother offered a dozen times to help in any way she could with our farmstead kraut business. One day when we were trying to figure out how to make giant shower caps, Kirsten came up with the idea of asking my mom to sew these bonnets for us. Mom was thrilled to help us. We got cute and functional caps made from vintage patterned material. Some fabric, elastic, and a needle and thread are all you need.

Airlocks

Jar airlock systems are popular; as a friend pointed out, "I find they allow me to neglect my ferments." These special lids, or airlocks affixed to lids, keep out oxygen and allow the CO_2 to escape, often without spilling the brine. Without an airlock, you must burp your ferment, or leave your lids loose to let CO_2 escape, which means keeping a closer eye for oxygen contamination and brine loss. An airlock can make the job of babysitting simpler and improve the flavor quality of the ferment by keeping "outside influences" in check.

Well then, you ask, why wouldn't we just always use an airlock? Because fermentation is so simple that you don't need one, and you may not want to bother. Or, if you are like us, you have

more ferments going than airlocks. Remember, this is about choosing equipment that makes the process happy and comfortable for you. If an airlock is the key, perfect; if you don't want another gadget in the drawer, that is fine.

There are many commercially available jar lids with built-in airlocks that are easy to use. Some of the most popular replace the flat of a canning jar with a silicone flat that has a one-way air valve, often an X incision in the silicone, but these are not our favorite type. They may work in the beginning but fail when the opening no longer closes properly, either because something is stuck in the opening or the silicone no longer returns to a fully closed state. If you do use these, carefully monitor the openings to make sure they are completely closing.

When filling a jar that you're going to top with an airlock, you will still need to make sure you have not over- or underfilled the jar. Everything must be snugly pressed into the jar with a follower to help keep things in place.

Tampers

Tampers, also called pounders, are often turned blocks of wood that are used to press the ferment into the vessel. Having a tool to compact your ferment is very helpful, as it can be difficult to maneuver your hand in a small jar, and pressing a ferment in a larger crock can turn into quite a workout. In some cases this tool can also be used to bruise shredded and salted vegetables to further release brine.

A proper tamper is a handy tool; however, a little ingenuity and a look through your utensils can produce a suitable alternative. For example, the plunger from a Vitamix blender will work, as will a solid straight-sided rolling pin.

Slicing, Shredding, Chopping

Much of the success of kraut or condiments is dependent on the finished texture, which is related to how you prep your vegetables. We had never given texture much thought when we bought a hand-cranked rotary slicer; we bought it to avoid hurting ourselves slicing case after case of cabbage with a 14½-inch blade of sharpened steel, a knife just short of a machete. With some of our first earnings we set out to find something safer, and we discovered a hand-cranked rotary slicer called the Nemco Easy Slicer.

The Nemco was perfect: It was versatile, affordable, accommodated most vegetables, and came with a variety of slicing and grating plates. It was made in the USA, quiet to operate, and definitely fit our green, off-the-grid technology. When the cabbage quarters lined up just right in the hopper, the slice was beautiful, but we were left with extra bits that didn't quite go through, so the total effect was not uniform. We called the texture "farmhouse," indicating its rustic hand-made character. Many customers told us that they especially liked this texture.

The texture of your chop affects the final result. For example, when working with cabbage a micro-thin slice is easy to bring to brine but may produce a softer kraut. A large, chunky chop provides a hearty finish but may take more massaging to produce sufficient brine. Finely slicing root vegetables creates a crisp, saladlike result, while grating them exposes more surface area, producing a more sour, krautlike ferment. Play around with how you prepare the vegetables and you will discover this, too, affects the flavor and your enjoyment of the final product.

KNIVES

You need a few sharp knives. The traditional chef's knife comes in a few sizes. The larger 10- or 12-inch sizes are nice for cutting through cabbages and thick-skinned squash. A smaller chef's knife is good for general chopping, slicing, dicing, and mincing. We also always keep a good paring knife handy for small tasks.

SLAW BOARDS

Every fermentista gets to a point when the question of slaw boards comes up. This happens when your batch sizes have moved beyond a knife and a cutting board. When we started

making sauerkraut, everyone with an old slaw board "donated" it to us. They are easy to find in antique stores, often without the sliding box that holds the cabbage while you move it across the series of blades. They look good hanging on the wall but can be a danger to the fingertips when in use. We preferred the Nemco Easy Slicer, mentioned previously.

You can find beautiful new slaw boards in kitchen stores and online. These boards are the same as the traditional design, just shiny, complete, and sharp. Unless you find one with a hand guard, you may want to pick up a pair of sturdy slash-resistant gloves while you are shopping.

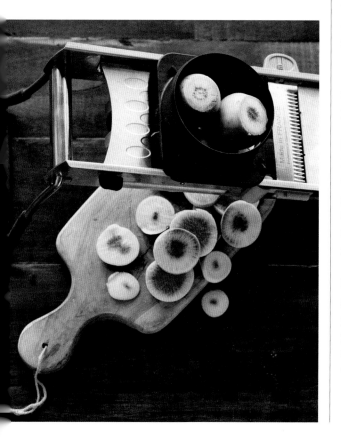

HAND GRATERS AND PEELERS

Hand graters and peelers come in every shape and size. A microplane grater/zester is wonderful for garlic cloves, citrus zest, or ginger and turmeric root.

We rarely peel our vegetables, but peelers are good for making ribbons of hard vegetables, such as carrots, daikon radishes, beets, or any other root. We use these ribbons to add whimsical strips of color and texture to ferments.

MANDOLINES

We have come to love the versatility of the mandoline with its numerous attachments, especially for the demands of our many condiments (relishes, chutneys, and salsas) that require, for example, micro-thin slices and tiny dices (see Chapter 5).

Mandoline slicers, with their shiny, sharp series of blades, can be intimidating. If you have a mandoline without a hand guard, we suggest you purchase a pair of sturdy slash-resistant gloves.

FOOD PROCESSORS

Food processors are convenient for various aspects of grating and for slicing certain vegetables. The grating attachment is perfect for harder root vegetables such as beets, carrots, and celeriac. The chopping blade is useful for chopping herbs and making pastes.

We find it doesn't save any time to slice cabbage with the food processor, as it's a battle just to get the cabbage small enough to fit down the hopper and through the slicing blade, at which point you might as well have sliced it with a knife. The slicing disk is useful, however, for thinly slicing vegetables.

Other Equipment

Here are a few other gadgets you may want in your fermentation tool kit.

DEHYDRATOR

Dehydration opens a whole range of possible techniques and ingredients for fermentation. We use it to reduce the water content in some vegetables (see page 80) and to dry fruit. Fresh fruit can have too much sugar to lacto-ferment well, but dried fruit—such as raisins, cranberries, and dried apple rings—can be a delicious addition. Tomatoes or mushrooms will taste off if they're fermented fresh, but when they're dehydrated, their concentrated flavor is delicious. Many fresh fruits and vegetables can be purchased already dehydrated, but what about fermented veggies? You might enjoy making your own probiotic-rich seasonings by dehydrating fermented veggies either to sprinkle on a salad or to flavor a meal (see Seasonings, page 142).

KITCHEN SCALE

These days, many home cooks use kitchen scales. Christopher, for one, is a convert to weight measurements, while Kirsten might feel the same . . . but only if she ever measured anything.

If you don't have a scale, don't worry; every recipe in this book has both volume and weight measurements.

PH TEST STRIPS AND METERS

Although it isn't necessary, you can make sure kraut is acidic enough by checking the pH level. A simple way to do this is with pH litmus strips. They are sold online and in brewing supply stores as dip sticks in a pack or in a small tape-dispenser-like roll. These testers come in all different ranges; look for ones that measure with some degree of accuracy in the acidic range (below 5). The full-range types aren't always specific enough. The strips are simple to use: Just dip the end in your kraut and match the color of the strip to the color chart on the box. Of course, all bets are off if you are looking to test a beet or red cabbage ferment with the strips.

A pH meter is a handheld meter that is calibrated against a known solution. The probe is then dipped into the brine, and the reading is shown on the screen. It's a fun gadget but can be expensive. The one we use we found at our local brewing supply and hardware store for less than $40. (For more about pH, see A Ticking Crock on page 36.)

PICKLE PRESS

For tsukemono, a Japanese pickling technique (see Chapter 6), watery vegetables must be pressed in salt before they are fermented. Pickle presses, also called tsukemonoki, are containers that include a spring press integrated into the lid, so that you can squeeze the water out of vegetables. Most are plastic, usually inexpensive, and available online or at larger Asian food markets. There are also glass basins with a thick glass weight that fits inside. Traditionally people used heavy rounded stones called tsukemono *ishi*.

Salt: Shaking Out the Differences

With just salt (and not very much of it) you can preserve fresh vegetables and their nutrients for months, even years. Our ancestors thought this was pretty great, so much so that armies marched across ancient landscapes just to be paid in salt. (Yep, salt is where our word *salary* comes from.) In this section, you'll find out which salt to put in your toolbox for the job of brining and about some of the many varieties available for the task.

NOT ALL SALTS ARE CREATED EQUAL

ISN'T ALL SALT THE SAME?

Not too long ago, table salt and kosher pickling salt were pretty much our only choices. Now we can taste our way around our planet with the salts of the earth and sea. Salts of all colors and flavors are available in even the most traditional grocery stores. We can choose red or black, finishing, milling, or cooking salts, in small crystals or large blocks.

With these amazing varieties, there is no reason to settle for kosher pickling salt or other highly refined salts, which contain additives that are not helpful to your ferment. These refined salts are salty in a way that assaults your taste buds. Different salts contain different ratios of sodium chloride to minerals, which changes the flavor drastically. We often begin our classes by passing around different salts to taste. Many times people are surprised at how sweet they can be. Have fun exploring salts. Find a good-quality, mineral-rich salt that suits your palate.

Minerals are an important subject in this time of depleted soils. The foods we have are no longer as rich in essential elements as they were in times past, and it can be challenging to nourish ourselves properly. We even saw it in our farm animals—keeping a small herd of dairy goats healthy became all about getting enough minerals into their systems. It stands to reason that we humans, eating from the same soil, should make sure our diets are mineral rich. Mineral-rich salt added to nutrient-dense food is a good solution.

Salts vary according to minerals, moisture content, and coarseness. Weighing salt gives you much more precision compared to measuring by volume. Fortunately, vegetable fermentations can tolerate a broad range of salt. This difference is partly why our recipes don't call for exact amounts—they are based on volume and using whole vegetables, so that you're not wasting parts if your beet is large or oversalting if your onion is small. We ourselves have experimented with making the same recipe using different salts and had very different results—another good reason to taste your ferments when salting.

WHICH SALT SHOULD I USE?

There is no correct answer. It depends on what feels right to you.

Mineral-Rich Salts of the Earth. These salts are extracted by mining. Redmond Real Salt, a rock salt mined in central Utah, and Himalayan Crystal Salt, mined in and around Pakistan, are both salts from remnants of ancient seabeds. These deposits were subjected to considerable heat and pressure to form densely compacted crystals that contain many beneficial trace minerals. These salts of the earth have a very low moisture content. Both have a beautiful pink color and are finely ground, which works well for krauts. The high mineral content can give your ferment a subtle sweetness. Rock salt can make pickling brine a bit gritty, but this grit will sink to the bottom of the crock and will not affect the quality of the vegetable.

Mineral-Rich Salts of the Sea. Sea salt is minimally processed, and therefore treads more lightly on the planet. The taste and color are indicative of where and how the salt was harvested. Maldon, from the United Kingdom, is light and flaky. The French salts *sel gris*, which means gray salt in French, and *fleur de sel*, which literally means flower of salt, are commonly known as Celtic sea salts. Increasingly there are tiny salt companies along our coastlines. Sea salts can provide a lot of nuanced flavors. In general, their higher moisture content makes them heavier. They are harvested by evaporating seawater in large pans, leaving the salt behind. Also left behind in this unprocessed sea salt are microscopic bits of plankton, minerals (calcium, magnesium, iron, and potassium), micronutrients, and, unfortunately, microplastics. The amount of microplastics in a given sea salt has a lot to do with where it was manufactured. One study found more than 200 microplastics per cup of salt originating in China, whereas another study of salts from eight different countries found much less.[7] At this point, it is just something to be aware of.

Sea salts are quite sweet and wonderful to ferment with. Often, however, they are coarse, which means they are slower to dissolve as you work them

into the kraut and build the brine. This can make your job of getting the vegetable to release the brine more difficult. This is solved by lightly crushing the salt before using it.

Iodized Table Salt. We don't recommend common table salt. It is said that the antimicrobial properties of iodine inhibit the very bacteria we encourage. Industrialized refined salt with added iodine could inhibit fermentation and cause a discolored product. Refined salt has been bleached and has had minerals leached out and iodine and anticaking agents such as calcium silicate and bone ash added. The amount of iodine added can be up to 300 percent more than the amounts occurring naturally in unrefined salt. To be clear, the naturally occurring iodine in unrefined salts does not cause a problem in fermentation.

Kosher Pickling Salt. These flaked crystals have more surface area and are intended to draw out moisture more efficiently; they are used for curing charcuterie or to remove surface blood in kosher meals. Its structure means you may need to use more of it than is called for in a volume measurement, and we find that it can taste more briny and a little metallic. It is 99.9 percent refined sodium chloride. Most often it begins in a salt deposit in the earth or is dehydrated out of seawater. A brine is made by pumping water into the raw salt. The resulting salt water is treated with carbon dioxide and sodium hydroxide to separate out the undesirable solids such as calcium. This refined liquid is boiled off at high heat in open pans until flaky salt crystals form. Some brands of kosher salts then add sodium ferrocyanide and other chemicals as anticaking agents. We prefer not to use this salt for vegetable fermentation.

Part 2

Mastering the Basics

Kraut, Condiments, Tsukemono, Pickles, and Kimchi

*Eat some foods that have been predigested by
bacteria or fungi.*

—MICHAEL POLLAN, *FOOD RULES: AN EATER'S MANUAL*

When we began selling sauerkraut at the market, people sought us out, and it wasn't always to buy our kraut. Sometimes they just wanted to taste our samples, chat, or learn. We were happy to oblige because we love to see people taking an active role in their food. Our classes were born from this experience, and so was this book.

In this section, you'll encounter the soul of fermentation. Mastering these techniques will ensure success, no matter your goal. We hope that fermenting becomes intuitive and part of your regular routine.

You'll find the master processes, illustrated step by step with photos, for each type of ferment. (Throughout part 3, we'll refer you to these chapters for details and guidance, although once you've made the basic recipes a few times, you won't need much help.) You'll also find storage directions and a troubleshooting section, and you can always turn to the appendix on page 414 to visually guide you through this thing called scum!

Before You Get Started

People often ask: Do I have to use organic vegetables? We encourage organics where possible for many reasons, but they are not always a realistic choice, and that is fine. Nonorganic, conventional produce is still teeming with microbes—a testament to its resilience—and will ferment naturally.

Before prepping produce, wash your hands with simple soap and warm water; avoid antibacterial soaps, as they might inhibit the fermentation process. Rinse your vegetables, but don't wash them with soaps, vegetable washes, or antimicrobial rinses.

And remember, we are not canning here, so there is no need to sterilize your vessels or tools. Clean your equipment with warm, soapy water, avoiding any products that will kill our friends the lactobacilli. Many people use just warm water to rinse out their stoneware crocks, believing that this promotes the most amiable environment—perhaps even aiding in the microbial process by allowing the helpful bacteria to survive from one batch to the next.

The Fermentista's Mantra: Stay Under the Covers

There are two protective layers that keep your ferment in delicious safety. The first is the brine that keeps ferments safely below and out of reach of mold and yeasts. The second is carbon dioxide, which is heavier than normal air, so it likes to sit on the surface of the brine. After some strong fermentation, that layer of headspace on top of the ferment will be nearly 100 percent

CO_2, adding another level of protection against all the microbes we don't want joining our fermentation party.

To keep your fermentation safe, mind the covers. When appropriate, have enough brine so that your ferment is fully submerged (a bonus is with extra brine on top). When you burp your ferment, do it very quickly, to relieve the pressure while preserving that layer of carbon dioxide.

This simple phrase is all you need to remember to keep your ferments safe to eat:

Stay Under the Covers.

It's Just a Crock: Your Safety Checklist

Fermenting is a simple process. Things can go awry, but if you follow the directions, you'll end up with ferments that are safe and delicious.

» Clean all work surfaces, tools, and your hands with warm, soapy water—no antibacterial soaps.

» Rinse vegetables in cool water without soap.

» Keep your ferments anaerobic.

» During fermentation, put the jar and crock in ambient temperatures.

» Store cured ferments in the refrigerator.

» Don't eat anything that smells rotten or looks wrong in any way.

WATER-WISE

If a recipe calls for water, use the best water you can. We advocate for using nonchlorinated water, as chlorine can inhibit fermentation (although we've also seen successful ferments made with chlorinated water).

If your tap water is chlorinated, you can use regular bottled water (not distilled water). Or you can boil your tap water for 15 minutes and let it cool, or just let it sit out overnight to allow the chlorine to dissipate.

However, you may want to check with your water provider. Increasingly, municipal water systems are adding a combination of chlorine and ammonia, called chloramine, that does not evaporate. To remove chloramine, you need a filtration system that employs first a carbon filter to remove the chlorine from the chloramine molecule and then a reverse-osmosis filter to remove the remaining ammonia.

CHAPTER 4

Mastering Sauerkraut

In this chapter, you'll learn everything you need to know about making sauerkraut. We'll walk you through the process, showing you the steps in photographic detail, to set you on the path to becoming a fermentation (c)rock star. Once you understand how the process works, you can make any variations that strike your fancy.

Cabbage: Your Raw Material

Our essential vegetable, the cabbage, comes in a variety of sizes, ranging from tiny, dense heads not much bigger than your fist to ones as big as soccer balls. For our purposes, we are assuming that one cabbage is a 2-pound, tightly packed head.

SELECTING THE CABBAGE

Through the miracle of cold storage and refrigerated shipping, you can always find cabbages. They're a staple. Unglamorous. Peasant food. But they're also quite amazing in their variety: There are summer cabbages, fall cabbages, and winter cabbages in many colors and shapes (who isn't enchanted by the ones shaped like a gnome's hat?).

Cabbages are a hardy cool-season crop. In northern climates, the harvest season begins when the spring-planted cabbages ripen in June and July and can last through January or February. This is something to be aware of when you want to make a big batch of kraut and are looking for the freshest cabbage possible. Out-of-season cabbages may be dry from long hauling and storage times. Increasingly, the storage varieties have been bred to be drier and drier so that they won't spoil, which can be difficult when you are trying to manage those microbes to ferment. If your cabbage is exceedingly dry, you have gotten one of these varieties. See Help! I Don't Have Enough Brine in My Kraut, on page 63.

So what do you look for? You want firm heads with crisp, shiny leaves. (They become dull as they lose vitality.) That said, if you have forgotten one in your fridge for longer than you care to mention and those leaves are a little dull, don't toss the head—ferment it! Check for damage on the outer leaves. If a head is cracked or bruised, chances are there's interior damage. Bypass precut; they're already losing nutrients.

If you're harvesting from the garden, cut a head off the root but let some outer leaves remain. It'll sprout baby cabbages from the sides of the root core. Giant homegrown cabbage that's about to set seed becomes slightly cone-shaped and will eventually open when the core develops into a flower shoot. You can still make kraut, but if it opens too much, the leaves are drier, tougher, greener, and the flavor is different.

Adding Salt

Time to add salt. The salt brings out the moisture of the cabbage, creating the brine. Because no water is added, we call this dry brining. While encouraging bacteria seems like a project for the science lab, you don't need to worry about being precise; the microbes will tolerate a wide range of salt and will still make brine and a successful ferment. Just as in cooking, there is a degree of flexibility.

As mentioned, you can use your entire vegetable in our recipes, so you won't end up with extra halves and pieces of this or that. While we recommend a certain amount of salt in each recipe, it is best, because vegetable sizes vary, to begin with half that amount of salt. Taste. You want to taste the salt, but not be overwhelmed by it. Slowly build up to the recommended amount, but don't be afraid to stop if your mixture is beginning to taste too salty. You want it salty like a chip—present but pleasing. If you find it is too salty, add more cabbage or other vegetable.

If you are comfortable with weight measures, you can do the math to determine the precise amount of salt you need to add to produce the salinity percentage you desire. You will weigh the prepared vegetables in grams and multiply this weight by the percentage. For most vegetables in a temperate climate, we find 1.5 percent salt works

well, and in a tropical climate this is 3 percent. For example, if your vegetables weigh 829 grams, which is just about perfect for a quart-jar ferment, and you live in a temperate climate, multiply 829 by 0.015 to get your salt quantity. In this case, you will need to add 12.5 grams of salt.

Add the salt after all the cabbage and any accompanying veggies are shredded. If you're doing a very large batch, sprinkle in the salt as you shred and transfer the cabbage to a bowl. This will begin to break down the cell walls and to release the juices even before mixing and will help ensure that the salt is spread throughout the batch.

Once the salt is added, massage it in with your fingers. The process of massaging cabbage is similar to kneading bread dough. Pick up some in your hands and squeeze it. Think deep-tissue Swedish massage, not a gentle back rub. Repeat this process, working through the entire batch. Almost instantly, the cabbage will start glistening, looking wet and limp. A puddle of liquid will pool at the bottom of the bowl. For a large batch, massaging becomes more of a workout. If this is difficult, thoroughly work in the salt and let the batch sit, covered, for about an hour before tossing and massaging it again for a few minutes. The salt does the work for you—when the brine has built up at the bottom, the mixture is ready to be pressed into your vessel.

Help! I Don't Have Enough Brine in My Kraut

You have salted, mixed, and massaged your shredded kraut, but when you squeeze, it is like milking the proverbial turnip. No liquid. Sometimes this happens when veggies are drier than usual or because the veggies were not sliced thinly enough. Here are some solutions.

First, taste the cabbage one more time. If you think it can take more salt, sprinkle in just a bit, massage again, and see if that helps draw out the brine. If you still don't have enough brine, maybe just a little time apart will help the relationship. Cover your bowl and set it aside for about an hour. When you return, the salt should have continued to break down the cell walls of the cabbage, and you should have more brine.

If you *still* don't have enough brine, you could try going right ahead and packing the kraut into a crock or jar. When you press the cabbage down,

you might find a thin brine layer at the top—and thin is enough, as long as the cabbage is lightly submerged. If you still don't have enough brine to cover the cabbage, put it back in the bowl. You have some choices.

The simplest option is to add other veggies that are known to give off a lot of liquid. Believe it or not, turnips are one of them. (Maybe you *can* milk a turnip!) Grate some turnips, carrots, or beets into the cabbage, or add very thinly sliced onions. (In this book, when we say "grated" we mean processed with a medium grater blade unless otherwise specified.)

The next option is to add some kind of liquid that will enhance the quality of your kraut. We don't advocate adding salt water as a first choice, but we do recommend a few tablespoons of lemon juice, bottled or fresh. The taste of lemon in the finished kraut will be subtle, as it gets lost in the acidity that is created with the fermentation. In fact, if you want to boost the lemon flavor, add

NO WHEY?

You might be wondering about adding whey to your kraut brine. A lot of sauerkraut recipes call for whey to inoculate the vegetables. The theory of adding whey to a vegetable ferment comes from two assumptions: first, that vegetables can't start a good fermentation without added bacteria, and second, that LAB is LAB is LAB.

Whey, which is the liquid left over from making cultured cheeses, contains live lactic acid bacteria (LAB), but they aren't the same as the bacteria that are useful for fermenting vegetables. Whey bacteria are different strains with different needs. This is not to say there is no overlap, but the main players are very different because milk sugars and plant sugars are very different. You wouldn't put the plant-eating bacteria in your cheese, and you shouldn't put the cheese eaters in your sauerkraut.

We also avoid using whey because our priority is flavor, and sometimes whey can leave a slightly "cheesy" or "sour milk" flavor.

the zest also. You can also use freshly squeezed orange, lime, or grapefruit juice. If you have left-over fermented brine from previous batches of krauts, or pickle juice, you could use a little of that as well, keeping in mind the potential effect on flavor.

If you really want simple unadulterated cabbage sauerkraut, you can bring out the pounder and beat out more liquid. With too vigorous an effort you risk softer kraut, but pounding the cabbage is a time-honored practice. Or, add a little bit of brine. Use Low-Salt Basic Brine on page 102.

Packing Your Vessel

Start by placing a small amount of your mixture in the bottom of your vessel, about an inch or so. Compress this with your fist or a flat-bottomed tamper (see page 49). When this layer is compacted, add a bit more and press again. Make sure that you are forcing out any air bubbles as you go. As you move up through the vessel, you will notice that the liquid is increasing. Meanwhile, the volume in your bowl is decreasing, and you might now be wondering if you made enough. It's always a surprise how much it compacts. Keep pressing.

Your vessel will be full when you have space between the brine and the rim; this is called *head-space*. In a 5- or 10-gallon straight-sided crock, you should aim for 4 to 6 inches of headspace. Water-seal crocks need enough room to fit the split weight in place. In a jar, the vegetables should reach to just below the shoulder. These parameters leave enough room so that even with a follower and a weight, all your hard-fought-for brine won't bubble out onto the counter.

FERMENTISTA'S TIP

No room left in the crock and you still have half a bowl of limp vegetables? Find an appropriately sized jar and follow the same instructions. Or, if you like the taste, this might just be the vegetable salad you needed for dinner or prechopped vegetables you wanted for soup.

This is the time to add the *primary follower* (see page 45), which in this case can be a large outer cabbage leaf, to keep the shredded bits from floating. Tuck the leaf under the shoulder of the jar or crock to secure it. Then, if need be, place a weighted follower (or a secondary follower with a weight) in your crock or jar. Wedge it into place, with the brine covering it.

If your vessel has a lid, put it on. Tighten the lid if you're planning to burp the ferment (see page 44). Otherwise, loosely cover the top of the vessel with a clean tea towel or muslin to keep out fruit flies or anything else that could fall into the brine.

Even if you left a lot of headspace, put your vessel on a plate or a rimmed baking sheet to catch escaping brine. Never underestimate the power of exhaling bacteria. In fact, watch for the level of kraut rising above the brine. Check every day at the start, during the active phase. You may need to apply pressure to force out the air and to allow the brine to return to cover the kraut, especially in a small jar.

Placing Your Ferment

Now there is nothing left to do but place your nascent ferment in a corner of your kitchen and wait. As a general rule, it's better to keep it out of direct sunlight and in your daily space, rather than in an out-of-the-way closet where it will be forgotten.

Most recommendations are to ferment at temperatures between 55 and 75°F/13 and 24°C.

Our preferred fermenting temperature is around 65°F/18°C because the ferment progresses more slowly, stays crunchy, and develops good flavor before eventually becoming very sour. That said, we have found that if the ferment starts in that sweet zone for a few days, it can then be moved to a spot that's below 55°F/13°C (such as a cellar or garage) and will keep fermenting at a slower rate, which can have advantages in developing the flavor. If you get below 45°F/7°C for sustained periods, it will ferment slowly and steadily as if it were in a refrigerator. Above 75°F/24°C, the entire fermentation process speeds up, although it will continue to work until temperatures are above 100°F/38°C for any sustained period.

Practically speaking, what does this mean in your home? No one knows the climate of your home better than you. If your kitchen counter is too warm in the height of summer, a closet or basement is probably better. Even a tile floor where the thermal mass is enough to keep the temperature constant will help. In winter in a cold climate, placing the crock on top of a water heater could help keep fermentation active.

FERMENTISTA'S TIP

Climate Control

A trick we learned in cheesemaking is to control the climate with a portable ice chest. We would put ripening feta in the cooler and leave it open outside on the porch during cold evenings. In the morning, we would close it and put it in a cool spot inside. In the heat of the summer, we would add an ice pack. This was enough to maintain a relatively stable temperature. If it isn't enough, go ahead and ferment in the fridge after the first day. Conversely, a cooler can be used to keep your ferment a bit warmer in a cold situation.

Curing Your Ferment: Maintaining the Active Ferment

In your vessel things are happening. You wake up to a pool of brine on your counter; the bubbling is active. This sign of fermentation is comforting and easy to read. But for the novice fermentista, questions begin to arise. Perhaps the bubbling has stopped, or nothing is happening, or the bubbling never started, as far as you can tell. Possibly something questionable is forming on top (for this we have provided a gallery of scum; see page 417).

In a perfect world, you will begin to see action in your kraut the day after you've packed it. If you're fermenting in a jar, you will see the little bubbles moving up through the cabbage like champagne. If you're fortunate enough to own a crock with a water seal, you will begin to hear an occasional *bloop* as the CO_2 escapes. Sometimes, even though the kraut is actively fermenting, these signs are less obvious or they don't last long. This is all within the range of normal. Krauts can be anything from explosively active to seemingly dead, and usually both are fine in the end.

Your job during active fermentation is a bit of a balancing act: You're responsible for keeping those veggies submerged, but at the same time you must try not to disturb the ferment too much, as this can invite in unwelcome microbes and oxygen.

The Waiting Period

How long you'll have to wait depends. "Finished" is a bit subjective, and "doneness" isn't always clear, especially if you consider all the different techniques and flavor goals you may have. There are, however, two things to consider: acidity level and taste. Acidity level is a clearly defined goal—anything below a 4.6 pH. Taste is a matter of personal preference.

There are as many opinions about active fermentation length as there are kraut makers. Some people will not even consider eating any kraut before it's had 6 weeks of curing time. On the other hand, one person wrote in an online forum that they never left a batch on the counter for more than 4 days (keep in mind, such a short ferment may compromise the acidity level in some batches). From a scientific perspective, the main things that affect the fermentation time are the carbohydrate content of the ferment, the temperature, the salt content, and to a lesser extent the size of the batch. Fermentations of vegetables with a higher sugar content are often more active, and while they may be sour sooner, they will continue actively fermenting longer. In warm weather, a batch might be ready in as little as 3 days, but the same batch might take 3 weeks in a cool environment. A higher salt content will slow things down. A very small batch will be ready much sooner than a larger batch. But don't worry, the recipes will guide you, and as you ferment and observe, you will develop a sense for what you like and will understand how to manipulate these "dials," as we like to call them, to steer your projects.

Your ferment is not quite there if it doesn't smell acidic and tastes dull, like a wilted salad. Eventually the vegetables will start to taste acidic, as though lemon has been squeezed into them. Although 4.6 pH is your goal, we have found most finished krauts are even more acidic—below 4 pH. Once you have reached that acidity level, "done" is again subjective. Let your senses make the decision for you.

How long do you ferment your pickles? 'Til they're perfect. Depending on the type of pickle, this can be anywhere from 24 hours to a year or more.
—ALEX HOZVEN, OWNER, CULTURED PICKLE SHOP, BERKELEY, CALIFORNIA

When Is the Ferment Ready?
» **Look:** somewhat translucent and the color of cooked cabbage (more yellow than green)
» **Smell:** sour
» **Touch:** firm to soft, but not slimy
» **Taste:** pleasingly sour and pickle-y, but without the strong acidity of vinegar

You can do your first taste test on smaller batches in a few days; on multigallon batches, you'll have to wait 1 to 2 weeks. Carefully lift off your weights and follower with clean hands. With a clean, nonreactive utensil (stainless steel is fine), remove some of your veggies and taste them. Then replace the weights and follower carefully, keeping everything submerged. Your weight will probably have some sediment on it; rinse it off with hot water before replacing.

Your kraut should already taste a bit sour. But it may still be a bit "green." In other words, it will be like a half-sour pickle, without the full-bodied rounded flavor of the acidity and spices that a pickle develops, falling somewhere between the cucumber and the pickle it is becoming. Young sauerkraut is the same way. If you prefer this "half" flavor, you can put the ferment in the refrigerator to arrest the process. The spice flavor will still deepen as it sits in the refrigerator. We think the best answer to the question "When is my kraut done?" is "When it tastes great."

FERMENTISTA'S TIP

Make sure you don't set your jar or crock too close to a refrigerator's motor or fans; they could heat up your ferment without you knowing it. Then again, this location can help warm up a ferment in a cool house or during the winter.

▶ Rinse the vegetables in cool water and prepare according to the recipe directions; transfer to a large bowl.

▶ Add half the salt in the recipe and, with your hands, massage it in (as if you were kneading dough), then taste. You should be able to taste salt, but it should not be overwhelming. If it's not salty enough, continue massaging in small amounts of salt and tasting, until it's to your liking. Remember: If it's tasty fresh, it will be delicious fermented.

▶ The vegetables will quickly look wet and limp. Depending on the amount of moisture in the vegetable and your efforts, some amount of liquid will begin to pool in the bowl. If you've put in a good effort and don't see much brine, let the vegetables stand, covered, for 45 minutes, then repeat the massage.

▶ Transfer the vegetables to a crock or jar. Press down on the vegetables with your fist or a tamper; this will release even more brine. There should be some brine visible on top of the vegetables when you press. (Don't worry if the brine "disappears" between pressings.) If not, return the vegetables to the bowl and massage again.

▶ When you pack the vessel, leave 4 to 6 inches of headspace for a crock and 2 to 3 inches for a jar. (*Headspace* is the area between the brine and the top rim of the vessel.)

▶ Top the vegetables with one or two cabbage leaves. This *primary follower* keeps the shreds from floating above the brine.

▶ Seal the jar with its lid, if you're planning on burping the ferment (see page 44). Otherwise, top it with a *weighted follower*. For a crock the follower may be a plate that fits the opening of the container and nestles over as much of the surface as possible; then weigh down the plate with a sealed water-filled jar. For a jar, you can use a sealed water-filled jar or ziplock bag as a follower-weight combination. (*Note:* Use a ziplock bag that fits the diameter of the vessel and will be heavy enough to submerge the vegetables when filled.) Then cover it all with a large kitchen towel or muslin.

▶ Set the jar or crock on a plate or a rimmed baking sheet in a spot where you can keep an eye on it, out of direct sunlight, with an ambient temperature between 55 and 75°F/13 and 24°C. Ferment for the time indicated in the recipe.

▶ Check daily to burp or make sure the vegetables are submerged, pressing down as needed to bring the brine back to the surface. You may see scum on top; it's generally harmless, but if you see mold, scoop it out.

(Continued on Next Page)

▶ When it's time to taste-test, use a clean, non-reactive utensil to remove some of the kraut and taste it. It's ready when:

» It's pleasingly sour and pickle-y tasting, without the strong acidity of vinegar.

» The flavors have mingled.

» The veggies have softened a bit but retain some crunch.

» The color is that of the cooked vegetable.

If it's not ready, rinse the followers and weight, put everything back in place, and continue monitoring.

▶ When the kraut is ready, carefully skim off any scum on top. If you fermented in a crock, transfer the kraut into a jar (or jars). If you fermented in a jar, you can store the kraut in it. Leaving as little headspace as possible, tamp down to make sure the kraut is submerged in its brine. Screw on the lid, then store in the refrigerator.

THE TASTE TEST: NAVIGATING THROUGH THE SCUM TO THE KRAUT ON THE OTHER SIDE

When it's time to taste-test your ferment, be warned: There may be blooms of yeasts or molds on top of your followers or even on your ferment. Take your time and follow these directions.

1. Remove the weight, if it's separate from the secondary follower.

2. Wipe the inside of the vessel with a clean towel carefully so as not to disturb the ferment or the scum.

3. Gently remove the secondary follower. There is often sediment on top of the follower; try not to disturb it too much.

4. Now lift out the primary follower (cabbage leaves, parchment paper, silicone mat, or whatever material you used), gently folding it to catch any stray floating vegetable bits, scum, or sediment. Discard any scummy leaves or paper if necessary and replace with new ones.

5. If the ferment is completely under the brine, it will be good. If the brine level is low and close to the surface of the ferment, there may be some soft or off-color areas; simply scoop out these parts. The ferment underneath will be fine and ready to taste.

1. Thinly slice the cabbage.

2. Work in the salt with your hands.

3. Massage the cabbage until brine develops.

4. Press the cabbage firmly into a fermenting vessel, pressing out air pockets.

5. A properly stuffed crock

6. Place a primary follower on the surface.

7. Add a follower and weight, forcing the brine to the top.

8. Cover with a cloth and set aside in a cool place.

9. During fermentation, press to release CO_2 and maintain brine coverage.

10. Taste to test doneness.

11. Firmly pack storage jars and refrigerate.

CHAPTER 5

Mastering Condiments

DRY BRINING TECHNIQUES

Exploring the breadth and depth of vegetable fermentation is an endeavor of infinite possibilities. We love fresh flavor and whole foods, but when it comes to the dinner crunch time, we are lazy cooks. We use flavorful fermented condiments to perk up any meal.

Whole-leaf fermenting is a tasty way to preserve herbs and to create delicious ingredients and garnishes for a cook's arsenal. Fermented pastes and bases can function as a seasoning foundation on which to build a meal. Think whole-food seasoning packets—a dollop or dash of leek, garlic, or another herbal paste added to a soup, sauce, or dressing at the end of the cook time provides a final burst of flavor for your meal. Most ferments can also become an instant vegetable side, or a whole soup, as you learned from Soirée-Leone (page 22). Ferments have become convenience foods for us, to the point that one shelf in the door of our fridge is dedicated to fermented herbs and pastes. Using fermentation to provide instant summer flavor year-round has been our best discovery in this culinary journey.

As you explore this chapter, you'll see most of the techniques are no different from that of making kraut (Chapter 4). But you will also learn that sometimes we first remove moisture to create our condiment. Even then, the secret to a successful fermentation is still pressing your ingredients under brine, keeping them under that brine and anaerobic, and letting the lactic acid bacteria do the work.

With condiments, the biggest challenge can be feeling like you have enough brine. There are a few reasons for this: In some of these recipes, the larger vegetable pieces have less "damaged" surface area than shredded veggies and will weep less brine; some ingredients, such as fresh leafy herbs, simply don't have as much moisture content; and last, condiments are often small-scale ferments, and when there is not a lot of vegetable, there is not a lot of brine. Just remember: You don't need a lot of brine, just enough to not have air pockets. The recipes will guide you through these conditions to a successful result.

Relishes/Chutneys/Salsas/Salads

The distinction between these four types of condiments is in the size and shape of the produce, the spices and herbs used, and the cultural ties associated with the condiment. Essentially they are all fermented or "sauered" vegetables that have been prepared in a way that is not just shredding and salting. They may be sliced, chopped, diced, or pulsed in a food processor and dried, salt-pressed, or a mixture thereof, depending on the texture desired. As you will learn, the preparation of the ingredients is one of the ways you can design the condiment you desire. Because many of our favorite condiments are sweet, we find you can add dried fruits or vegetables to layer in sweetness and texture. In some cases, you might add sugar after fermentation to create that sweet condiment, but also add vinegar so the sugar won't awaken the microbes and cause the ferment to sour further.

Use condiment making as a strategy to rescue a ferment that didn't quite live up to your expectations. The inadequacy could be about texture, such as a limp pickle (see Sweet Dill Relish, page 218), or a dull flavor, where adding spices or dried fruit can brighten it up. Or it could be too much flavor: We once made a pickle medley with jalapeños that was too spicy to eat. We blended the entire batch, added brine, and *voilà!* Hot sauce.

The process for making these types of ferments is essentially the same as for kraut (see page 67), with a few variations illustrated in the photos that follow.

▶ Vegetables in these types of recipes may be sliced, diced, pulsed in the food processor, dried, or pressed.

▶ When you press the vegetables into your vessel, you should see brine above the veggies. Don't worry if it "disappears" between pressings. If it fills the gaps, you have enough.

▶ Top the ferment with a primary follower. Then add a weighted follower. For a crock, you can use a plate topped with a sealed water-filled jar. For a jar, you can use a sealed water-filled jar or a ziplock bag as a follower-weight combination (or you can use the burping method; see page 44).

▶ Once it's finished and in storage, the less headspace above a ferment, the longer it will last, so fill each jar to the rim and transfer the ferment to a smaller jar as you use it.

1. Work the salt into the prepared vegetables.

2. Press the vegetables under the brine.

3. Submerged and weighted = a healthy environment for fermentation

4. Ready for long-term storage

Pastes

Worldwide, many gastronomic traditions are based on thick, robust pastes. Herbs and spices are ground together and used to flavor sauces to be served over grains. In North Africa berbere chili pastes warm many a dish, in Indonesia sambal pastes instantly add bling to a meal, and in Thailand red or green curry pastes are the basis for many dishes. In these pages you'll find, for example, Thai Basil Paste (page 155), Garlic Scape Paste (page 238), and Pepper Paste (page 295). One or all of these, combined with coconut milk, can turn a simple stir-fry into a Thai-style curry.

When taste-testing a paste, be aware that it may taste somewhat saltier than a kraut or relish because it's meant to be a concentrate, like bouillon.

The process for making these types of ferments is essentially the same as for kraut (see page 67), with a few variations illustrated in the photos that follow.

▶ Pastes are pulsed to a paste consistency in a food processor. When you mix in the salt, the vegetables will become juicy immediately. There is no need to massage to get the brine.

▶ When you press the mixture into a jar, there will be only a small amount of a thicker, sometimes syrupy brine that may be hard to distinguish from the vegetables. Don't worry; as long as the paste can be pressed with no air pockets, you have enough brine.

▶ Pastes need to be carefully packed in order to keep the vegetables under the brine and protected from the air. In the recipes we recommend the burping method first, as it is our preferred method and doesn't use single-use plastic. However, a water-filled ziplock bag, which acts as follower and weight, is a very successful strategy that we have recommended for years, especially if you don't think you will have the time or patience to burp. You choose what works for you. For the bag method, press the plastic down onto the top of the ferment and around the edges before you fill it with water and seal.

▶ Once it's finished and in storage, the less headspace above a ferment, the longer it will last, so fill each jar to the rim and transfer the ferment to a smaller jar as you use it. Keep a small round of parchment paper directly on top of the paste to prevent evaporation.

1. Chop or pulse the veggies to a fine consistency.

2. Press the paste into a jar to remove air pockets and to bring brine to the surface.

3. Place a ziplock bag, if using, on the surface of the ferment, and fill the bag to the rim of the jar with water to create weight.

4. Ready for long-term storage, with a piece of parchment paper in place to impede evaporation

Whole-Leaf Ferments

Think of whole-leaf ferments as an alternative to drying aromatic leafy herbs from the garden. Some herbs, such as basil, lose their flavorful volatile oils to the drying process, but fermentation captures and intensifies them. Whole-leaf ferments are made by salting the whole leaves, which shrink considerably. Don't expect a lot of brine in these ferments; depending on the herb used, they can seem nearly dry, but they will ferment beautifully.

Use fermented whole leaves as a garnish or a zesty addition to dressings, sauces, stir-fries, pasta dishes, or soups. Add them at the end of the cooking time for freshest flavor.

The process for making these types of ferments is essentially the same as for kraut (see page 67), with a few variations illustrated in the photos that follow.

▶ Remove the leaves from the stems.

▶ After salting, gently toss the leaves. They will wilt immediately and start to brine.

▶ Press the leaves into a jar, tamping to remove the air pockets. The leaves will become wilted and a deep green color, and you will get a tiny amount of a dark-colored brine.

▶ When this ferment is ready, the amount of visual change will depend on the particular leaves, and because of their low-sugar aromatic nature, when you taste-test the ferment the sour will not be as obvious as the salt.

▶ Once it's finished and in storage, the less head-space above a ferment, the longer it will last; fill each jar to the rim and transfer the ferment to a smaller jar as you use it. Keep a small round of parchment paper directly on top of the ferment to prevent evaporation and oxygen contamination.

1. Remove the leaves from their stems.

2. Add salt and toss.

3. Press the wilted leaves to remove air pockets and to bring brine to the surface.

4. Taste-test for doneness.

5. For long-term storage, set a piece of parchment paper on top to impede evaporation.

Reducing Moisture: Pressing and Drying Vegetables

Removing water from the vegetables that you intend to ferment may seem counterintuitive if you think about the all-important brine that keeps your ferment anaerobic and safe. However, for vegetables with high water content, removing moisture is an important step to reduce degradation and to keep the vegetables crunchy, with a pleasing mouthfeel and less watery texture. For example, large zucchinis and overgrown cucumbers do not ferment well—they break down and become mushy, with no redeeming flavors. But if you first remove their excess water, you get vastly better textural results. Removing moisture also intensifies flavors by concentrating the compounds in the food.

The two most common ways to rid vegetables of excess water is by salt pressing (using salt and pressure to draw out the juices) or drying (using air or sun to evaporate the moisture).

Around the world today, people are using these methods to create some fantastic contemporary condiments, but removing moisture from foods as a prelude to fermentation is not a new technique. Many traditional ferments rely on it—achars of the Asian subcontinent, Japanese tsukemono, traditional and modern pickling beds, and hundreds more. One notable example is a Himalayan khalpi made from a variety of cucumber that, when fully ripe, is *huge*—so big and fleshy and watery that most Western gardeners would consider it inedible. But when the seeds are scooped out and the flesh partially dehydrated before being chopped and packed with spices and oils, the result is a delicious and shelf-stable condiment.

In many traditional techniques, the vegetables are pressed or dried whole because the makers are producing large quantities during harvest season. In this case, using whole vegetables is more efficient, and the large quantities ensure enough mass to achieve even pressure across the vegetables. In home kitchens, where the scale is much smaller, it makes more sense to slice the vegetables before pressing or drying them.

SALT PRESSING

Salt pressing has a few advantages. Along with removing moisture, salting can extract bitter flavors that may be off-putting. As the vegetables are being pressed, they are also beginning to ferment, which means you don't need to worry if you can't get to the vegetables immediately after the prescribed time, as long as all the vegetable pieces are fully submerged in the brine.

For a successful outcome, you must apply even pressure across the entire quantity of vegetables. Here are some ways to evenly press vegetables:

» Two same-size casserole dishes, food-grade storage containers, or 5-gallon plastic buckets, one nested in the other, with the vegetables in the bottom one and the weights piled in the top one

» A casserole dish, bowl, or pot with a plate that fits inside and rests on the vegetables, weighted down evenly

» A crock with its weights or split weights, with more weight piled on top

» Two cutting boards, one on top of the other, with the vegetables in between them and the top board weighted, set up so that the liquid will drain into the sink (appropriate for recipes that don't require foods to ferment in the brine)

» Other weights: jars of water or large, clean rocks. Anything that is reactive, for example, canned foods or plastic that is not food-safe, such as barbell weights, can be piled on when there is no possibility for contact with the vegetables or salt.

» A purchased pickle press, or tsukemonoki

The particulars of a salt pressing vary slightly depending on the recipe, but here's the general process.

▶ Prepare vegetables by slicing them into rounds or strips that are ½ to ¾ inch thick. (If you choose to press whole vegetables, the pressing will take 2 to 3 days and need more weight.)

▶ Lightly salt all exposed sides of the vegetables.

▶ Place the vegetables in a crock, jar, glass casserole dish, or other nonreactive container.

▶ Place a significant amount of weight on top: 4 to 5 pounds or more, depending on the type and quantity of vegetable. Leave on counter.

▶ The pressing time will vary according to the recipe, vegetable, and desired outcome. In general, vegetables should be visibly reduced in size and liquid should be pooling. If not, let them sit for a few more hours.

▶ If the recipe calls for combining the pressing with fermentation, then after 24 hours (or as instructed by the recipe) you will add water to submerge the vegetables, if needed.

How Much Salt?

A good rule of thumb is to weigh the vegetables and to use no more than 5 percent of the weight of the vegetables in salt. Anything more than that and you risk oversalting. In many cases, you can use just 1.5 to 3 percent. Anything less than that, though, and you risk texture issues. Our recipes indicate the recommended amount.

Don't worry if the amount of salt seems high. Remember, the purpose of the salt is to draw out the moisture. The resulting salty liquid is discarded (or reused elsewhere), and the vegetables are rinsed and patted dry.

1. Thickly slice vegetables.

2. Lightly salt the vegetables on all sides.

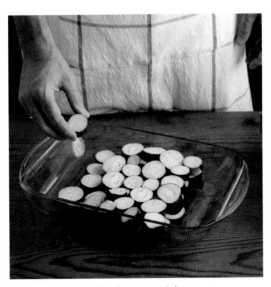

3. Place the vegetables in your container.

4. Weigh down the vegetables.

5. The vegetables are done when they are visibly smaller and liquid pools.

DRYING FOR FERMENTATION

Drying is an ancient technique for reducing moisture in vegetables, prolonging their shelf life. In many traditions, foods would be dried or partially dried in the sun and then fermented, offering double protection against the organisms that spoil while also boosting flavor and nutritional benefits.

We sometimes dry fruits or vegetables to help them retain their sweetness through fermentation. Dehydration is like locking away the sugar bowl—the fermenting microbes cannot as easily access the sugar in the fruit or vegetable, and so it stays sweet rather than being converted to sour. You'll see this technique in some recipes in this book.

The particulars of drying will vary by recipe and your chosen drying technique. You might sun-dry, air-dry, oven-dry, or use a dehydrator. You might simply lay out greens or herbs on racks or flat baskets to wilt. Drying cages that hang in the breeze are also great and keep bugs away.

In most cases, you'll dry the fruits or vegetables until their outer skin is dry and they have a somewhat rubbery or wilted consistency. If you're following a recipe, it will provide instructions.

CHAPTER 6

Mastering Tsukemono and Pickling Beds

Japanese methods of fermenting vegetables are particularly artful, producing delicious tastes and crisp textures. The often-intense flavors are meant to be consumed as small bites alongside grains and fresh vegetables. *Nani wanakutomo ko no mono* is a Japanese proverb that translates roughly to "There may be nothing else but as long as I have pickles."

The Japanese practice of tsukemono is both uncomplicated and elegant. *Tsukemono*, pronounced *skay-mo-noh*, is a generic term: *tsuke* means "pickled, marinated, or steeped," and *mono* means "things." These pickled things might be napa cabbage given a quick rub with salt and pressed for a few hours or daikon radishes fermented for a year or more in sake lees. Many delicious variations are an essential part of Japanese meals, an element incorporated in both simple home-cooked meals and elaborate dinners.

Many types of tsukemono are fermented in "pickling beds"—containers layered with vegetables and microbe- and enzyme-rich pastes that ferment, flavor, and preserve fruits and vegetables with very little effort and time. Although they can be used to make quick pickles, pickling beds double as a long-term preservation medium (yearslong, in fact!). The technique likely arose as a way to find uses for the by-products of other food productions. For example, *kasu-zuke* are pickles fermented in sake lees (*kasu*), the mash of rice and yeast that is a by-product of making sake. *Nuka-zuke* are fermented in rice bran (*nuka*), a by-product of polishing rice. Interestingly, eating nuka-zuke was shown to reduce the occurrence of beriberi, a disease that comes from vitamin B_1 deficiency and is a result of widespread consumption of polished rice.

Tsuke becomes *-zuke* when it's used as a suffix for another word. For example, *shio-zuke* is something marinated in salt (*shio*), and *miso-zuke* is something steeped in miso. Tsukemono include not just vegetables but also preserved fruit, fish, tofu, seaweed, and flowers.

Alex Hozven and Kevin Farley: Pioneers in Modern Fermentation

As we wrote this second edition, Alex Hozven and Kevin Farley of The Cultured Pickle Shop were celebrating 25 years of creating inspired ferments in Berkeley, California. They are considered by many to be pioneers in the modern fermentation movement. Their peerless creativity is due in part to many years of honing their relationship with their staff of tiny chefs—the microbes. "We think about the science of fermentation while we work about as much as we think about the science of respiration while we breathe," says Kevin.

Their story is rooted in food as medicine and began with a love of miso, which became their entry point into tsukemono. In the summer of 1995, they strung up turnips to air-dry, purchased a goldfish bowl as a fermenting vessel, and buried the shriveled turnips in a dark, rich barley miso.

Fermenting What Is Available

Alex sees the world of tsukemono as a way of taking people out of the mindset of "pickle = sour," as many tsukemono ferments are more balanced in flavor. The practice, developed in monasteries, is an elegant and efficient way to deal with the by-products of food production.

"I understand that there is tradition and beauty," Alex says, but she points out that monks used everything that was available to them. She explains, "Kasu-zuke is generally always done with bitter melon or eggplant, certain types of rice bran pickling is generally done with daikon, or umeboshi is always done with a particular type of fruit. Yet, one can use these techniques with the utmost of respect and reverence and apply the basic understanding of microbial transformation and preservation to what people have available within their own foodshed." The Cultured Pickle Shop approach playfully melds technique and place to create a unique sensibility.

Rice & Pickles

Some years ago, Alex and Kevin began weekend events called Rice & Pickles. The bowls represent feeding people good food that their bodies can digest. One weekend guests might be treated to rice topped with Frisée & Radicchio Yuzu Kosho, Romaine Lettuce Kimchi, Sea Kraut, Sweet Potato White Miso, Red Onion Umeboshi, Beet Kasuzuke, Burdock & Red Daikon Koji, Kale & Date Chile Paste Brine, or Spring Onion & Nori Lemon Gomashio. Pickles chosen for each weekend's offering might be 5 days or 2 years old. Alex says, "The shop operates so much better; by-products and waste streams are recycled into the lunch service in a beautiful way. It is the thing about the business that is the most genuine and good."

Alex told us, "You are never going to convince people verbally that this is the way they should eat. It has to come from within themselves. Feed them well and they will eat better because it is what their body desires. At the end of the day, eat food and eat plants and eat them as close to their natural form as possible. Fermentation allows you to do that in a way that satisfies all sorts of cravings for nourishment and diversity."

Rather than brine, vinegar, or soy sauce, a pickling bed uses a solid medium, such as a paste, to simultaneously ferment and marinate vegetables. The enzymes and microbes in the pickling medium work to break down and ferment the vegetables. Some of these pickling mediums can be reused a few times, and some can hold a ferment for years. With care, a nuka pot (see page 96) lasts indefinitely.

Some form of partial dehydration is important. If the vegetables aren't somewhat dehydrated, the pickling medium will become moist or even liquid, which is not conducive to a long-term ferment. Most vegetables benefit from some water reduction, but this is especially important when you're working with vegetables that have a high water content, such as radishes, eggplant, celery, cucumbers, zucchini, and so on.

▶ Decide how you want to prepare the vegetables. You may keep them whole, chunky, or cut them. The thinner you cut the vegetables, the sooner they will be finished and the more deeply the flavors of the pickling medium will penetrate.

▶ Prep your vegetables by salt pressing or partially drying them, or at a minimum tossing them with a little salt in a bowl and letting them sit for an hour or so.

▶ If you've salted the vegetables, they will be wilted and sitting in a pool of salt water. Rinse and pat dry.

▶ To start a pickling bed, spread half of the pickling paste in a small, square glass container. Place the vegetables in a single layer on top of the paste, then spread the rest of the paste on top. If the bed is already made, just poke your veggies down into the paste. The important thing is to make sure the vegetables are completely covered by the paste. (Another method is to place the vegetables in a ziplock plastic bag, or vacuum seal bag, and spoon in a few tablespoons of the paste. Seal the bag, removing as much air as possible, and squish the vegetables around a bit to make sure they are completely coated. Then press the vegetables and the sauce together to the bottom of the bag.)

▶ Place a cover, preferably sealed, on your container.

▶ Let the vegetables sit in the pickling bed for at least a few hours and up to 3 days (or more). It will depend on the pickling bed medium and your climate, but most should be left on the counter. You can also keep it in the fridge for a longer, slower fermententation, or in extra-warm conditions. Taste periodically to evaluate the flavor.

▶ When the vegetables are cured to your liking, pull them out and wipe them off. Whether you leave some of the paste on them or clean it off entirely depends on the presentation and intensity of flavor desired, among other considerations.

▶ Eat the fermented vegetables immediately or store them in an airtight container in the refrigerator, where they will keep for up to a week. Refrigerate the pickling bed between uses.

1. Make the pickling paste.

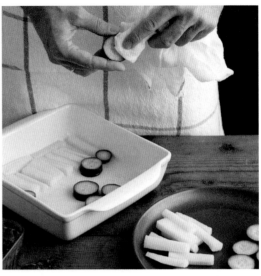

2. Prepare your vegetables by partially dehydrating them (by salt pressing, drying, or salting). Rinse off any salt water and pat dry.

3. Spread half of the pickling paste in a small rectangular glass container.

4. Place the vegetables in a single layer on top of the paste.

5. Spread the rest of the paste over the top of the vegetables. The vegetables should be completely covered. Cover the container with a lid.

6. Let the vegetables sit on the counter for a few hours to a few days. Taste periodically to evaluate the flavor.

7. Pull out the vegetables and wipe off some or all of the pickling paste, as desired.

8. Place the vegetables in a storage container and keep in the refrigerator. Store the pickling paste in the refrigerator between uses.

Make Your Bed: Options for Various Mediums

Here are a few recipes for traditional tsukemono pickling mediums. The consistency of these mediums varies from thick paste to saucy porridge. For consistency and ease in the recipes we will refer to all these mediums as pastes; just be aware some will be a true paste consistency and others a bit looser. You will find a nontraditional herbal paste that uses leftover herb stems as a pickling medium to deeply flavor other vegetables on page 246. In Japan, these pastes are traditionally used with specific vegetables, but they work wonderfully for any vegetable we've ever tried them with.

Once made, the best-by time of these pickles varies greatly. In the recipes you will see that the pickles removed from their medium—or bed—will keep in the refrigerator for a week. However, depending on moisture content, time fermented, medium used, acidic levels achieved, and how they are stored, this keeping time can be much longer. The flavors, however, will change and lose luster. If you want longer preservation, many of the pickles are best left to age in the medium.

KOJI-ZUKE

Koji-zuke are pickles created with the magic of koji, which is the superpower behind miso, soy sauce, sake, and many other Japanese fermentations. As the fungus *Aspergillus oryzae* grows on rice and other substrates, it creates enzymes that are the catalyst for fermentation. The enzymes break down carbohydrates and other large molecules, enhancing vegetables' natural sweetness and umami. Koji fermentation provides delicious pickles overnight, with little to no sour flavor.

We are including simple instructions for making three koji-based pickling pastes: ama-koji, sour ama-koji, and shio koji. While you can purchase koji-based pastes, they are not necessarily raw and unpasteurized. The key to koji is active enzymes; a pasteurized paste is merely a marinade. Dried rice koji is available online, from artisan makers of koji products, and at many Asian markets (usually in the refrigerator section).

» **Ama-koji** enhances the sweetness of vegetables; it is a good choice to encourage children or other ferment-shy eaters to join you on this journey. *Ama-koji* means "sweet koji" and is very similar to amazake, but is a bit thicker and traditionally used a little differently. *Amazake* translates to "sweet sake" and is the sweet beverage or base that is fermented into sake. Both can be used for making sweet pickles.

» **Sour ama-koji** is simply ama-koji that has naturally soured over time. It creates a crunchy lacto-fermented pickle with all the funk, some of the sweet, and none of the salt—and that combination can be mind-blowing. It is also a great method for folks looking to ferment without salt.

» **Shio koji** is similar to ama-koji but with salt, which plays an important role in bringing out the savory notes in vegetables.

Using Koji Pickling Pastes

Koji-zuke are generally made in a bowl as a quick pickle rather than a traditional pickling bed. Use fresh vegetables that haven't been dried or salt pressed. The koji mixture draws the moisture from the vegetables, leaving them with a pleasing light, crisp texture. Place the veggies in a bowl and cover with the ama-koji, sour ama-koji, or shio koji. Let marinate as desired. In general, koji-zuke are quick pickles, fermented for a few hours, overnight, or up to a week. The flavors evolve the longer they sit.

Once the pickles are ready, you can eat them immediately. If serving them fresh, they are delicious with the fermented rice liquid they are in. Or, you may pull them out and wipe off any lingering paste for serving or storing. Store the pickles in an airtight container in the refrigerator, where they will keep for about a week. The paste will be more liquidy after use and usually too weakened to reuse for fermentation, but don't toss it—it is tasty stuff; see box on page 93.

Ama-koji Pickling Paste

This basic ama-koji has a fairly thick, porridge-like consistency.

Note: Don't use distilled water to cook the rice, as the fermentation needs trace amounts of calcium.

> 1½ cups (330 g) brown, sweet brown, or white rice (to make 4 cups cooked rice)
> 1½ cups (300 g) koji rice

1. Cook the rice (using the appropriate amount of water, which will vary depending on the type of rice you're using) in a rice cooker or on the stovetop. Let it cool to 135°F/57°C.

2. Add the koji rice to the warm cooked rice and mix well. Pour the mixture into a 2-quart mason jar and tighten the lid.

3. Set the jar somewhere warm, preferably at a temperature between 135°F/57°C and 138°F/59°C. We use our dehydrator, set to 135°F/57°C. You can also wrap the jar in towels and put it in your oven with the light on, or place it in a picnic cooler with jars full of very hot water. Incubate the mixture for 6 to 10 hours, or until it has a floral aroma and a mild, sweet taste. (The cooler the incubation, the longer it will take.) Stir the mixture after the first hour and again once or twice during the incubation.

4. If you want the ama-koji to be sweeter, let it ferment a little longer. It will also become a little more liquidy. It will continue to sweeten, but only up to a point. When it hits its limit, the flavor will start to turn slightly sour and have some bitter or alcoholic notes. If this happens don't worry, you can still use it to pickle; it will just be more like the sour ama-koji below.

5. When the ama-koji is finished, put it in the refrigerator to halt the fermentation. It will keep for 3 to 4 months in the refrigerator, or for 6 months in the freezer.

SOUR AMA-KOJI

To make sour ama-koji, place a bit of your sweet ama-koji in a jar, add an equal amount of water, and put on the lid, but don't tighten it. Let sit at room temperature for a week, then use it or transfer it to the refrigerator.

Shio Koji Pickling Paste

2 cups (473 ml) water
1½ cups (300 g) koji rice
3 tablespoons (50 g) sea salt

1. Bring the water to a boil, then let it cool to 135°F/57°C. Combine the warm water, koji, and salt in a bowl. Mix well.

2. Place the mixture in a quart jar. Cover with cheesecloth and secure the cloth with a rubber band. Let sit at room temperature for 7 to 14 days. (The speed of fermentation is dependent on the temperature.) Stir daily.

3. Use the shio koji as is, or if you prefer a smooth consistency, press it through a sieve with a wooden spoon or blend in a blender. Like miso, shio koji is quite stable. Stored, sealed, and at room temperature, it will keep for at least 6 months and in the fridge possibly indefinitely.

MISO-ZUKE

Miso-zuke are pickles fermented in a *miso-doko*, a simple, light, and sweet miso pickling bed that can be made in minutes. After a few hours in the paste, the vegetables develop a mellow flavor. After a few days, they become boldly flavored small bites to be used in small servings or as garnish. While not required, it is a good idea to salt-press or partially dry your vegetables beforehand (see page 80). This step will also keep your miso-doko vibrant for longer.

The flavor of the miso pickling paste is heavily influenced by the type of miso you use. Use a sweet white miso and your vegetables will have a sweet, light flavor similar to that of ama-koji. If you use a deep, dark, earthy miso, those flavors will carry through to the final product. We recommend starting with red miso, as it is in the middle ground and has a lot of depth of flavor. You can also use a mixture of miso types.

OTHER PICKLING MEDIUMS

Anything that is a delicious environment for microbes is a candidate for further flavor building in making tsukemono-style pickles. We make pickling beds from leftover (or forgotten!) herbs. For example, you know that parsley bunch you bought, used some, and then forgot about until you found it wilting in the bottom of the vegetable drawer? Well, maybe that doesn't happen to you, but it does to us. We freeze that wilting bundle, along with any other herbs or trimmed-off herb stems, until we have a few cups. Then we use those herbs and herb bits to make a fermented paste and use the paste to stuff into a vegetable, as in Georgian-Style Fermented Green Tomatoes (page 334), or to make a pickling bed.

For a recipe based on this concept, see Jessica Alonzo's Herbal "Quick Pickling Bed" & Condiment on page 246.

Miso Pickling Paste

This miso paste will last for numerous pickle batches, but its vibrant, salty sweetness will eventually dissipate. You will know the bed is getting "tired" when it becomes watery and the flavors become thin. At this point, you can use the miso mixture to flavor another dish, a stir-fry, or a soup stock.

Miso can be expensive to use in this quantity. This is why we want to use the miso as many times as possible. You can add salt and extra mirin and sake to freshen it up. Or, if you do not want to maintain a bed, thinly coat the vegetables with miso and place them in a ziplock bag, removing as much air as possible. Place this on the counter for a few hours, or longer in the fridge.

You can use any type of miso or tasty paste. This is also a good way to use a homemade miso that may not have turned out as hoped or become too sour. If you are using an imperfect miso or tasty paste that is low in salt, add another 1 percent salt by weight for deeper flavor.

- 1 cup (237 ml) miso
- 3 tablespoons (44 ml) mirin, sherry, or rice vinegar (see note)
- 3 tablespoons (44 ml) sake

1. Combine the miso, mirin, and sake in a small bowl and mix well.

2. Use the miso paste to prepare a pickling bed as described on page 87, layering the paste with fresh vegetables (for short fermentations) or partially dried or salt-pressed vegetables (for longer fermentations).

3. Taste the miso-zuke to determine doneness. They are finished whenever they are flavored to your liking, which can be anywhere from a few hours to a few days. Once the pickles are ready, pull them out of the pickling bed, wiping off any lingering paste, and store them in an airtight container in the refrigerator, where they will keep for about a week.

4. Store the miso paste in the refrigerator when not in use. We like to store it in a small, square glass container that can serve as the vessel for both storage and a pickling bed.

Note: The alcohol content of the sake and mirin helps keep the medium from developing surface yeast or off-flavors, but they can be omitted if avoiding alcohol.

Uses for Already-Used Pickling Pastes

Once a pickling paste is past its prime, don't toss it—even if it's not potent enough to be used for tsukemono, it has a lot of life still left. Try using it as a flavoring agent in sauces, soups, and dressings, or use it as the liquid for savory baked goods. Another option is to dehydrate it and use it as a flavoring powder.

Nao Sadewic: Teaching Traditional Japanese Cooking

Nao Sadewic was born and grew up in Miyazaki, a semitropical region in southern Japan. She came to the United States in 1991 to take a break from her job "as a corporate warrior" and never went back, settling in Santa Fe in 2004. She taught traditional Japanese cooking classes in her kitchen for many years, focusing on fermentation and digestion. "My goal in life is to empower people in my community with the knowledge of how to make nourishing food," she says. "If people are making miso and koji after I leave this world, I couldn't be happier!"

A Part of Life

As Nao told us, tsukemono are just another way to preserve, everybody does it, and it is just a part of life. It can be as simple as cutting vegetables and sprinkling on salt and putting them in a container for shio-zuke. Nao explained *asa-zuke* is tsukemono that is ready in a short time frame, lightly pickled and wilted overnight, whereas *nara-zuke* is a type of kasu-zuke that may sit in the kasu for years. Making tsukemono is part of Nao's weekly routine. A big farmers' market supporter, she only buys vegetables in season, so she is always looking for good ways to help them last longer.

Making tsukemono is a practical and personal endeavor, and Nao has her own variations. When Nao is making miso, she uses an inch-thick layer of kasu (from sake maker Arizona Sake in Holbrook, Arizona) to seal the top of the miso fermentation vessel so that "nothing funny grows in there." Although it's not a common practice, Nao says, people who do it call it *sakekasu futa* (*futa* means lid). As the fermentation is happening, the kasu sucks up the miso's tamari and the flavor is pure gold. She uses this tamari-infused kasu for marinating pickles, among other things. It can be used a few times for vegetables, and if it is used for fish or meat it then becomes soup flavoring.

Nao's current *nukadoko* (nuka pot) is 4 or 5 years old. It's based on the rice bran that comes from preparing the brown rice for her koji making. She adds koji to her nukadoko because it makes the medium more forgiving, she says—with koji, the nuka pot does not need stirring every day. Once in a while she adds rice bran, salt, and powdered koji or shio koji to refresh the medium.

Contributing to Community

During the COVID-19 pandemic, Nao pivoted from structured teaching to concentrate on fundraising through her miso and koji making. She sends what she makes from the sale of her products to local farmers, and they donate the fresh, organically grown produce that her funds "bought" to an organization that provides food boxes and lunch bags to people in need—no questions asked. Nao says, "It feels like I've found a perfect way to contribute to the community."

"My goal in life is to empower people in my community with the knowledge of how to make nourishing food."

KASU-ZUKE

The practice of fermenting with kasu, the lees or mash left over from making sake, evolved more than a millennium ago in the Kansai region of Japan. The lees have both residual yeast and alcohol, making kasu great for preservation. With a high protein content and plenty of vitamins B_1, B_2, and B_6, it packs a nutritional punch as well. Kasu sold by artisan sake makers is usually pressed into a cake that is thick and slightly damp, such as ricotta or tofu. Mechanically pressed kasu from larger makers comes in very dry sheets, which need to be reconstituted with water before use. The powdered version no longer contains alcohol. If you happen to live near a sake maker, you may be able to purchase kasu relatively inexpensively. It is sometimes available in Asian grocery stores as well and is readily available online.

Kasu can be used just as is but is often doctored up with mirin for consistency, sugar for flavor and keeping those microbes fed, and a little salt for control.

Kasu pickles are sweet, not so much sour, and only lightly salty. As with any ferment, the flavor will vary from mildly sweet to pungently strong, even developing slightly alcoholic flavors, as time goes on.

Kasu Pickling Paste

Get creative with this base recipe. Add herbs and spices to your kasu pickle bed—we like basil, shiso leaves, or dried citrus peel. If you are feeling particularly adventurous, play around with the lees from other ferments. We have used both cider lees and vinegar lees as a pickling medium, with varying results.

- 3 cups (710 ml) sake kasu*
- 3 tablespoons (50 g) sea salt
- 1 tablespoon (12.5 g) sugar, and more if desired
- 2 tablespoons (30 ml) mirin, sherry, or rice vinegar

*If using mechanically pressed sheets, tear them into small pieces and massage them with a bit of water until they achieve a paste consistency.

1. Combine the kasu, salt, sugar, and mirin in a bowl and mix well.

2. Use the kasu paste to prepare a pickling bed as described on page 87, layering the paste with partially dried or salt-pressed vegetables.

3. For kasu-zuke, the vegetables will ferment for a few days to 18 months or more. Check the fermentation regularly during the first weeks; there will be a lot of CO_2 action, and you'll want to make sure that the vegetables stay submerged in the kasu mixture.

4. Once they are cured to your liking, pull the kasu-zuke out of the pickling bed, wipe off any lingering paste, and store them in an airtight container in the refrigerator, where they will keep for about a week.

5. Store the kasu mixture in an airtight container in the refrigerator. It can be used for additional batches for several weeks.

Nukazuke

A nuka pot (or nukadoko) is an ongoing pickling bed made of rice bran and salt. As with a sourdough starter or a kombucha SCOBY, this bed comprises a community of microorganisms working in harmony with one another. Like fine cheeses and wines, a nuka pot has terroir, a unique flavor of place. This flavor matures over time, becoming smoother and more complex. Nukazuke are crunchy, with a tangy, salty, yeasty, earthy flavor. You can add these highly seasoned vegetables to dishes at will.

But unlike aging wine and cheese, this medium requires almost daily care. To sustain the microbial equilibrium, the nuka bed must be used frequently. But you have great flexibility in regard to the vegetables you use and how long you ferment them. Both fresh and salt-pressed or partially dried vegetables can be pickled in a nuka bed. And you can have long-term pickling projects going on in the bed while also using it for quick pickles that ferment for just hours or days.

FERMENTISTA'S TIP

Nukazuke make great tempura. If you like fried okra, for example, sink okra whole in the pot, remove when cured, batter, and fry.

Making and Using a Nuka Pot (Nukadoko)

At the start, this recipe uses some dried koji, which is available online or at Asian markets. Simply put it in a blender to create koji flour. Omit the koji if it's not available.

Sonoko Sakai, whom you will meet on page 303, said that while growing up in Japan you could smell the nuka in homes. For her, it is a familiar and comforting smell, but it is so much less common now as most people purchase their nukadoko. Nuka beds are traditionally kept in cedar tubs, but any lidded vessel will do, as long as the lid isn't airtight. Many people use a ceramic crock with a lid. Though the lid shouldn't be airtight, you do want a covering that keeps out dust, bugs, and other contaminants.

- 2 pounds (900 g) dry rice bran
- ½ cup (100 g) dried koji ground to flour, or fresh if available
- ½ cup (135 g) sea salt
- ½ ounce (14 g) kombu, broken into pieces
- 8 cloves garlic, sliced
- 1 (1-inch/2.5 cm) piece ginger, minced
- 1 tablespoon (7 g) ground cayenne pepper
- 1 tablespoon (5 g) powdered yellow mustard
- 1 or 2 dried shiitake mushrooms, run through a blender to make a powder (optional)
- 6 cups (1.42 l) water, or as needed
- Vegetable scraps, as needed

1. Place the rice bran in a large skillet over medium heat and toast for 5 to 10 minutes, until lightly browned. Stir frequently to keep the bran from scorching.

2. Combine the toasted bran, koji, salt, kombu, garlic, ginger, cayenne, mustard, and shiitake mushroom powder, if using, in a 1- to 2-gallon glass or ceramic lidded vessel. Mix well with your hands, adding the water in a few batches until the mixture has the consistency of moist beach sand, like what you would build sandcastles with. You want it to be damp and clumping but not a wet slurry. Make sure you get any dry spots out of the corners.

3. Bury a handful (around ½ cup) of vegetable scraps in the mash. Cover the vessel and place it in a spot that is on the cool side of ambient home temperatures (in the lower to mid-60°s Fahrenheit/15°–19°C). Let sit for 1 day.

4. After 1 day, remove the veggies, scraping the paste back into the pot. Discard the scraps and add fresh ones. (You can eat the used scraps but the flavor will be bland.) Stir the mixture from top to bottom to aerate (which discourages mold) and manage temperature, moisture, and flavor. For the first month, you will repeat the stirring process daily. You can add new scraps once a week.

5. After the first month, begin adding veggies that you want to eat, such as carrot or daikon sticks. Vegetables are ready to eat in 8 to 24 hours. Watery veggies such as celery, eggplant, and cucumbers should be pressed with salt (see page 80) and allowed to sit for an hour or two before being put in the pickling bed.

6. After 6 to 8 weeks, the nuka flavors become more mature. At this point, the pot should have a pleasant earthy smell. Refresh the pot monthly with additional bran as needed (we usually do ¼ to ½ cup depending on use), salt (use 13 percent by weight of the rice bran you're adding), optional tablespoon of koji flour, and a few flavoring spices.

MAINTAINING THE BED

To sustain the microbial equilibrium, the bed must be used frequently. This means regularly adding fresh vegetables as well as continued frequent stirring from top to bottom to aerate. If you can't keep up with the nuka pot's demands, you can put the pot in the refrigerator, which works once it is established, especially if you will be traveling or the weather is very hot. If you know you will not be using it for a longer period of time, Nao suggests putting the pot in the freezer. We've put ours to hibernate for around 6 months at a time. When you are ready to use it, thaw it slowly by putting it in the fridge first, then back on the counter.

WASTE NOT

We found that when we needed to feed the pot but didn't have anything we wanted to pickle, we could put in vegetable scraps, such as carrot tops or cucumber peels, for a day. Some scraps, such as kale stems, were reborn in the nuka pot—when chopped finely, they became a delicious garnish, similar to capers, but different.

TROUBLESHOOTING NUKADOKO

The vegetables taste too salty or not sour enough. If your pot is young, it might not be ready. Keep priming the bed with vegetable scraps until the vegetables have a nice acidic flavor.

The nukadoko is wet. Vegetables with a high moisture content will lose water in the bed and make it watery. Pour off any excess water that is sitting on top of the bed, or add more rice bran and salt. Do this as soon as you see it, as too much moisture will smother the bed and it will sour.

Something is off. If your pot smells sour or alcoholic, or if it has white mold on top, something is out of balance. Yellow mustard powder can be used to bring it back into balance. In the case of mold, scoop it off first. Add 1 teaspoon of yellow mustard powder and turn the nukadoko two times a day for 1 week. Uncover it and set it in a sunny spot if you can. It should start smelling earthy and yeasty in a couple of days. If not, you can try a little more mustard, but if this doesn't help after about a week, the bed might be beyond saving. If the bed does return to normal, try aerating it a little less frequently; you don't want to overoxygenate the bacteria.

The pot developed a green or pink mold. Discard immediately and start again.

Zero-Waste Tip: Make a Cuppa Miso

Another way to reuse miso pickling paste is to drink it. A warm cup of miso—or miso pickling paste—is not only tasty but offers these benefits:

Short-Term Benefits

» Stimulates digestive fluids in your stomach, which aids in digestion and assimilation of food
» Provides beneficial probiotics
» Offers high levels of antioxidants
» Contains all essential amino acids
» Serves as a good (vegan) source of B vitamins (including B_{12})

Longer-Term Benefits

» Strengthens the immune system and helps lower LDL cholesterol
» Reduces risk for breast, prostate, lung, and colon cancers
» Strengthens quality of blood and lymph fluid
» Protects against radiation and heavy metals due to dipicolonic acid, an alkaloid that chelates heavy metals and discharges them from the body

TO MAKE A CUPPA MISO

A cup of miso is just miso and warm water—not a classic soup made with broths. It can replace that first morning cup of coffee (okay, that might be asking too much) or serve as a savory afternoon pick-me-up. This "recipe" is for using watered-down pickling miso, but you can use fresh miso if you don't have pickling paste to upcycle.

Different varieties of miso have different flavors, and of course those flavors will be altered by having been through some pickling. Your cup may be rich and gingery if you used the miso for a ginger pickle or more vegetal if you were curing carrots.

Add 1 to 2 tablespoons (17–34 g) of miso pickling paste to your favorite mug. Heat 1 cup (237 ml) of water to 180°F/82°C. Pour a few tablespoons of the hot water into your mug and work with a spoon until mixed well. Top with the remaining hot water. Stir and enjoy.

CHAPTER 7

Mastering Brine Pickling

Many people think of pickles as cucumbers preserved in vinegar. That is one type of pickle, but not the only kind. Technically every process we talk about in this book is pickling. However, as the conversation around lacto-fermented pickling increases, so does the collective confusion around the difference between fermenting and pickling. All vegetable fermentation is pickling, but not all pickling is fermentation.

This is in many ways more a question of semantics than process. The first point of confusion is that pickled cucumbers are so ubiquitous that most of us think the word *pickle* denotes some version of a cucumber—garlic dills, bread and butter, and so on. But the definition of the verb "to pickle" is "to preserve or flavor (food) in a solution of brine or vinegar." Many kinds of food can be pickled, but in this book, we're talking (mostly) about vegetables.

Recipes for canned vinegar pickles use precise measurements because it is crucial that the added acidity brings the pH of everything in the jar to 4.6 pH or below, so that they are safe to consume. This acidic pH gives pickles their sour pucker. Adding vinegar is one way to create that pH level, but not the only way.

Fermentation also acidifies vegetables. When we set up vegetables to ferment, the microbes get busy doing what microbes do: transforming the carbohydrates into acid. The cool thing about fermentation as pickling is that the microbes do the work for you and the recipes don't have to be precise because they acidify everything equally, well below our magic 4.6 pH.

In this chapter, you will learn how to create lacto-fermented pickled vegetables that are either whole or cut into large pieces. Unlike shredded, thinly sliced, or finely diced veggies, these vegetables cannot create their own brine, so we submerge them in a prepared salt brine. The brine interacts with the vegetables through the process of osmosis, which begins the lactic acid fermentation.

Understanding Brine

Brine keeps the fermentation anaerobic (without oxygen), dissuades malevolent bacteria from intruding, and controls the pace of fermentation for maximum flavor and a crisp texture. Controlling the brine controls the fermentation. Understanding the nuances of brine gives you the power to trust the process and turn the dials as you want. To keep this simple, we have created three brines that work well for a variety of applications. There is no need to do any calculations.

To make brine, always use the best water you can find, preferably unchlorinated water. Many recipes recommend boiling the water for the brine. We skip this as it takes more time and energy resources, and we never add so much salt that we need heat to dissolve it. We do recommend boiling if your water source is questionable.

For cucumbers and other vegetables with a high water content, the ratio of salt to water is higher than what is appropriate for denser vegetables; it is important for proper preservation and texture and to achieve that deli taste. We call this High Brine, and we use ¾ cup salt per gallon of water. If you want less salt, you can experiment with reducing the amount—but just a little, and don't go lower than ½ cup salt per gallon of water.

With less watery veggies, for example root crops and denser vegetables, you can use a more dilute brine solution, which we call Basic Brine. This is our go-to brine. For those of you who want to experiment, we've included a slightly lower-salt version of Basic Brine.

Our Soaking Brine has the highest salt ratio (7 percent), and it's used for fermentations such as kimchi that rely on brine to draw out the moisture from vegetables before fermentation. This brine doesn't get used in the final fermentation.

Remember, with all these brines, this doesn't include the vegetable weight so the final salt concentration is lower.

BASIC BRINE (3% SALT)
- 1 gallon (3.78 l) water
- ½ cup (134 g) unrefined salt

LOW-SALT BASIC BRINE (2.5% SALT)
- 1 gallon (3.78 l) water
- 5 tablespoons plus 1 teaspoon (91 g) salt

HIGH BRINE (5.25% SALT)
- 1 gallon (3.78 l) water
- ¾ cup (200 g) unrefined salt

SOAKING BRINE (7% SALT)
- 1 gallon (3.78 l) water
- 1 cup (269 g) unrefined salt

WASTE NOT
If you've happened to make too much brine, save the extra. You will often need to top up a jar or crock to keep the fermenting vegetables submerged; it will keep in the fridge for about a week.

Before you throw it out, consider reclaiming the salt. Simply place the unused brine on a plate or other shallow container. Divide among a few plates if needed. During the next few days the water will evaporate, leaving the salt crystals to be reused.

ADDITIONS TO BRINE SOLUTIONS
Sugar. Some brine recipes in this book contain added sugar. Sugar will feed the microbes that ferment your vegetables and help make sure your brine—or any ferment, really—has enough carbohydrates for the bacteria to create strong acidity. We have observed that adding sugar to a brine often makes it less susceptible to Kahm yeast growth, and we suspect that this is because

Calculating Your Own Brine Ratios

The brines in this book are based on a simple ratio of salt weight to water weight. This means that after you add your vegetables, your actual ratio of salt weight to ferment weight is less. For example, the actual pickle Basic Brine yields is lower than a 3 percent salt ratio. We do this because it is simple, and it works. Vegetable fermentation for most applications does not require fine precision. If you are looking for more control and nuance in your fermentation practice, you may choose to create specific brine ratios. To do this, you will need a kitchen scale.

To make a brine, take the volume of water in milliliters or its weight in grams (which will be the same number: 1 ml water = 1 g) and multiply it by the desired brine strength to find the number of grams of salt you should add. For example, to calculate how much salt we should add to 1 quart (946 ml) of water to make a 2 percent brine, we use the following equation:

$$946 \times .02 = 18.92$$

We round this up to 19. So we must add 19 grams of salt to the quart of water.

For a simple brine that takes the vegetable weight into account, place your vessel on the scale. Tare it to zero. Place the vegetables in the vessel, then add water to the level desired. Take the weight. Multiply this weight by the desired salt ratio. Let's say you have 439 grams of vegetables + 420 grams of water = 859 grams. If your desired brine strength is 3.5 percent, multiply 859 by .035, which yields a salt amount of 30 grams.

the sugar helps lower the pH of the brine to less than 3.5.

That being said, we don't recommend adding sugar to ferments of vegetables with a high carbohydrate content. With too much sugar, the ferment could acidify too quickly and become too acidic for the lactic acid bacteria to continue the fermentation. This would mean the vegetables themselves don't get fully fermented. More on this in a minute.

Vinegar. There are as many family recipes for pickles as there are grandmothers who made them. We've been asked about recipes calling for brine solutions that contain both salt and vinegar. It's not a good idea to use both in fermentation. The salt solution is ideal for promoting the succession of lactic acid bacteria. While a bit of acetic acid

(vinegar) is created during the fermentation, the ratio works. When acetic acid is introduced from the outside, the balance is disrupted and it will stunt or even stop the development of the pickles.

But what about that classic bread-and-butter pickle flavor—all vinegary and sweet at the same time? This flavor cannot be achieved by fermentation alone. Instead, ferment your cucumbers fully, then remove some of the brine and replace with a 50:50 solution of raw vinegar and honey or sugar.

Tea. It can be fun and delicious to create brines with tea. Black and green teas add tannins that help keep veggies crisp. The teas add flavor, including some bitter notes, and dark color. We like jasmine green tea, genmaicha, and Earl Grey to change things up now and then. Herbal teas (tisanes) are wonderful as well—chamomile, hibiscus, and so on will give your brines special color and flavor. Use the water that you will use to make your brine to brew your tea or tisane. You will want to make it stronger than you would for drinking.

LEAVES

We top our pickle batches with large leaves to help keep everything—from pickles to spices—submerged. You can use any large edible leaf. Cabbage, collards, and lettuce are common. We use leaves that contain tannins as followers but also place them in the batch with the vegetables, as they help maintain crispness; our favorites are grape and horseradish leaves. Grape leaves are conveniently shaped. The horseradish is also large and offers wonderful flavor. Other tannic options include raspberry leaves, currant leaves, sour cherry leaves, and oak leaves. Oak leaves are high in tannins and can add a little more bitterness than what you are looking for, so use them sparingly. Be sure to use only leaves that have not been treated with pesticides. Because tannic leaves all come from perennial shrubs, vines, and trees, you might consider preserving some grape leaves just for winter pickling (page 241).

PICKLE FACTS TO IMPRESS YOUR FRIENDS

» The practice of pickling cucumbers began in India 4,000 years ago.
» *Pickle* comes from the Dutch word *pekel*, which actually means "brine."
» When both salt concentration and temperature are low, the dominant bacteria at work are *Leuconostoc mesenteroides*. This strain produces a mix of acids, alcohol, and aroma compounds. At higher temperatures, we see *Lactiplantibacillus plantarum*, a.k.a.

lactic acid bacteria. Many pickles start with *Leuconostoc* and progressively change to *Lactiplantibacillus* as acidity increases.

The Vegetables

You can ferment any fruit or vegetable in brine. How salty your brine needs to be is based on the texture, or structure, of the fruit or vegetable and its inherent sugar content.

Softer vegetables will need a higher-salt brine for pleasing crispness and mouthfeel. Let's face it: For whatever reason, if a food or a vegetable doesn't have a texture we like, we don't want to eat it—even if our mind tells us that it's healthy, the flavor is good, and there is nothing inherently wrong with it. Another way to keep that crispness or to achieve it in a softer vegetable is to salt-press or partially dry such vegetables before fermenting them further.

We are going to get a little nerdy for a moment, because some of us just can't help but be fascinated by the little particulars. If that is not you, feel free to skip the next paragraph and to use the recipes as written.

Vegetables that are more dense may not need as much salt to stay crisp. However, if the vegetable is very dense, such as a whole carrot or a Brussels sprout, it may not fully acidify. There are two main reasons this might happen. The first is easy to guess—it's just too dense. This can easily be solved by cutting the carrot into slices or sticks or the Brussels sprouts in half. The other reason is that dense vegetables need more time to fully ferment and tend to have a higher carbohydrate content. As you know, carbohydrates give the lactic acid bacteria more food, which means more acid development. A good thing, right? Yes, but it also can cause a problem. The microbes may enjoy a gluttonous feast, causing too much acid to develop too quickly. If the brine then falls below a pH of 3.0, the microbes will have created an environment they themselves cannot tolerate. Most will then be out of the game, and the fermentation could halt before the dense vegetable is acidic throughout.

SEAWATER BRINE

Yes, brine can be made from seawater. In some places, people have been doing so for a long time. Kirsten tasted amazing Aegean Sea water–cured olives made by a grandmother in Greece. The average salt concentration is 4 percent, which is on point for many pickles. A study[8] that looked at using seawater as brine to preserve vegetables in areas where water is limited showed that the seawater improved the firmness and color of the pickles due to the calcium and magnesium content of the water. To use, run the seawater through a coffee filter, boil, and allow to cool before submerging your vegetables in it.

ABOUT PICKLE MEDLEYS

You can use just about any vegetable to make brined pickles, just not necessarily together. There are some things to keep in mind when making medleys:

» Consider the type of vegetables. You want the textures to be similar; for example, you might not want to use zucchini and beets in the same ferment, as fermentation and long-term preservation rates are different.

» Alliums such as onions and garlic work well in any pickle.

» Sliced peppers tend to get very soft. They may require a little more salt in the brine, or might do better if dried. You could also use the small pickling varieties, such as pimientos, and ferment them whole.

▶ Prepare a salt water brine according to the recipe directions.

▶ Rinse the vegetables in cold water and prepare according to the recipe directions.

▶ Place any spices in the bottom of your fermentation vessel.

▶ Pack the vegetables into the vessel, leaving 4 inches of headspace in a crock or wedging them under the shoulder of a jar to help keep them submerged.

▶ Pour in enough brine to cover the vegetables completely. In a jar, this may be quite close to the rim; in a crock you'll need to leave room for a weighted follower. Store any leftover brine in the fridge (it will keep for a week; discard thereafter and make a new batch, if needed).

▶ If using grape leaves or other tannin-rich leaves (oak, horseradish, sour cherry, currant, and so on), place them over the vegetables as a *follower*.

(CONTINUED ON NEXT PAGE)

▶ If you're using a crock, add a *secondary follower*, which could be the weight that came with the crock, or use a plate that will rest on top of the pickles, and a *weight*, such as a sealed water-filled jar, to keep things in place, and cover the crock with its lid or a clean towel. In a jar, the tightly wedged vegetables usually stay in place on their own, so you won't need to hold them down. If your jar has a lid, put it on loosely and cover the jar with a towel, or tighten the lid if you intend to release CO_2 with the burping method (see page 44).

▶ Set the jar or crock on a plate or a rimmed baking sheet in a spot where you can keep an eye on it, out of direct sunlight, ideally with an ambient temperature between 55 and 75°F/13 and 24°C. Ferment for the time indicated in the recipe.

▶ During the fermentation period, monitor the brine level and top off with reserved brine solution, if needed, to cover. You may see some harmless scum on top; scoop it out. Veggies peeking up out of the brine will quickly get soft and spoil. If you see anything even a *tiny bit* out of the brine, use a utensil to poke it back under or, if it's begun to soften or turn pinkish, pluck it out.

▶ As the vegetables ferment, they begin to lose their vibrant color and the brine becomes cloudy. This is when you can start to test your pickles. Using a clean, nonreactive utensil, remove some of the vegetables and taste. They're ready when:
  » They're pleasingly sour and pickle-y tasting, without the strong acidity of vinegar.
  » The flavors have mingled.
  » They're softer than they were when fresh but retain some crispiness.

If they're not sour enough for your palate, rinse the followers and weight, put everything back in place, and continue monitoring the brine level and watching for scum or mold.

▶ When the pickled vegetables are ready, carefully skim off any scum on top. Transfer the pickled vegetables into jars if you fermented in a crock. If you fermented in jars, you can store the vegetables in them. Add enough fresh brine to completely submerge the vegetables. Cover with fresh grape leaves, if available, tighten lids, and store in the refrigerator.

▶ After about 1 day, check to be sure the pickles are still submerged, topping off with more brine if necessary.

1. Make the brine.

2. Cut the veggies into chunks, if desired.

3. Place any spices in the bottom of a jar, then pack in the vegetables.

4. Pour in brine until the veggies are submerged.

5. Place a leaf or other follower on the surface.

6. Make sure the leaf is over the veggies and below the brine.

7. Put on the lid. Unless you plan to burp your jar (see page 44), leave the lid loose so CO_2 can escape.

8. Cover with a cloth and set aside to ferment.

9. Taste the veggies when the brine begins to appear cloudy.

10. Finished pickles

11. Transfer to smaller jars for long-term storage.

12. For storage, pickles should be fully submerged.

Continuous Fermentation Brines

People often ask: Can I reuse my brine after I've eaten the last pickle? The answer is annoyingly vague: It depends. In most cases, we recommend enjoying the fabulous elixir to sip, to flavor other dishes, or to make crackers (page 369). In a way, there is no technical advantage to reusing a brine. It isn't like sourdough starter, where you begin with a cultivated community of microbes. However, dropping in a few veggies for a quick pickle (for flavor and not necessarily full fermentation) is fun. Reusing brines can result in less tasty pickles if the brine oxidizes or Kahm yeast move in. One of the things we love about fermentation is that there are few steadfast rules.

Traditions and microbe collaboration are vast and varied. In parts of China, a fermented pickle called Pao Cai is made with a perpetual brine. Once this brine is established, it can be used for years. It will pickle vegetables in just a few hours or overnight. This method is less about preservation and more about processing vegetables for bright flavors. The results can be served raw but are more often cooked in a dish.

The crocks that house these brines are made of glass, porcelain, or glazed ceramic. They have a distinctive shape with a wide belly and narrow opening to decrease oxygen exposure. The rim has a flared trough that serves as a water seal for the lid to nestle into. The top is an inverted bowl that functions as both lid and serving vessel. A crock with a continuous brine is a source of pride for the maker and requires care and upkeep. A relationship develops, beginning with the maker's hands. Each maker has a unique microbiome that enhances the flavor of the pickles. Makers do not let the hands of others dip into their pots, as it may spoil the brine.

As with a nuka pot, a continuous brine needs a few weeks to develop its flavor, will get stronger over time, and will be healthiest if used regularly. After it is established, it can be used for quick pickles. It can be replenished with salt, sugar, and spices as needed, indefinitely.

Mara Jane King:
Reassessing Our Ideas of Food Heroes

The scent of fermenting soy sauce from a nearby soy sauce manufacturer wafted through Mara's childhood. Mara grew up in Hong Kong, where stalls selling fermented foods filled the markets and where salted eggs, fermented mustard greens, and preserved meats dotted the rice bowls served to her. Many of the simple, nourishing, delicious home-cooked meals she enjoyed as a child were prepared by Kai Ma, her god-grandmother (*kai ma* means godmother), who tended to the family's cooking and most of the childminding of the extended family.

Unsung Food Hero

Kai Ma, whose name was Han Huan Zhi (韩焕枝), is one of Mara's food heroes. A small, hardworking woman who was beloved by her family, Kai Ma— like most of the people who show up daily to nourish their loved ones—will never receive the recognition she deserves, Mara feels. Knowing this, Mara works to redesign and reassess our ideas of food heroes. She features home cooking in her work as a chef, educator, and writer because it is in many ways forgotten, approachable, and deeply satisfying. She believes that good food is an inherent part of good living, and she is always looking for ways to put food knowledge into practice.

Growing Her Passion

Mara's journey with fermentation began with kombucha and expanded when she was the head chef at a sushi restaurant in Boulder, Colorado, where she still resides. Because she was tasked with building the menu, she began fermenting kimchi and other vegetables. Mara credits kombucha, kimchi, and sauerkraut as her nexus ferments. In 2011, she and her friend Willow King began to explore the idea of a ferment-forward deli. On the advice of a friend, they pared this down to the part they loved the most— making pickled vegetables. In 2012, their small fermentation business, Ozuke, began to take wing. The ride took them from home kitchen to commissary kitchen to a dedicated factory with eight full-time employees and a pet forklift named King Tub.

Mara told us the same thing we've been hearing from many small artisan food producers over the last decade: Our food system just isn't designed for the small maker to succeed; the distributors and retailers hold the power and make the most money from the products. It is hard work. In 2019, Mara and Willow sold the business, but the Ozuke brand lives on. And Mara's passion for fermentation hasn't moved aside. She is now the director of fermentation at IE Hospitality and is working on a book, *Chinese Fermentation*.

Mrs. Ding's Continuous Pickling Brine

See photo on page 188

Mrs. Ding lives in Chengdu, in southwestern China, and generously shared her home and her recipe with Mara King, Mara's mom Judy King, Sandor Katz, and filmmaker Mattia Sacco. You can see Mrs. Ding in her kitchen making her pickles in Episode 1 of the YouTube series *People's Republic of Fermentation*. Mara transcribed and shared this recipe.

This is both a recipe and a springboard. Mara notes that she has heard of other continuous brines made with different seasonings, such as turmeric, ginger, bay leaf, and celery seed.

Finally, an important note: Sugar is not inconsequential. Continuous brines traditionally use malt sugar, and this less-refined sugar has a relatively high mineral content that supports the bacteria. Mara suggests that if you have to use refined cane sugar, supplement with a couple of teaspoons of coconut sugar, molasses, or something similar.

> 5 cups (1.18 l) water
> 2 teaspoons (11 g) unrefined salt
> 2 teaspoons (18 g) maltose (or barley malt sugar, rice syrup, unrefined sugar, or brown cane sugar)
> 3 slices ginger
> 2 teaspoons (3 g) Sichuan peppercorns
> 5 pieces dried chiles
> 2 black cardamom pods
> Veggies to pickle in the brine, such as radish, daikon radish, cabbage, onion, carrot, and cucumber

1. Bring the water to a boil, then pour it into a ½-gallon jar. Add the salt, maltose, ginger, Sichuan peppercorns, chiles, and cardamom pods. Let cool to room temperature.

2. Add the vegetables to the jar. Make sure they are submerged. Set the lid on top, leaving it slightly ajar to release CO_2, or tightening it if you intend to burp the jar (see page 44).

3. Let ferment for 1 to 2 weeks, until the vegetables are sour, keeping an eye on the jar to make sure the vegetables stay submerged and, if necessary, to burp it. Remove all the vegetables, and eat them if you like.

4. The brine is now "primed," so you can add more vegetables and they will be done pickling in only a day or two. The pickles should be nice and crisp and sour. The more seasoned the brine, the faster the pickle.

5. To keep brine active and strong, move a rotating supply of vegetables through it. If the brine is not in use for a period of time, seal the jar and place it in the refrigerator.

Note: Keep your hands clean when handling the pickling brine to avoid contaminating it. If it develops a yeast layer on top, add a tablespoon or so of hard alcohol. Mrs. Ding uses baijiu, China's ubiquitous sorghum spirit, but a splash of vodka or gin would also do the trick. We've used a similar trick for years on any ferment that develops surface yeast. We keep a neutral vodka in a spray bottle and spritz the top of the misbehaving ferment.

Accelerated Calcium Fermentation (A-Ferm) for the Home Fermentista

By Lisa Moeller

The calculations for this calcium chloride brine will work for jalapeños, carrots, green tomatoes, and cauliflower, which are easily fermented without salt. Other vegetables will not work as well with these ratios; you'd need to know the sugar content of the vegetables in order to dial in the correct ratios to control the fermentation.

The concentration of calcium chloride and potassium sorbate, both of which can be purchased online, is based on total volume, rather than weight, which makes it simple. In other words, whether a 1-gallon vessel has 50 grams, 500 grams, or 1,500 grams of produce doesn't matter so long as the final volume is 1 gallon.

For a 1-gallon crock or jar, you'll need:

- **37** grams calcium chloride
- **3–4** grams potassium sorbate
  Starter culture that favors lactic acid production (use the amount recommended for the culture you have)

Prepare the jalapeños, carrots, green tomatoes, or cauliflower by pricking, dicing, slicing, or shredding them to expose more surface area. Use them to fill a gallon crock or jar.

Add the calcium chloride, potassium sorbate, and starter culture. Top with water.

Set the fermentation vessel in a warm spot, around 86°F/30°C. In this environment it will likely ferment within a week. Fermentation is finished when pH is below 3.5.

Store the pickled vegetables in the brine with the lid tightened. When you're ready to use them, rinse them. If they are still bitter, cook or use with other ingredients as the calcium chloride will be diluted and the bitterness won't be perceived.

PICKLES IN ANCIENT CHINA

One notable window into China's fermentation diversity is the 2,100-year-old tomb of Xin Zhui (辛追), a noblewoman from the Han Dynasty, discovered in the 1970s. This oxygen-starved subterranean tomb lay in perfect conditions for unparalleled preservation, becoming a time capsule of ancient consumption. Xin Zhui was laid to rest surrounded with baskets, bags, and ceramic pots full of foodstuffs. The variety of food is staggering, but of particular interest to us is that among these afterlife comestibles were pickles in their pots. And, if that wasn't discovery enough, she was also accompanied by a stunning collection of books and tablets containing information on health and well-being, as well as preparation techniques for the pickles.

Lisa Moeller:
Making the Pickling Industry More Sustainable

The ways in which we employ microbes to process our food are changing by leaps and bounds as scientists, innovators, and experimenters work to answer the question: How can fermentation be used for the good of the world? For example, we regularly come across interesting research looking into ways in which fermentation can transform the by-products of food processing, such as avocado or mango pits, for example, from waste to useable nourishment.

A Sustainable Pickle

We want to introduce you to Lisa Moeller, whose passion is promoting sustainability in the pickle industry, which she's been part of for more than 35 years. Her work comes at this from two angles: The first is by introducing a process that can help reduce food waste by allowing more vegetables to be fermented and held in a stable state until they can be combined with other ingredients. This helps with products that combine fruits and vegetables with different harvest seasons. For example, the vegetables in a taqueria-style mix—cauliflower, carrots, jalapeños—could be harvested locally (less shipping) in their season, fermented for storage, and then mixed after all ingredients are in from the fields.

The second is eliminating the need for salt in the fermentation process, which reduces salt contamination of the environment—groundwater, stormwater, and soil structure. Lisa, based in North Carolina, works with companies worldwide to shift their fermentation processes to those that improve consistency and flavor, reduce energy use, allow for closed systems that can attain zero waste, and eliminate the what-happens-to-the-tons-of-solid-salt-waste problem.

Let's back up a moment and start with the journey from freshly harvested vegetable to pickles on the grocery store shelves. Vegetables are harvested, then plopped in a 10,000-or-so-gallon tank to ferment. The veggies are now soaking in 6.9 percent salt brine, and for those of you who like fun facts, that is about 5,838 pounds of salt per tank. As an interesting aside, up until 1988 these tanks used a 13 percent salt brine, and today's 6.9 percent is seen as the lowest concentration the industry can use to avoid loss. This brine also has a bit of calcium chloride for crunch and potassium sorbate to control yeast and mold. The microbe population is a mix of many but dominated by *Lacticaseibacillus casei*, *Lactiplantibacillus plantarum*, and *Levilactobacillus brevis*.

Once fermented, the veggies are able to stay in the tanks for some time until they are called upon to become, oh, let's say relish. Now the salt is discharged in order for that relish to have a 1.5 percent salt content. Finally, vinegar and flavors are added, the veggies are packed in jars and pasteurized, and off they go to sit on a shelf.

Enter No-Salt Fermentation

No-salt fermentation uses calcium chloride. Vegetables are diced, sliced, or pricked and placed in a 1.0 percent calcium chloride solution. This process, originally patented by Bill Scott, is called

Accelerated Calcium Fermentation, trademarked under the name A-Ferm. It is a game changer. It produces a faster fermentation that is more stable over longer periods of time with no refrigeration. The vegetables are held in a stable brine with a pH that drops to near 3.0. Common brine problems, such as shrinkage or the blow-out of the middle of a cucumber, although not major concerns for home fermenters, cause considerable waste in the industry. With just calcium chloride, potassium sorbate, an added culture of *L. plantarum* to ensure a robust microbial population, and no sodium chloride (salt) at all, these issues are eliminated.

There is a downside: At 1 percent concentration, calcium chloride is bitter. In the industry, which is already set up to rinse off salt, this isn't an issue, and the calcium chloride causes no harm to soils when rinsed. In the home situation, it does not produce a ferment that you make and enjoy straight out of the jar. Therefore, for most home fermenters, A-Ferm may not be a solution. However, for small productions and folks who have big gardens, this could be an interesting way to save your harvest when it's at the peak, in a way that does not require refrigeration or canning—both of which demand a lot of energy.

Potassium sorbate is an ingredient that may raise eyebrows. It is used in the food industry for preservation, and while it is part of the commercial pickle-making process, it does not have to be put on the product label because it breaks down. It is used to limit the growth of that pesky Kahm yeast (page 414). In the case of accelerated calcium fermentation, potassium sorbate is used to kill off the wild yeasts that are naturally present on vegetables. They're held in check in a high-salt environment but need an inhibitor in this no-salt process. (Although of course you may decide to experiment without potassium sorbate.)

As we mentioned, Lisa is passionate about creating a more sustainable industry, and as we talked, it was clear that her love of our planet is her motivator. We were happy when she agreed to share this process for the small-scale fermenter (see page 113). To us, this feels a little bit like citizen science. So take this idea and feel free to experiment!

Common brine problems, such as shrinkage or the blow-out of the middle of a cucumber, although not major concerns for home fermenters, cause considerable waste in the industry.

CHAPTER 8

Mastering Kimchi Basics

Preserved in soybean paste, kimchi tastes good in the summer, whereas kimchi pickled in brine is served as a good side dish during the winter. When the root of the Chinese cabbage grows larger in the ground, it tastes like a pear, especially after the first frost in the autumn harvest season.

—FROM THE POEM "SIX SONGS ON THE BACKYARD VEGETABLE PLOT"

BY LEE GYU-BO (이규보 / 李奎報) **(1168–1241),**

IN *GOOD MORNING, KIMCHI!*, **BY YOON SOOK-JA** (윤숙자 / 尹淑子)

The quote above is the first written record of kimchi pickled in brine. Lee Gyu-bo was a twelfth-century Korean senior government official who left his work behind for a simple life in the woods as a poet. His story is one that is still being played out. Trying to get back to the land, it turns out, is nothing new.

Kimchi famously hit the world media in 2008 during an outbreak of avian flu. There was not one recorded case of the flu in Korea, which was attributed to their population's daily kimchi consumption.[9] Indeed, research has shown that at least two of the major bacteria responsible for kimchi fermentation—*Lactiplantibacillus plantarum* and *Leuconostoc mesenteroides*—act as probiotics, promoting healthy immune responses against influenza and other infectious diseases.[10, 11, 12] And it's believed that the immune-boosting properties of garlic and hot pepper, two prime ingredients in kimchi, are magnified by fermentation. So it is not surprising that soon after the global COVID-19 pandemic began, people started asking if kimchi and other fermented vegetables could help either prevent infection or reduce symptoms during infection.

Making kimchi is a Korean tradition. Neither of us has a Korean background, nor did we apprentice with a master kimchi maker to learn the art. Our kimchi résumé is simply that we read as much as we could, we made a lot of it, and many people enjoyed what we created and sold. From that experience, we hope to provide a basic primer on making kimchi in this chapter.

Kimchi is generally distinguished by its staple ingredients: Chinese or napa cabbage, radish, garlic, scallions, ginger, and red chile pepper. However, as is the case for so many other ancient domestic arts, there are as many correct ways to make kimchi as there have been mothers passing down knowledge to their daughters. The exacting recipes that we are accustomed to today would not have been an option for most families. Through much of history, people haven't had the luxury that comes with supermarkets and year-round vegetables. The variability of each year's harvest season dictated the composition of kimchis.

As we trend toward more local food systems, we are returning more to the old ways. The home cook realizes that although there is no daikon available, for example, the farmers' market is bursting with red, purple, and pink Easter egg radishes. And so the recipe shifts and the flavor of that moment is captured. The next time, it might be turnips that take center stage.

Understanding Kimchi

Kimchi is the common name for *any* vegetable pickled in the Korean style of lactic acid fermentation. The most familiar type of kimchi in the United States is a dazzling sunset-orange color with a fiery, spicy flavor to match. It's called *tongbaechu* and its main ingredient is napa cabbage.

In Korea, there are nearly 200 documented varieties of kimchi, and probably an exponential quantity of family recipes. Kimchi is more than a side dish or condiment; it's a cultural symbol and a great source of national pride, as evidenced by the national museum dedicated to the dish.

In this book, we've included recipes for the two broad types of kimchi: the regular type of kimchi, such as *tongbaechu*, which is similar to chunky kraut in consistency, and water kimchi, which is a vegetable pickle in prepared brine. Water kimchis are made by following the same process as brine pickling (see Chapter 7). The biggest difference between water kimchis and their Western pickle counterparts is the spice profile. Instead of dill and mustard seed, water kimchis often include ginger, chile pepper, garlic, and sugar in the brine, which adds extra effervescent sparkle. Using this array of ingredients allows for experimentation—changing the ratios can radically change a recipe. There are many excellent books available on kimchi. A few of our kimchi recipes are adapted from a book by Yoon Sook-ja called *Good Morning, Kimchi!*

Many traditional recipes contain a starch, often rice or wheat flour, which is made into a paste to act as a thickener and more food for the microbes. The fermented paste *gochujang* can also be used as the paste in kimchi making. (If you buy it be sure to look for a fermented one. Many are created with corn syrup and other additives and are no longer fermented.) We have chosen to keep the kimchi recipes in this book simple, and so we have not included recipes using starch-based pastes.

Getting Started

The traditional process for kimchi can be thought of as a hybrid of brine pickling and dry brine fermentation. The napa cabbage soaks in a brine solution for 6 to 8 hours; then it is mixed with spices and other vegetables that have not been in brine. While this extra step takes some time and planning, it yields a crunchier texture.

As the cabbage soaks in brine, salt penetrates it by osmosis and reduces the moisture content (page 80).

Korean Pepper Powder, a.k.a. Gochugaru

The traditional red chile pepper in kimchi is *gochugaru* (*gochu* means chile; *garu* means powder). It's a vibrant red and has a bit of sweetness, like Hungarian paprika. Unlike most paprika, however, most gochugaru is hot.

You'll find this Korean chile powder at some grocery stores and most Asian markets. You'll want to make sure the gochugaru doesn't contain salt or other additives—some do. If you can't find it, you can substitute red chile pepper flakes, but use much less as they are hotter.

SPRING RADISH PICKLES

▶ In a crock or large bowl, combine the brine ingredients according to the recipe directions and stir to dissolve.

▶ Rinse the vegetables in cold water and prepare according to the recipe directions.

▶ Submerge the vegetables and leaves you'll use as a primary follower in the brine. Use a plate as a weight to keep the vegetables submerged. Set aside, at room temperature, for 6 to 8 hours.

▶ Drain the brined vegetables for 15 minutes. Set aside the leaves you'll use as a follower. Reserve about 1 cup of the brine solution.

▶ Meanwhile, combine the seasonings and any unbrined vegetables, blending thoroughly.

▶ Chop the brined vegetables according to the recipe instructions, then put them in a large bowl. Add the seasoned vegetables and massage together thoroughly.

▶ Transfer the vegetables into a crock, jar, or onggi pot, a few handfuls at a time, pressing with your hands as you go. Add reserved brine as needed to submerge the vegetables. Leave about 4 inches of headspace for a crock or onggi pot or 2 to 3 inches for a jar.

▶ Cover with the reserved leaves and a *weighted follower*. For a crock or onggi, this may be a plate that fits the opening of the container and nestles over as much of the surface as possible, with a sealed water-filled jar or ziplock bag on top for weight. For a jar, you might use a sealed water-filled ziplock bag as a follower and weight. Cover loosely with a lid and/or towel, or tighten the lid if you're planning to use the burping method (see page 44).

▶ Set the fermenting vessel where you can keep an eye on it, out of direct sunlight, ideally in a spot with a temperature between 55 and 75°F/ 13 and 24°C. Ferment for the time indicated by the recipe.

▶ Check daily to make sure the kimchi is submerged, pressing down as needed to bring the brine back to the surface. You may see foam on top; it is harmless. Scoop out yeast or mold.

▶ Using a clean, nonreactive utensil, remove some of the kimchi and taste it when the recipe directs. It's ready when:
   » It's pleasingly sour and pickle-y tasting, without the strong acidity of vinegar.
   » The flavors have mingled.
   » The vegetables have softened a bit but retain some crunch.

If it's not ready, rinse the followers and weight, put them back in place, and continue monitoring the brine level and watching for scum and mold.

▶ When the kimchi is ready, carefully skim off any scum. Transfer the kimchi into small jars for storage. Tamp down to make sure the ferment is submerged in its brine. Leave as little headspace as possible. Screw on the lids; store in the refrigerator.

1. Make the brine.

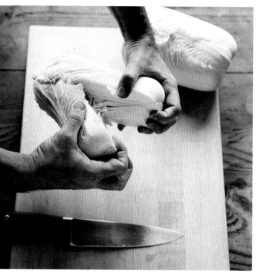

2. Cut through the end of the cabbage and pull apart to split in half.

3. Submerge the cabbage in the brine, weighing it down to keep it submerged.

4. Drain the cabbage after 6 to 8 hours of soak time.

5. Prepare the remaining vegetables and seasoning mixture.

6. Combine the brined and seasoned vegetables and massage together.

7. Press the kimchi firmly into the fermenting vessel to remove air pockets and to bring brine to the surface.

8. Add a follower and weight.

9. Cover with a cloth and set aside to ferment.

10. Carefully scoop off any mold if it develops.

11. Rinse off the weight before replacing for further fermentation time.

12. Transfer to smaller jars for long-term storage or to give as gifts.

CHAPTER 9

Practical Matters

STORAGE AND TROUBLESHOOTING

Now that you're well on your way to mastering the processes of basic fermentation, there are a few more things you may be wondering about. What's the best way to store your creations, and how long will they keep? What if something looks like it's going wrong? And what if, along the way, you still have unanswered questions? You'll find answers in this chapter.

Nurturing Ferments: Storage Considerations

In this section, you'll find out how long you should store your ferments and get tips on the best way to keep and prolong the life of your creations, both in the fridge and out.

HOW LONG CAN I STORE MY FERMENT?

Acidity is what preserves the vegetables; once they've achieved a pH of 4.6, they can be stored as safe ferments indefinitely. However, whether or not they stay "good" (as in tasty) varies greatly by the type of vegetable. Each vegetable has its own properties that aid in preservation (garlic) or diminish quickly (cucumbers). The other factor

is oxygen exposure during storage—too much headspace will cause color change and oxidation, even if there is no yeast or mold. The final factor, of course, is your personal palate.

The most important thing to remember is that fermented vegetables are a live food, so the rules are different than for, say, a jar of home-canned strawberries. The strawberries sit sealed and relatively stable on the shelf until opened, when the race toward spoiling is set into motion. Fermented vegetables are always changing; even when the jar is sealed in the refrigerator, the bacteria continue ever so slowly to acidify your food. This doesn't mean it's going bad; it will just taste different, perhaps changing your idea of what is no longer fit to eat. As long as it isn't contaminated throughout with mold, yeast, or other clear spoilage, it is safe.

As a general rule of thumb, fermented vegetables will keep their texture for 6 to 12 months. However, there is no reason to toss something out at year's end if it is still tasty and viable; even ferments that have become soft can be saved by being made into something else, like crackers (page 369) or seasonings (page 142). We have herbal ferments and hot sauces that are many years old and more delicious than ever. The lower the temperature, the longer the shelf life. Refrigerate all ferments in airtight containers for long-term storage. Recipes note special considerations.

Don't forget that fermented vegetables can vary from batch to batch because of the season, the crop, the sugar content of the vegetables, or the type of herbs used. It's not always predictable, but that's what makes it fun. We just have to reclaim our own judgment skills; observation and taste have served humans well for a long time.

KEEPING LIVE FOOD ALIVE: HOW TO STORE FERMENTS

We choose to store our ferments in the fridge to capture the bounty of each season and to preserve the flavor at its peak, for both the short and long term. For us, having a second refrigerator has been the best way to preserve our harvest while enhancing our family's diet.

That said, this is a pre-refrigeration preservation technique after all, right? If maintaining an extra fridge is not an option, see Going Off the Grid, on the facing page, for other ideas.

Refrigerated Storage Tips

» Transfer ferments to jars that are an appropriate size for the batch. This can be gallon jars or a series of small pint jars. Just make sure the jars are firmly packed to within 1 inch (1.5 cm) of the top.

» Rotate your ferment into smaller jars as it is consumed. Less headspace increases the freshness and longevity of your ferment.

» Ferments stay freshest if you tamp down the vegetables tightly in the jar after each use. It's okay if the ferment doesn't have a lot of brine. Using a nonreactive utensil, push down any stray pieces on the side of the jar, then press it all down. Tamp to remove air bubbles—compressed kraut stays fresh.

» Any ferment that has been opened and is being consumed on a somewhat regular basis keeps best in your refrigerator.

» For brine pickles, make sure nothing is bobbing above the brine. Position a leaf or piece of parchment paper to assist. If you're actively consuming them, they'll be fine for the weeks it takes to enjoy them.

» For drier ferments, for example, whole leaves, press a small round of parchment or wax paper on top of the vegetables. This will help keep oxidation at bay.

» For pickles, check the brine level every few months by looking into the jars without opening them. If you see an issue, top off with fresh, unfermented brine solution. For krauts, brine evaporation isn't usually a problem, but if it is, top only with previously fermented brine.

» Most jar lids are metal. For storage lasting a month or more, place a bit of parchment or wax paper over the top of the jar before screwing on the lid or ring to keep rust from forming.

» If you're using plastic lids, make sure they are airtight; many are not.

What about freezing? Or freeze drying?

Freezing is an option when you don't have other ways to store your abundance. With proper freezing you can avoid oxidation and other "spoilers." However, as most of the cell walls of both the vegetables and the probiotics themselves expand and rupture, you will experience textural changes and most of the probiotics will no longer be alive.

While expensive, the popularity of home freeze-drying equipment is on the rise. We have not tasted freeze-dried fermented vegetables but our research indicates that freeze-dried vegetables show no major changes in color and microbiological properties, as the freeze-drying process does not affect the number of bacteria.

Going Off the Grid: Unrefrigerated Storage

It takes energy to preserve food—the sun's energy (drying), stored sun energy (fuels), and human energy. Fermentation uses less energy than many modern forms of preservation, yet maintaining an extra ferment refrigerator demands energy and space. Humans have been storing ferments for thousands of years without one of these cold boxes. The main thing to remember is that oxygen is the enemy of your ferments, and your job is to keep it out of them.

While the fermentation process continues under refrigeration, it slows down enough to achieve a sort of suspended animation and food therefore can go months without perceptible changes. When foods are kept unrefrigerated, fermentation happens faster than if they were refrigerated, and this may leave the ferment with flavors (more sour) and textures (softer) that we are not accustomed to. While flavors may not stay the same, the food will not rot if starved of oxygen. Once all the food for the microbes has been consumed, fermentation will cease and the food will be stable if in an anaerobic state.

The best trick we have found is to ferment in the same jars that you will store your ferment in. Fill the jar as much as possible and use the burping method (see page 44) to release CO_2. Once the active fermentation slows, burp the jar one last time and then seal the lid tight. The burping

works because the lighter air containing the oxygen sits on top of the CO_2 and gets forced out first. Your ferment will now be stable as long as you don't open it, and you can store it in a cool but unrefrigerated spot. You will find that some vegetables do better than others in this unrefrigerated state.

If using airlock lids, make sure you manage the lid. Some have a vacuum pump, which works well. If there is a water trap seal, you will need to maintain that; if it dries out once, your ferment has had oxygen contact. Silicone one-way valves aren't designed to keep out oxygen once the pressure of the CO_2 is gone, so these are not recommended for longer storage.

We don't recommend storing ferments in crocks, refrigerated or not. They require quite a bit of management. If you use crocks for fermenting, transfer the ferment to jars while the fermentation is at least still somewhat active, so that you can burp the jars once to push out the oxygen.

Ideally, top your unrefrigerated ferments with generous amounts of brine and store them in a space that stays consistently less than 50°F/10°C and above freezing. (The USDA recommends 42°F/5.6°C.)

In many traditional fermentation practices, the fermented vegetables are dehydrated for storage. This solves the issues of space constraints, oxygen management, and therefore spoilage.

Water-bath canning is another option for unrefrigerated storage. Although it requires more energy and time, it yields a product that doesn't need any maintenance while in storage, won't oxidize, and doesn't need refrigeration. Of course, heating your ferments will deactivate the probiotics, but as we discussed earlier (see page 25), even deactivated probiotics offer health benefits. And by preserving your locally grown harvest of fresh veggies, you are still capturing the peak energy of the vegetable, and you can't do better than that for good, clean food. Follow the USDA guidelines for boiling-water canning for both raw- and hot-packed vegetables. See the ferment and pickle pages on the website of the National Center for Home Food Preservation, where you can also download a PDF of the USDA's *Complete Guide to Home Canning*.

Troubleshooting Your Ferment: FAQs and What-Ifs

Because ferments are live foods with all the quirks and personality of any live being, there can be many variations of normal. Often the fermentista (even one with years of experience) will look into a crock and wonder, "What the heck?"

This section is a result of interacting with the fermenting community—newbies, experts, and everyone in between—while teaching, while working the market or events, and through emails and social media messages. We are sure there are many more questions out there, but this is a list of the most common issues we've heard of from fermentistas who are teaching themselves.

Collectively, through much of the world, we've lost much of our ancestors' shared story of fermenting. It will return, but until then we must all share our own experiences as we rediscover and reinvent this culinary art. Remember: Be brave, but trust your gut. If a ferment truly feels, tastes, and seems wrong, take it to the compost to build soil and try again.

And if something looks especially dubious, do consult the scum appendix (page 414), where we've compiled mug shots of the most common culprits.

Should I sterilize my crocks and jars?

It's not necessary to sterilize your fermentation vessels and other equipment, although good hygiene is always important. You will avoid the risk of yeast and other contaminants just by making sure your work surfaces, implements, jars, and vegetables are clean. However, do not wash your vegetables with antimicrobial soap, extract, or any of the commercial vegetable washes on the market.

Oops! I've oversalted the kraut.

One strategy is to take the portion you plan to eat and soak it in clear, cold water. Pour this off. Repeat until it tastes pleasant. We haven't done the lab work required to know whether all the probiotic benefits go down the drain, but other advantages of fermented food do stay intact.

Alternatively, overly salty ferments are great for adding to salt stews, soups, or sauces instead of salt. Use some salty ferment as you might any flavor enhancer.

To avoid oversalting, taste your ferment as you make it. If it is too salty, add vegetables to the ferment until the mixture tastes properly salty—not briny, but present and pleasing.

The kraut tastes too sour.

This is a matter of personal preference. If a batch is too sour for you, taste the next batch sooner and more frequently during fermentation; that way you know to refrigerate it when you like it best.

The kraut tastes bad or weird.

Unwanted microbes may have found their way in. Trust your gut. If it tastes bad, compost it, and don't be discouraged from trying again. Weird can be what has become known as funky.

These flavors of funk can be the sourness or yeasty flavors. Yeasty flavors are especially prevalent in ferments from vegetables with a higher sugar content. If the lactic acid bacteria don't consume all the sugar fast enough, the yeasts will help. This isn't bad; it will just give the ferment a strong yeast or even slightly alcoholic flavor.

The kraut isn't sour enough.

Repack your ferment and continue to ferment outside the refrigerator. Check again in a few days. If you like things "super sauer," you can add a touch of sugar to your ferment as you are making it to encourage the lactic acid bacteria—½ teaspoon of sugar per 2 pounds of vegetables should do it.

There's mold!

First, make sure it is mold. (See the Scum Gallery, page 417.) White film across the top is often mistaken for mold but is usually a surface yeast called Kahm yeast. Believe it or not, greenish or grayish mold on the top layer of ferments is okay and not out of the realm of normal. Just scrape off the moldy layer. But if the mold is black, pink, or orange, or your ferment smells or tastes off, then send it to the compost pile.

The jar won't open.

There are two possibilities:

1. Active ferment has continued to build up CO_2 pressure behind the lid.

2. Salt has caused corrosion that makes the jar band stick.

In either case, run the lid under a bit of warm water. Try again with a cloth for traction. Corroded bands are difficult to remove but generally don't affect the contents of the jar. If you are faced with a corroded lid, use your best judgment as to whether the ferment is edible. A small spot of rust on the bottom of the lid has likely not done anything to taint the ferment.

The kraut is too dry.

Sometimes it might seem like all your brine went away when you put your kraut in the refrigerator. The brine doesn't go anywhere, but as the ferment chills, it contracts. Just compress the kraut. As you eat kraut from your jars, always tamp back to a tight pack. You can top off a jar of kraut with some fermented brine from another batch, but do not add water to a finished ferment.

The kraut is too soft.

The fermentation may have happened too quickly, or the salt strength was insufficient, or the salt was not evenly distributed. Usually, though, the reason is not enough salt. Soft kraut can also result from kraut that was not packed properly, leaving air pockets. Air pockets develop when the weight is not heavy enough to keep the brine in the vegetables during the most active stages of fermentation.

The brine looks like snot.

We know that nothing seems okay about gooey, viscous brine surrounding your ferment. It's rare (in all our fermenting, we have encountered it only a handful of times), but it is a normal result of the bacteria eating their way through the starches and creating acidity. In our experience, this condition is more likely to occur when a ferment is fermenting very slowly because of cool temperatures. If you come across a gelatinous brine but all other indications are good, just tuck that ferment back in place, move it to a slightly warmer spot, and give it another week or so.

WASTE NOT

If your kraut is soft but otherwise fine, you can still eat it. If you don't find soft kraut pleasing, you can use it to cook with: in a frittata (page 359), a chocolate cake (page 411), and any long-simmered soups and stews.

The pickles got soft in storage.

This means they were exposed to air. If most are okay, remove any soft pickles. They can be upcycled for flavor—pickle seasoning, anyone? (See page 142.) Add brine to top off the jar, seal tightly, and return it to the refrigerator. The ferment should stabilize and the remaining pickles keep for months. To avoid this problem, make sure pickles remain submerged under the brine while stored.

The ferment is discolored.

Ferments often darken from the top down, which occurs with exposure to oxygen. Remove the discolored portion and move the remaining ferment to a smaller jar with little headspace and an airtight lid. Some ingredients—for example, shiso—may give the kraut a pink hue. Otherwise, pink can indicate spoilage. Compost a ferment if the pink color occurs throughout.

The refrigerated jars pop and fizz when I open them.

That is okay. This is a live food and the CO_2 is escaping. The microculture is just continuing its natural cycle. Pressure increases when carbon dioxide builds in a jar without an escape route. Even when a ferment is technically done, as defined by correct acidity and good flavor, it can still be quite active, due to high carbohydrates in the vegetables. Your loved ones won't get sick from eating this food. (Rest assured, even when your jar is quiet, it is also fine.)

When you're opening a hissing, fizzing jar, do so over a clean bowl so that if the brine bubbles out you will be able to rescue it and pour it back into the ferment, or at least not make a mess.

IT'S ALIVE!

In the early stages of fermentation, called the heterofermentative stage, the microbes produce a lot of lactic acid and significant amounts of carbon dioxide. These early colonizing species of lactic acid bacteria that move in are very active. They are also a little more heat sensitive and not very tolerant of the lower acid levels they are producing. This sends the ferment on to the next wave of microbes that continue to produce lactic acid and carbon dioxide, although at much lower levels. This is called the homofermentative stage.

The kraut smells like dirty socks.

But does it smell putrid? Putrid is an unmistakably awful odor, like rotting potatoes. Other indicators—slimy texture, mold growth, off-color appearance—often accompany this kind of stench. If the ferment is not slimy, moldy, and putrefied, chances are that smell is just the perfume, fragrance, bouquet, or stink, if you will, of the fermenting vegetables. It's subjective.

Most ferments just smell acidic, but there are three ferment perpetrators that can cause offending odor. All are naturally occurring fatty acids. For reasons unknown, some batches produce one or more of these acids in quantities that affect the smell. (Vegetable ferments also experience what the wine world calls terroir— the flavor and mood are affected by season and place.) These same acids are present in other foods and, in many cases, used in the flavor industry.

The first is *n-propionic acid*, a fatty acid produced naturally by members of the *Propionibacterium* genus during the fermentation process. (It is a member of this family that causes the holes in Swiss cheese.) These bacteria break down the lactic acid and are often described as smelling like human sweat or dirty socks. The good news is that propionic acid has antimicrobial properties, which is why it is also used in bread making.

The second offender on this list is *n-caproic acid*. This fatty acid smells like goats, so much so that its name derives from the Latin word for goats, *caper*.

The last on our list of most common stinkers is *n-butyric acid*. This fatty acid smells like rancid butter. Again, it is harmless, and from the scientific research we consulted—the kind where everything is done under intense scrutiny in sterile laboratory conditions—it is unclear why some batches develop it.

If the ferment smells of sulfur, that's a sign of different compounds that will dissipate in the steam if the ferment is heated to 158°F/70°C.

Alleviating Fermentation Fragrance in Your Kitchen:

» Find a place to age your ferments that is out of the way and at least slightly ventilated.
» Work with a water-seal crock or airlock lids.
» Store in the fridge. Even the strongest-smelling krauts often lose a lot of their nasal punch when refrigerated. Chilled kraut tastes and smells milder than room-temperature kraut.

I have to leave a ferment for some time.

Sometimes things come up that won't allow you to tend to your curing ferment. If your ferment is immature, you can put it in the refrigerator—followers, weight, and all. It will slow way down, and when you come back, put it back on the counter. As it warms up, it will wake up and continue fermenting.

I don't see bubbles.

While bubbles are an obvious visual sign of fermentation, not observing them doesn't mean that fermentation isn't happening. Some ferments are just introverts quietly doing their thing without a lot of conversation and show. If you are unsure, check for acidity—if it is fermenting, the pH level will be dropping. You should be able to smell it and taste it. If you are unsure, use a pH strip or pH meter.

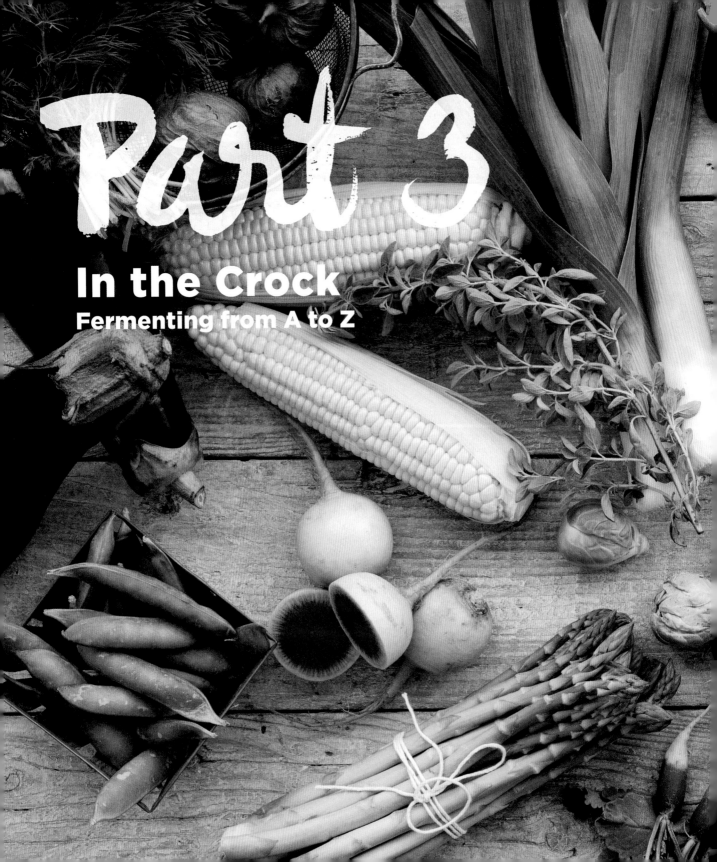

Part 3

In the Crock
Fermenting from A to Z

THINK OF A TIME when you first tasted a food that surprised and delighted you. Your eyes closed in a slow-chew moment.

That's what this section is about: enjoying new flavors that also happen to be good for you. For some people, that new flavor is tasting fresh lacto-fermented sauerkraut for the first time. For others, the addiction to lacto-fermented vegetables is already in place and they're ready to go beyond—way beyond—cabbage sauerkraut, kimchi, and brined pickles. This section provides recipes and complete instructions for archetypal ferments as well as unusual single-vegetable recipes and creative combinations and spins on the classics.

We invite you daring fermentistas to come up with your own combinations, using this section to guide you. We want your relationship with this book and your fermentation practice to be dynamic. Take notes in the margins; dog-ear the pages. Be adventurous. Technically you can ferment any vegetable, but a few are finicky or not worth it, and we point out possible pitfalls.

This part of the book is designed for exploring, discovery, and learning. We hope fermentation becomes intuitive and that this section inspires you to take our ideas and, well, ferment them. Let the journey begin.

How to Use This Section

We designed part 3 to be useful for eaters of vegetables, whether you garden, have a CSA share, or shop for them (you'll find a few fruits and herbs here, too, although we call the lot "vegetables" as a whole to keep things simple). Vegetables are presented alphabetically, from A to Z. Flip to the one you'd like to prepare in not-the-usual way, where you will find recipes and more. Each vegetable (or fruit or herb) has its own section.

Within each section you'll see **Your Raw Material**, which provides information specific to the fresh vegetable. **In the Crock** tells you how to use the vegetable—shredded, sliced, or diced—for dry brining, meaning fermented without the addition of a brine solution. **In the Pickle Jar** recipes are for brining whole (or chunked) vegetables, which of course you can do in a jar or a crock, and **Create Your Own Recipes** presents ideas for inventing your own ferments.

About the Recipes

Vegetable fermentation is like putting on a play.

It begins with a cast of characters. Some, such as the vegetables, the salt, and the spices, are onstage, in the spotlight: They're the leads. The majority, though, do their work behind the scenes. Lactic acid bacteria ride into a fermentation vessel on the coattails of the stars, but—like set designers, costumers, and the director—they're just as important. Regardless of the role, each performer has their own personality. It's the same with ingredients: They each have a special aroma, texture, and taste, which may change according to the season, the soil, your climate, and the ambient temperature of your home. You are the director. You can influence, direct, and manage, but ultimately when it is showtime they are in control. Thus, as in a play, no two performances are identical.

FERMENTATION TIME

Time is a major factor in fermentation. It is not always clear when things begin and when they end. Fermentation times can be only approximate. Use them as a guide or suggestion, but rely on your own senses to tell you when a ferment is ready: Watch for changes in the vegetable's appearance; taste and smell for that telltale pickle-y sourness.

Many factors can affect the time it takes your produce to ferment. The size of the batch can affect times; most recipes in this book are fairly small and will ferment fairly quickly. Larger batches—more than a gallon or two or 7 or so liters—will require a noticeable difference in time. For example, a quart on our counter might take a week and the same ferment in a 10-gallon crock will take 3 weeks.

Temperature will likely affect your times. We assume ambient home temperatures in the recipes. In each recipe you'll see a range of time. As a rule, the first number in the range is the potential minimum *warm-temperature* fermentation time and the second number will be your *cool-temperature* time. So when the recipe suggests fermenting for 5 to 10 days, consider the temperature of your room and know that your veggies will take longer to get "sauer" in a cool room than in a warm one.

VEGGIE WEIGHTS AND MEASURES

Unlike the chemistry in baking, which requires exact measurements—get the baking soda wrong and there are repercussions—fermenting vegetables leaves room for divergence, variation, and adaptation. This means you can substitute ingredients based on seasonality, availability, or your preferences. It also means that you can make larger and smaller batches of the recipes; just remember large batches take a little longer to ferment. In most of the ingredient lists, we refer to the whole vegetable. Although this may seem unconventional, recipes based on quantities of whole vegetables minimize waste of both vegetables and energy. Not including that bit of leftover cabbage because your measure is already at the designated weight seems to defeat the purpose of preservation, or—worse—perhaps there's more waste in the outer leaves than anticipated and you don't have enough cabbage to meet the volume or weight required.

Using precise measurements can be problematic. Let's look at volume, for example. Given the springy nature of sliced cabbage, consistent measurement in a cup is difficult. Is our packed cup tighter than your packed cup? There is no way to know. While we include approximate weights for our international audience, going by strict weight is also challenging for the same reasons; vegetables' weights vary. We believe you'll know how much to pick or buy, and that you'll use it all. Vegetable fermentation is a wonderfully forgiving way to start learning to trust your intuition in the kitchen.

Note: If you're using a grater or a food processor, use the medium grater blade when a recipe calls for grating or shredding, unless specified otherwise.

YIELD

Recipe yields are all approximate because you're working with different-size vegetables and varying water contents, often determined by season and freshness.

Use the yield approximation to determine your jar or vessel size. You want to make sure that whatever vessel you use will accommodate the ferment with enough room for CO_2 to bubble up without sending your brine out of the vessel.

LET'S GET SALTY

In the last few years, we have seen a trend toward calling recipes "formulas"—this goes for both fermented and nonfermented recipes. While we have nothing against that, we also find that there is so much to be gained with fermentation as your teacher. Intuitively cooking and fermenting build trust and confidence in yourself and the world around you. Our goal is to teach you to be comfortable fermenting vegetables so that you can do you!

Ultimately, the biggest recipe risk is not enough or too much salt. This is why the salt is given in a range to make up for the variation in ingredients. You can read more about calculating salt on page 103. We have done the math, so don't worry; your ferments will be fine if you follow the recipes.

We use fine Redmond Real Salt, which is a sea salt with a bit lower sodium chloride content and a subtle sweetness due to its higher natural mineral content. While most salt choices will work, we recommend that you use a salt with a regular table salt grain size (not coarse) that is unrefined and without additives.

How much salt is right? Something as seemingly simple as salt has variation in weight, sodium chloride content, and flavor. This is in addition to the varying moisture content of the vegetables and differing climates. For more discussion on salt concentration percentages, see page 102. Here's what to consider when you salt your ferments:

> » In most of the recipes, we ask that you taste for salt to accommodate different palates and varieties of salt. Let the amount in the recipes guide you. Add salt gradually and keep tasting, and you won't go wrong. Trust your taste buds!
> Aim for a pleasing amount of salt, like a salty chip that you cannot stop eating (we're saying it again because it is a cue that works), rather than saltiness that

is uncomfortable, like swallowing seawater. The exceptions are some brines, which are indicated in the recipes.

» If you know your fermenting environment will be consistently warm (more than 85°F/29°C), you might want to sprinkle in just a little more salt than the recipe suggests; this will help maintain the texture and develop the flavor. Otherwise, the kraut will be more acidic and somewhat softer, but still safe to eat.

» Note that for brine pickles, you're working with a salt brine recipe, so you won't be tasting for salt.

TAKE NOTES

Label your jars; believe us, you do forget. We give you permission to write in this book. We love seeing our books evolving with sticky notes and marginalia—it feels as if the books become alive in their own way with your ideas and microbes. Or use a journal if that feels wrong, but do keep track. It is wonderful to have something to refer to when you find a jar in the back of the fridge that you love and you can't remember what you did, or conversely you don't love and know you never want to try that combo again.

WHAT IS ON TOP OF MY FERMENT?

Where the top of the ferment meets oxygen is where other microbes might grow. You may see something growing on top that is not your ferment. It's generally harmless; consult the appendix to learn what it is and what to do.

STORAGE

We went over storing ferments on page 125; however, we want to remind you that if you are fermenting in a crock or a container much larger than the final ferment, be sure to put your ferment into one or more jars that are filled to the top. At this point, a heave of CO_2 is no longer a concern but an oxygen-filled headspace is.

BEST BY

In the recipes we share a range of times for when ferments, if refrigerated with a sealed lid, will still be at their best (their yummiest). The truth is that lacto-fermented vegetables last a very long time if oxygen-starved and cool. They will stay "good" (as in they won't hurt you) if you eat them past the recommended dates. (Most of us fermentation educators love to quote USDA microbiologist Fred Breidt, who says no one has ever died from properly fermented vegetables.) So, please don't toss something because you forgot about it. Open it up and use your five senses. Ferments will tell you when they are bad. We promise. If bad, things will look and smell off—as in rotten, gross, yucky. So ask yourself, how does it smell? How does it look? If the answers are normal, acidic, or I don't see anything off—then there isn't anything off. Often with older ferments the texture has become soft or even mushy, but if they still smell and taste acidic they are fine for consumption. (If the texture is off-putting, head to our Waste Not section, page 140, for ideas.)

If you're still not sure, check our scum gallery on page 417, but ultimately don't consume anything that doesn't feel right to you. Always, always, always trust your gut.

Christopher Writes

"I hate my sauerkraut!" someone behind me blurts out. It's a cry that would make any sauerkraut maker cringe.

I'm solo this Saturday. I'd told Kirsten I could handle everything today, but I'm regretting that decision.

My mind is racing as I fasten a cooler lid. Flight seems like a good idea, as does hiding under the table, but neither would be easy to explain to Kirsten later, so I try to compose myself before standing up to face my accuser.

Peering up at me is a sweet-looking woman with her hands placed firmly on the sides of our tasting tray. She's waiting for a reply.

"What don't you like about it?" I ask.

"It's wrong. It's just not, you know, good. I've followed the instructions in my cookbook and am just so damn frustrated that I thought I'd ask you what to do before I throw out this batch," she said. Then she noticed our tasting jars: six different krauts and kimchis. "Are all of these sauerkrauts?"

I stare at her while it slowly dawns on me that it's not one of our ferments she hates; it's her own. I start asking questions and learn it's a recipe that forgets to mention that ferments must remain below the brine line, which calls for a weight of some type. Without it, the vegetables eventually rise above the brine, and with exposure to the little bit of air in the closed jar, even in a refrigerator, undesirable microbes get in, causing the whole thing to go bad.

I explain this to her and encourage her to buy a couple of organic cabbages from one of the stands and give it another try.

"Would you like to try some samples to get an idea of what you want to create?" I ask.

Looking over our jars of Curtido, Lemon-Dill Kraut, Golden Beet Kraut, and Spicy Kimchi, she turns back to me: "Don't you make plain old sauerkraut?" We do, but it's sold out.

Other people push past her to taste, and I watch as she wanders over to our neighbor's produce stand.

The next week she returns and reports that her latest batch looks great. It's bubbling away, she tells me, and smells wonderful, but she's not convinced it'll be tasty. I hand her a bamboo skewer and point to a sample jar of our Naked Kraut (page 173), which is just cabbage and salt, glorious in their simplicity. She stabs at it, puts it in her mouth, then closes her eyes and slowly chews.

"That," she proclaims, "is what I want mine to taste like. I want to make that," she says, pumping the skewer at the sample jar for emphasis.

I forget about the interaction until late October, at the end of the market season, when she returns. She tells me she has her recipe down pat and produces so much fermented goodness that she shares it with her coworkers.

"I'm ready to try something new now," she says. Beginning with the closest jar, she tastes what we have out, eyes closed, chewing slowly, sighing with every bite, smiling.

WASTE NOT...

Change the form. Vary the use.
Expand your notions.
—KEVIN FARLEY, THE CULTURED PICKLE SHOP

In this new edition, we want to bring to the forefront how fermentation can be used as a strategy to make better use of our food. We have included new recipes and techniques with an eye toward preservation as a form of reducing waste. Zero waste, or at least full utilization, in your own kitchen has far-reaching effects. For example, you can explore ways to use wilted or imperfect vegetables to make perfectly nourishing foods, and trimmings and peels can also show up to boost flavors. There are tips and recipes scattered throughout the book, but we also want to give this concept space of its own by putting a few of the ideas and skills together here so that you can let your imagination soar.

LEFTOVER BRINE

One of the primary by-products of fermentation is brine. When you've eaten up all your ferment and are looking at a jar or crock full of brine, don't dump this tasty stuff down the sink just because you are unsure what to do with it—especially if there is a lot.

Culinary addition. You can use leftover brine as a flavorful addition to soups, sauces, or dressings. One of our longtime favorites is to make crackers and flax crisps (see the recipes on pages 368 and 369). We have found over the years that including any vegetables that got a little too soft with the brine makes these crackers even more delicious. We particularly like to use cherry tomato pickles (Cherry Bombs, page 333) to make fermented "sun-dried" tomato crackers.

Flavored finishing salt. When the reality hits that you don't have room in your refrigerator for any more brine, you can reclaim the salt. In many cases it will become beautiful finishing salt—small crystals with big flavor. This salt is also pretty enough to dress up in a cute jar and give as a gift.

To make it, you will use evaporation, just as people have been using evaporation to make sea salt for millennia. First decide whether to strain out any small vegetable bits or spices. Straining will give you a flavored salt. Leaving the bits will give you a seasoning salt: pickle salt, kimchi salt, and so on. Simply pour your brine into a noncorrosive, shallow, wide container (we usually use a plate) and put it on the counter, in a sunny window, or outside. Let evaporation do its magic.

Drink it. Brine is yummy. Use it as a refreshing electrolyte-type drink or in cocktails and mocktails.

Brine *g'spritzt.* The German word for spray or sprinkle is *spritzen*, which is where we get the word *spritzer*, meaning a bubbly drink. In Austria, fruit juice added to soda water is called *g'spritzt!* To make a brine version, pour a few ounces of any brine over ice in a tall glass, then fill the glass with soda water. Play around with this drink. You can use soda water, fruit juice, and a splash of brine to make a healthy probiotic soda that will delight even a brine-averse sweet tooth.

Brine-Ade

serves 4 to 6

If you're not ready to drink your brine straight up, this "brine-ade" might be a good way to dip a toe into the brine.

¾–1 cup (135–180 g) unrefined sugar or
       raw honey (177–237 ml)
   1 cup (237 ml) warm water
3–4 cups (710–946 ml) cold water
   1 cup (237 ml) sauerkraut brine
   1 whole lemon, thinly sliced
     Grated fresh ginger, to taste (optional)

1. Make a simple syrup by combining the sugar with the warm water and mixing until the sugar is completely dissolved.

2. Pour the syrup into a pitcher and add the cold water and sauerkraut brine. Add the lemon slices, giving them a twist to release some of the juice as you drop them in. Add the ginger, if using.

3. Let this mixture sit for about 30 minutes to allow the flavors to mingle.

4. Serve over ice for a refreshing summer beverage, or serve at room temperature for a soothing, healing beverage.

Christopher Writes

When we sold ferments at market, I loved tending the shot bar. I identified four types of drinkers:

» **The Natives.** Usually Eastern Europeans who grew up depending upon fermented brine after a late night at the discos. Given market day was on Saturday, we provided relief to more than a few.

» **The Skeptics.** Our small, chalk-written sign that read "Brine Shots $1" proved a siren's song, eventually pulling in folks with a crumpled dollar bill in hand who didn't want to taste kraut.

» **The Believers.** Some did their homework and understood gut biota. For them, a shot of brine was a quick infusion of the healthy microbes.

» **The Naughty Ones.** These people wanted to knock back a shot glass in the middle of the street in the middle of a market. They would often giggle or make a dramatic play of it, convinced they were somehow being mischievous.

SEASONINGS: A GREAT USE FOR OLD OR NOT-YOUR-FAVORITE FERMENTS

When you need to clear out old ferments from your fridge, don't toss them! You can make simple savory seasonings, soup mixes (such as "Onion Soup" Seasoning, page 287), or flavor dusts by dehydrating fermented veggies and grinding them in a coffee grinder or blender. You are left with the concentrated flavor of the vegetable and salt. For example, the Simple Beet Kraut (page 163) makes a lovely deep pink, tangy spice that is not only stunning sprinkled on top of food but also delicious. Fermented kimchi makes great instant kimchi spice.

First, drain the brine from the ferment by letting it sit in a strainer over a bowl for 30 minutes or by squeezing it in cheesecloth. You want to get the loose, drippy moisture out; don't forget to save that brine. There's no need for it to be completely dry. Then spread the ferment out on a tray and let dry for 8 to 10 hours, or overnight, in a dehydrator at 100°F/38°C. Leave as is for seasoning or soup mix, or grind for flavor dusts. The shelf life is 6 months at room temperature. Lower temps equal longer shelf life (for example, storing dehydrated ferments at 60°F/16°C increases viability to 12 to 18 months). Refrigerate or freeze in airtight containers for longer storage.

Jazz up your dehydrated ferments by mixing them with other herbs, spices, and seeds, like Shiso Gomashio (page 326).

TEXTURE-CHALLENGED FERMENTS

If your ferment didn't turn out with quite the right texture, you can dehydrate it and use it as a seasoning, as described above. Other options include puréeing it to a flavoring paste, simmering it to a thick reduction (especially great for brined mushrooms that are too mushy), or incorporating it into a relish (see Sweet Dill Relish, page 218).

BY-PRODUCTS, WASTE, REMAINS, DISCARDS, SURPLUS . . .

Normally you'd dispose of all those bits piled on the side of the cutting board after you are done processing a vegetable. What if we called them an opportunity? Let's look at those stems, stumpy cores, peels, butts, seeds, and leaves.

When time, energy, and creativity fail, save these bits in the freezer and use them for making delicious stocks. Corncobs also are delicious in stock, and in Kirsten's book *Homebrewed Vinegar*, you can learn to use the cobs to make vinegar.

Thick brassica stems and cores can be shaved or sliced finely (a mandoline is a dream for this). They are refreshing and crunchy when fermented or eaten raw as part of a salad, and when cooked they are tender, with a mild taste. They can be braised or fermented with miso or put in a nuka pot or continuous pickling pot to keep the microbes busy. It's like hiring a babysitter to keep the children busy and fed.

Citrus peels are versatile. One example is Lemon Habanero Date Paste (page 207), which uses lemon peels. At the very least, simply drying the zest you have peeled off a lemon, orange, lime, or other citrus will give you so much future flavor. When you have saved enough, you can put the dried zests in a spice grinder to powder. To turn the citrus zests into citrus salt, simply combine ½ cup (134 g) salt with 2 tablespoons (6 g) fresh citrus zest. Don't stop at citrus; other fruit and vegetable peels make delicious powders, too.

We use the butt ends of onions, celery, pak choi (bok choy), and napa cabbage or the top ends of beets or larger radishes as followers to keep our ferments under the brine. We also use vegetable stems to wedge in an X over pickles in a brine to keep vegetables from floating.

Fermented Orange & Fennel Spice Blend

by Meredith Leigh

I use this blend for sausages, dry rubs, poached fish, and pickles. You can ferment all the ingredients, or skip fermentation for the orange peel and chile flakes and lacto-ferment everything else. The result is a bright, salty umami.

- 3 parts dried orange peel (lacto-fermented or not)
- 2 parts lacto-fermented fennel powder
- ½ part hot chile flakes (lacto-fermented or not)
- ½ part lacto-fermented garlic powder

Combine all the ingredients and store in a non-reactive container away from light and heat. You can combine this blend with a fat, such as coconut oil or olive oil, to carry the flavor or use it as a dry rub.

Umami Dust

by Meredith Leigh

There are endless variations of this basic recipe, but in general it concentrates and combines the umami imparted by mushrooms and nearly any aromatic vegetable to create a secret base that pumps up soups, sauces, and gravies.

- 2 parts lacto-fermented mushroom powder
- 1 part garlic powder
- ½ part lacto-fermented celery powder (I use celeriac peels to make this!)
- ½ part lacto-fermented onion powder (I use onion skins to make this!)

Combine all the ingredients and store in a non-reactive container away from light and heat. This is a great mix for anchoring flavor in a roux, compound butter, soup, stew, or gravy. It can also be used in making sausage.

Lacto-Fermented Ranch Blend

by Meredith Leigh

I used to hate ranch dressing. Being from the South, this made me a bit of an outsider, so I dove in and experimented. The first thing I learned is that homemade ranch is a whole different story from school cafeteria ranch. And lacto-fermenting the ranch herbs and spices takes this classic flavor profile to a whole new level. My family affectionately calls this "ranchish." Try different combinations of dried fresh herbs and dried lacto-fermented herbs until you find your favorite.

- 1 part lacto-fermented parsley
- 1 part lacto-fermented green onion
- 1 part lacto-fermented basil
- 1 part cane sugar
- 1 part garlic powder
- 1 part ground Tellicherry peppercorn
- ½ part dried thyme leaves
- ½ part ground dried sweet pepper
- ½ part onion powder

Combine all the ingredients and store in a non-reactive container away from light and heat. To make ranch dressing, mix 1 part aioli (you can use mayonnaise if you're in a pinch) and 1 part full-fat buttermilk. Mix in the spice blend to taste. Store this ranchish dressing in the refrigerator in a jar, and shake before serving. It won't last long because you'll eat it up, but it will keep in the fridge for 2 weeks.

Meredith Leigh:
Using Vegetable Ferments in Charcuterie

As a specialist in agriculture, and livestock specifically, Meredith was focused on producing the best food from the soil up until she realized that post-harvest processing was an essential part of a resilient food chain. Her business focuses on food education and consulting through the lens of holism across the supply chain. She uses vegetable and fruit fermentation to augment and amplify the preservation of meat. Here she describes it in her own words.

Mind-Blowing Eating

"Fermentation remains one of the richest spaces of my work, where tradition and ingenuity continually combine to bring food (and soil) to the highest expression of vitality and nutrient density. I teach butchery, meat processing, and charcuterie (which is also fermentation!). Because shelf stability relies on a gradual loss of water activity, it often doesn't work to use fresh or fermented vegetables straight from the jar, so I began experimenting with drying fermented herbs and vegetable scraps to create unique flavor profiles in custom charcuterie and beyond. As we all know, salt by itself enhances inherent flavors, but then the processes of fermentation as well as drying doubly and triply concentrates flavor notes, resulting in mind-blowing eating experiences.

"For example, if I want to make use of fennel fronds in fermented products but don't like their pulpy texture, dehydrating the lacto-fermented fronds and grinding them into a fermented fennel salt is an option. And, when I'm trying to carefully control pH, the dried herbal blends are a clever way to get me where I'm going without a bunch of process tweaks. Last, we know that many fruits and vegetables store vital minerals and nutrients in their peels, rinds, and roots, so why not harness the processes of fermentation to capture those treasures, and see what flavor bonuses one can create? This has led to things such as a banana peel–daikon radish flavor bomb that blends the edgy spice of Asian radishes with the sweet, toasty flavor of dehydrated banana peels. Sometimes, each strange fermented and dried element by itself is too bitter, or sour, or spicy, but inventive combinations produce subtle balance that delivers for every taste bud.

"Development of these recipes comes from practicality and curiosity. Tired of composting my lush green onion tops but not loving their semi-slimy texture when fermented led to lacto-onion powder. In producing these creations, I usually aim for a 2 to 2.5 percent salt ratio to the weight of the ingredient, and depending on the combo I am planning, some ingredients will be dried without fermenting while others are greeted with a fermentation step. This prevents the final mix from being far too salty and creates a gigantic playground of variation in approach based on the desired result.

"Once each element is fermented (or not), and dried overnight at 115°F [46°C], I buzz it up in a coffee grinder (for large quantities use a burr grinder) and push it through a tamis or a spice sieve. Chunkier or higher-water-activity items may take several days to dry completely. Any larger pieces that don't powder properly are either processed again or tossed in a jar together for a fun and ever-changing 'soup salt.'"

Vegetables, Fruits, and Herbs

ARTICHOKES

This robust flower bud has a bit of a history, mythologically speaking. The maiden Cynara had the unfortunate luck of being seduced by Zeus, a scenario that never ends well. When his temper got the best of him, he turned her into an artichoke, and thus the scientific name *Cynara cardunculus* var. *scolymus*.

Artichokes are one of those Mediterranean foods that have all kinds of health benefits. They are in the top 10 list of antioxidant vegetables and are a rich source of potassium, vitamin C, inulin (prebiotics), and polyphenols, which are enhanced by fermentation.[13] Pliny the Elder said that artichoke cured baldness, strengthened the stomach, freshened the breath, and promoted the conception of male children—hmmm, was that before or after fermentation?

YOUR RAW MATERIAL

Artichoke season in many areas is April, May, and June, as is fitting for flowers. Artichokes are grown year-round on California's central coast, where they thrive in the mild temperatures and fog.

Smaller artichokes are more convenient for stuffing in a jar, but we have fermented quite large artichokes with good results.

BANNED GOODS

In New York City in the early twentieth century, artichokes were banned. Ciro "Whitey" Terranova (a.k.a. the "Artichoke King") obtained all artichokes shipped to New York from California, mob-style, and built a produce company. He resold the artichokes at a profit of 30 to 40 percent. Threats abounded on both coasts. The mayor declared a ban on all artichokes but lifted it three days later because he loved artichokes, too.

IN THE PICKLE JAR

Fermented Artichokes

See photo on page 244

yield: 1 gallon (3.8 l)

technique used: Mastering Brine Pickling (page 101)

These pickled artichokes have a pleasing saltiness and citrusy acidity. The texture is perfect. We eat them raw, in salads, or sautéed in plenty of butter or olive oil. After fermentation, you can also drain them and pack them in olive oil with dry herbs and spices (see page 336 for the method).

This recipe uses High Brine prepared with lemon and (sometimes) seasonings, which gives us the best result. With lower levels of salt in the brine, our results were inconsistent, and we battled Kahm yeast and a softer artichoke. If you find the final product too salty, we invite you to experiment with the salinity of the brine.

A 1-gallon fermentation equates to about 30 baby artichokes or 4 or 5 large ones. We ferment the whole artichoke, cutting off only the top and the external petals so that we can eat as much as possible. Feel free to halve or quarter them for fermentation, though. As tough as they seem, as soon as you start peeling back the thick outer petals, artichokes will begin oxidizing. Make the brine before you get started.

We Are Family: Cardoon

A cardoon (*Cynara cardunculus*) is a badass Mediterranean thistle and a close cousin of the artichoke. It is a member of the daisy family and a long-standing food in Mediterranean cuisines. Artichoke domestication began in Sicily about a thousand years before the cardoon was cultivated in Spain and France. DNA reveals that they share the same wild cardoon ancestor.

While the artichoke is grown for its large, meaty immature flower bud, the cardoon is harvested for its thick leaf ribs, which are spiky and look a little threatening. They are peeled and roasted and taste similar to the artichoke heart. The cardoon's smaller, spinier flower does have some culinary and fermentation interest, but not as a vegetable. The dried purple stamens from the flowers have enzymes that will coagulate milk and have been used for this since Roman times. Interestingly, the enzymes will produce unpleasant bitter amino acids in cow's milk, but in sheep and goat's milk they produce cheeses with just a light residual bitterness that complements the flavors. Certain European cheeses still use the cardoon stamens for their enzymes, especially on the Iberian Peninsula.

Cardoon ferment well following the same process described here for artichokes, except you ferment the ribs. The leaves with barbed hairs are removed with the outer skin and the strings. Place in lemon water to avoid browning. The salt and lemon leave them delicious, with no sign of bitterness. We ate some immediately after fermentation, raw and fried, then tucked the rest in the "long storage" fridge, where they migrated to the back and we forgot about them for 3 years. Upon their rediscovery, we poached and fried some of them, and they were still tasty. The rest went into a stew, which is another traditional Mediterranean use.

Note: You can also use this recipe and technique to pickle unopened small sunflower heads (see Capers on page 233), which can taste surprisingly similar. If you do so, use Basic Brine with lemon, instead of the high brine.

2–3 **quarts (1.9–2.8 l) High Brine (3 tablespoons/ 50.4 g unrefined salt per quart unchlorinated water)**

4 **medium lemons**

4 **pounds (1.8 kg) artichokes**

Garlic, chiles, juniper berries, bay leaves, cumin, or any other flavorings you desire (optional)

1. To make the brine, combine the water and salt, and mix to dissolve. Juice the lemons, then add the juice to the brine. Reserve the squeezed lemons.

2. Prepare the artichokes by peeling back and snapping off the external petals until you reach the tender inner layer. These will look yellowish or white at the base. Cut off the bottom woody end of the stem, keeping as much intact as possible, as it is tasty. Peel the skin off the remaining stem. Finally, slice the spiky top off the artichoke, about halfway up from the base. Place each artichoke in the brine immediately after trimming it.

3. Pack the artichokes into your fermenting vessel, and pour in enough brine to cover them. Reserve any leftover brine in the fridge (it will keep for 1 week; discard thereafter or dry out and reclaim salt, and make a new batch of High Brine, if needed).

4. Pack the top with the reserved lemon halves; this will keep the artichokes submerged in the brine and add a little more lemon essence to the mix. Let soak (ferment) for 12 to 24 hours.

5. Bring a pot of water to a boil. You will be keeping the brine. Remove the lemons from the brine and discard the lemons. Then remove the artichokes from the brine and add them to the boiling water. Blanch the artichokes for 2 minutes.

6. Place the blanched artichokes in a colander to drain and cool. Then return them to your fermenting vessel with any optional spices or flavorings. Add more brine if needed to submerge the artichokes.

7. Follow instructions for your fermenting vessel. In a jar, the tightly wedged artichokes usually stay submerged on their own, so you won't need to weigh them down. Put on the lid loosely and cover the jar with a towel, or tighten the lid if you intend to release CO_2 with the burping method (see page 44).

8. Set your fermentation vessel on a plate in a spot where you can keep an eye on it, out of direct sunlight, and let ferment for 10 to 14 days. During the fermentation period, monitor the brine level and top off with the reserved brine, if needed, to cover. As the artichokes ferment, they begin to lose their vibrant color and the brine will get cloudy; you can taste-test by picking off an outer petal and tasting the tender bottom. The artichokes are ready when they are pleasingly sour.

9. These will keep, refrigerated, for about 12 months.

Note: When you're ready to eat the pickled artichokes, cut them in half and use a spoon to scoop out the fuzzy spines in the center if they haven't softened.

ARUGULA

Arugula, native to the Mediterranean region, is popular in Italian cuisine. Ancient Romans valued it for its peppery leaves, and they used its seed as a spice. Believing arugula to be an aphrodisiac, they recommended it as a side dish to accompany any meal.

YOUR RAW MATERIAL

Arugula (also known as salad rocket) is a member of the crucifer family with important sulfur-rich phytonutrients. Cooking destroys the enzymes that activate those phytonutrients; fermenting enhances them.

Sounds great, but here's the thing: When we experimented with using arugula in a Korean water kimchi, we discovered that its nutty-peppery flavor, so tasty in a mesclun salad, can become bitter in fermentation—but only at first. As this ferment sits in the fridge, the bitterness mellows, and it disappears over time.

Another way to ameliorate the bitterness is to chop the arugula and add it to a combination kraut, or to use it instead of mustard greens in a kimchi.

IN THE PICKLE JAR

Arugula Kimchi

Adapted from the cookbook *Good Morning, Kimchi!* by Yoon Sook-ja

yield: about 1 pint (473 ml)
technique used: Mastering Brine Pickling (page 101)

This ferment is a water kimchi (which employs the same process as brine pickling). The brine boasts a lot of flavor, and it is good all by itself as a brine shot or for making crackers (page 369).

1 tablespoon (13 g) unrefined sugar
2 cups (473 ml) Low-Salt Basic Brine (1 teaspoon/5.6 g unrefined salt per cup unchlorinated water)
1–2 bunches arugula
3 thin slices fresh ginger
3 cloves garlic, sliced
1–2 dried red chiles or 1–2 slices dried sweet red pepper
1 grape leaf or parchment paper, to top the ferment (optional)

1. Add the sugar to the brine and mix to dissolve. Place the arugula leaves in the brine and let sit for a few hours or overnight, until softened.

2. Gently form the softened arugula into little bundles. Put the bundles in a pint jar and add the ginger, garlic, and chiles. Pour in enough of the same brine to cover.

3. Cover with a grape leaf or parchment paper, if using. Use an airlock lid or the burping method (page 44) to release CO_2; make sure there is little headspace at the top of the jar, then seal the lid tightly.

4. Set the jar on a plate in a spot where you can keep an eye on it, out of direct sunlight, and let ferment for 4 to 5 days. During the fermentation period, burp as needed, monitor the brine level and top off with the reserved brine, if needed, to cover. Begin taste-testing when the brine is cloudy and the leaves are faded. If the arugula is a little bitter, keep fermenting until it has a pleasant sour flavor.

5. When it's ready, tighten the lid of the jar and store in the refrigerator, where the kimchi will keep for 6 to 8 months.

Create Your Own Recipes

Fresh arugula makes a wonderful pesto. Try fermenting the leaves as a paste with garlic, a little cracked black pepper, and lemon, following the instructions for making pastes (page 76). To serve, mix in some chopped pine nuts and grated Parmesan.

Add chopped arugula to any condiment or kraut that you want to level up with some extra greens. You can also ferment it similarly to mustard greens (page 269).

ASPARAGUS

The ancient Romans had a saying to describe a task swiftly accomplished: "faster than cooking asparagus."

How times change! That wasn't the prevailing opinion in the United States of 1871. *The White House Cook Book: A Comprehensive Cyclopedia of Information for the Home*, a book thick with advice to the homemakers of the era, claimed to "represent the progress and present perfection of the culinary art." Treasures abound within old, forgotten books; this one, however, recommended boiling asparagus for 20 to 40 minutes!

The Romans had the right idea. Reputedly, their royalty prized asparagus enough to keep a fleet just to fetch it. They would have liked the slightly crisp, al dente texture of our pickled asparagus.

YOUR RAW MATERIAL

Ferment asparagus in the spring, when it's in season; the sooner these spears go from ground to jar, the better. The diameter of the spears, pencil thin or thumb thick, doesn't matter. What counts is that they're of fairly uniform size within each batch.

IN THE PICKLE JAR
Asparagus Pickles

See photo on page 323

yield: about 1 quart (946 ml)
technique used: Mastering Brine Pickling (page 101)

Bring these pickles to a potluck when you want to show off—they're food art, in both flavor and appearance, and easy to make. You'll need to trim the spears to fit in a 1-quart jar, but you can use any leftover nonwoody pieces to make a jar of bite-size pickles. To fill two narrow-mouthed pint jars instead, cut the spears to 3¾ inches long.

1–2 pounds (454–907 g) asparagus spears
3–4 cloves garlic
  1 teaspoon (2 g) black peppercorns
  ½ teaspoon (2.7 g) chile pepper flakes
  1 bay leaf
3–4 dried red chiles (cayenne if you want spicy; sweet if you want pretty but without heat)
2–3 cups (473–710 ml) High Brine (2¼ teaspoons/12.6 g unrefined salt per cup unchlorinated water)
1–2 grape leaves or parchment paper, to top the ferment (optional)

1. Snap the woody ends off the spears (compost them or save them for making broth). Cut the spears to fit in a 1-quart jar or crock; 5 inches is about the right length to leave room for the brine to cover them. Lightly crush the garlic cloves with the flat side of a knife.

2. Put the peppercorns, chile flakes, and bay leaf in the bottom of your fermentation vessel. Arrange the spears upright in the vessel, wedging the garlic and dried chiles between them. Pour enough brine over the spears to cover them. Store leftover brine in the fridge (it will keep for 1 week; discard thereafter or dry out and reclaim salt; make a new batch, if needed). Put the grape leaves or parchment paper, if using, on top of the spears.

3. When the spears are tightly packed they tend to stay in place, so you won't need a weighted follower, which could damage the delicate sprout ends. If your fermenting vessel has a lid, put it on loosely and cover with a towel, or tighten the lid if you intend to release CO_2 with the burping method (see page 44).

4. Set your fermentation vessel on a plate in a spot where you can keep an eye on it, out of direct sunlight, and let ferment for 5 to 8 days. During the fermentation period, monitor the brine level and top off with the reserved brine, if needed, to cover. The pickles are ready when the spears are a dull olive green and the brine is cloudy. They will be softened (not mushy) and have a pickle-y, not vinegary, flavor.

5. Top off with brine as needed, tighten the lids, and place in the refrigerator. The next day, check to be sure the asparagus spears are still submerged, topping off with more brine

if necessary. These pickles will keep, refrigerated, for 12 months. They will begin to soften after 8 months.

Asparagus Kimchi

yield: about 1 quart (946 ml)
technique used: Mastering Brine Pickling (page 101)

In this recipe, classic kimchi vegetables and spices are packed around whole asparagus spears, then a little brine is added to keep everything submerged. Serve a few spears topped with the shredded veggies as a pungent fermented side salad. Gochugaru pepper is pleasantly spicy, and red pepper flakes more so. Adjust pepper levels to suit your palate.

- 1–2 **pounds (454–907 g) asparagus spears**
- 1 **medium carrot, grated**
- 1 **(4-inch/10 cm) chunk daikon radish (or any variety), grated**
- 1 **(1½-inch/3.8 cm) piece fresh ginger, grated**
- 4 or 5 **cloves garlic, grated**
- 1 **tablespoon (5 g) gochugaru powder or chile pepper flakes**
- 1 **cup (237 ml) High Brine (2¼ teaspoons/ 12.6 g unrefined salt per cup unchlorinated water)**
- **Grape leaf or parchment paper, to top the ferment**

1. Snap the woody ends off the spears (compost them or save them for making broth). Cut the spears to fit in a 1-quart jar or crock; 5 inches is about the right length to leave room for the brine to cover them.

2. Combine the grated carrot, daikon, ginger, and garlic in a bowl. Add the gochugaru powder and massage into a coarse paste.

3. Arrange the spears upright in a crock or jar, wedging them in and packing the paste around them as you go. Pour enough brine over the spears to cover them, and top with a grape leaf or parchment paper to keep the paste under the brine. Store leftover brine in the fridge (it will keep for 1 week; discard thereafter or dry out and reclaim salt and make a new batch, if needed).

4. When the asparagus spears are tightly packed they tend to stay in place, so you won't need a weighted follower, which could damage the delicate ends. If your fermenting vessel has a lid, put it on loosely and cover with a towel, or tighten the lid if you intend to release CO_2 with the burping method (see page 44).

5. Set your crock or jar on a plate in a spot where you can keep an eye on it, out of direct sunlight, and let ferment for 5 to 8 days. During the fermentation period, monitor the brine level and top off with the reserved brine, if needed, to cover. These pickles are ready when the spears are a dull olive green and the brine is cloudy. We generally don't taste-test this ferment if it is in a jar because it is nice to keep the spears tightly packed.

6. Top off with brine, if needed, tighten the lid, and place in the refrigerator. The next day, check to be sure the asparagus is still submerged, topping off with more brine if necessary. These pickles will keep, refrigerated, for 1 year.

AVOCADOS

We were often asked: Can you ferment an avocado? To find out, we experimented and asked the "why ferment?" questions. The first two are: Does fermentation add flavor? Does fermentation preserve the avocado? After several trials, it turns out the answer to both is yes.

Fermented avocados can be a little funky; they are decidedly different than fresh but not particularly yeasty or sour, which would be our usual definition of fermentation funk. They are quite soft, which may be off-putting for some, but useful for spreading on toast or using in guacamole. Is it worth it? We mostly eat our avocados fresh, but we find fermentation worthwhile when there is a particularly good sale or we want to preserve the abundance of seasonal avocados.

A third question is, Does fermentation add remarkable nutritional benefits? Again, the simple answer is yes. We found a study that investigated whether lacto-fermentation would enrich the bioactive compounds (the good and healthy parts) of the avocado fruit. Interestingly, the researchers were looking to put all this goodness into pill form. They learned that fermentation resulted in high levels of total free amino acids, strongly increased antioxidant activity, and possibly the transformation of oleic and linoleic acids to high levels of mono, di-, and trihydroxy-octadecenoic acids.

One final note: Turns out the seed is the most nutrient-dense part of an avocado. Seventy percent of the avocado's antioxidants are locked up in it, and it's edible but mostly gets tossed out. In our explorations, we found that scientists are looking at how, with fungus-based fermentation, they can turn avocado seeds, a current waste product, into a nutritional product. We don't think their focus is culinary (yet), but we are imagining an avocado pit miso.

IN THE PICKLE JAR

Whole Avocados Fermented in Brine

yield: about 1 quart (946 ml)
technique used: Mastering Brine Pickling (page 101)

Choose rock-hard unripe avocados for this recipe. You will be fermenting them in a brine, not making guacamole. The idea here is that you ferment the whole avocado, either peeled with the pit in or peeled, halved, and pitted, simply to preserve it, and then later you use it to make guacamole or another condiment. Leaving the pit in keeps the avocado a little more intact and less soft, but fermenting the halves is much easier when packing the jar.

You'll see there's a bit of sugar in the brine. The pH of this ferment does get to a sufficient acidity, usually 4.0 to 4.2, without the sugar, but the sugar gives the bacteria more to work with and brings about a more robust fermentation.

We tried adding spices, lemon wheels, and other flavors to the brine. Ultimately, we preferred them plain. Feel free to experiment. Make sure that you have a jar with a mouth wide enough to fit the avocados. Finally, be careful if using a crock. Only add enough weight to keep the avocados under the brine. You don't want to add so much weight that everything squishes together when fermented.

2–4 small to medium unripe avocados
1 teaspoon (5 g) sugar
3–4 cups (710–946 ml) High Brine
(2¼ teaspoons/12.6 g unrefined salt per cup unchlorinated water)

1. Peel the avocados. Pack them, either whole or halved and pitted, into a crock or jar. Add the sugar to the brine mixture, stir until dissolved, and pour in enough brine to cover the avocados completely. Store any leftover brine in the fridge (it will keep for 1 week; discard thereafter or dry out to reclaim salt and make a new batch, if needed).

2. Follow the instructions for your fermentation vessel. In a jar, the avocados usually stay submerged on their own, so you won't need to weigh them down. Put on the lid loosely and cover the jar with a towel, or tighten the lid if you intend to release CO_2 with the burping method (see page 44).

3. Set your fermentation vessel on a plate in a spot where you can keep an eye on it, out of direct sunlight, and let ferment for 12 to 20 days. During the fermentation period, monitor the brine level and top off with the reserved brine, if needed, to cover. As the avocados ferment, the brine will get quite cloudy. They're ready when they are pleasingly sour.

4. Top off with brine, if needed, tighten the lid, and place in the refrigerator. The next day, check to be sure the avocados are still submerged, topping off with more brine if necessary. These will keep, refrigerated, for 3 to 6 months.

BASIL

Every summer we grow a flat of sweet basil and a flat of Thai basil among our flowers. We used to make pounds of pesto to freeze. It was expensive to invest in all the other pesto ingredients, so now we save money, time, and freezer space by preserving the basil in a ferment.

Drying diminishes this herb's aromatic volatile oils. Fermenting, on the other hand, retains the essential basil flavor while unleashing a unique pickled quality—a fresh yet concentrated flavor. We ferment whole leaves to toss into a dish at serving time, and we make concentrated spice pastes to use during meal preparation.

YOUR RAW MATERIAL

Humans have enjoyed basil's fragrant flavor for more than 5,000 years. This member of the mint family is native to India and Asia. There are more than 40 varieties of basil, in colors ranging from pale to deep green, rich aubergine purple, and a variegated lace of golden yellow, and with a wide range of textures, fragrances, and flavors. Perhaps the best-known species is sweet basil (*Ocimum basilicum*).

Basil leaves are tender and easily bruised. Harvest them early in the morning just after the dew dries and use as soon as possible. If purchasing basil, choose bundles with vivid green leaves without black spots.

THAI AND HOLY BASIL

Thai basil is a purplish variety of sweet basil, *Ocimum basilicum*. It has a distinct flavor that shows notes of licorice, cinnamon, and a hint of mint.

Another variety you find often these days is holy basil (*Ocimum tenuiflorum*), sometimes called tulsi, which has a sweet floral flavor with a delicate mint quality. Holy basil is antioxidant-rich and a digestive aid, and it is said to be a balm for mind, body, and spirit. Fresh and dried leaves of any variety of tulsi enhance many ferments.

WE ARE FAMILY: MINT

Mint has played a significant role in traditional herbal pharmacopoeias throughout history. Its wonderful scent and flavor have also made it a leading player in the kitchen, where it adds a cool, refreshing taste to dishes. Of the many varieties of mint, spearmint, curly mint, and peppermint are the most common culinary types, but there are also fruity varieties, such as apple, pineapple, and orange mints. The flavor of the various mints holds up well in fermentation. If you want to add mint to one of your own ferment recipes, use it in quantities similar to what you would use in a fresh salad or veggie dish, and add it to the ferment when you combine the rest of your vegetables, just before salting. Chopping the leaves will release a little more flavor in the ferment. Mint lends itself well to whole-leaf or paste preparations, too (see Chapter 5). Our favorite way to use mint is in Lemon-Mint Kraut (page 177).

IN THE CROCK
Whole-Leaf Fermented Basil

technique used: Whole-Leaf Ferments (page 78)

This ferment is wonderful to have on hand; the leaves retain their texture and shape and can be used in any of the same applications as fresh basil. Toss some in a salad, stir-fry, or pasta dish (after the dish has been removed from the heat if you want to preserve the probiotics).

For this recipe, use any quantity of basil and any kind, or mix and match: lemon, cinnamon, sweet, Thai, you name it.

Tip: Keep those stems. They are full of flavor and can be used to flavor brines in pickles or vinegars, or add to condiments and then remove before consuming.

**Basil leaves, in ¼-pound (113 g) bunches
¼ teaspoon (1.4 g) unrefined salt per bunch of basil**

1. Lightly sprinkle the basil with salt until you can taste it. (It takes very little.) Massage the salt into the leaves; they'll quickly bruise and turn dark. There's no waiting time for the brine to develop. *Note:* The leaves will shrink down to what seems like nothing—that's okay, because the flavor is concentrated.

2. Press the leaves into an appropriately sized jar. More liquid will release as you press, and you should now see a little brine. If using the burping method (page 44), make sure there is little headspace, top with a round of parchment paper, and seal the lid tightly. Watch the lid for pressure building up. With this recipe you may never need to burp, or at most just once. Alternatively,

top the paste with a quart-size ziplock bag. Press the bag down onto the top of the ferment, then fill it with water and seal.

3. Set the jar on your counter, out of direct sunlight, and let ferment for 7 to 14 days. As the leaves ferment, they begin to lose their vibrant color and the brine will get cloudy; this is when you can start to taste-test. The ferment is ready when lightly sour.

4. To store, tamp down the fermented leaves to make sure they are submerged in the brine, press a small round of parchment paper directly on top, and seal the jar with the lid. This ferment will keep, refrigerated, indefinitely.

Basil Garlic Paste

technique used: Pastes (page 76)

This paste ferments in the same way as whole-leaf basil (at left). The advantage here is that you can use some of the basil stem, which increases your yield. If the flowers are just starting to appear, that's fine, but as they mature they might impart bitter flavors. Taste them to decide.

The combination of basil and garlic makes this paste an excellent pesto starter kit. Just add the paste to your favorite pesto ingredients—olive oil, nuts, and Romano or other hard cheese. Or you can use the paste to flavor sauces, soups, and salad dressings.

**Basil, in ¼-pound (113 g) bunches of leaves
and nonwoody stems
⅓ teaspoon (2 g) unrefined salt per bunch
of basil
3 cloves garlic per bunch of basil**

1. Process the basil to a paste consistency in a food processor. Sprinkle in the salt. The basil will become juicy immediately.

2. Press the paste into an appropriately sized jar. More liquid will release as you press, and you should now see a little brine. If using the burping method (page 44), make sure there is little headspace, top with a round of parchment paper, and seal the lid tightly. Watch the lid for pressure building up. With this recipe you may never need to burp, or at most just once. Alternatively, top the paste with a quart-size ziplock bag. Press the bag down onto the top of the ferment, then fill it with water and seal.

3. Set the jar on your counter, out of direct sunlight, and let ferment for 7 to 14 days. As the basil paste ferments, it begins to lose its vibrant color and the brine will get cloudy; this is when you can start to taste-test. It's ready when lightly sour.

4. To store, tamp down to make sure the ferment is submerged in its brine, press a small round of parchment paper directly on top, and seal the jar with its lid. Store in the refrigerator, where the paste will keep for 2 years or more.

Thai Basil Paste

technique used: Pastes (page 76)

This handy paste is a tasty addition to any dish prepared with coconut milk, or dollop it on rice or noodles. This is one of our favorite homemade convenience foods, and we invite you to play with it.

The bottled fish sauce in this recipe provides the salt necessary to start the ferment. You won't need additional salt.

Thai basil, in ¼-pound (113 g) bunches
  of leaves and nonwoody stems
2 cloves garlic per bunch of basil
1 tablespoon (15 g) grated galangal or
  fresh ginger per bunch of basil
½ teaspoon (2.5 ml) fish sauce per bunch
  of basil

1. Process the basil, garlic, galangal, and fish sauce to a paste consistency in a food processor.

2. Press the paste into an appropriately sized jar. More liquid will release as you press, and you should now see a little brine. If using the burping method (page 44), make sure there is little headspace, top with a round of parchment paper, and seal the lid tightly. Watch the lid for pressure building up. With this recipe you may never need to burp or at most just once. Alternatively, top the paste with a quart-size ziplock bag. Press the bag down onto the top of the ferment, then fill it with water and seal.

3. Set the jar on your counter, out of direct sunlight, and let ferment for 7 to 14 days. As the basil paste ferments, it begins to lose its vibrant color and the brine will get cloudy; this is when you can start to taste-test. It's ready when lightly sour.

4. To store, tamp down to make sure the ferment is submerged in its brine, press a small round of parchment paper directly on top, and seal the jar with its lid. Store in the refrigerator, where the paste will keep for 2 years or more.

BEANS, GREEN

Common wisdom has it that green beans should not be consumed raw due to varying concentrations—less in young beans, more as they mature—of lectins, potentially toxic proteins (see the sidebar). It's a matter of balance: Enjoy young, succulent green beans as a fermented pickle; don't make them a staple in a raw-food diet. Or, deactivate the lectins by steaming your green beans for 2 minutes or boiling for 4 minutes. This is a viable option for the dilly beans. The ferment will still have enough LAB from the other ingredients to get going. We find the beans ferment well; the texture is just softer.

YOUR RAW MATERIAL

There are many beautiful varieties of green beans, among them some that aren't even green. Yellow wax beans and green beans retain their colors when fermented, but the purple beans and the beautiful pintoed red-and-white beans turn drab during fermentation, their colors bleeding into the brine.

Choose pods that are firm and slim, with a slightly downy bright skin—indicators of young beans. As the green beans mature on the vine, they become tough and will not break down properly in fermentation. If the shape of the seeds is evident through the skin, they're too mature.

Christopher Writes

When I was young, my brother and I had the job of snapping beans every summer. The job description was simple: Pinch one of the pointy ends, use it to pull the string down the side of the bean and off, then snap the bean into pieces.

Lectin Facts

There's a lot of information (and misinformation) on the subject of eating raw green beans, from touting their health benefits to the warning that they're antinutrient thugs you should stay clear of. Conflicting information can make us afraid of our food.

The fact is that much of what we eat, healthy or not, contains something "toxic." As it happens, lectin proteins are present in varying concentrations in almost everything we eat.

According to T. Shibamoto and L. Bjeldanes, the authors of *Introduction to Food Toxicology*, "Toxicity has been shown in feeding studies with the pure lectin comprising 0.5–1.0% of mice or rat diets. Lectins appear to inhibit nutrient absorption in the intestine and inhibit growth of the animals. Meals that contain raw or fermented green beans should be of no cause for concern, as any lectins present would be too small of a dose to have any effect on nutrient availability. It is unknown if lactic acid fermentation has any effect on lectin content of green beans, since lectins are a group of proteins and glycoproteins."

In other words, the amount of lectins present in any quantity of raw or fermented green beans that a human being might reasonably consume is no cause for concern.

All our garden bounty was canned and stashed in our basement, and it was my job to go down there when called upon to fetch a can or two for dinner. I was terrified of the basement. The monsters that I knew lived down there might grab my legs from under the stairs, or drop on me from the exposed floor joists, or best yet, reach out and grab my hands as I reached for a jar . . . I really did see eyes and often heard breathing, and more than once I dropped and broke a jar as I sprinted for my life up the stairs.

Somehow, no matter what canned good my mother sent me to get, it was always the green beans that died at my hand, and here's where it gets weird. Upon breakage of the bean jar, my mother would go into hazmat mode: She'd direct the family to stand well back, pull on her bright yellow dishwashing gloves, meticulously clean up, and then douse the crime scene with Pine-Sol or bleach—or both. I remember wondering, "Why are green beans radioactive when the jar breaks, but otherwise we just dump them in a pot and eat them?"

IN THE PICKLE JAR
Dilly Beans

See photo on page 304

yield: about 1 gallon (3.8 l)
technique used: Mastering Brine Pickling (page 101)

Dilly beans are the gold standard of green bean pickles, but don't feel limited. If you want to try making a different kind of bean pickle, we encourage you to use this process and your favorite spice combination.

- 15 **cloves garlic**
- 6 **pounds (2.7 kg) green beans, trimmed**
- 12 **dried red chile peppers**
- 6 **bay leaves**
- 2 **tablespoons (24 g) pickling spice (see page 158 for a recipe)**
- 1 **gallon (3.8 l) Basic Brine (½ cup/134 g unrefined salt per gallon unchlorinated water)**
- **A few grape or other tannin-rich leaves (see page 105) or parchment paper, to top the ferment (optional)**

1. Lightly mash the garlic cloves with the side of a knife. Layer the beans in four widemouthed quart jars (the visual effect is stunning if you can arrange them vertically) or a 1-gallon jar or crock, incorporating the garlic, chile peppers, bay leaves, and pickling spice as you go.

2. Pour enough brine over the beans to cover them. Reserve any leftover brine in the fridge. (It will keep for 1 week; discard thereafter or dry out and reclaim salt and make a new batch, if needed.)

3. Put the grape leaves or parchment paper, if using, over the beans to keep everything submerged. Follow the instructions for your fermentation vessel. In a jar, the tightly wedged beans usually stay in place on their own, so you won't need to weigh them down unless they are loosely packed. Put on the lid loosely and cover the jar with a towel, or tighten the lid if you intend to release CO_2 with the burping method (see page 44).

4. Set your fermentation vessel on a plate in a spot where you can keep an eye on it, out of direct sunlight, and let ferment for 6 to 10 days. During the fermentation period, monitor the brine level and top off with the reserved brine, if needed, to cover. Like many green vegetables, the beans begin as a vibrant green but lose color as fermentation commences, eventually turning a drab olive, a result of the acids interacting with the chlorophyll. The brine will become cloudy; this comes from the production of lactic acid. On day 6 you can start to taste-test. The beans are ready when the brine is cloudy, the color is drab, and their acidity is like cucumber pickles.

5. Top off with brine, if needed, tighten the lids, and place in the refrigerator. The next day, check to be sure the beans are still submerged, topping off with more brine if necessary. They will keep, refrigerated, for 1 year.

Kirsten Writes

When Christopher and I were newly married, we had dinner with his parents one night, and I remember his mom lamenting that it was too late to prepare canned green beans. Dinner was still an hour away, but she explained that it would take a minimum of 2 hours to cook them. I had no idea what she meant. It turns out that my new mother-in-law was concerned about botulism, which is a rare form of food poisoning but nonetheless can be a real threat in canned low-acid foods.

As with any "threat," we all learn to respect it and live by the rules around it. My lesson came when we started our commercial kitchen 20 years later; I had to spend 2 days memorizing everything about botulism in order to get certification (part of our state's licensing requirements).

My mother-in-law was right, if overcautious with 2 hours of cooking time. Heat does kill the botulism bacteria at the boiling point. And generally people are told to boil for 10 minutes to make sure the entire batch has cooked evenly.

MAKE-YOUR-OWN
Pickling Spice

¼ teaspoon (0.3 g) cumin seeds
2 teaspoons (4.4 g) dill seed (or 3 or 4 fresh dill seed heads)
1½ teaspoons (4 g) whole black peppercorns
1½ teaspoons (4.5 g) mustard seeds
1 teaspoon (2.4 g) coriander seeds

Combine all the ingredients.

FERMENTISTA'S TIP

Fermentation and Botulism
Clostridium botulinum, *which manifests as botulism, is rare but still the bogeyman of canning, whether at home or in commercial production. As recently as 2007,* C. botulinum *was discovered in commercially canned green beans.*

We don't worry about botulism because fermentation uses acidity to preserve vegetables (and to control microbes) and takes place at a pH below 4.6. The C. botulinum *spore cannot hatch or grow in that sort of acidic environment.*

Fermented Three-Bean Salad

See photo on page 189

yield: about 1 quart (946 ml)
technique used: Mastering Brine Pickling (page 101)

This isn't your great-grandmother's Three Bean Salad. We use fresh or frozen edamame and green chickpeas (harvested younger and not dried) for a fun, fresh texture, plenty of nutrition and protein, and a crisp, sour flavor. Instead of the calico color combination of the classic, this is a multihued green dish. If you cannot find fresh or frozen green chickpeas, canned chickpeas or soaked and boiled dried chickpeas (not too mushy) work beautifully.

Eat as is right alongside your meal, or drizzle with olive oil to serve it like a salad.

- 2 cups (520 g) fresh or frozen green chickpeas, shelled
- 1 cup (83 g) green beans, cut into 1- to 2-inch (2.5–5 cm) lengths
- 8 ounces (227 g) frozen shelled edamame, thawed
- 8 ounces (227 g) pearl onions or 1 cup (115 g) thinly sliced yellow onions
- 1 stalk celery, cut diagonally in very thin slices
  A few sprigs of your favorite herb (our favorites are tarragon and thyme)
- 1 quart (946 ml) Basic Brine (2 tablespoons/ 34 g unrefined salt per quart unchlorinated water)
  Grape leaves or parchment paper, to top the ferment

1. Combine the chickpeas, green beans, edamame, onions, celery, and herbs in a bowl and toss to mix.

2. Transfer the mixture to your fermentation vessel. Pour enough brine over the beans to cover them. Store any leftover brine in the fridge (it will keep for 1 week; discard thereafter or dry out and reclaim salt and make a new batch, if needed).

3. Put the grape leaves or parchment paper, if using, on top of the mixture to keep things submerged. Follow the instructions for your fermentation vessel. For a jar, if using the burping method (page 44), make sure there is little headspace and seal lid tightly. Burp daily or as needed. Alternatively, top the ferment with a quart-size ziplock bag. Press the bag down onto the top of the ferment and then fill it with water and seal.

4. Set your fermentation vessel on a plate in a spot where you can keep an eye on it, out of direct sunlight, and let ferment for 7 to 10 days. During the fermentation period, monitor the brine level and top off with the reserved brine, if needed, to cover. As the beans ferment, they lose their vibrant color and the brine turns cloudy; this is when you can start to taste-test. The beans are ready when they're pleasingly sour, the flavors have mingled, and the brine is cloudy.

5. Top off with brine, if needed, tighten the lids, and place in the refrigerator. The next day, check to be sure the beans are still submerged, topping off with more brine if necessary. They will keep, refrigerated, for 6 to 12 months.

ONION AND PEPPER
RELISH (made with
habanero), *page 286*

PICKLED GARLIC
SCAPES, *page 239*

SWEET PEPPER SALSA,
page 297

NAKED KRAUT, *page 173*

FERMENTED FENNEL
CRANBERRY CHUTNEY,
page 229

SIMPLE BEET KRAUT,
page 163

FERMENTED SHISO
LEAVES, *page 325*

CHIPOTLE SQUASH
KRAUT, *page 347*

BEETS

People seem to have a strong opinion about beets. It's either "I adore the earthy flavor of beets" or "Beets taste like dirt."

Beets add color, fun, and flavor to your table. They are readily available and often fairly inexpensive.

The health benefits of beets are tremendous. The striking crimson color is beautiful and also part of what makes beets healthy. Interestingly, traditional Chinese medicine sees red foods as blood food—nourishing, building, and keeping things moving. Western medicine, with its scientific analysis, confirms that beets improve blood flow and arterial health while reducing blood pressure. The high folate content and bioflavonoids keep our blood and bodies strong. To these things, add the health benefits of raw probiotic-rich and vitamin-enhanced fermented vegetables, and the result is a real power food. The question really becomes: why not?

YOUR RAW MATERIAL

There's a difference in how spring beets and overwintered roots ferment. Once beets freeze in the ground, the roots develop a lot more sugar, which affects the ferment—the bubbling and energy are amazing. The brine is also thick and syrupy, at times even gooey. Most winter vegetables contain more sugar than other vegetables; they store these carbohydrates for their big push in the spring. This can make it a little more challenging for fermentation—mostly in the form of extra CO_2 and mess, but the extra sugar can turn a lactic acid fermentation more yeasty or even alcoholic. These flavors are sometimes described as funky. A little funk can be tasty to some palates and yucky to others. Funk level is a personal thing. Winter beets are especially sugary, even syrupy, and our little microbe yeast buddies can thrive so alcoholic flavors in a beet ferment are very possible.

FOR BEST RESULTS

» **Slice, don't grate.** Thinly slice beets on a mandoline rather than grate them into shreds. Less surface area means the fermentation will be slower, more manageable, and both less sour and less "funky."

» **Dilute, dilute, dilute.** All root veggies that have gone through frosts are particularly high in sugar, and this is amplified for beets. Instead of making a pure beet ferment, dilute them with other vegetables, such as cabbage or celery.

» **Finally, give it space.** This means don't fill your vessel to the top. Give beets an extra few inches of headspace to allow that bubbling "heave" to have the space it needs. Then it won't push your brine and ferment out the top.

Fermented red beets are a rich and deep crimson. With other types of beets, the colors aren't always what you might expect. For example, golden beets don't retain their sunset gold for very long. Be aware, too, of Chioggia beets. They'll lure you with their concentric candy-cane rings. You'll think about how sexy they'll look in the jar. You might take the candy-cane image further—sugar and spice and everything nice—and make a Chioggia pickle with cinnamon sticks and whole cloves. You'll pour in the brine and start daydreaming of your great idea coming to fruition . . .

Fast-forward a few days, to the moment you check the jar and find only gray slices. The beautiful pink stripes have fallen out of the beets and into the brine. Oh, the disappointment! Your only consolation is that the flavor is still good.

IN THE CROCK

Beets blend nicely with many other vegetables, but they'll turn everything else fuchsia. (Even the smallest addition of beet is dominant.) And your hands will also turn red. Use gloves if you're going out . . . it takes a lot of scrubbing to remove the staining.

Peel overwintered beets. Thin-skinned spring beets don't need peeling, although peeling will mitigate the earthy flavor. In general, beets are tough to grate. If you need to grate them, it's easiest to quarter them and run them through the grater attachment of a food processor. Hand grating works, too, though, and builds up your muscle strength.

Simple Beet Kraut

See photo on page 161

yield: about 2 quarts (1.9 l)
technique used: Mastering Sauerkraut (page 61)

The nature of beets might cause this brine to be heavier than usual, more like a syrup. This is normal. If it's too thick for you, use more cabbage than beets.

> *The beet kraut is a monster! Keeps exploding and knocking the jars sideways and burping over. I punch it down and add some kraut brine to try to thin the syrup a bit. Gad!*
> —MARY ALIONIS, WHISTLING DUCK FARM, GRANTS PASS, OREGON, COMMENTING ON MAKING HER FIRST BEET KRAUT TO SELL AT HER FARM STAND

1 **head cabbage**
1½ **pounds (680 g) beets (2 medium beets)**
1–1½ **tablespoons (17–25 g) unrefined salt**

1. Remove the coarse outer leaves of the cabbage. Rinse a few unblemished ones and set them aside. Rinse the rest of the cabbage in cold water. Quarter and core the cabbage, thinly slice or shred, and transfer to a large bowl. Rinse the beets, peel if desired, grate them, and then transfer to the bowl with the cabbage.

2. Add 1 tablespoon of the salt and, with your hands, massage it into the vegetables. Then taste. You should be able to taste the salt without it being overwhelming. Add more salt if necessary. The beets are especially quick to release brine and will look wet and limp, and liquid will begin to pool. However, if you don't see much brine, let the mixture stand, covered, for 45 minutes, then massage again.

3. Transfer the cabbage-beet mixture to a 2-quart jar, crock, or other vessel a handful at a time, pressing down to remove air pockets. You should see some brine on top of the mixture when you press. If you don't, return the mixture to the bowl and massage again.

4. Top the kraut with the reserved outer cabbage leaves to keep everything submerged, pressing them down under the brine. Add a weight if you have one. Follow instructions for your fermentation vessel. For a jar, if using the burping method (page 44) make sure there is little headspace and seal lid tightly. Alternatively, top the ferment with a quart-size ziplock bag. Press the bag down onto the top of the ferment and then fill it with water and seal.

5. Set your fermentation vessel on a plate in a spot where you can keep an eye on it, out of direct sunlight, and let ferment for 4 to 14 days. Check regularly to make sure the kraut is submerged, pressing down, as needed, to bring the brine back to the surface. If you're using the burping method, check often; with all the sugar in the beets, this is a lively fermentation. The foam may be a little brackish after a few days; this is within the realm of normal. Just skim off the foam; underneath it the kraut will be perfect. Start taste-testing after 4 or 5 days. The kraut will be a little raw this early, but some people like it that way. We find it tastiest after about 2 weeks. You'll know it's ready when it's pleasingly sour and pickle-y tasting, the veggies have softened a bit but retain crunch, and the color is a rich deep fuchsia.

6. When the kraut is ready, transfer to smaller jars, if necessary, and tamp down. Pour in any brine that's left. Tighten the lids, then store in the fridge. The kraut will keep, refrigerated, for 6 months.

Curtido Rojo

yield: about 1 gallon (3.8 l)
technique used: Mastering Sauerkraut (page 61)

This is our fermented take on Guatemala's version of a vinegar-pickled sauerkraut. It's usually served as a quick, fresh side dish. Whether you use red or green cabbage, the ferment will turn a beautiful purple.

- 1 **head red or green cabbage, thinly sliced or shredded**
- 2 **beets, shredded**
- 1 **large red onion, thinly sliced**
- ½ **pound (227 g) green beans, sliced in ½-inch (1.3 cm) pieces**
- 2 or 3 **cloves garlic, minced**
- 1 or 2 **fresh jalapeños, seeded and minced (for extra heat, keep the seeds)**
- 1 **tablespoon (8.4 g) cumin seed**
- 1 **tablespoon (6 g) grated orange zest or lime zest**
- 1 **tablespoon (5.4 g) dried oregano, crumbled**
- ½ **teaspoon (2.7 g) chile pepper flakes**
- 1–2 **tablespoons (17–34 g) unrefined salt**
- 1 or 2 **bay leaves**

Follow the recipe for Simple Beet Kraut (page 163), combining the cabbage with the beets, onion, beans, garlic, jalapeños, cumin seed, orange or lime zest, oregano, and chile flakes. Massage in the salt. When the brine has developed and it's ready to pack, lay the bay leaves in the bottom of a 1-gallon jar or crock and continue with the recipe instructions.

> **FERMENTISTA'S TIP**
>
> ### Ch-ch-ch-changes
>
> *Let's talk about color. Sometimes a red beet kraut will take on a faint orange color with age, but if it gets brown, it has fully oxidized. When you see color changes in any ferment that start from the top (where the oxygen hits) and go down—especially if a ferment has been sitting—it is most likely due to oxidation. Color changes during fermentation are normal. You will notice some vegetables such as beets "lose" their color in the brine. This means the pigment is water soluble. Other vegetables such as carrots or red peppers don't; their pigments are oil soluble. When these oil-soluble pigments change colors, you can be sure it is due to oxidation.*

Curried Golden Beets

See photo on page 226

yield: about 2 quarts (946 ml)
technique used: Mastering Sauerkraut (page 61)

Another variation on Simple Beet Kraut, this is earthy, warm, and delicious. Work quickly once the beets are shredded; they'll retain more of their golden color the sooner you can get them tucked under the brine. The optional dried currants in the recipe make this ferment thicker and sweeter.

1	head cabbage, thinly sliced or shredded
2	golden beets, grated
1	teaspoon (2 g) curry powder (or make your own; see recipe at right)
½	cup (72 g) dried currants (optional)
1–1½	tablespoons (17–25 g) unrefined salt

Follow the recipe for Simple Beet Kraut (page 163), combining the cabbage with the beets, curry powder, currants (if using), and salt.

Kirsten Writes

When a farmer friend called and asked if we would like to make kraut with golden beets, our immediate reaction was *absolutely*. We envisioned a radiant yellow, like van Gogh's sunflowers, beaming beet love throughout the market, pulling customers to our table. Later that week, as we enthusiastically grated beets, their vibrant color faded before our eyes, turning into a rather unappetizing grayish brown. Oxidation was taking place before fermentation's anaerobic acidity could save the color. Then we had a "eureka" moment: "Turmeric!" The beets fermented thick and syrupy and the color of saffron. We sold 6 gallons' worth in 2 weeks.

MAKE-YOUR-OWN

Curry Powder

- ¼ teaspoon (0.3 g) cumin seeds
- ¼ teaspoon (0.75 g) mustard seeds
- 1 teaspoon (2 g) ground turmeric
- ½ teaspoon (2.5 g) grated fresh ginger
- ⅛ teaspoon (0.4 g) ground black pepper
- ⅛ teaspoon (0.4 g) ground cayenne
- ⅛ teaspoon (0.4 g) ground cinnamon

In a dry skillet, toast the cumin and mustard seeds; transfer to a bowl, then stir in the rest of the spices. Store in a spice jar for up to 6 months.

Beet-Celery Fermented Salad

See photo on page 244

yield: about 1 quart (946 ml)
technique used: Mastering Sauerkraut (page 61)

This fermented salad is based on Eastern European flavor profiles; it highlights the beets, while the celery brings a lightness to the flavor. The biggest trick here is to make sure the beets are sliced thinly—we use a mandoline.

- 4 small beets
- 1 medium bunch celery
- 1 medium red onion
- 1 tablespoon (17 g) unrefined salt
- 1 teaspoon (2 g) whole peppercorns, freshly ground (1½ teaspoons ground)
- ¼–½ teaspoon (0.5–1 g) ground allspice
- 3 whole cloves, freshly ground (¼ teaspoon ground)

1. Rinse and peel the beets. Slice as thinly as possible, ideally with a mandoline. Place in a large bowl. Use the mandoline on the same thin setting to slice the celery and red onion and add them to the bowl with the beets. Save the top round of the onion or the butt of the celery to use as a follower.

2. Add the salt, plus pepper, allspice, and cloves and massage them into the vegetables, using your hands. Then taste. You should be able to taste the salt without it being overwhelming; add more salt if necessary. (Because the celery has natural salts, you may not need any more salt.) The vegetables should begin to look wet and limp, and liquid will pool. However, if you don't see much brine, let the mixture stand, covered, for 45 minutes, then massage again.

3. Transfer the mixture to a 2-quart jar or crock, a handful at a time, pressing down to remove the air pockets. You should see some brine on top of the mixture when you press. If you don't, return the mixture to the bowl and massage again.

4. Top the kraut with the reserved onion top or celery butt to keep everything submerged. Follow the instructions for your fermentation vessel. For a jar, if using the burping method (page 44) make sure there is little headspace and seal lid tightly. Burp daily or as needed. Alternatively, top the ferment with a quart-size ziplock bag. Press the bag down onto the top of the ferment and then fill it with water and seal.

5. Set your fermentation vessel on a plate in a spot where you can keep an eye on it, out of direct sunlight, and let ferment for 4 to 14 days. Check regularly to make sure the kraut is submerged, pressing down, as needed, to bring the brine back to the surface. Start taste-testing after 4 or so days. This kraut has a rich, deep flavor. You'll know it's ready when these flavors are developed, with an acidic or pickle-like undertone, and the colors have melded to a magical fuchsia.

6. When the kraut is ready, transfer to smaller jars, if necessary, and tamp down. Pour in any brine that's left. Tighten the lids, then store in the fridge. The kraut will keep, refrigerated, for up to 10 months.

IN THE PICKLE JAR

Beet slices, beet spears, tiny whole peeled beets—they all make wonderful pickles. However, for people accustomed to the soft, sweet, acidic flavor of vinegar-pickled beets, these are a surprise, as the beets stay quite firm—their texture is that of raw beets. Slice them thinly.

Beet Kvass (*Russel*)

yield: about 1 quart (946 ml)
technique used: Mastering Brine Pickling (page 101)

One of our market regulars always wanted to buy jars of straight beet brine. She wanted to have this elixir whenever her mood was low. One day she brought a small paperback cookbook—*The Complete American-Jewish Cookbook* by Anne London and Bertha Kahn Bishov (1952)—to show us a recipe for *russel*. That was the first time we'd heard of this traditional Jewish cooking brine.

   That recipe was simple: 12 pounds (5.4 kg) of beets in water for 3½ weeks. Our recipe isn't much different—just less time and a bit of salt. Try this as a base for your favorite borscht recipe. The rough chop in this recipe gives the beets enough surface area to ferment without the sugars breaking down too quickly, thus leading to alcohol; don't grate the beets.

  1½ **pounds (680 g) beets, scrubbed or peeled**
   1 **quart (946 ml) unchlorinated water**
   2 **teaspoons (11 g) unrefined salt**

1. Chop the beets into ½-inch pieces and put them in a ½-gallon jar. Add enough water to fill the jar and mix in the salt (you'll need minimal headspace). Cover loosely.

2. Set the jar on a plate on your counter, out of direct sunlight, and let ferment for 7 to 21 days, stirring daily. You will see some bubbling. For more effervescence, seal the jar with its lid and use the burping method (page 44).

3. Start to taste the liquid on day 7. It should have a light effervescence; an acidic quality, like lemonade; and a slight saltiness. It will, of course, taste like beets. If you want something more like vinegar, ferment longer, taste again, and repeat until it's just right. Occasionally this ferment will take much longer to get started. If you don't see it fermenting, as long as it isn't spoiled, keep waiting.

4. Pour the liquid off the beets and into a clean jar. Seal tightly. (The beets themselves are a by-product of the process; however, they can be used to make a second batch of *russel*, shredded into salad, or cooked in soup.) This tonic is meant to be made regularly and consumed quickly; nonetheless, it will keep, refrigerated, for many months.

ABOUT BEET KVASS

Beet kvass is the sour, salty liquid that comes from fermenting beet cubes. Depending on the region or ethnicity, this same liquid is also called *russel*, which is the Yiddish or Slavic word for brine, and brine it is. It's a fermented, ruby-colored beet "vinegar" used to flavor soups, preserve and color horseradish, and make drinks. This brine has a reputation as a tonic, cleanser, appetite builder, and hangover cure.

   The word *kvass* comes from the old Slavic word meaning "yeast" or "leaven." It's a common brew throughout Eastern Europe, usually made by fermenting dark rye bread. In Russia, *rassol* is cucumber pickle brine, touted for the same virtues as kvass and the identifying ingredient in *rassolnik*, a traditional soup made with meat and barley.

BROCCOLI

Broccoli is versatile. Raw, steamed, sautéed? Yes. Lacto-fermented? You'd rather not. When we tried brine-pickling broccoli florets, we came up with a lot of comments that weren't exactly flattering. When we chopped the florets and stalks and added them to a basic cabbage sauerkraut, it had a nice-enough earthy flavor for the first few weeks, and then a strong broccoli-gas taste developed, almost like sulfur. As it aged, this became even more acrid. Fermentation just isn't a long-term preservation solution for broccoli florets.

The stems are another story. They are the sweetest part of this vegetable once you get past the woody layer under the peel. Generously peel the stem with a paring knife to get to this "marrow," then grate, dice, or thinly slice the inner stems. They are a delicious addition to any kimchi, kraut, or condiment. Use them as you would kohlrabi.

You can use broccoli in quick fermentation projects. For example, broccoli florets that have been in shio koji (see page 92) for a few hours are quite delicious.

Waste Not

Sometimes broccoli stems make up more than half the weight of the broccoli you paid for, not to mention the energy the plant put into producing it. These chunky stems are an excellent source of much-needed dietary fiber (more than in the florets). Plus the stems boast slightly more vitamin C, calcium, and iron than their showy tops, which makes one wonder when they became a by-product. If you are fortunate enough to have some broccoli leaves, they have the highest levels of antioxidants. Treat them as you would kale or collards in fermentation.

BRUSSELS SPROUTS

Pickling Brussels sprouts came early in our fermentation experimentation ('cuz tiny cabbages . . .). Our first attempts were awful. We suspected that the tight leaves were too dense to allow the acidification to penetrate to the centers. We quickly learned that cutting the sprouts in half or quarters before pickling creates a delicious product.

YOUR RAW MATERIAL

Brussels sprouts are increasingly available fresh year-round. However, they're a cold-season crop usually best from September through January in the northern hemisphere. When purchasing, check the stems (if sold cut from the stock) for dehydration. The longer it has been since they were harvested, the more likely it is they will be sulfuric instead of sweet.

Hot Smoky Sprouts

See photo on page 280

yield: about 1 quart (946 ml)
technique used: Mastering Brine Pickling (page 101)

This recipe is inspired by our love for Brussels sprouts sautéed with plenty of bacon. We use just a small amount of smoked salt in the brine, as it can become overpowering.

- 1 tablespoon (17 g) smoked salt
- 1 quart (946 ml) Low-Salt Basic Brine (4 teaspoons/22 g unrefined salt per quart unchlorinated water)
- 1 pound (454 g) Brussels sprouts, halved
- 4 or 5 cloves garlic
- 1 tablespoon (8 g) peppercorns
- 1 tablespoon (16 g) chile pepper flakes
- 2 or 3 jalapeños, cut into strips or rounds
- 1 grape leaf or parchment paper, to top the ferment (optional)

1. Add the smoked salt to the brine and mix to dissolve. Prepare sprouts by removing any yellowing outer leaves, rinse, and halve.

2. Put the garlic cloves, peppercorns, and chile pepper flakes in the bottom of a quart jar or crock. If using a jar, arrange the Brussels sprouts and jalapeños so they're wedged below the shoulder. Pour in enough brine to cover the vegetables. Store any leftover brine in the fridge (it will keep for 1 week; discard thereafter or dry out and reclaim salt and make a new batch, if needed).

3. Place the grape leaf or piece of parchment paper, if using, over the vegetables to keep things submerged. Follow the instructions for your fermentation vessel. For a jar, if using the burping method (page 44) make sure there is little headspace and seal lid tightly. Burp daily or as needed.

4. Set your fermentation vessel on a plate in a spot where you can keep an eye on it, out of direct sunlight, and let ferment for 7 to 14 days. During the fermentation period, monitor the brine level and top off with the reserved brine, if needed, to cover. As the sprouts ferment, they begin to lose their vibrant color and the brine will get cloudy. Start to taste your pickles after a week. They're ready when the sprouts are sour enough for your palate.

5. Top off with brine, if needed, tighten the lids, and place in the refrigerator. The next day, check to be sure the sprouts are still submerged, topping off with more brine if necessary. The pickles will keep, refrigerated, for 1 year.

Create Your Own Recipes

Brussels sprouts are versatile. You can pickle them in a variety of ways—on their own in regular brine, with other vegetables in a medley, or sliced thinly on a mandoline to make "sprout kraut." Or add garlic, spice, and ginger to make a kimchi.

BURDOCK (GOBO)

The reputation of burdock (*Arctium lappa*) ranges from a nuisance weed for flower gardeners to an essential ingredient for herbalists and chefs. Burdock has anti-inflammatory, antioxidant, and antibacterial properties. It's said to aid digestion and to alleviate arthritis and some skin disorders. This list goes on, and the reason is that this "weed" belongs to the class of herbs known as adaptogens, which work to balance the system. This group of highly nutritive and broad-spectrum medicinal plants includes perilla, spikenard, nettle, and ginseng. Burdock originated in the Siberian region of northern Asia. In Europe, it was used during the Middle Ages both as a medicinal herb and as a vegetable. It's a popular vegetable in Japan (where it's known as *gobo*) and is important in the Chinese herbal pharmacy.

YOUR RAW MATERIAL

Although it's a biennial, most gardeners and farmers cultivate burdock (*A. lappa* var. *edule*) as an annual and harvest it for the long, thin taproot, which may be 4 feet long with a 1-inch diameter. If you let it go to seed, in the "right" environment (for example, a garden), burdock will quickly get away, at which point you have as much as you like.

If you're not growing or foraging it, you'll often find it in the vegetable section of natural-foods stores. Look for roots that are still firm, not limp like an old carrot. Select those that are about the thickness of your thumb; any bigger and they tend to be woody.

Burdock, or gobo, is a wonderful addition to sauerkraut. It imparts a mild sweetness, only subtly perceptible against the stronger taste of the cabbage.

BURDOCK LEAVES

If you are a gardener or a wildcrafter and come across burdock, it's good to know that its tender leaves make a nice salad green (if you don't mind the small hairs on them). Shred a leaf or two—they're big—and add to a kraut; the fermentation will take care of the fuzzy texture.

IN THE CROCK

Burdock root oxidizes to an unappetizing gray-brown when grated and exposed to the air. Although in the beginning the color makes you think the burdock must have been scraped off the forest floor, after some hours in the anaerobic, soon-to-be-acidic environment of the brine, the brighter color of the freshly grated root returns.

Grated or thinly sliced burdock root works nicely with other vegetables. If you have a lot of it, as in the recipe for kimchi (facing page), it's better to slice the roots thinly. They become a little too starchy when grated for use by themselves.

Kirsten Writes

When I first started working with burdock, I wanted to make a burdock-only ferment. I peeled and grated the root, but it soon began to oxidize. I added freshly squeezed orange juice; I thought the flavor would complement that of the burdock and was hoping the acidity would balance the color, much in the way lemon juice does with sliced apples.

As it fermented it became increasingly starchy and thick, and there was no recognizable brine. The orange juice did nothing for the color or flavor; the ferment became slightly alcoholic, and that was the least of its problems. It all went straight to the compost bin.

So much for an all-burdock ferment.

Burdock Kimchi

yield: about 1 quart (946 ml)
technique used: Relishes/Chutneys/Salsas/Salads
(page 74)

This root never bubbled to the top of our gotta-have-it list—until we fermented it. After much experimentation, we found this kimchi to be a perfect (and tasty) way to incorporate burdock into our diet. A dollop of Burdock Kimchi on a few slices of cheese is a satisfying afternoon snack.

The heat is up to you. Use a pinch of hot pepper flakes for mild heat or a small spoonful to make it fiery hot.

- 2 carrots, thinly sliced
- 1 bunch scallions, greens included, cut into 1-inch (2.5 cm) slices
- 1 bunch mustard greens, thinly sliced
- 2 cloves garlic, minced
- 1 tablespoon (11 g) finely grated fresh ginger
- 2 pounds (900 g) burdock root
  Zest and juice of 1 lemon
- 1 tablespoon (9 g) sesame seeds
  Chile pepper flakes or salt-free gochugaru, to taste
- 1–2 teaspoons (6–11 g) unrefined salt or ½ cup (152 ml) fish sauce
  Grape leaves or parchment paper, to top the ferment

1. Combine the carrots, scallions, mustard greens, garlic, and ginger in a large bowl. Mix well and set aside.

2. Peel the burdock root and thinly slice crosswise; then quickly squeeze the juice of the lemon over the root slices to help them retain their color. Add the burdock, lemon zest, sesame seeds, and chile flakes to the bowl, mixing to combine.

3. Sprinkle in the salt or fish sauce and work it in with your hands; if you are not getting much brine, let the mixture sit, covered, for 30 to 45 minutes. Then toss and massage again for a few minutes to get everything mixed. At this point, you should see brine at the bottom of the bowl.

4. Transfer the vegetables, a few handfuls at a time, to your fermentation vessel, pressing down as you go to remove air pockets. You should see some brine on top of the mixture when you press.

5. Place grape leaves or a piece of parchment paper and weight, if using, on top of the vegetables to keep everything submerged, pressing them down under the brine. Follow the instructions for your fermentation vessel. For a jar, if using the burping method (page 44) make sure there is little headspace and seal lid tightly. Burp daily or as needed. Alternatively, top the ferment with a quart-size ziplock bag. Press the bag down onto the top of the ferment and then fill it with water and seal.

6. Set your fermentation vessel on a plate in a spot where you can keep an eye on it, out of direct sunlight, and let ferment for 7 to 14 days. Check daily to make sure the vegetables are submerged, pressing down, as needed, to bring the brine back to the surface. Start taste-testing when the vegetables start to lose their vibrant color and the brine becomes cloudy. The kimchi is ready when it is pleasingly sour.

7. When the kimchi is ready, transfer to smaller jars, if necessary, and tamp down. Pour in any brine that's left. Tighten the lids, then store in the fridge. The kimchi will keep, refrigerated, for 1 year.

Burdock-Carrot Kimchi
See photo on page 280

Follow the recipe for Burdock Kimchi on page 171, adding 2 pounds (900 g) of thinly sliced carrots and omitting the mustard greens and sesame seeds.

Create Your Own Recipes

For a burdock kraut, follow the recipe for Naked Kraut (page 173) and add 4 large or 5 medium burdock roots, peeled and grated. Burdock is also a great choice for a pickling bed—nuka, miso, kasu, or your own invention.

CABBAGE, GREEN AND SAVOY

Cabbage, n: a familiar kitchen-garden vegetable about as large and wise as a man's head.
—FROM *THE DEVIL'S DICTIONARY*, 1906, BY AMBROSE BIERCE

The lowly cabbage, round and plain and generally inexpensive in the grocery store, is a rock star of lactic acid fermentation! This simple-looking vegetable is one of the most beautiful in the garden—a magnificent "flower" when surrounded by all its deeply colored leaves, peeling back as the plant appears to bloom.

Cabbage, in its many varieties, is the basis of most of the traditional ferments around the world. Fermented cabbage has always been, and continues to be, an important staple in nourishing people around the globe: German *sauerkraut*, Dutch *zuurkool*, Polish *kapusta*, Korean *kimchi*, Japanese *tsukemono*, Chinese *suan cai*, French *choucroute*, Swedish *surkål*, Russian *shchi* . . . the list goes on.

YOUR RAW MATERIAL
Winter cabbages are as beautiful as they are welcome for their freshness. January King, with outer leaves that are a deep fuchsia, matures just when we're in the darkest of days, reminding us it's time to make kraut to savor with thick, hot soups through the bleak months of February and March. However, winter cabbages are sometimes not fresh-from-the-field varieties but long-term storage varieties that are being brought out in winter. Because these are bred to last and last and last, they can have very low moisture content and therefore are more difficult to ferment. Look for heads with plump, juicy leaves.

In spring, nature brings us flowers and salad greens, but the big, overwintered cabbage heads you see are ready to do what's in their genetic makeup: bolt and go to seed. We have found that they often release less brine.

Summer and fall cabbages are the archetypal pale green. They're crunchy and moist, perfect for putting up a year's supply of kraut. Savoy, beautiful and crinkly, is a late-fall variety. Its taste is generally milder than that of other cabbages; fermented, it has a similar flavor but the leaf has a thinner quality. When we made Lemon-Dill Kraut with Savoy cabbage, it was different enough that we renamed the kraut Lemon-Dill's Curly Cousin. It's somewhat drier and produces less brine.

In general, for the recipes in this section, 1 cabbage head equals 2 to 3 pounds (0.9 to 1.4 kg).

A Note on Goitrogens

Crucifers (the backbone of the canon of fermented vegetables) contain goitrogens, which some people with hypothyroid conditions should avoid, as the goitrogen suppresses thyroid function. Cooking breaks down goitrogen compounds; fermentation will not, so we spent a good deal of time testing krauts and kimchis based on vegetables not from the cabbage family.

To balance or counteract too much goitrogen, add sea vegetables (see Natural Iodine, page 177) to crucifer-based ferments. Or, make sure you cook the ferments that will be an issue for you.

Alternatively, try Escarole Kimchi (page 228), Beet-Celery Fermented Salad (page 166), and celeriac or carrot krauts, as just a few examples of ferments from other vegetable families that have just as much pizzazz and flavor as does anything with cabbage.

The ferments pictured on pages 304–305 are all free of goitrogens.

IN THE CROCK

Naked Kraut

See photo on page 160

yield: about 2 quarts (1.9 l)
technique used: Mastering Sauerkraut (page 61)

This is pure cabbage deliciousness. We used to teach our students a mantra for kraut success: Shred, salt, submerge, conquers evil every time! Remember this for this and all your ferments.

   1–2 heads (3½ pounds/1.6 kg) cabbage
   1–1½ tablespoons (17–25 g) unrefined salt

1. To prepare the cabbage, remove the coarse outer leaves. Rinse a few unblemished ones and set them aside. Rinse the rest of the cabbage in cold water. Quarter, core, and thinly slice the cabbage, then transfer to a large bowl.

2. Add half the salt and, with your hands, massage it into the cabbage, then taste. You should be able to taste the salt without it being overwhelming. Add more salt if necessary. The cabbage will look wet and limp and liquid will pool. If you've put in a good effort and don't see much brine in the bowl, let it stand, covered, for 45 minutes, then massage again.

3. Transfer the mixture to a 2-quart jar or crock, a handful at a time, pressing down to remove air pockets. You should see some brine on top of the mixture when you press. If you don't, return the mixture to the bowl and massage again.

4. Top the kraut with the reserved outer cabbage leaves to keep everything submerged, pressing them down under the brine. Add a weight if you have one. Follow the instructions for your fermentation vessel. For a jar, if using the burping method (page 44) make sure there is little headspace and seal lid tightly. Burp daily or as needed. Alternatively, top the ferment with a quart-size ziplock bag. Press the bag down onto the top of the ferment and then fill it with water and seal.

5. Set your fermentation vessel on a plate in a spot where you can keep an eye on it, out of direct sunlight, and let ferment for 4 to 14 days. Check regularly to make sure the kraut is submerged, pressing down, as needed, to bring the brine back to the surface. Start to taste-test when the cabbage begins to turn the color of cooked cabbage and the brine becomes cloudy. The kraut is ready when it is pleasingly sour and pickle-y.

6. When the kraut is ready, transfer to smaller jars and tamp down. Pour in any brine that's left. Tighten the lids, then store in the fridge. The kraut will keep, refrigerated, for 6 months.

Charred Cabbage Sauerkraut

See photo on page 263

yield: about 2 quarts (1.9 l)
technique used: Mastering Sauerkraut (page 61)

When we had our first charred cabbage salad in a restaurant, Kirsten immediately thought about making a charred sauerkraut. It worked, and the family loved it—lightly smoky and bitter notes from the char combine perfectly with the salty sour. The char is just on the edges, and the middle of the cabbage stays sweet and uncooked. We have no need to add live brine to this recipe; it ferments beautifully as is. That said, there is no harm in adding some if you have it and want the assurance.

We experimented with many other flavors but ultimately love this simple and plain one. The runner-up was flavored with toasted cumin seed.

1–2 **heads (3½ pounds/1.6 kg) cabbage**
1–1½ **tablespoons (17–25 g) unrefined salt**
2 **teaspoons toasted cumin seeds (optional)**

1. To prepare the cabbage, remove the coarse outer leaves. Rinse a few unblemished ones and set them aside. Cut the cabbage in half through the core, and then, keeping the core intact, cut each half into 2 or 3 wedges.

2. Heat a grill or large cast-iron pan over medium-high heat.

3. Grill the cabbage wedges until charred on their cut sides, 4–5 minutes per side. You are charring the edges, which will get blistered; the cabbage is getting somewhat cooked but the inside of the wedges will still be raw. Place on a cutting board to cool.

4. When the cabbage is cool, thinly slice and place in a large bowl. Add half the salt and the cumin, if using, and, with your hands, massage it into the cabbage. Then taste. You should be able to taste the salt without it being overwhelming. Add more salt if necessary. The cabbage will look wet and limp and liquid will pool. If you've put in a good effort and don't see much brine in the bowl, let it stand, covered, for 45 minutes, then massage again.

5. Transfer the mixture to a 2-quart jar or crock, a handful at a time, pressing down to remove air pockets. You should see some brine on top of the mixture when you press. If you don't, return the mixture to the bowl and massage again.

6. Top the kraut with the reserved outer cabbage leaves to keep everything submerged, pressing them down under the brine. Add a weight if you have one. Follow the instructions for your fermentation vessel. For a jar, if using the burping method (page 44) make sure there is little headspace and seal lid tightly. Burp daily or as needed. Alternatively, top the ferment with a quart-size ziplock bag. Press the bag down onto the top of the ferment and then fill it with water and seal.

7. Set your fermentation vessel on a plate in a spot where you can keep an eye on it, out of direct sunlight, and let ferment for 10 to 14 days. Check regularly to make sure the kraut is submerged, pressing down, as needed, to bring the brine back to the surface. As the cabbage ferments, the brine will become cloudy and start to smell pickle-y; this is when you can start taste-testing. The kraut is done when it is pleasingly sour.

8. When the kraut is ready, transfer to smaller jars and tamp down. Pour in any brine that's left. Tighten the lids, then store in the fridge. The kraut will keep, refrigerated, for 6 months.

> **FERMENTISTA'S TIP**
>
> **The Bacteria with a Buttery Flavor**
>
> Pediococcus cerevisiae, *one of the members of the microbial fermentation team, is the bacterium that gives lacto-fermented sauerkraut its buttery flavor. This occurs because Pediococcus produces diacetyl, a compound that tastes, well, buttery. The creamy flavor profile imparted by this bacterium makes it a good influence on cheeses and yogurt; wine and beer makers, however, view the little guy as a contaminant.*

Three Cs

See photo on page 339

yield: about 3 quarts (2.8 l)

technique used: Mastering Sauerkraut (page 61)

The three Cs are cabbage, carrots, and celeriac. This kraut combination was one of the first products we sold at the market. Each of the vegetables provides a subtle flavor that doesn't overwhelm the others.

Follow the recipe for Naked Kraut (page 173), adding 1 packed cup each of shredded carrot and celeriac to the cabbage and ¼–½ teaspoon (1.4–2.8 g) additional salt.

Smoky Kraut or Hot and Smoky Kraut

yield: about 2 quarts (1.9 l)

technique used: Mastering Sauerkraut (page 61)

This is one of our favorite recipes, still, after all these years.

Follow the recipe for Naked Kraut (page 173), but replace half of the regular salt with smoked salt. After you've shredded the cabbage, add 1 sliced onion and 1 diced red bell pepper for a mild smoky kraut; for the hot version, add 2 or 3 diced jalapeños instead.

ABOUT SMOKED SALTS

There are many varieties of smoked salts, each imparting different character and smoky notes. We use applewood, as it is delicious and readily available where we live. We encourage you to start with your region's specialty, such as alder, hickory, or mesquite. Some smoked salts are quite strong—in that case, use half smoked and half regular salt. The goal is for the smoky flavor to be noticeable but not overwhelming.

Curtido

See photo on page 323

yield: about 1 gallon (3.9 l)
technique used: Mastering Sauerkraut (page 61)

Curtido tied Lemon-Dill Kraut for our bestseller, and people who were adamant that they didn't like fermented vegetables liked curtido. The name comes from the Spanish verb *encurtir*, which means "to pickle." Curtido is traditional in the cuisine of El Salvador, where it is often served with pupusas. We find it to be a refreshing replacement for pico de gallo, which helps any efforts to eat local, as it's not reliant on a fresh tomato traveling hundreds of miles to get to your winter table.

2	heads (about 6 pounds/2.7 kg) cabbage
1 or 2	carrots, thinly sliced
1	onion, thinly sliced
4	cloves garlic, grated
2	tablespoons (11 g) dried oregano, crumbled
1	tablespoon (16 g) chile pepper flakes
½	teaspoon (1 g) ground cumin, or to taste
2½	tablespoons (40 g) unrefined salt

Follow the recipe for Naked Kraut (page 173), shredding the cabbage and combining it with the carrot, onion, garlic, oregano, chile flakes, cumin, and salt.

Juniper-Onion Kraut

See photo on page 280

yield: about 1 gallon (3.9 l)
technique used: Mastering Sauerkraut (page 61)

This ferment was our first foray into beyond-cabbage kraut, when we had no idea what would lie ahead. Kraut and onions are a delicious combination on their own, but the sweet piney notes of juniper really bring the flavors together. Some people love to bite into the whole berries for an intense burst of sharp flavor—not unlike a shot of gin.

3–4	heads (8 pounds/3.6 kg) cabbage
2	large sweet onions, thinly sliced
2	tablespoons (10 g) juniper berries, lightly crushed
3	tablespoons (50 g) unrefined salt

Follow the recipe for Naked Kraut (page 173), shredding the cabbage and combining it with the onions, juniper berries, and salt. *Note:* Lightly crush the berries with the handle of your knife to release the flavorful oils.

Lemon-Mint Kraut

yield: about 1 quart (946 ml)
technique used: Mastering Sauerkraut (page 61)

Lemon is a player in this sprightly kraut as well as in the lemon-dill one that follows, but in this recipe we accentuate it even more with the use of the zest. The cooling quality of the mint and the freshness of the lemon make this a superb summer kraut. It's particularly nice on a Mediterranean platter (the flavors were inspired by our love of Greek food).

> 1 cabbage
> ½ cup (30 g) finely chopped fresh mint leaves, such as spearmint (see **We Are Family: Mint**, page 153)
> Juice and zest of 1 lemon
> 1 tablespoon (17 g) unrefined salt

Follow the recipe for Naked Kraut (page 173), shredding the cabbage and combining it with the mint, lemon juice and zest, and salt.

FERMENTISTA'S TIP

Natural Iodine

Consumption of large quantities of the goitrogens in raw cruciferous vegetables is not recommended for those with a sensitive thyroid. The best way to consume them is fermented with seaweed (see page 328). It naturally contains iodine, which the body does not produce on its own, and which is important for the proper function of the thyroid.

Although some say iodine inhibits fermentation, we've never had a problem with it, nor do we know anyone else who has.

Lemon-Dill Kraut

See photo on page 339

yield: about 1 gallon (3.8 l)
technique used: Mastering Sauerkraut (page 61)

One of our sons was going backpacking and wanted to bring a kraut, something refreshing that would provide some electrolytes to go along with the cheese, crackers, and trail mix that made up his standard fare. The sauerkraut we came up with soon became our bestseller and the one we recommend to people who "don't like sauerkraut." We received an email from a customer off-season, right before Christmas, asking if we had any Lemon-Dill Kraut. Her 7-year-old had written to Santa and requested only two things: a bathrobe and a jar of our lemon kraut. 'Nuff said.

> 2 heads (about 6 pounds/2.7 kg) cabbage
> ¼ cup (59 ml) lemon juice
> 1–2 tablespoons (3–6 g) dried dill weed (to taste)
> 1½–2 tablespoons (25–34 g) unrefined salt
> 4 or 5 cloves garlic, finely grated

Follow the recipe for Naked Kraut (page 173), shredding the cabbage and combining it with the lemon juice, dill, and salt. When the cabbage is glistening and you have a small pool of liquid in the bottom of the bowl, mix in the garlic.

Senfkraut (Mustardkraut)

yield: about 2 quarts (1.9 l)
technique used: Mastering Sauerkraut (page 61)

This is a showy kraut, with turmeric adding that bright, sunny color, as it does for so many of our foods, including classic yellow mustard. It is delicious on sausages (meat or plant-based), mashed potatoes, and Reubens. This recipe has its roots in a traditional mustard pickle recipe Kirsten found in a German American cookbook from 1888.

> 3 tablespoons (27 g) white mustard seeds
> ¼ cup (59 ml) unchlorinated water
> 1 head cabbage (about 3 pounds/1.4 kg)
> ½ medium onion, thinly sliced
> 3 cloves garlic, minced
> 1 tablespoon (6 g) grated fresh ginger
> 3 teaspoons (15 g) ground turmeric or
>   2 tablespoons (14 g) freshly grated
>   turmeric
> 1½ tablespoons (4 g) dried dill weed
> 1–1½ tablespoons (17–25 g) unrefined salt
>   A few bay leaves
> ½ teaspoon (1 g) whole peppercorns

Follow the recipe for Naked Kraut (page 173). Combine the mustard seeds with the water in a blender and blend just enough to break up the seeds; you don't need to blend until thick and smooth. Shred the cabbage and add it to a large bowl with the mustard seed slurry, onion, garlic, ginger, turmeric, dill, and salt. Place the bay leaves and peppercorns at the bottom of your vessel.

Shiso Kraut

See photo on page 338
yield: about 2 quarts (1.9 l)
technique used: Mastering Sauerkraut (page 61)

Both shiso and sauerkraut are digestive stimulants, so this kraut does double duty. That shouldn't be your only motivation, though; this kraut has a wonderful subtly floral flavor. The leaves turn a dark and nondescript color, but if you use red shiso, a beautiful pink halos the leaves in the kraut.

Add 1 bunch (4 ounces/113 g) shiso leaves to the shredded cabbage in a batch of Naked Kraut (page 173). *Note:* Because it's such a small quantity of shiso, it will have little effect on the amount of salt the kraut needs, perhaps requiring only an extra gram or two. As always, taste before packing.

Wine Kraut

See photo on page 227
yield: about 2 quarts (1.9 l)
technique used: Mastering Sauerkraut (page 61)

We wanted to make a lacto-fermented wine sauerkraut that retained the flavor of the wine. Wine added to raw cabbage at the beginning of the ferment time became vinegary. Not bad, but not wine. We thought of trying to infuse the flavor by fermenting in an old barrel from one of the local wineries, but 55 gallons of kraut was a larger-scale experiment than we were up for. In smaller trials, we learned to add the wine at the end of the fermentation.

Ferment Naked Kraut (page 173) for 2 weeks, then add 1 cup (237 ml) of a good red wine. Because the kraut is already fermented, just let it sit on the counter with the wine infusion until you like the flavor. It will taste like a wine kraut immediately, but a day or two on the counter lets the flavors commingle and deepen.

Za'atar Kraut

yield: about 2 quarts (1.9 l)
technique used: Mastering Sauerkraut (page 61)

Za'atar is a blend of herbs traditionally used in Middle Eastern cooking. In the Mediterranean countries east of Italy, za'atar is believed to make the mind alert and the body strong, and it is often incorporated into breakfast to prepare for a big day. If you'd like a bold kraut as part of your morning meal, this one's nice in an omelet.

Follow the recipe for Naked Kraut (page 173), adding 2 tablespoons of za'atar with the salt.

About Sumac

Sumac, a red-flaked spice with a tart flavor reminiscent of lemon, is an essential spice in much of the Middle East. It has a long culinary history, having served as the tart, acidic element in food before the ancient Romans brought lemons to the region.

MAKE-YOUR-OWN

Za'atar Spice Blend

¼ cup (29 g) ground sumac
2 tablespoons (3.4 g) dried marjoram
2 tablespoons (10.8 g) dried oregano
2 tablespoons (12 g) dried thyme
1 tablespoon (16 g) roasted sesame seeds

Combine all the ingredients, and there you have it!

Big-Batch Kraut

yield: about 4 gallons (15 l)
technique used: Mastering Sauerkraut (page 61)

The basic process is the same for a large batch as for a small one. The differences have to do in part with the equipment needed to manage a vast pile of cabbage, especially before it breaks down, but the bigger factors are that the fermentation time is usually longer and the brine management duties are less (because the weight of the shredded vegetables and larger quantity of brine achieves a critical mass that helps keep everything in place). It is interesting to note that large batches need less manipulation for the cabbage to release its juices. If the cabbage is evenly salted, the mass, weight, and gravity help this happen on its own in a few hours.

Prep the cabbage in the largest bowl you have or a large, food-grade plastic container. Add salt as you go. This jump-starts the breakdown of the cell walls, releasing juices even before you begin to work at it.

40 pounds (18 kg) cabbage
1 cup (269 g) unrefined salt

1. To prepare the cabbage, remove the coarse outer leaves. Rinse several unblemished ones and set them aside. Rinse the rest of the cabbage in cold water. Quarter and core each head and shred or thinly slice. As you slice, transfer the cabbage to a very large bowl or food-grade tub, sprinkling a little of the salt onto each batch.

2. When all the cabbage is shredded, continue to massage with your hands to evenly distribute the salt, then taste. It should taste slightly salty without being overwhelming. If it's not salty enough, continue adding salt and tasting, until it's to your liking. You should see plenty of brine accumulating in the bottom of your vessel. Cover the bowl with clean cloths and set aside for 1 to 3 hours to allow more brine to release.

3. Put 2 to 3 inches of the cabbage in the bottom of a large crock and press with your fists or a tamper to remove air pockets. Repeat with the remaining cabbage. When the vessel is packed, you should have pressed out all the air pockets and see a layer of brine on top. Leave at least 4 inches of space between the top of the brine and the rim of the crock.

4. Arrange the reserved leaves, or another primary follower, on top. Add a plate that fits the opening of the container and covers as much of the cabbage as possible; weigh it down with a sealed water-filled 1-gallon jar. Usually this is enough weight, but after a day or two of fermentation, you may need two or three jars.

5. Set the crock aside to ferment, somewhere nearby, out of direct sunlight, and cool, for 2 to 4 weeks. Check daily for the first few days to make sure the vegetables are submerged, pressing down to bring the brine back to the surface.

If the cabbage is "lifting" above the brine or your brine seems to have decreased, add more weight. You may see scum on top; it's harmless, but check the appendix if you are concerned.

6. Start to taste-test after 2 weeks. You'll know the kraut is ready when it's pleasingly sour and pickle-y tasting, without the strong acidity of vinegar; the flavors have mingled; the cabbage has softened a bit but still has some crunch; and it is more yellow than green and slightly translucent, as if it's been cooked.

7. When it's to your liking, spoon the kraut into jars and tamp down, leaving as little headspace as possible. Pour in any remaining brine to cover. Tighten the lids, then store in the fridge, where the kraut will keep for 1 year.

SWEETENING THE CROCK

For a sweet-flavored kraut, add stevia to the ferment. Although it's sweet, it doesn't have the carbohydrates that bacteria convert to acid. Stevia is extremely sweet; a pinch goes a long way. Use the dried leaves, which are a whole food. The white stevia powder you find in grocery stores is a processed food.

Pears contain sorbitol, which is another unfermentable sugar. Unless you dry them, European pears tend to get mushy in fermentation, but Asian pears keep a decent texture and add nice sweet notes.

Remember: Adding regular sugar is adding food for the bacteria and will only make your creation more sour.

Big-Batch Curtido

yield: about 8 gallons (30 l)
technique used: Mastering Sauerkraut (page 61)

This is a super-size batch of Curtido (page 176). The process is a variation of the Big-Batch Kraut (page 179), but this yield is bigger still.

- 60 **pounds (27.2 kg) cabbage**
- 10 **pounds (4.5 kg) carrots, thinly sliced**
- 10 **pounds (4.5 kg) onions, thinly sliced**
- 4 **heads garlic, cloves separated and grated**
- 1 **cup (86 g) dried oregano**
- ½ **cup (128 g) chile pepper flakes**
- ⅓ **cup (45 g) ground cumin**
- 1 **pound (454 g/about 1 pint) unrefined salt, plus more to taste**

Follow the recipe for Big-Batch Kraut (page 179), shredding the cabbage and combining it with the carrots, onions, garlic, oregano, chile flakes, and cumin, then adding the salt.

Big-Batch Lemon-Dill Kraut

yield: about 8 gallons (30 l)
technique used: Mastering Sauerkraut (page 61)

This recipe makes enough to last a year for a big family (a very big family)—as in, once fermented, it will take 40 quart jars to store it! It's somewhat labor-intensive; it'll take two people at least 2 hours to cut and prepare the cabbage.

- 80 **pounds (36.3 kg) cabbage**
- 3 **cups (710 ml) lemon juice**
- 1–1½ **cups (50–74 g) dried dill weed (to taste)**
- 1¼ **pounds (680 g) unrefined salt**
- 7 **heads garlic, cloves separated and grated**

Follow the recipe for Big-Batch Kraut (page 179), shredding the cabbage and adding the lemon juice and dill with the salt. When the cabbage is glistening and you have a small pool of liquid in the bottom of the bowl, add the garlic.

OlyKraut's Eastern European Sauerkraut

yield: about 1 gallon (3.8 l)
technique used: Mastering Sauerkraut (page 61)

This recipe was shared with us by OlyKraut, a woman-owned, B Corp–certified fermented food company in Olympia, Washington, that's been around since 2008. It perfectly blends the crisp, fresh taste favored by the modern palate with the deep, traditional flavor of sauerkraut with caraway. The recipe is based on one that OlyKraut founding member Kai Tillman learned from their grandmother. The OlyKraut team tested batch after batch, adjusting as they went, until it was just right. It won Good Food Awards in 2012 and 2020!

OlyKraut is now run by Sash Sunday, who is driven by a vision of healthy, sustainable, regional food systems. The company is committed to working with smaller regional farms where workers are treated well and the cabbages are delicious. The team loves encouraging the consumption of raw fermented vegetables because they believe healthier people are just at their best.

- 5 **pounds (2.3 kg) cabbage**
- 1 **large yellow onion**
- 2 or 3 **carrots**
- 1 **tart apple**
- **Juice of 1 grapefruit**
- 3–4 **tablespoons (50–67 g) unrefined salt**
- **Sprinkling of caraway seeds**

1. Slice the cabbage and onion and transfer to a large bowl. Grate the carrots and the apple into the bowl, then add the grapefruit juice and salt and sprinkle on the caraway seeds.

2. Using your hands, mix everything together, then pack it into a crock.

3. Weight, cover, and let ferment until it's delicious!

4. Ladle the kraut into jars and tamp down. Pour in any brine that's left. Tighten the lids, then store in the refrigerator, where the kraut will keep for 1 year.

Create Your Own Recipes

So many krauts, so little time. Cabbage is the base for just about anything you can think of, kraut-wise. Use your imagination and have fun!

CABBAGE, NAPA OR CHINESE

Napa, or Chinese, cabbage is a staple throughout Asia. Napa leaves are typically more tender, juicy, and delicate than those of other types of cabbage, yet they have a crispy, fresh texture when fermented. Depending on the recipe, you may use it whole, slice it diagonally or lengthwise, quarter or halve it, roll it, or stuff it.

YOUR RAW MATERIAL

There are many varieties of Chinese cabbage. Some are short and stalky; some, long and thin. All work well as long as they're fresh. Choose cabbages with a tight body and light green outer leaves. The inner leaves should be almost white, with no browning on the edges (use your judgment here—are they still fresh but need a little trimming?). Bolting or sprouting heads are fine. They are mild, neither bitter nor tough.

IN THE CROCK
Kimchi
See photo on page 323

yield: about 1 gallon (3.8 l)
technique used: Mastering Kimchi Basics (page 117)

This is our basic kimchi recipe. We make it in the fall in a 3-gallon batch, which almost lasts through the winter. It's a good recipe to use as a springboard for experimentation. Remember to plan ahead, as this recipe requires a brining period, 6 to 8 hours or overnight.

In traditional kimchi making, after brining, the cabbage can be sliced in a variety of ways: chopped, quartered, halved, or left whole. In the United States, it's most commonly cut into bite-size pieces, but slice it however you like. Remember that standard chile flakes are generally quite a bit spicier than gochugaru. As with salt, manage your chile pepper additions by adding a little at a time and tasting as you go.

1 gallon (3.8 l) Soaking Brine (1 cup/269 g unrefined salt per gallon unchlorinated water)

2 large napa cabbages

½ cup (256 g) chile pepper flakes or salt-free gochugaru

½ cup (75 g) shredded daikon radish

¼ cup (25 g) shredded carrot

3 scallions, greens included, sliced

½–1 head garlic, cloves separated and minced

1 tablespoon (15 g) minced fresh ginger

1. Pour the brine into a crock or large bowl. Rinse the cabbages in cold water and remove the coarse outer leaves; keep a few to use as a follower. Trim off the stalk end and cut the cabbage in half. Submerge the cabbage halves and the reserved outer leaves in the brine. Use a plate as a weight to keep the cabbages submerged. Set aside, at room temperature, for 8 hours or overnight.

2. Using a colander set over a bowl, drain the cabbage for 15 minutes, reserving the brine. Set aside the brined outer leaves.

3. Combine the chile flakes, daikon, carrot, scallions, garlic, and ginger in a large bowl and blend thoroughly.

4. Chop the brined cabbage into bite-size pieces, or larger if you prefer, and add them to the bowl. Massage the mixture thoroughly, then taste for salt. Usually the brined cabbage will provide enough salt, but if it's not to your liking, sprinkle in a small amount of the reserved brine, massage, and taste again.

5. Transfer the vegetables, a few handfuls at a time, into a crock, jar, or onggi pot, pressing as you go. Add any liquid left in the bowl, and top off with enough of the reserved brine, if needed, to submerge the vegetables. Discard any excess brine or reclaim salt.

6. Cover the kimchi with the brined leaves or parchment paper and weight if you have one. Follow the instructions for your fermentation vessel. For a jar, if using the burping method (page 44) make sure there is little headspace and seal lid tightly. Burp daily or as needed. Alternatively, top the ferment with a quart-size ziplock bag. Press the bag down onto the top of the ferment and then fill it with water and seal.

7. Set your fermentation vessel on a plate in a spot where you can keep an eye on it, out of direct sunlight, and let ferment for 4 to 14 days. As the kimchi ferments, it begins to lose its vibrant color and the brine will get cloudy; this is when you can start to taste-test. It's ready when it is pleasingly sour.

8. Top off with brine, if needed, tighten the lids, and place in the refrigerator, where it will keep for 9 to 12 months.

Su-In Park: Achieving Zero Waste Through Kimchi

Su-In Park is a daughter, mother, and kimchi maker (see her recipe for Kimchi Pancake on page 380). Below, Su-In describes the roots of her love of fermented foods and how she started her New York–based company, forward ROOTS.

Everything from Scratch

"I was born in the Jeolla province of Korea, in a small village, Hwasun. We immigrated to Canada when I was a young child. As the eldest daughter from a traditional Korean family, I inherited certain responsibilities. Early on, I was given the task of tasting and seasoning the final dishes. I participated in the annual kimjang (collective kimchi making in late autumn) with my mother, aunts, and her friends. I spent a great deal of time watching, tasting, and learning. My mother was her own biggest critic; she never recognized what a great cook she was. She made everything from scratch. I thought every household was doing the same only to discover years later, not many did—especially not the whole pantry!

"My mother preserved and fermented a lot. She made kimchi, gochujang (red chili pepper paste), cheonggukjang and doenjang (soybean paste), jang (soy sauce), and jeotgal (fermented fish/seafood). She took immense pleasure in the transformation of simple ingredients resulting in complex, pungent, flavor-powered cooking essentials that seasoned our foods. If you grew up eating homemade, you know nothing industrial compares to personal touch, intentions, and love invested at home. Korean foods and ingredients have always occupied my thoughts."

Preserving Our Heritage

"When I met my husband, I moved to New York City. In 2017, I decided to take the jump and create forward ROOTS. It filled the gap of losing my mother years before. When she was alive, I felt her near through her care packages, but after her departure, I felt a deep loss. To this day, I still hold on to the last of her fermented goodies. She had cleaned out all her crocks and filled them with newly made ferments and said that she wanted to present that particular batch in beautiful containers, so that I could experience the simple joy of receiving, as one would an exquisitely packaged gift.

"Forward ROOTS is a celebration of the flavors that formed my palate. It is a connection that bridges the gap from my mother to my daughter. It is about preserving our heritage. It is a journey of moving and growing from our ancestral and cultural roots to where I am—influenced and experienced through friends, travels, and life. For my daughter, I am representing something deeply rooted in our history, our culture. Years ago, my daughter asked if kimchi was Korean because the only folks we saw selling and talking about kimchi in public were non-Koreans. She ate it at home,

"Our motto is: Preserve Through Kimchi, Zero Waste Through Kimchi."

with her grandparents, and in Korean restaurants—environments that are less public. I have absolutely no issue with non-Koreans making and selling kimchi, but what was often missing was the genuine association of the food to the people and culture. For us, it's not a new discovery or trend; it's a part of our past and present. We are a small company, so each kimchi sauce and condiment was made with my hands, using the large stainless steel bowls from childhood that I inherited. Everything is personal, with love and good intentions.

"We launched forward ROOTS with fermented kimchi sauces. I started making the sauce on its own, breaking the kimchi-making process into separate functions and making kimchi as needed. This helped deal with the stress that can come with making large volumes and running a business seven days a week. The kimchi sauces are fermented to naturally extend the shelf life, to be used as needed. They can be added to freshly made kimchi to give it the fermented tang or used to kick-start fermentation and make the kimchi-making process approachable. The sauces are the gateway to kimchi making, to encourage cooks to reduce food waste in the home.

"Our motto is PRESERVE THROUGH KIMCHI, ZERO WASTE THROUGH KIMCHI. You read about how much food is wasted in this country—it is appalling and disrespectful, given how much food insecurity exists. It negatively impacts people, the economy, and the environment, none of which should be taken lightly. Wasting food is a big no-no in our family. My parents grew up during the occupation and the war, when food was scarce, and it remained so for a long, long time after the war. We were taught to eat every grain of rice in our bowl. After each meal, we poured barley tea into our bowls and drank it to make sure no grain was lost. We peeled fruits and vegetables very close to the skin, to avoid losing anything. We grew some of our own produce and ate all parts of the plant from root to tip; we ate the fruit, blanched and marinated the leaves, and dried the peels or roots for medicinal use or to add flavor. Our motto is about being aware of scarcity, if not your own, then that of others.

"Kimchi comes in many variations; the vegetables and ingredients used depend on region, climate, season, and family recipes. I remind folks that kimchi can be made with just about any produce and all its parts. Many of us who are fortunate enough end up with odds and ends, excess harvest, and CSA baskets; all these can easily be made into kimchi to preserve for later. There is so much benefit from making your own: preventing food waste, eating healthy probiotics, consuming more nutrient-dense foods, getting more fiber, being open to learning about another culture, and enjoying endless deliciousness."

Pineapple Kid-chi

yield: about 1½ quarts (1.4 l)
technique used: Mastering Kimchi Basics (page 117)

We've rarely met a kid who doesn't instantly take to mild kimchi, sauerkraut, or pickles. We realize this may not be your reality—it wasn't ours either—but when we present these foods to kids at events, they usually can't get enough, especially when their parent says, "You aren't going to like that." (Oh, stab me with a fork.) You don't have to be a kid to love this, but it is a good recipe to make and enjoy with kids.

Look for pineapple rings that have been dehydrated with no added sugar. We find these have the best final texture, but use what you can find. The dried pineapple will retain much of its sweet flavor, adding to the appeal. You may use fresh pineapple, but it will be a very different ferment because the fresh pineapple will ferment vigorously, its flavors becoming more sour and yeasty. If you use fresh pineapple, add a bit more of the salt brine to the ferment to raise the salt level. This will help control the sugar frenzy that the microbes will be in. If you feel like doing some kitchen science, put dried pineapple in half the recipe and fresh pineapple in the other half, ferment in separate containers, side by side, and watch the difference.

Be sure to plan ahead, as this recipe requires a brining period, 6 to 8 hours or overnight.

- 1 gallon (3.8 l) Soaking Brine (1 cup/269 g unrefined salt per gallon unchlorinated water)
- 1 large (about 2 pounds/1 kg) napa cabbage (see note)
- 1 medium carrot, grated
- 1 scallion, greens included, cut crosswise
- 8 dried pineapple rings (2 ounces/57 grams), chopped into bite-size pieces
- 6 pieces candied ginger (1.5 ounces/43 grams), chopped finely
- 3 cloves garlic, finely grated

Follow the recipe for kimchi (page 182). Add the pineapple, candied ginger, and garlic to the rest of the vegetables, mix together, and add to brined cabbage.

Note: If napa cabbage is unavailable, feel free to substitute with a green cabbage. If you do, chop it more finely and prepare it like a sauerkraut (page 173), forgoing the typical first brining step of kimchi.

Sea-Chi (a.k.a. Sea Kimchi)

See photo on page 226

yield: about 1 gallon (3.8 l)

This is a mild variation of our basic kimchi recipe, using two sea vegetables instead of the chile pepper flakes. Despite all the great health reasons for eating seaweed, some people find its typical "ocean" smell unappealing. Others love the plant-based umami created by these sea veggies. Whatever camp you fall in, we think you will like this recipe. Dulse comes in small flakes and adds pretty purple flecks to the ferment. Sea palm has a mild flavor; when rehydrated in kimchi, it retains a nice crunch. If you can't imagine kimchi without a little heat, feel free to add 1 to 2 tablespoons of chile pepper flakes.

You'll need to plan ahead for this recipe, as it requires a brining period, 6 to 8 hours or overnight.

- 1 gallon (3.8 l) Soaking Brine (1 cup/269 g unrefined salt per gallon unchlorinated water)
- 2 large heads napa cabbage
- ½–1 head garlic, cloves separated and minced
- 1 tablespoon (15 g) minced fresh ginger
- 3 scallions, sliced
- ½ cup (75 g) shredded daikon radish
- ¼ cup (25 g) shredded carrot
- ½ cup (10 g) sea palm fronds, broken or cut into bite-size pieces
- 1 tablespoon (5 g) dulse flakes

Follow the recipe for kimchi (page 182), adding the sea palm and dulse when you add the seasonings, daikon, and carrot.

> ### FERMENTISTA'S TIP
>
> #### Salting with Sea Vegetables
> *Seaweed brings its own salt to the mix, and that salt is unrefined, full of minerals, and bioavailable. For these reasons, many people omit some salt for a ferment heavy with seaweed. If you're adding a significant amount to, say, a sauerkraut, cut the added salt by half. That way, you get a bit of both.*
>
> *You don't have to presoak dried seaweed, but keep in mind that when it reconstitutes in the ferment, it will swell to 5 times the size. See Seaweed Primer (page 328) for more information.*

Lemon Kimchi

See photo on page 262

yield: about 3 quarts (2.8 l)
technique used: Mastering Kimchi Basics (page 117)

Crisp and lemony, this recipe is basically a fermented lemon and napa cabbage salad that adds freshness to the plate. Although based on the kimchi-making process, it is not really a condiment because it can be eaten in a good amount. We enjoy it as a side dish. The lemons are fermented peel-on, so we suggest finding organic lemons. They add complexity in the form of a light bitterness and floral citrus notes. The recipe calls for two lemons, but feel free to omit one if you want less flavor of the peel. Substituting Meyer lemons will also mellow out the citrus flavor.

- 1 gallon (3.8 l) Soaking Brine (1 cup/269 g unrefined salt per gallon unchlorinated water)
- 1 large (about 3 pounds/1.4 kg) napa cabbage
- 2 lemons
- 2 bundles scallions
- 1 cup (155 g) grated daikon radish (or other radishes)
- 2 tablespoons (22 g) finely grated fresh ginger
- 6 large cloves garlic, finely grated

Follow the recipe for kimchi (page 182). After soaking the cabbage, quarter the lemon(s) lengthwise, and, leaving the peel on, slice as thinly as possible, removing the seeds as you go. Add the lemon slices to the scallions, daikon, ginger, and garlic and toss gently to incorporate, and ferment as instructed.

FERMENTED CARROT ACHAR, *page 275*

RADICCHIO QUINCE FERMENTED SALAD, *page 313*

PEARL ONIONS FERMENTED IN MRS. DING'S CONTINUOUS PICKLING BRINE, *page 112*

SOUR CORN, *page 212*

BAVARIAN-STYLE SWEET MUSTARD, *page 274*

BE GOOD TO YOUR GUT
FENNEL CHUTNEY,
page 230

CHOW-CHOW,
page 334

FERMENTED THREE-BEAN
SALAD, *page 159*

FERMENTED MIREPOIX/
SOFRITO MIX,
page 224

CABBAGE, RED

Beyond a mild, pleasantly sweet flavor and a great color, red cabbage is packed with nutrition. During the Middle Ages, botanists encouraged the red pigment, which we now know as anthocyanin. Studies suggest that certain anthocyanins have anti-inflammatory, antiviral, and antimicrobial properties. The amounts of anthocyanin and vitamin C in red cabbage are superior to those of green cabbage.

YOUR RAW MATERIAL

When fermented, the violet-red of the raw cabbage is modified by a cooling blue hue that makes the whole affair a fuchsia-infused purple, the color of royalty, military honors, religious ceremonies, and the '60s haze of psychedelic drugs.

Red cabbage is sturdier than green, giving krauts a different texture and longer storage time under cool conditions.

Look for heads that are crisp and brightly colored; avoid cabbage that looks old or wilted. Choose the heads with the deepest red, as this pigment is what gives nutritional value. A dull color or leaves separating from the stem indicate that the cabbage is no longer fresh.

IN THE CROCK

Blaukraut

See photo on page 338

yield: about 1 gallon (3.8 l)
technique used: Mastering Sauerkraut (page 61)

The flavor here is decidedly more acidic than the traditional Bavarian sugar-sweetened cooked version, but it's delicious and a satisfying accompaniment to anything. Serve as a side dish just as it is, dress it up with blue cheese and walnuts

(page 390), or turn it into Braised Blaukraut (page 403). It also makes a nice layer in a sandwich or wrap.

- 2–3 heads (about 6 pounds/2.7 kg) red cabbage
- 1½–2 tablespoons (25–34 g) unrefined salt
- 2–3 crisp tart apples, cored, quartered, and thinly sliced
- 1 medium onion, thinly sliced
- 2 tablespoons (17 g) caraway seeds (or to taste)

1. Remove the coarse outer leaves of the cabbage. Rinse a few unblemished ones and set them aside. Rinse the rest of the cabbage in cold water. Quarter and core the cabbage, thinly slice or shred, and transfer to a large bowl.

2. Add half the salt and, with your hands, massage it into the cabbage. Then taste. You should be able to taste the salt without it being overwhelming. Add more salt if necessary. Add apples, onion, and caraway seeds and mix to combine. The cabbage will begin to glisten and liquid will pool. If you've put in a good effort and don't see much brine in the bowl, let it stand, covered, for 45 minutes, then massage again.

3. Transfer the mixture, several handfuls at a time, to your crock or jar, pressing down to remove air pockets. You should see some brine on top of the mixture when you press. If you don't, return the mixture to the bowl and massage again.

4. Top the kraut with the reserved outer cabbage leaves to keep everything submerged, pressing them down under the brine. Add weight if you have it. Follow the instructions for your fermentation vessel. For a jar, if using the burping method (page 44) make sure there is little headspace and seal lid tightly. Burp daily or as needed. Alternatively, top the ferment with a quart-size ziplock bag. Press the bag down onto the top of the ferment and then fill it with water and seal.

5. Set your fermentation vessel on a plate in a spot where you can keep an eye on it, out of direct sunlight, and let ferment for 7 to 14 days. Check regularly to make sure the kraut is submerged, pressing down, as needed, to bring the brine back to the surface. As it ferments, the color will turn more blue and the brine will get cloudy; this is when you can start to taste-test. The kraut is ready when it is pleasingly sour.

6. When the kraut is ready, transfer to smaller jars and tamp down. Pour in any brine that's left. Tighten the lids, then store in the fridge. The kraut will keep, refrigerated, for 6 months.

APPLES

Worldwide, there are more than 7,500 varieties of apples, and you can ferment any of them—each has its own character. In some Eastern European nations, apples are traditionally brined and fermented, sometimes with a bit of rye flour in the brine.

Fresh apples add appeal to kraut, but not for the reason you might think. They don't mellow the acidity or incorporate sweetness. Instead they add a delightful fresh crispness, and as you may be realizing by now, wherever there is sugar there is more sour—or in the case of apples, bright acidic notes.

Try adding crisp apples to any ferment. Grating imparts a hint of apple taste and a certain lightness of texture. For more texture and greater apple flavor, slice them thinly. To retain an apple's sweetness, incorporate sliced dried apple rings into your ferments.

CARROTS

The day is coming when a single carrot, freshly observed, will set off a revolution.
—PAUL CÉZANNE, POST-IMPRESSIONIST FRENCH PAINTER

You can't go wrong putting carrots in any ferment, for taste, color, a hint of sweetness, and crunch. Our first introduction to pickled carrots were ones prepared by a Ukrainian neighbor. She never got used to the abundance in our American supermarkets and could not help saving every scrap of food (certainly not a bad habit to be in). She fermented the miniscule carrots gleaned from thinning the garden. It took her hours to clean and prepare them. They were adorable in the jar and scrumptious, so we adopted the practice of fermenting our carrots, too. We invite you to make each of these recipes to explore how different a ferment can be just by changing how you prepare the vegetables. Carrots can give you a hands-on experience in turning the dials you the maker can control to make your ferments just the way you love them. The size of the *chop* in each recipe varies, exposing differing amounts of the broken cell structure to the fermentation. You can read more about this on page 31.

Carrot Kraut has a thicker brine and heavier texture than the slices in the Fermented Carrot Salad. The Fermented Carrot Sticks are, of course, whole pickles—easy to pack, easy to eat.

YOUR RAW MATERIAL

Carrots come in myriad colors and are available year-round. They pair well with most vegetables and transform any ferment—you'll find recipes throughout this A–Z guide that include carrots. You decide if you want to peel your carrots. We peel larger overwintered carrots when the skins are tough or bitter. Carrots with tender skin get a good wash and are left as is.

FERMENTISTA'S TIP

Yeasty Business

Ferments that contain a significant quantity of carrots are more susceptible to surface yeasts, which can cause funky flavors.

IN THE CROCK

Carrot Kraut

yield: about 2 quarts (1.9 l)
technique used: Mastering Sauerkraut (page 61)

This is an adaptation of Sally Fallon's gingered carrots. Although it's a colorful and refreshing side dish, we like it best in carrot cake. The kraut adds moisture, and with the cream-cheese frosting, life is good. *Note:* Due to its high sugar content, this kraut continues to ferment in the refrigerator and will sour more with time.

> 4 pounds (1.8 kg) carrots, grated
> 1 tablespoon (15 g) grated fresh ginger
> Juice and zest of 1 lemon
> 1½–2 tablespoons (25–34 g) unrefined salt
> Grape leaves or parchment paper, to top the ferment

1. Combine the carrots, ginger, and lemon juice and zest in a large bowl. Add 1½ tablespoons of the salt and, with your hands, massage it into the veggies. Then taste. You should be able to taste the salt without it being overwhelming. Add more salt if necessary.

2. Transfer the mixture to your fermentation vessel, a few handfuls at a time, pressing down to remove air pockets. You should see some brine on top of the carrots when you press. If you don't, return the mixture to the bowl and massage again.

3. Place grape leaves or a piece of parchment paper, if using, on top to keep everything submerged. Add weight if you have it. Follow the instructions for your fermentation vessel. For a jar, if using the burping method (page 44) make sure there is little headspace and seal lid tightly. Burp daily or as needed. Alternatively, top the ferment with a quart-size ziplock bag. Press the bag down onto the top of the ferment and then fill it with water and seal.

4. Set your fermentation vessel on a plate in a spot where you can keep an eye on it, out of direct sunlight, and let ferment for 7 to 14 days. Check regularly to make sure the carrots are submerged, pressing down, as needed, to bring the brine back to the surface. Start taste-testing on day 7. You'll know the carrots are ready when they have a crisp-sour flavor and the brine is thick and rich.

5. When the carrots are ready, transfer to smaller jars and tamp down. Pour in any brine that's left. Tighten the lids, then store in the fridge. The carrots will keep, refrigerated, for 1 year, but are better within 6 months.

Fermented Carrot Salad

Use the same ingredients and process, but instead of grating the carrots, slice them crosswise as thinly as possible. Use a mandoline, or food processor with 2 mm blade.

WASTE NOT

If your carrots have come with their feathery leafy fronds, consider yourself fortunate as you now have two ingredients. Use the leaves as you would parsley, make pesto or Chimichurri (page 290), or chop finely and add to any ferment that could use a lovely infusion of a peppery carrot flavor.

IN THE PICKLE JAR
Vietnamese Pickled Carrot and Daikon

yield: about 2 quarts (1.9 l)
technique used: Mastering Brine Pickling (page 101)

This is a variation on a pickle that's an important ingredient in *banh mi*, the Vietnamese version of a hoagie, a hero, or a sub. The traditional ingredient is a vinegar pickle, but this lacto-fermented one carries itself just as well in this and other sandwiches.

- 2 **tablespoons (24 g) sugar**
- 1 **gallon (3.8 l) Basic Brine (½ cup/134 g unrefined salt per gallon unchlorinated water)**
- 2 **pounds (907 g) carrots, julienned or sliced in thin medallions**
- 2 **pounds (907 g) daikon radishes, julienned or sliced in thin medallions**
- 1 or 2 **grape leaves or parchment paper, to top the ferment**

1. Add the sugar to the brine and stir to dissolve.

2. Arrange the carrots and daikon, wedging them under the shoulder of a jar or leaving 4 inches of headspace in a crock. Pour in enough brine to cover the vegetables completely. Reserve any leftover brine in the fridge. (It will keep for 1 week; discard thereafter or dry out and reclaim salt and make a new batch, if needed.)

3. Place grape leaves or a piece of parchment paper, if using, on top of the vegetables. Follow the instructions for your fermentation vessel. For a jar, if using the burping method (page 44) make sure there is little headspace and seal lid tightly. Burp daily or as needed.

4. Set your fermentation vessel on a plate in a spot where you can keep an eye on it, out of direct sunlight, and let ferment for 7 to 14 days. During the fermentation period, monitor the brine level and top off with the reserved brine, if needed, to cover. The carrots will not lose their color, but the brine will get cloudy; that's when you can start to taste-test. They're ready when they are pleasingly sour and pickle-y.

5. Top off with brine, if needed, tighten the lids, and place in the refrigerator. The next day, check to be sure the vegetables are still submerged, topping off with more brine if necessary. These pickles will keep, refrigerated, for 1 year.

Fermented Carrot Sticks

See photo on page 280

Pickled carrot sticks can be a child's gateway into fermented food. They're crunchy and so convenient; just pull them out of the jar and serve with nut butter.

Follow the recipe for Vietnamese Pickled Carrot and Daikon (page 193), using only the carrots and cutting them into sticks. For a less sour ferment, omit the sugar from the brine. For a little more flavor, add a sprig of rosemary or 3 or 4 lemon slices to the fermentation vessel.

CAULIFLOWER

Cauliflower, as its name suggests, is a bundle of flowers. It probably developed in Asia Minor from wild cabbage, which grew in gardens of that area around 600 BCE. Botanists believe it started off looking somewhat like today's collards. It hit the culinary scene in the sixteenth century as *cauli-fiori*, from Genoa, then made its way to France, where it was called *chou-fleur*. It was prized for its delicacy. Cauliflower has a hefty amount of vitamins C and K. Raw, a serving fulfills 77 percent of the daily C requirement; cooked, that number is reduced to 46 percent.

Cauliflower is delicious fermented, but some folks find it a little tricky. It is just a little more of a diva. Don't treat it quite right and you will pay with some pretty dank smells. Not enough salt and you can find yourself with some epic mush.

At some point Kirsten thought it would be cool to make a whole fermented cauliflower head. Three whole heads fit in one of our crocks, so in they went with garlic, spices, and brine. When they were done fermenting, she pulled them out and our daughter said from across the house, "That smells like dirty socks." It did! We weren't sure why—the salt was sufficient, and the cauliflower head had been poked so fermentation had commenced throughout it—but we suspect that a healthy layer of surface yeast had a part to play. Even after years of experience, we can find ourselves skunked. Don't let one experience turn you off.

YOUR RAW MATERIAL

Cauliflower's head is called a *curd*. When you examine the curd, it should be compact. Separation in the bud clusters, or a rough or loose texture, means the head has matured past its prime, which doesn't mean it is unfermentable, just different. Cut off any brown spots, as they are a sign of age.

Orange cauliflower, developed in Canada in the 1970s, has a sweeter taste and boasts 25 percent more vitamin A. The origins of the purple cauliflower are unclear, but it's said that it developed naturally. The color comes from anthocyanin, a beneficial antioxidant. Both ferment well.

For us, green cauliflower and Romanesco are hit-or-miss, perhaps because these varieties are a cross between cauliflower and broccoli, and broccoli is problematic.

CauliKraut

See photo on page 281

yield: about 1 quart (946 ml)
technique used: Relishes/Chutneys/Salsas/Salads (page 74)

When making this tasty kraut, the key is to slice the cauliflower ribbon-thin. Use a mandoline or the slicing option on a microplane grater. The latter works well enough, but be aware that the brittle cauliflower bits tend to snap and fly off the counter—just corral them and toss them back into the bowl. Second tip: Don't skimp on the salt.

      1 **head (1½ pounds/680 g) cauliflower**
      2 **jalapeños, minced**
  1½–2 **teaspoons (8–11 g) unrefined salt**
         **Grape leaves or parchment paper, to top
         the ferment**

1. Rinse the cauliflower. Cut it into florets and slice as thinly as you can. Place in a bowl with the jalapeños. Sprinkle in 1 teaspoon of the salt, working it in with your hands; let rest for 30 minutes. It may seem too dry, but don't worry, it's fine. Toss and massage the salted cauliflower again for a few minutes just to get everything mixed.

2. Pack the cauliflower tightly into a jar or your fermentation vessel. It may still feel too dry, but it will continue to weep as fermentation begins. Go ahead and tuck it in.

3. Place grape leaves or a piece of parchment paper, if using, on top of the cauliflower. Add a weight if you have one. Follow the instructions for your fermentation vessel. For a jar, if using the burping method (page 44) make sure there is little headspace and seal lid tightly. Burp daily

or as needed. Alternatively, top the ferment with a quart-size ziplock bag. Press the bag down onto the top of the ferment and then fill it with water and seal. If you don't feel there's enough brine, wait about 8 hours, remove the weight or bag, and press down to get the brine to the surface. If there are still air pockets, make a small amount of Basic Brine (page 102) to top off. Replace the bag.

4. Set the jar on a plate in a spot where you can keep an eye on it, out of direct sunlight, and let ferment for 4 to 8 days. Check daily to make sure cauliflower is submerged, pressing down on the ferment as needed to bring the brine to the surface. Start taste-testing on day 4. You'll know the kraut is ready when it's pleasingly sour and the flavors have mingled.

5. Tamp down to make sure the kraut is submerged, screw on the lid, and store in the fridge, where it will keep for 10 months.

Curried CauliKraut

yield: about 1 quart (946 ml)
technique used: Relishes/Chutneys/Salsas/Salads (page 74)

This is an ocher-yellow, Indian-spiced variation of CauliKraut. Toasting the curry spice seeds intensifies their flavor; feel free to substitute 2 teaspoons of curry powder (page 165).

    1 **teaspoon (3 g) mustard seeds**
    ½ **teaspoon (1.2 g) coriander seeds**
    ½ **teaspoon (0.5 g) cumin seeds**
    ½ **teaspoon (2.5 g) turmeric powder**
    1 **head (1½ pounds/680 g) cauliflower, cut
        into florets and sliced very thin**
    2 **carrots, shredded**

Juice of 1 orange (⅓ cup/79 ml)
1 spring onion, greens attached, sliced
1½–2 teaspoons (8–11 g) unrefined salt

1. In a dry skillet, toast the mustard, coriander, and cumin seeds until fragrant.

2. Follow the recipe for CauliKraut on page 195, omitting the jalapeño and adding the rest of the ingredients, including the toasted seeds, to the bowl with the sliced cauliflower.

Piccalilli

See photo on page 245

yield: about 1 quart (946 ml)

technique used: Relishes/Chutneys/Salsas/Salads (page 74)

In piccalilli, South Asian pickles (such as achar; see page 275) collided with British colonialization in a cultural mashup. Time and immigration continued the flavor journey of this relish. Now, beyond the British style, there are regional piccalilli variations in the United States as well as a spicy Surinamese version.

This fermentation has two steps: first, the main fermentation, and second, after fermentation, adding the thick, mustardy sauce. Once added, the sauce is left to ferment for a day or two to allow the flavors to meld.

1 small cauliflower, cut into small florets, with stems diced
4 pickling cucumbers, gherkins, or small Persian cucumbers, diced (remove the seeds if they're large)
8 ounces (227 g) pearl onions, peeled and quartered
2 tablespoons (30 g) capers, rinsed
1 tablespoon (17 g) unrefined salt

4 tablespoons (56 g) butter
3–4 tablespoons (23–30 g) all-purpose flour (or gluten-free alternative)
2 teaspoons (4 g) ground turmeric
1–2 teaspoons (2–4 g) ground mustard
1–2 tablespoons (12–24 g) unrefined sugar or your favorite sweetener

1. Combine the cauliflower, cucumbers, pearl onions, and capers in a bowl. Add the salt and massage everything together. The mixture will become wet and liquid should pool.

2. Transfer the mixture into an appropriately sized jar, pressing as you go to remove air pockets. You should see brine on top. If not, wait a little; the cucumbers will continue to release liquid.

3. If you plan to use the burping method (page 44) to release CO_2, make sure there is little headspace at the top of the jar, then seal the lid tightly. Alternatively, top the jar with a quart-size ziplock bag. Press the plastic down onto the top of the ferment, then fill it with water and seal shut. This will act as both follower and weight.

4. Set the jar on a plate in a spot where you can keep an eye on it, out of direct sunlight, and let ferment for about 5 days. It's ready when the colors are muted, the brine is cloudy, the ferment has a pleasing acidic smell, and it tastes pickle-y, with an effervescent zing.

5. When it is ready, drain off and reserve the brine. Place the vegetables in a bowl and set aside. Time to make the sauce.

6. Melt the butter in a pan over medium heat. Add the flour, whisking it in until smooth. Add the reserved brine and cook for a few minutes, until thickened. Whisk in the turmeric, mustard powder, and sugar, if using, and remove from heat. Let the sauce cool to about body temperature (less than 100°F/38°C) to avoid damaging the probiotics in the ferment.

7. Mix the sauce into the vegetables, then transfer to an appropriately sized jar. Screw on the lid and let ferment for a day or two, until the flavors have melded.

8. Store the piccalilli in the fridge, where it will keep for 6 months or more.

IN THE PICKLE JAR

Cauliflower is a natural choice to brine-pickle in any vegetable medley. To prepare it for pickling, first remove the outer leaves, if present. (Be sure to save these and enjoy as you would collards or kale. They are delicious.) Turn the curd upside down and remove the core with a paring knife. Pull apart and separate the florets into bite-size pieces. The stems and core can also be pickled in bite-size pieces or used in other ferments.

Edgy Veggies

See photo on page 339

yield: about 1 gallon (3.8 l)
technique used: Mastering Brine Pickling (page 101)

One year Kirsten proudly traded homemade feta for a big box of cauliflower. (The family didn't share her enthusiasm.) That year our garden produced an abundance of jalapeños. Inspired by the pickled carrots and jalapeños served in many Mexican restaurants, she brined the cauliflower with the jalapeños plus onions, carrots, and a lot of garlic. Crisp and spicy, the cauliflower took on all those flavors beautifully. In this new guise, cauliflower became a new family favorite.

This medley can range from spicy to fiery, depending on the jalapeños. A gallon might seem like a lot, but you'll see they go quickly.

- 1–2 tablespoons (5–11 g) dried oregano, crumbled
- 2 pounds (907 g) carrots, peeled and sliced
- 1 pound (454 g) jalapeños, cored and cut into rounds (see note)
- 1 head cauliflower, cut into florets
- 5 cloves garlic (or more, if desired), whole or halved
- 1 onion, cut into wedges
- 1 gallon (3.8 l) Basic Brine (½ cup/134 g unrefined salt per gallon unchlorinated water)
- Grape leaves or parchment paper, to top the ferment (optional)

Note: In the off-season, substitute 2 tablespoons (32 g) chile pepper flakes for the jalapeños, adding them with the oregano, and include a few more carrots and cauliflower florets.

1. Place the oregano and any other spices in the bottom of your fermentation vessel. Add the carrots, jalapeños, cauliflower, garlic, and onion, mixing as you go, wedging them under the shoulder of the jar or leaving 4 inches of headspace in a crock. Pour in enough brine to cover the vegetables completely. Reserve any leftover brine in the fridge. (It will keep for 1 week; discard thereafter and make a new batch, if needed.)

2. Put the grape leaves or a piece of parchment paper, if using, on top of the vegetables. Follow the instructions for your fermentation vessel. For a jar, if using the burping method (page 44) make sure there is little headspace and seal lid tightly. Burp daily or as needed.

3. Set your fermentation vessel on a plate in a spot where you can keep an eye on it, out of direct sunlight, and let ferment for 7 to 21 days. During the fermentation period, monitor the brine level and top off with the reserved brine, if needed. The vegetables are done when their colors are muted, the brine is cloudy, there is a pleasing acidic smell, and the taste is pickle-y, perhaps with an effervescent zing.

4. Top off with brine, if needed, tighten the lids, and place in the refrigerator. The next day, check to be sure the veggies are still submerged, topping off with more brine if necessary. These pickles will keep, refrigerated, for 1 year.

Pink Giardiniera

See photo on page 244

yield: about 2 quarts (473 ml)
technique used: Mastering Brine Pickling (page 101)

The vegetables in this classic Italian relish vary a bit from region to region, but most include a combination of cauliflower, carrots, celery, and red bell peppers submerged in vinegar and oil. In this remix, we swapped out red bell peppers (which get soft in fermentation) for Hungarian wax peppers (which are sturdier) and then used purple carrots and red pearl onions to give the giardiniera color.

This fermented version of giardiniera is crisp and confident but not the least bit abrasive.

- 1 small head cauliflower, cut into florets
- 2 stalks celery, cut in 1-inch diagonal slices
- 1 medium purple carrot, cut in diagonal slices
- 1 cup (83 g) chopped green or wax beans
- 2 Hungarian wax peppers, sliced into rings

- 8 ounces (227 g) red pearl onions or small cipollini onions, peeled and left whole
- ½ teaspoon (1.2 g) black peppercorns
- ½ teaspoon (1.4 g) whole cloves
- ½ teaspoon (2.7 g) juniper berries, lightly crushed
- 1 or 2 bay leaves
- 1 quart (946 ml) Basic Brine (2 tablespoons/ 34 g unrefined salt per quart unchlorinated water)
- Grape leaves or parchment paper, to top the ferment (optional)

AFTER FERMENTATION
- ½ cup extra-virgin olive oil

Follow the recipe for Edgy Veggies (page 197). When the pickles have fermented to your liking, add the olive oil; you may need to pour off a small amount of the brine to make room for it. (Don't toss it; drink it for a little probiotic boost.) Store in an airtight container in the fridge. These pickles will keep, refrigerated, for 8 to 12 months.

Create Your Own Recipes

Combinations of pickled produce show up all over the world. Persian *torshi*, a mixture of soured vegetables such as cauliflower, Persian cucumbers, chopped cabbage, celery, bell peppers, eggplant, onions, and garlic, is just one example. Herbs might include fresh parsley, cilantro, or dill. Spices might include *loomi* (dried lime), nigella seeds, fennel seeds, angelica powder, coriander seeds, hot peppers, or turmeric. As is common in traditional cuisines, there are as many variations of *torshi* as there are makers. Most recipes use vinegar for pickling, but there is no reason you couldn't make a *torshi*-inspired ferment.

CELERIAC

Unfortunately everyone seems to be completely baffled by celeriac, but it's beautiful in soups or thinly sliced into salads. When roasted it goes sweet and when mixed with potato and mashed it's a complete joy.

—JAMIE OLIVER, *HAPPY DAYS WITH THE NAKED CHEF*, 2001

Celeriac, although lacking in conventional beauty (it's really not pretty), is delicious fermented, but even more important, it's one of our favorite bases for crucifer-free kraut (good for people who are crucifer intolerant; see page 173). Grated or sliced, it holds up in fermentation and has good consistency. It has a mild celery flavor, which other vegetables and spices complement. Celeriac spears are also delicious in a pickle medley.

FERMENTISTA'S TIP

Working with Celeriac

Celeriac should be peeled; the peels have a tough texture when fermented. However, it is a bit difficult to peel. Using a paring knife, carefully cut off the skin on the tops and side. On the bottom, you'll find a tangled mass of roots with bits of dirt wedged in. Either spend a lot of time trying to salvage most of the tangle of roots or cut off the bottom and move on. These bits can be rinsed and used in a vegetable stock.

IN THE CROCK
Naked Celeriac Kraut

yield: about 1 quart (946 ml)
technique used: Mastering Sauerkraut (page 61)

This is fermented celeriac, plain and unassuming, delicious and versatile. The instructions here call for shredding the celeriac for a kraut-like consistency; however, for a salad-like presentation, slice the celeriac thinly on a mandoline.

> 2 pounds (907 g) celeriac root, cleaned, peeled, and shredded
> 1–1½ teaspoons (6–8 g) unrefined salt
> Grape leaves or parchment paper, to top the ferment

1. In a large bowl, combine the celeriac with 1 teaspoon of the salt and massage well. Then taste. You should be able to taste the salt without it being overwhelming. Add more salt if necessary. The celeriac will become limp and liquid may begin to pool. (Celeriac root is dry, and sometimes the brine isn't obvious until the celeriac is pressed into the fermentation vessel.)

2. Transfer the mixture to your fermentation vessel, a few handfuls at a time, pressing down to remove air pockets. You should see some brine on top of the mixture when you press. If you don't, return the mixture to the bowl and massage again.

3. Place grape leaves or a piece of parchment paper, if using, on top of the celeriac to keep everything submerged. Add weight if you have it. Follow the instructions for your fermentation vessel. For a jar, if using the burping method (page 44) make sure there is little headspace and seal lid tightly. Burp daily or as needed. Alternatively, top the ferment with a quart-size ziplock bag. Press the bag down onto the top of the ferment and then fill it with water and seal.

4. Set your fermentation vessel on a plate in a spot where you can keep an eye on it, out of direct sunlight, and let ferment for 5 to 10 days. Check regularly to make sure the celeriac is submerged, pressing down, as needed, to bring the brine back to the surface. Start taste-testing on day 5. It's ready when it's pleasingly sour. *Note:* The texture will be softer than that of a cabbage-based kraut.

5. When the kraut is ready, transfer to smaller jars, if necessary, and tamp down. Pour in any brine that's left. Tighten the lids, then store in the fridge. The kraut will keep, refrigerated, for 1 year.

Hungarian-Inspired Celeriac Kraut

See photo on page 305

yield: about 2 quarts (473 ml)
technique used: Mastering Sauerkraut (page 61)

In our hands-on classes, vegetables are piled high for students to choose from. We start by tasting krauts so people get a sense of what they like. This kraut never ceases to surprise and delight students, not only because it's delicious but also because most people have never thought to ferment celeriac. When it's time to make the kraut, there's often a mad dash to the vegetable pile for this gnarled root.

> 2 pounds (907 g) celeriac root, shredded
> 5 or 6 wax peppers (use Hungarian for heat, banana for sweet), thinly sliced
> 1 generous tablespoon (8 g) caraway seeds
> 1 teaspoon (3 g) ground paprika
> 1–1½ teaspoons (6–8 g) unrefined salt

Follow the recipe for Naked Celeriac Kraut (page 199), adding the peppers and spices with the celeriac.

CELERY

Don't overlook celery when it comes to fermentation. We find it delicious in celery-forward ferments and a great addition to many other fermented salads and condiments. It imparts flavor and, more important, great texture and crunch to any ferment. You will see it in many recipes in this book.

Where does celery fall on the nutritional scale? Urban legend has it that celery takes more calories to consume than it contains, and that it's all water, which leads some people to think of it as a diet food or empty food. Instead, celery boasts numerous benefits. Suffering from sleeplessness, mild anxiety, high blood pressure, arthritis, kidney stones, or gallstones? Need relaxation, a cancer preventive, a sexual stimulant? Celery. Nothing empty about it.

YOUR RAW MATERIAL

Celery can be anywhere from mild and sweet to bitter. The leaves, too often tossed, are a green herb in their own right. Use them in ferments or other dishes as you would parsley. Celery is wonderful for fermentation because of its natural juiciness and sodium content. It stays delightfully crunchy and brings that to the ferments it is added to. Homegrown and heirloom celery are greener with more leaves, denser stems, stronger flavor, crunchier texture, and less moisture than your typical store-bought celery.

You can use lovage as a substitute for celery in fermentation recipes, but be aware that lovage has a much stronger flavor. It is delicious in its own right, though, and because it is a perennial, you can have it in your garden and cut a rib or two for celery-like additions when you are fermenting throughout the growing season.

Waste Not

Keep the butt for use as a topper—that is, a follower and weight—for the top of a ferment.

IN THE CROCK

Celery "Stuffing"

See photo on page 305

yield: about 1 quart (946 ml)

technique used: Relishes/Chutneys/Salsas/Salads (page 74)

This "bready" name may seem ridiculous for a vegetable ferment, but you'll be surprised. It's not a relish, a kraut, a kimchi, a pickle, or a paste. It is, though, a substantial presence in the mouth, and the thyme and sage suggest a turkey dinner. Whether you call it stuffing or dressing, this can be a gluten-free option to stuff poultry or to eat

alongside as a raw dressing. If you aren't feeling the poultry vibe, replace the herbs with 6 sprigs of mint and a bundle of scallions.

1½	**pounds (680 g) celery, including the leaves, chopped**
8–10	**fresh sage leaves, thinly sliced**
1	**tablespoon (6 g) chopped fresh thyme**
1	**teaspoon (6 g) unrefined salt**
1 or 2	**grape leaves or parchment paper, to top the ferment (optional)**

1. Combine the celery, sage, and thyme in a large bowl. Mix in the salt, a little at a time, tasting as you go, until the saltiness is evident but not overwhelming. Massage the mixture and let sit, covered, for 30 minutes.

2. Pack the mixture, a few handfuls at a time, into your vessel or a quart jar, pressing as you go to remove air pockets and to release brine; because of the texture, it will take some effort to get it tightly packed. This pressure will release more brine. Store-bought celery will likely produce a noticeable layer of brine, while homegrown celery may produce just enough brine to barely cover the vegetables. Leave 1½ inches of headspace in the jar and top with the celery butt.

3. Because of the low brine content, make sure this ferment is weighted well (the pressure of the butt against the lid works well in a jar with a tightened lid to burp). If you don't use the butt, top with the grape leaves or a piece of parchment paper and weight if you have it. Use a sealed water-filled jar or ziplock bag as a combination follower and weight.

4. Set the jar on a plate in a spot where you can keep an eye on it, out of direct sunlight, and let ferment for 5 to 10 days. Check daily, burp as needed (page 44), or make sure the celery is submerged, pressing down as needed to bring the brine back to the surface. Start tasting the ferment on day 5. When it's ready, it will be crunchy, with a flavor of sage and a mild, light sourness—very different from the bold sourness of most krauts.

5. When it's sour enough for your palate, tamp down the ferment under the brine, screw on the lid, and store in the refrigerator. Because of its high natural nitrate content, celery keeps well, if it remains submerged, and will last for more than a year, but you will want to eat it well before then.

Create Your Own Recipes

Honestly, celery can go in anything. Ferment whole celery sticks in Basic Brine (page 102), with or without spices. Be sure to remove the strings—otherwise it's like eating fermented dental floss.

CHARD

Have a huge crop of chard and want to preserve it? We can help you with the stems, but sorry, the leaves on their own just don't shine. However, chopped finely, leaves can be added to other ferments.

IN THE PICKLE JAR

Chard stems take on the flavors of any herb you ferment with them, and with the rainbow of color options—ruby, fuchsia, orange, yellow, and white—they look delightful in a jar. Use your favorite pickling flavorings, Basic Brine (page 102), and the directions for brine pickling (page 105).

CILANTRO (CORIANDER)

Some people love cilantro. Some don't. If you dislike it intensely—okay, you loathe it—just skip this section. In the I-love-cilantro camp? Keep reading.

Cilantro's sensitive aromatic oils seem to disappear when dried. Enter flavorful preservation. Fermented cilantro is slightly salty, with a touch of lemon flavor and a powerful, pure cilantro-ness.

YOUR RAW MATERIAL

Select bunches that show bright leaves with no signs of yellow or wilting. To make it last a bit longer, store it like a bouquet, with the stems submerged in a glass of water.

In the United States, the dried seeds of cilantro are called coriander. Whole coriander is indispensable in a pickling spice mix (see page 158).

We like to ferment green coriander seeds, an ingredient for which you'll probably need to grow your own cilantro, as you likely won't find the green seeds in stores. To harvest, pluck the seeds before they develop fully, when they're still green and tender. The flavor is somewhere between the coriander it's becoming and the cilantro that it was. The seeds are in this magical state for only a few days, after which they become woody.

IN THE PICKLE JAR
Pickled Green Coriander

yield: about 1 cup (237 ml)
technique used: Mastering Brine Pickling (page 101)

These tiny green pickles are delicious, and the size of your batch is a testament to your patience. The best way we have found to bring some efficiency to the task of removing the small, round seeds from the stalk of the seedhead is to use a pair of scissors. You will not need to make much brine, so if it's possible to time this fermentation with another pickle project, you can just take a little brine for your itty-bitty coriander pickles.

Less patience? Add some seeds to other ferments. Or make a paste with the entire bolting plant, seeds and all (see the following recipe).

½–1 cup (40–80 g) green coriander seeds
1 cup (237 ml) Basic Brine (1½ teaspoons/ 8 g unrefined salt per cup unchlorinated water)
Grape leaf or parchment paper, to top the ferment (optional)

1. Place the seeds in a small jar, leaving a few inches of headspace. Pour in enough brine to cover the seeds completely. Place a grape leaf or piece of parchment paper, if using, over the seeds. Make sure there is little headspace in the jar and seal lid tightly. Burp daily (page 44) or as needed.

2. Set the jar on a plate in a spot where you can keep an eye on it, out of direct sunlight, and let ferment for 4 to 7 days. Check daily to make sure the seeds stay submerged. As the seeds ferment, they begin to lose their vibrant color and the brine will get cloudy; this is when you can start to taste-test. They will be pleasingly sour and taste like tiny pickles, with a cilantro finish.

3. When they're ready, screw a lid on the jar and store in the refrigerator, where they will keep for 6 months.

IN THE CROCK
Cilantro Paste

yield: about 1 cup (237 ml)
technique used: Pastes (page 76)

We use this recipe to preserve fresh cilantro when it is ready to bolt in the garden. We can then use it for cooking or in other ferments later in the season. If you don't grow cilantro, don't worry. This is still delicious with purchased cilantro. If you have access to the root, use it. The cilantro-y flavor of the root is so strong that it helps keep the ferment cilantro-forward.

2–3 bunches (7 ounces/200 g) cilantro, leaves, tender stems, and roots
¾ teaspoon (4 g) unrefined salt
½ teaspoon (2 g) sugar

1. Put the cilantro in a food processor, sprinkle with the salt and sugar, and process to a paste. Don't expect a lot of brine; this is almost a dry ferment. It should taste salty but still pleasing; if not, then add a bit more salt.

2. Press the paste into a pint jar. More liquid will release as you press, and you should now see a little brine. If using the burping method (page 44), make sure there is little headspace, top with a round of parchment paper, and seal the lid tightly. Watch the lid for pressure building up. With this recipe you may never need to burp or at most just once. Alternatively, top the paste with a quart-size ziplock. Press the bag down onto the top of the ferment and then fill it with water and seal.

3. Set the jar on a counter, out of direct sunlight, and let ferment for 7 to 14 days. It will become a deep green wilted color, with a cloudy brine. When you taste-test it, the salt should be more obvious than the sour.

4. To store, tamp down to make sure the ferment is submerged in its brine, press a small round of parchment paper directly on top, and screw on the lid. Store in the refrigerator, checking periodically to make sure the ferment stays submerged. It will keep, refrigerated, for 1 year.

Fermented Cilantro Coconut Sauce

See photo on page 245

yield: about ½ pint (473 ml)
technique used: Pastes (page 76)

This sauce is a staple in our fridge. For years we made it without the coconut and loved it; it was bright and sour and often began a salad dressing. So, if you don't like coconut, feel free to omit it. But once we fermented it with coconut milk, we never looked back. It becomes rich and creamy, with lighter acid notes. The color stays much brighter. You can make it spicy with jalapeños or mild with green bell peppers, or mix it up.

At nearly every meal at our house, someone says, "Grab the green yummy sauce." We admit we might have a problem. Therein lies another problem: We have never managed to hide and store this sauce long enough for a true test of shelf life in the fridge. We know you've got at least a month of goodness.

½ cup (118 ml) creamy coconut milk
  Juice and zest of 1½ limes, or ¼ cup (59 ml) lime juice
½ large green bell pepper or 2 jalapeños, seeded and roughly chopped
3 cloves garlic, peeled
2 scallions, roughly chopped
1 teaspoon (6 g) unrefined salt
1 bunch cilantro (about 3.5 ounces/100 grams), trim just the ends of stems and rough chop

1. Place the coconut milk, lime juice and zest, bell pepper, garlic, scallions, and salt in a high-powered blender, if you have one, or a food processor. You want the liquid at the bottom so that every ingredient blends well. Adding the cilantro in two or three batches, process until you have a creamy sauce.

2. Pour the sauce into a jar that leaves a couple of inches (3 cm) of headspace. You will not see any separation of the brine. It is too saucy to place a weight or follower on. Tighten the lid to seal.

3. Set aside the jar, somewhere nearby and out of direct sunlight, in a cool spot, and let ferment for 7 to 14 days. Burp daily (see page 44), or as needed. If you see separation or bubbles, shake the jar or open it and give the contents a stir. The sauce is ready when it is pleasingly sour. The coconut will get thicker and more creamy, like yogurt.

4. To store, transfer to the refrigerator, where the sauce will keep for at least 1 month.

CITRUS FRUITS

Citrus juice and zest can find a happy home in ferments. Pickled lemons and limes are common in the cuisines of Morocco, India, and other regions, either whole or in achars. Preserved citrus has become an important staple in our larder. We dice finely, or make a paste of the preserved citrus to add to anything that needs an instant citrus kick.

Use the Preserved Lemon recipe (page 207) as a process guide to using any cirtrus. We love preserved lemons and have preserved every variety—those pink lemons look dreamy in a jar. We use all varieties of limes, including Persian, Key, makrut, sweet limes, or finger limes. Blood oranges make a delicious ingredient as well. Black limes (*loomi*) are a delicious example of fermented flavor. Hailing from Persia, these limes have been boiled in salt water and then dried whole until their insides turn jet black and their interior sugars ferment slightly.

The peels and seeds of citrus are high in pectin. This means that sometimes you will notice a ferment has more or less of a gelled brine. The peels of fresh fruit have a much higher amount of pectin than do the peels of fruit that has been in cold storage for months, which might affect quality. Because the seeds are high in pectin, you will find that if you leave them in, you will also have a thickened ferment. We take the seeds out of our condiments because we don't want to bite into them accidently; however, we leave the seeds in salt-preserved citrus because we like this gelatinous quality. For some fun kitchen science, place a tablespoon or so of seeds in a small jar and cover with a bit of water overnight. The next day you will see that they've created gel. You can add this gel to any preserve. In this same vein, we have started to experiment with adding fresh citrus seeds (tucked into a cheesecloth bundle) to non-citrus-fermented condiments that we want to thicken up.

The citrus flavor of the zest stays intact through fermentation, such that you can distinguish the flavor of lemons, limes, oranges, and even grapefruit in your ferments. Always save the zests from freshly squeezed uses; you can freeze it for use in ferments or dry it to use as a flavor dust (see page 142).

Citrus juices retain less flavor in ferments but come in handy when you need a little more brine or want to quickly begin acidification.

Preserved Limes

See photos on pages 262 and 281

yield: about 1 quart (946 ml)
technique used: Relishes/Chutneys/Salsas/Salads (page 74)

This is an intensely flavored condiment; a little goes a long way. In India, Persian limes are pickled as an accompaniment to many dishes. They can be sweet, salty, or hot, depending on additions. The pickles we eat at a local Indian buffet inspired this recipe. We'd been enjoying them for years before we finally asked for the ingredients. The chef didn't share much, just enough to let the experiments begin.

We use Key limes, but feel free to use other varieties. Key limes are especially nice in this recipe as they are smaller than Persian limes. They are picked prematurely and are known for their tart-acidic flavor. (When they ripen on the tree, they're yellow and sweeter.) Because their skins are thin, they have a short shelf life; they will turn brown soon after they are brought home—just another good reason to preserve them with fermentation!

- 2 **pounds (900 g) Key limes, or limes of your choice**
- 5 **sun-dried tomatoes, thinly sliced**
- 3 **fresh Fresno chiles or 1 sweet red pepper, diced**
- 4–6 **cloves garlic, minced**
- 3 **tablespoons (50 g) unrefined salt**
- 2 **tablespoons (24 g) sugar**
- 1 **tablespoon (5 g) coriander seeds**
- 1 **tablespoon (11 g) fenugreek seeds, lightly crushed**
- 1 **tablespoon (6 g) grated fresh ginger**
- 2 **teaspoons (4 g) ground turmeric**
- ½ **teaspoon (1 g) ground cumin (optional)**
  Grape leaves or parchment paper, to top the ferment

1. Rinse the limes in cold water. Quarter the limes, remove the seeds, and place in a bowl. Mix in the tomatoes, chiles, garlic, salt, sugar, coriander, fenugreek, ginger, turmeric, and cumin, if using.

2. Press the mixture into your fermentation vessel to release the juicy brine. Put grape leaves or parchment paper and weight, if using, on top.

3. Follow the instructions for your fermentation vessel. For a jar, if using the burping method (page 44) make sure there is little headspace and seal lid tightly. Burp daily or as needed. Alternatively, top the ferment with a quart-size ziplock bag. Press the bag down onto the top of the ferment and then fill it with water and seal.

4. Set your fermentation vessel on a plate in a spot where you can keep an eye on it, out of direct sunlight, and let ferment for 1 to 3 months.

Check periodically to make sure the limes are submerged.

5. Start taste-testing the ferment on day 30. Because the limes started out as acidic, your readiness clue is a little more subtle: The flavor should be no longer the bright citrus of fresh lime but taste instead of garlic and the other spices; it should be pungent and the lime flavor is stronger and deeper, as the oils from the zest have permeated the pickle.

6. When the limes are ready, transfer the ferment to smaller jars, if necessary, leaving as little headspace as possible and tamping down the limes under the brine. Tighten the lids, then store in the fridge, where the limes will keep indefinitely.

Christopher Writes

On my first trip into the countryside of Andhra Pradesh, I learned two things right away: just how efficient a meal can be, and that preserved lemons in India are spicy.

We spent the morning shuttling among government projects in cramped taxis. The success of every project may have been narrated by a different official each time, but the message was always clear: With more money, they could do so much more. By noon, I was exhausted from the heat and humidity, the montage of bright colors, the loud sounds, the strong smells.

As we washed our hands and gathered in an open, concrete government building, I could only wonder how they would cater for the dozen of us waiting to be fed. Then in walked a man carrying beautiful, stacked stainless steel containers, delivering enough food for a dozen people. Among the dishes was a preserved lemon pickle that blew my mind and almost melted my forehead.

Preserved Lemons

See photo on page 262

yield: about 1 quart (946 ml)

technique used: Relishes/Chutneys/Salsas/Salads (page 74)

With its salty-sour, lemony flavor, this recipe is so versatile when your dish needs a little lift. The citrus brings with it umami and saltiness, so don't salt the dish until after you've incorporated the preserved lemon. And if you like preserved lemons, be sure to check out our Lemon Kimchi recipe (page 187).

If you find the flavor too strong, try preserving Meyer lemons. They have floral, fruity notes and less pucker than regular lemons. This is much more of a process than a recipe; please use any citrus you are inspired to try.

- **8 whole lemons**
- **½–1 cup (134–269 g) plus 2 tablespoons (34 g) unrefined salt**
- **Freshly squeezed lemon juice, as needed**
- **Grape leaves or parchment paper, to top the ferment**

1. Rinse the lemons in cold water. Trim about ¼ inch from the tip of each one. Cut the lemons as if you were going to slice them in half lengthwise, starting from the tip, but end the cut before you're all the way through. Then cut in the other direction, so the lemons are in quarters but still attached at the base. Remove the seeds. Rub generous amounts of salt in and around each lemon.

2. Pack the lemons in your fermentation vessel, pressing so juice rises to the top. Make sure the lemons are submerged in the juice brine—if they're not, add freshly squeezed lemon juice.

Sprinkle 2 tablespoons of salt over the surface. Place grape leaves or parchment paper on top.

3. Follow the instructions for your fermentation vessel. For a jar, if using the burping method (page 44) make sure there is little headspace and seal lid tightly. Burp daily or as needed. Alternatively, top the ferment with a quart-size ziplock bag. Press the bag down onto the top of the ferment and then fill it with water and seal.

4. Set your fermentation vessel on a plate in a spot where you can keep an eye on it, out of direct sunlight, and let ferment for 21 to 60 days. Check periodically to make sure the lemons stay submerged.

5. The lemons will be ready after 21 days but can go longer if you like. Taste and decide; the changes are in the richness of the thick brine and infusion of the zesty flavor. The peels will continue to soften.

6. When the lemons are ready, transfer the ferment to smaller jars, if necessary, tamping down the lemons under the brine. Lay parchment paper over the top. Tighten the lids, then store in the fridge, where the lemons will keep indefinitely.

Lemon Habanero Date Paste

yield: a small but mighty ½ cup (118 ml)

technique: Pastes (page 76)

This spicy, thick paste came about when Janine Lane gifted us a box of fresh Medjool dates for the sole purpose of fermenting. What a gift! Kirsten was tasked with experimenting with dates (we know there are worse assignments). Because dates are so high in sugar, many became vinegar, and the leftover paste made amazing date bars. As far as lacto-fermentation, we found that dates are good to add in small amounts to any ferment that needs a little something sweet, but they can get very active and yeasty. This recipe keeps the moisture low enough that the ferment is slow and stable. This recipe, though, came about in looking for a way to use lemon peels, after we'd squeezed out the juice. Because this recipe is based on using a by-product, we kept it to the peels of two lemons, but feel free to double.

This paste hits all the flavors, and the lemon zest candies a bit from the sugar in the dates. We love putting it on a charcuterie board—a little cracker, some cheese, and a dab of this.

2 lemons
6 fresh Medjool dates, seeded and chopped
3 habaneros, seeded and minced
1 teaspoon (3 g) minced candied ginger
1 teaspoon (6 g) unrefined salt
Parchment paper, to top the ferment

1. Slice the zest off the lemons, taking care not to get too much of the white pith. Slice into small strips. Place in a small bowl. Add the dates, habaneros, candied ginger, and salt. Massage the ingredients together with gloved hands or a spoon.

2. Pack the mixture into a small jar, pressing to remove air pockets as you go. Place a piece of parchment paper on top. Top with a weight (a small, clean stone will work). Then screw on the lid.

3. Set aside the jar, somewhere nearby and out of direct sunlight, in a cool spot, and let ferment for 7 to 14 days. Burp daily (see page 44), or as

needed. The paste is done when the flavors are deliciously mingled.

4. When it's ready, store the jar in the fridge, where it will keep for 1 year. (Actually, this paste will keep for a long, long time. We forgot about one of our jars, and when we found it 3 years later, it was just as we had left it. We don't recommend forgetting, though. Just eat and enjoy.)

Create Your Own Recipes

» Add your favorite spices or herbs to preserved citrus. Traditional additions are cinnamon sticks, peppercorns, whole cloves, coriander seeds, juniper seeds, and bay leaves.

» Preserve limes or lemons with garlic, onions, coriander, cilantro, and plenty of hot pepper. Chop fine and add to fresh tomatoes for a salsa or to a ceviche.

» Use grapefruit juice or sections of the fruit in various ferments to add citrus notes to the acidic flavor—we love grapefruit with radishes. If you add a lot, be sure to up the salt level to 3 percent minimum.

» Add orange zest or juice to ferments and chutneys; they hold their flavor through the fermentation process.

» Don't forget other citrus—kumquats (amazing on a cheese board, just saying), makrut limes, Buddha's hands, finger limes, yuzu, and the many other members of this family also ferment well.

COLLARD GREENS

Fermented collards are somewhat chewy, although not unpleasant. They don't soften the way cooked collards do. We like to ferment these greens with aromatic and pungent spices.

YOUR RAW MATERIAL

Collards are available year-round, but in cold climates they're best in the winter months, when they're sweet and juicy. During the heat of summer, they can be tough and slightly bitter. Select leaves that are deep green and pliable.

Christopher Writes

We were on the road with 7 hours of driving ahead of us to get home and the morning was already blazing at 110°F/43°C. When we stopped at a small farmers' market in central California to get provisions for lunch, the vegetables and flowers were as wilted as the farmers who grew them.

At one stand, a woman was preparing Eritrean food. Many Eritrean meals are based on a spongy fermented-teff flatbread called injera, with spicy sauces and stews poured over it. On her menu was a meal with three sauces and collard greens as the foundation.

We explained we were traveling. "Oh," she said, smiling. "Well, you don't have to worry about it spoiling in this heat. We don't have refrigerators in Africa. The spices will keep it good."

Hours later, the food was indeed delicious, perfect for that sweltering day.

Ethiopian-Inspired Collard Ferment

See photo on page 226

yield: about 1 quart (946 ml)
technique used: Relishes/Chutneys/Salsas/Salads (page 74)

This recipe is based on an Ethiopian stewed collard dish known as *gomen*. There are variations on the herbs that flavor it, and we played with the quantities and came up with this recipe.

It's a spicy ferment, and in Ethiopia it might be served with buttermilk curds or yogurt and a flatbread to temper the heat.

2	bunches (about 1½ pounds/680 g) collard greens
1–1½	teaspoons (6–8 g) unrefined salt
5	cloves garlic, minced
2	jalapeños or other hot chiles, minced
1	large onion, chopped
2–3	tablespoons (22–33 g) finely grated fresh ginger
½–¾	teaspoon (1.2–1.8 g) ground cardamom
	Grape leaves or parchment paper, to top the ferment

1. Rinse the collard leaves and remove the stems. Place the leaves in a pile and roll them into a tight bundle, then slice thinly. (Rolling the leaves makes it easier to get a thin slice.) Transfer the sliced greens to a large bowl. Keep the stems for another make, or slice crosswise finely to add to this ferment.

2. Sprinkle in 1 teaspoon of the salt, working it in with your hands. Then taste. You should be able to taste the salt without it being overwhelming. Add more salt if needed. Then add the garlic, jalapeños, onion, ginger, and cardamom. Toss and massage again to get everything mixed. At this point, brine should be building at the bottom of the bowl.

3. Press the vegetables into your fermentation vessel. More brine will release at this stage. Place grape leaves or parchment paper on top, and weight if you have it.

4. Follow the instructions for your fermentation vessel. For a jar, if using the burping method (page 44) make sure there is little headspace and seal lid tightly. Burp daily or as needed. Alternatively, top the ferment with a quart-size

ziplock bag. Press the bag down onto the top of the ferment and then fill it with water and seal.

5. Set your fermentation vessel on a plate in a spot where you can keep an eye on it, out of direct sunlight, and let ferment for 5 to 10 days. Press down as needed to bring the brine back to the surface. Start taste-testing on day 5. It's ready when the flavors have mingled and it tastes mildly acidic.

6. Store in the same jar, or transfer to a jar if you fermented in a crock. Tamp down to submerge the collards, screw on the lid, and store in the refrigerator, where they will keep for 6 months.

CORN

Our "next-door" neighbors (a mile of wooded ridge separates our farms) John and Frances have a big farm stand along the highway sporting a sign year-round that announces CORN, a sad reminder that for 10 months it's not sweet corn season. Then one day you'll see a single ear of corn wired to the sign and you know it's on. Fresh sweet corn has such a fleeting season, the season of long, lazy days and golden sunshine— perhaps that is why it's a national favorite for fresh eating and preserving.

Kirsten has been determined to make a Three Sisters ferment, with jars upon jars of variations on the theme of dried beans, corn, and squash. In several tests she used cooked hominy kernels, and while a few weeks of fermentation yielded many tasty contenders, after a few months of storage the hominy had hardened, as if it were dry

and raw. Fresh corn works, but many of the ferments using cooked beans were also disappointing. Again, a couple of weeks after fermentation they were perfect, but after 6 months every one of the fermented beans had softened everything else in the jar to inedibility. Still, the experiments continue. We'll keep you posted.

YOUR RAW MATERIAL
Because there are more than 200 varieties of sweet corn, let's assume your local farmer is growing the best variety for your region. Your job is to make sure you choose fresh ears. Start with the husks—you want green, not dry, papery, or brown. The silk should be pale and a bit sticky. The next step (which may not be appreciated by the grower) is to peek at the kernels; they're fresh when they have a milky juice. This indicates

tender corn, as this sugary juice turns to starch as soon as the corn has been picked. So the sooner you eat that corn (or get it fermenting), the less tough it will be.

Sweet Corn Relish

yield: about 1 quart (946 ml)
technique used: Relishes/Chutneys/Salsas/Salads (page 74)

This tangy relish has a Tex-Mex flavor. The short fermentation time retains the sweetness of the corn, but over time, the sweet notes will be replaced by the sour. Corn kernels can get lightly fizzy. Use only young zucchinis, or omit them entirely for a longer storage.

For a different flavor, omit the cilantro and chile and sprinkle in ½ teaspoon (1 g) celery seed.

    3 cups (495 g) raw sweet corn kernels
        (see note)
    1 red bell pepper, finely diced
    1 red onion, finely diced
    ½ cup (63 g) finely diced small zucchini
    1 serrano or jalapeño chile, finely diced
        (optional)
    3 tablespoons (11 g) chopped cilantro
 1–1½ teaspoons (6–8 g) unrefined salt
        Grape leaves or parchment paper, to top
        the ferment

AFTER FERMENTATION
    1 tablespoon (21 ml) raw honey

Note: You'll need 5 or 6 ears of corn to get 3 cups of kernels. You can also use frozen corn.

1. Combine the corn, bell pepper, onion, zucchini, chile, and cilantro in a large bowl. Sprinkle in 1 teaspoon of the salt, working it in with your hands. At this point, brine should be building at the bottom. (If you don't have enough liquid, add some lemon or lime juice.)

2. Press the mixture into a jar or crock. Place grape leaves or parchment paper on top, and weight if you have it.

3. Follow the instructions for your fermentation vessel. For a jar, if using the burping method (page 44) make sure there is little headspace and seal lid tightly. Burp daily or as needed. Alternatively, top the ferment with a quart-size ziplock bag. Press the bag down onto the top of the ferment and then fill it with water and seal.

4. Set your fermentation vessel on a plate in a spot where you can keep an eye on it, out of direct sunlight, and let ferment for 3 to 4 days. As the mixture ferments, the brine will get cloudy; this is when you can start to taste-test. The relish is ready when it tastes slightly sour but retains some of the sweetness of the corn.

5. Add the honey when you're ready to consume it. If you don't serve it right away, store in a sealed jar in the fridge. With the honey mixed in, it will keep for about 1 month (it will be fine, just very fizzy and potentially yeasty); without honey, it will keep for 1 year.

Sour Corn

by Soirée-Leone (see profile on page 22)

See photo on page 188

technique: Mastering Brine Pickling (page 101)

Sour corn is a favorite I love to share with people exploring fermentation. It looks just like fresh corn even when fermented for a couple of years, which adds to the intrigue as someone bites into it. Each kernel explodes with a salty, sour tang. Sour corn has roots in Indigenous American foodways. Corn is fermented in other traditions around the globe, and I first learned of it in *The Art of Fermentation*. I love taking a food that has a very short harvest window and enjoying it in the winter. Freezing isn't an option with limited freezer space and pressure canning corn is time and resource intensive.

Sour corn can be fermented on the cob for a dramatic presentation or off the cob. I ferment 5 or 6 dozen ears each summer, which fit in two 23-liter glass jars. Cutting the ears into three or four pieces can make it easier to pack the container. Whole spices can be added, such as black peppercorns, black cardamom, bay leaves, fresh split hot peppers, whole garlic cloves, or cinnamon sticks. I like black peppercorns, red hot chiles, and whole garlic cloves.

I use the corn silk to make a tincture and I use the husks to wrap and inoculate wheat and soybeans to make shoyu. If you cut the corn off the cob before or after fermenting, the cobs are a terrific addition to broths and stocks.

Sour corn can be enjoyed right out of the jar and included on appetizer platters. It can be cut off the cob and added to soups, stews, corn bread, or a personal favorite: tacos. Dehydrate, pulverize, and add to a homemade seasoning blend, dust corn bread or muffins, or mix with cornmeal for dredging foods before baking or frying.

Corn on the cob

Enough High Brine (3 tablespoons/50.4 g unrefined salt per quart unchlorinated water) to cover the corn

Grape leaf or parchment paper, to top the ferment (optional)

1. Remove the husks and the silk from the corn. Cut each cob into three or more pieces.

2. Pack the corn into your fermentation vessel, wedging in place. Pour in enough brine to cover the corn. Reserve any leftover brine in the fridge (it will keep for 1 week; discard thereafter or dry out to reclaim salt, and make a new batch, if needed).

3. Top with a grape leaf or parchment paper. Follow the instructions for your fermentation vessel. For a jar, if using the burping method (page 44) make sure there is little headspace and seal lid tightly. Burp daily or as needed.

4. Set your fermentation vessel on a plate in a spot where you can keep an eye on it, out of direct sunlight, and let ferment for 4 to 7 days. During the fermentation period, monitor the brine level and top off with the reserved brine, if needed, to cover. The corn will not lose color, but the brine will get cloudy. It's ready when it is pleasingly sour and pickle-y.

5. The corn will keep, refrigerated, for 1 year or more.

Create Your Own Recipes

Use corn, still on its cob, in summer pickles. One particularly delicious and beautiful combination that we made had green tomatoes, sweet corn on the cob, onions, sunflower buds, and garlic.

CRANBERRIES

The cranberry, *Vaccinium macrocarpon* and *V. oxycoccos*, is one of the three commercial fruit crops indigenous to the North American continent. They're native from Maine west to Wisconsin and south along the Appalachians to North Carolina. They're an introduced crop in the Northwest (Oregon, Washington, and British Columbia). Cranberries are water-lovers: They grow in bogs and marshes.

Some Indigenous American peoples used cranberries extensively, as food and medicinally as a poultice against food poisoning. They ate them raw, used them in pemmican (a sort of meat jerky "bar"), or sweetened them with maple syrup. The tart red berries are loaded with antioxidants, they're anti-inflammatory, and with regular consumption, they may protect against various cancers.

You get all this when you ferment the berries, but without all the sugar and other additives that go into a commercial bottle of cranberry juice.

YOUR RAW MATERIAL

Cranberry season generally begins in September and runs through December, which is a good time to put in a crock or two. Why limit this fruit to the holidays? You'll want to enjoy them all year long. We ferment them both as relish and whole.

IN THE CROCK
Cranberry Relish

See photo on page 339

yield: about 1 quart (946 ml)
technique used: Relishes/Chutneys/Salsas/Salads (page 74)

This is a simple conversion of the traditional cranberry sauce to a fermented relish. Adding juice-sweetened dried cranberries balances the tartness of fresh ones. If it's not sweet enough for your taste, simply splash in a bit of maple syrup or honey when serving.

  2 oranges
  2 (8-ounce/227 g) packages fresh cranberries (see note)
  ½ teaspoon (2.8 g) unrefined salt
  1 cup (130 g) dried cranberries sweetened with fruit juice
  1 tablespoon (13 g) chopped candied ginger (optional)
  Grape leaves or parchment paper, to top the ferment

Note: You can make this relish with frozen cranberries. It'll have a softer consistency but otherwise is just as scrumptious.

1. Zest one of the oranges, peel and section both, then remove the membranes from the sections (the chewy, sometimes bitter membranes can negatively affect the texture of the ferment). Chop the sections and set aside.

2. Rinse the fresh cranberries and put them in a food processor; pulse until lightly chopped. Transfer to a bowl, add the salt, and massage it in for a minute to develop the brine. Add the dried cranberries, the orange zest and sections, and the ginger, if using.

3. Press the mixture into your fermentation vessel, making sure there are no air pockets. The brine will be a little thick. Place grape leaves or parchment paper on top.

4. Follow the instructions for your fermentation vessel. For a jar, if using the burping method (page 44) make sure there is little headspace and seal lid tightly. Burp daily or as needed. Alternatively, top the ferment with a quart-size ziplock bag. Press the bag down onto the top of the ferment and then fill it with water and seal.

5. Set your fermentation vessel on a plate in a spot where you can keep an eye on it, out of direct sunlight, and let ferment for 5 to 7 days. Taste the ferment starting on day 5. It will be the same deep crimson color of cooked relish and will have two sour notes: one from the cranberries and one from fermentation.

6. When the relish is ready, transfer to smaller jars, if necessary, and tamp down. Tighten the lids, then store in the fridge. The relish will keep, refrigerated, for 1 year.

IN THE PICKLE JAR

Pickled Cranberries

See photo on page 281

yield: about 1 quart (946 ml)
technique used: Mastering Brine Pickling (page 101)

These delightful little orbs pop in your mouth with a salty-tart burst. They are lovely as garnishes on baked goods or pancakes. The trickiest part about pickling cranberries is that they really want to float. Be sure to use a follower of some kind. We find that food-plastic screening (page 45) cut to the size of the jar or crock works well.

2 (8-ounce/227 g) packages fresh cranberries
5 slices fresh or candied ginger
2 cinnamon sticks
1 tablespoon (6 g) whole cloves
1 quart (946 ml) Basic Brine (2 tablespoons/ 34 g unrefined salt per quart unchlorinated water)
Grape leaves or parchment paper, to top the ferment (optional)

1. Rinse the cranberries in cold water. Place the ginger, cinnamon, and cloves in the bottom of your fermentation vessel.

2. Add the cranberries to the vessel. Pour in enough brine to cover the cranberries completely. Reserve any leftover brine in the fridge. (It will keep for 1 week; discard thereafter or dry out to reclaim salt, and make a new batch, if needed.)

3. Place a primary follower such as a few leaves, parchment paper, or a round of food-grade screening to keep the berries from floating out of the brine. Follow the instructions for your fermentation vessel. For a jar, if using the burping method (page 44) make sure there is little headspace and seal lid tightly. Burp daily or as needed.

4. Set aside on a plate to ferment, somewhere nearby, out of direct sunlight for 7 to 21 days. During the fermentation period, monitor the brine level and top off with the reserved brine, if needed, to cover.

5. As the mixture ferments, the brine will become slightly cloudy and have the hue of rosé wine. You can start to taste-test as soon as 7 days. The ferment is ready when the brine tastes acidic, like spiced vinegar, and the berries taste pickled.

6. Store in jars, adding fresh brine to cover if needed. Top with a follower, then screw on the lids and store in the fridge. These pickles will keep, refrigerated, for 12 months.

CUCUMBERS

Fresh cucumbers don't last long, so it is no surprise that pickled cucumbers appeared on the culinary scene around 4,000 years ago in India. Modern Indian cuisine boasts hundreds of cucumber achars, pickles, and chutneys (we explore these traditions in detail in our book *Fiery Ferments*), and, of course, the concept has since spread around the world.

YOUR RAW MATERIAL

Although you can pickle any cucumber, pickling cucumbers are best if you're looking for that classic pickle. They're a challenge to find in a grocery store as their season is brief and they last only a few days before they show signs of age: dull, wrinkly skin and dark, pocked bumps. Don't buy these or any cucumbers that have yellowed; they've been left too long on the vine.

The best place to find pickling cucumbers is at a farmers' market. They should be available for a few weeks in late summer. Ask farmers early in the season if they'll have them. Because they require daily picking and are a specialty crop with a short shelf life, many farmers don't want to take the risk of growing them.

FERMENTISTA'S TIP

Cucumbers pickle quickly because the juice contains elements that encourage the growth of Lactiplantibacillus plantarum.

Try growing your own. White Wonders and other compact varieties can be grown in pots. Our neighbor introduced us to this ivory-skinned cucumber. We thought it was a brand-new hybrid. It was brand-new all right—in 1893. It's an open-pollinated heirloom acquired by the seedsman W. Atlee Burpee from a customer in western New York State. It's our favorite for its sweet flavor and crisp texture.

Small Persian cucumbers are increasingly available and work well also. Large cucumbers are best fermented when their seeds are scooped out and they've been pressed or partially dried to reduce some of their moisture (page 80), much in the same way as you will see in the Watermelon Rind–Zucchini Salsa on page 344.

BITTER CUCUMBERS

Cucumbers can be bitter, and fermenting doesn't solve that problem—you will just have bitter pickles—but salt pressing (page 80) can mitigate it. All cucurbits (members of the gourd family, such as squash) produce bitter organic compounds called cucurbitacins. They hang out in the leaves, but if the plant is stressed (by, for example, deep fluctuations in temperature, uneven watering, or extreme heat), they enter the fruit. Unfortunately, once a plant starts to produce bitter fruit, it will continue to do so.

Occasionally the bitterness is in just the ends of the cucumber. If that's the case, slice them off.

New York Deli-Style Pickles

yield: about 1 gallon (3.8 l)
technique used: Mastering Brine Pickling (page 101)

In the United States, the archetype for the lacto-fermented cucumber pickle is the kosher dill—the cool, crisp, garlicky deli dills that came out of a barrel as "full sours" and "half sours." As was the case for Kirsten's Ukrainian great-grandfather in the early part of the twentieth century, the first business an Eastern European immigrant could start was often that of a pushcart vendor. Pushcarts were cheap to rent and mobile, and the market for pickles was good. Many vendors eventually bought their own carts, then stores. In New York, these were concentrated in Manhattan's Lower East Side in an area that became known as the Pickle District. However, this was nothing new to NYC. Dutch settlers in the seventeenth century pickled Brooklyn cucumbers, which they sold in Manhattan.

When a cucumber transforms to a pickle, the white interior flesh turns a waxy and translucent color as the air is forced from the cells. The half sours usually look mottled; the translucent flesh of the pickle mixes with the fresh white flesh of the cucumber. Full sours are fully translucent inside.

- 20 pickling-type cucumbers (not waxed)
- 15 cloves garlic
- 1 or 2 dried red chiles
- 6 bay leaves
- 2 tablespoons (24 g) pickling spice (see page 158 for a recipe)
- 1 gallon (3.8 l) High Brine (¾ cup/200 g unrefined salt per gallon unchlorinated water)

Grape, horseradish, or other tannin-rich leaves, or parchment paper, to top the ferment (optional)

1. Scrub the cucumbers in water. Trim off the stems and scrape off the blossom ends (they contain an enzyme that will soften the pickles). Lightly mash the garlic cloves with the back of a knife.

2. Pack the cucumbers, incorporating the garlic, chiles, bay leaves, and spices as you go, into four widemouthed quart jars or a 1-gallon jar or crock. Take time to wedge them tightly as you go so they stay in place. If you can't do this, wedge some toothpicks in an X over the follower to keep everything in place. Pour in enough brine to cover them.

3. Place leaves or a piece of parchment paper, if using, on top of the cucumbers. Follow the instructions for your fermentation vessel. For a jar, if using the burping method (page 44) make sure there is little headspace and seal lid tightly. Burp daily or as needed.

4. Set your fermentation vessel on a plate in a spot where you can keep an eye on it, out of direct sunlight. Cucumbers are one of the few ferments for which we have a firm fermentation timeline: For half sours or long storage, let ferment for 3 days (1 day in hotter climates, before refrigerating). For full sours you intend to eat soonish, ferment for no more than 6 days. (They will continue to ferment while in storage in the fridge.) During the fermentation period, monitor the brine level and top off with the reserved brine, if needed, to cover. The cucumbers begin a vibrant green—the colors look almost larger than life—but turn a drab olive as the fermentation progresses, the result of the acids interacting with chlorophyll. The brine will become cloudy.

5. When it's ready, top off with brine, if needed, then tighten the lids and place in the refrigerator. The next day, check to be sure the pickles are still submerged, topping off with more brine if necessary. The pickles will keep, refrigerated, for 1 year.

IPA Pickles

yield: 1 gallon (3.8 l)
technique used: Mastering Brine Pickling (page 101)

These hoppy pickles are not only tasty but also practical. Hops have incredible preservative qualities, which help with a longer, crisp shelf life. And fresh hops, which conveniently bloom when cucumbers are on, impart a lovely floral flavor, one not as evident in dried hops. Look for hops in the bulk herb section of health food stores or at brewing suppliers. Use whole hops, not pellets.

20 or so pickling cucumbers
3 or 4 cloves garlic
2 tablespoons (24 g) pickling spice (see page 158 for a recipe)
1 or 2 dried red chiles, such as cayenne
10–12 hop blossoms
1 gallon (3.8 l) High Brine (¾ cup /200 g unrefined salt per gallon unchlorinated water)
Grape, horseradish, or other tannin-rich leaves, or parchment paper, to top the ferment (optional)

Follow the recipe for New York Deli-Style Pickles (facing page).

Hop Vines

We have hop vines on the south side of our house for shade. In spring, they may grow more than 12 inches a day, and by the time it's hot, we have a pretty green wall shielding the house from direct sunlight. In late summer, the smell is entrancing. As the days chill, the vines die back. We cut them down, toss into the compost, and the winter sun is free to warm the house.

In a Pickle

Some cucumbers are too big and a few are too soft (Armenian cucumbers, for example) to ferment whole—here are some suggestions.

1. Preserve slices! If the seeds in your cucumbers are well developed, scoop them out, as the seeds (like the blossom end) contain enzymes that will soften the slices. (See the photo on page 281.)

2. If the seeds are quite mature, cut the cucumbers in half, scoop out the seeds, and reduce the water by salt pressing or partially drying (see page 80).

3. Make pickle kraut, because why choose between relish and kraut when you can have both? Follow the recipe for Naked Kraut (page 173), replacing one-third of the cabbage with thinly sliced cucumber. Add an extra ¼ teaspoon (1.4 g) of salt, a few grated garlic cloves, some dill weed, and a pinch of coriander seeds and mustard seeds to the mixture before fermenting.

Sweet Dill Relish (or Save-the-Pickle Relish)

yield: about 1 quart (946 ml)

Sometimes a fermentista has to do what a fermentista has to do to help along a less-than-stellar ferment, and why not a sweet pickle relish? This is a great way to use flat or hollow pickles—and you can even use perfect ones!

> 2 pounds (900 g) lacto-fermented dill pickles, chopped in a food processor
> ½ cup (80 g) finely chopped onion
> 1 tablespoon (12 g) raw cane sugar
> ½ teaspoon (1.5 g) mustard seeds
> ½ teaspoon (0.25 g) ground turmeric
> 1–2 tablespoons (15–30 ml) raw apple cider vinegar

1. Mix all the ingredients in a large bowl. Taste. Add more sugar or vinegar if either isn't strong enough. When it's pleasing, put the mixture in a 2-quart jar.

2. Make sure the vegetables are submerged, then cover loosely with the lid. Set aside for 1 day to allow the flavors to ripen and the onions to acidifiy.

3. Screw on the lid, put in the refrigerator, and wait a few days for the flavors to enhance.

IN THE CROCK (BEYOND PICKLES)
Pickle Kraut

Why choose between relish and kraut when you can have both in one? This condiment is one of our favorite ways to use cucumbers that are either the wrong variety (such as slicers) or too large to make a great pickle. We used to add fermented cucumbers to fermented cabbage, which you can totally do; however, if you know you are aiming for Pickle Kraut—just ferment them together. Use the Naked Kraut recipe (page 173) as your base, then add about a pound (454 g) of sliced cucumbers, a tablespoon (12 g) of pickling spice, a bay leaf, 3 cloves of minced garlic, and 2 teaspoons (8.5 g) salt. Mix together and follow fermentation instructions for Naked Kraut (page 173).

WE ARE FAMILY: BITE-SIZE PICKLES

For any of these, use the seasonings for New York Deli-Style Pickles (page 216) or whatever pickling spices strike your fancy. Common cornichon herbs and spices are tarragon, cloves, bay leaves, and thyme.

Lemon cucumbers can be too seedy to ferment well when they're matrue, but when you're overwhelmed by the amount you have in the garden, you can pickle the babies. Trim off the stems and make sure to scrub off the blossom ends.

Cornichons and gherkins are pickling cucumber varieties that are picked when they are quite small. Often they are cured with salt and vinegar, but you can ferment and store them just like any other pickle.

Cucamelons (a.k.a. mouse melons) look like tiny watermelons that are the size of grapes. They ferment deliciously, just like pickles.

TROUBLESHOOTING CUCUMBER PICKLES

Cucumbers have a few nuances not associated with the other vegetables. One is that they require a higher-salinity brine, as you'll see in our recipes. If you follow the recipes, you'll have delicious, crispy pickles every time. Read on for other typical cucumber pickle problems.

» **White sediment in the pickle jar.** This is not a problem. Instead, it's a good sign that all is well.

» **Hollow pickles.** Interestingly, this can be caused by the pressure difference between the brine and the inside of the cucumber. In our experience, it is more likely to happen when cukes are too big or there was a long delay between harvest and brining. Hollow pickles are perfectly *safe* to eat.

» **Shriveled pickles.** Shriveling comes from moisture loss during the osmosis process. Either the brine was too salty or the cukes were too old at brine time. Shriveled pickles are unappetizing, but they're *safe* to eat. In fact, make them into a relish (try the recipe on page 218).

» **Mushy or slimy pickles.** Mush and slime happen when the brine didn't contain enough salt, there were high temperatures, or there was yeast contamination. Other possibilities: The cukes came up over the level of the brine, or the blossom ends hadn't been scrubbed off. Discard these pickles.

» **Discolored pickles.** Discoloration can come from hard water. Changes caused by hard water are *safe*. Sometimes discoloration is only the result of the spices or colorful veggies. This is *harmless*.

DANDELIONS

Dandelion (*Taraxacum officinale*) is a common wild plant found growing along roadsides and in yards and vacant lots. One cup of dandelion greens is said to supply 112 percent of the USDA recommended daily allowance of vitamin A and 535 percent of vitamin K. The roots are a powerful medicinal and good for gut health, and their qualities can be enhanced by fermentation.

YOUR RAW MATERIAL

Dandelions can be found everywhere, but be picky. Dandelions growing in rich soil will have larger leaves and roots. Avoid roadside specimens, and only harvest from lawns you are confident have not been sprayed with pesticides or chemically fertilized in many years.

Early spring leaves are the most tender and are least bitter before the flower appears. As spring progresses, you can harvest the flower buds for capers (see page 220). The taproot is edible year-round but best when the plant is dormant, in late fall to early spring.

Italian dandelion (*Cichorium intybus*) can be found in markets. As a member of the chicory family, it is slightly more succulent but will still ferment beautifully.

IN THE CROCK

Use dandelion greens and roots as part of other ferments. Add a handful of greens to any kraut or kimchi.

Digestive Bitters Kraut

yield: about 2 quarts (1.9 l)

While there are some bitter notes, as it should be for digestive health, this recipe is mellowed out by the cabbage. It came to us from Kirsten's mom, Nadine Levie, who practiced traditional Chinese medicine as a licensed acupuncturist and herbalist. (For another digestive ferment, see Be Good to Your Gut Fennel Chutney, page 230.)

    1 tablespoon (7 g) grated fresh dandelion root
    1 teaspoon (2 g) grated fresh ginger
    ½ teaspoon (1.2 g) dried cardamom
    ½ teaspoon (1 g) dried citrus peel
    ½ teaspoon (1 g) dried gentian

Follow the recipe for Naked Kraut (page 173), mixing these herbs into the cabbage before fermentation.

IN THE PICKLE JAR
Fermented Dandelion Capers

yield: about 1 pint (473 ml)
technique used: Mastering Brine Pickling (page 101)

When selecting flower buds to pickle, be sure to pick buds that are still tightly closed, not flowers that have simply closed for the night, which will have bits of petals sticking out. Use these small pickles as you would capers.

    2 cups (80 g) dandelion buds
    1–2 heads garlic, cloves separated
    1 onion, sliced into wedges
    1 (1-inch/2.5 cm) piece fresh ginger, chopped
    2 tablespoons (14 g) red goji berries
    1–2 cups (237–473 ml) Basic Brine
        (1½ teaspoons/8 g unrefined salt per cup
        unchlorinated water)

1. Combine the dandelion buds, garlic, onion wedges, ginger, and goji berries in a jar. Pour in enough brine to cover. The dandelion buds will want to float; place some of the larger onion wedges on top to keep everything under the brine. Reserve any leftover brine in the fridge. (It will keep for 1 week; discard thereafter or dry out and reclaim salt and make a new batch, if needed.)

2. Put the grape leaves or a piece of parchment paper, if using, on top of the buds. Follow the instructions for your fermentation vessel. For a jar, if using the burping method (page 44) make sure there is little headspace and seal lid tightly. Burp daily or as needed.

3. Set the jar on a plate in a spot where you can keep an eye on it, out of direct sunlight, and let ferment for 5 to 7 days. During the fermentation period, monitor the brine level and top off with the reserved brine, if needed, to cover. As the buds ferment, they begin to lose their vibrant color and the brine will get cloudy; this is when you can start to taste-taste them. When done, the buds will be dull green and taste slightly sour, with ginger and garlic notes.

4. Top off with brine, if needed, tighten the lids, and place in the refrigerator. The next day, check to be sure the buds are still submerged, topping off with more brine if necessary. Store the jar in the fridge, where the "capers" will keep for up to 1 year.

GOJI BERRIES

Goji berries (*Lycium barbarum*), also called wolf-berries, add bright red polka dots to ferments. They have received lots of attention in recent years as a superfood with countless benefits. Use them as you would raisins.

EGGPLANT

For at least a year, a jar of fermented eggplant sat in our refrigerator. It remained steadfastly in its place while hands reached past it for other jars—even though a 2-quart jar took up a lot of real estate in our crammed refrigerator. The kids tended to ignore unknown things in jars anyway, wary of their mother's experiments. Meanwhile, their mother, also wary, kept looking at this gray-ish ferment and thinking, *Maybe tomorrow.*

That unappetizing color was a hurdle. One day Kirsten bravely reached into the refrigerator, pulled it out, and tasted. We were all sur-prised—the texture was not mushy and it had an unexpectedly pleasant lemony flavor. The journey continued. That first eggplant pickle was chunks of eggplant in its own brine with some herbs. For a number of years this is how we made fermented baba ganoush. Enter salt press-ing, a technique that has been used throughout the world to make eggplant enjoyable. While we use salt pressing as part of our cooking, it took a while to bring it to our fermentation practice. It's a game changer! We knew the true magnitude of our success when our seriously eggplant-averse grandchildren and their father said they liked it. The 4-year-old said, "That's not eggplant!"

YOUR RAW MATERIAL

Eggplant, or aubergine, is botanically a fruit (seeds inside). This member of the nightshade family is believed to have originated in India.

The late-summer farmers' baskets at the market are beautiful, filled with the small round, large oblong, and long slim varieties of eggplant in shades of green, white, yellow, striped, and, of course, purple. All these varieties are great for fermenting.

Once picked, the fruit degrades quickly, so make sure your eggplant is fresh. Look for smooth, shiny skin that's free of blemishes of any kind. It is simple to detect aging fruit: The skin has a saggy quality. When eggplants brown inside, they don't ferment as well.

IN THE CROCK
Fermented Eggplant in Olive Oil

See photo on page 245

yield: about 1 quart (946 ml)
technique used: Salt Pressing (page 80)

Oil-preserved eggplant is a quintessential part of an Italian antipasto platter. Salting and pressing give the eggplant a pleasing and substantial chewy texture. This recipe will work with any type of eggplant; if you don't want the seeds, choose the smaller young ones or the longer Asian varieties.

If you try adding other vegetables to this recipe—onion slices or red pepper rings, for example—be sure to ferment them. You can add dried spices to the oil at the end, but everything fresh must be fermented first to a pH of 4.6 or below.

This pickle is quite beautiful. The aubergine color of the skin dyes the brine, giving the ferment a pink hue.

3 medium firm eggplants (around 2 pounds/ 907 g), cut into rounds about ½ inch (1.25 cm) thick

2 tablespoons plus 2 teaspoons (50 g) unrefined salt

5 or 6 cloves garlic, peeled and sliced

AFTER FERMENTATION

1 teaspoon (1.8 g) dried oregano
Chile pepper flakes, as desired (optional)
1 bay leaf
1½–2 cups (355–473 ml) olive oil

Preserving in Oil

Submerging vegetables in oil prevents exposure to oxygen, inhibiting oxidation and deterioration. And let's just be honest: Oil-preserved vegetables are beautiful and unbelievably delicious. They also have a reputation for being dangerous. Let's take a look at why.

That same oxygen-starved environment that offers protection from most microbes provides the perfect environment for one particularly annoying one. *Clostridium botulinum* spores thrive in this warm, moist, anaerobic environment and produce neurotoxins. Garlic is the most famous culprit, although any low-acid vegetable could harbor this bacteria; in the 1980s there were several outbreaks of food-borne botulism arising from improperly preserved garlic in oil. The USDA advises against submerging raw, low-acid vegetables in olive oil for preservation—in or out of the refrigerator, as they are not considered safe. Most vegetables are low acid in their raw, natural state. However, when done properly, oil and fermentation go together beautifully. The acid produced by proper fermentation inhibits the growth of botulism.

With a little care and time, this technique is safe and delicious. Salting removes excess moisture, and time allows the lactic acid bacteria to ferment the vegetables, creating that all-important acid. When the vegetables are fully fermented and preserved, dousing them in oil poses no threat.

Typically, once they are oil-cured, you will want to consume your veggies within 1 to 3 months so the oils don't become rancid. Traditionally, these types of preserves were kept somewhere cool and dark. In our time, a refrigerator is perfect. Okay, we know it is annoying to have the oil harden in the refrigerator, and to have to wait for it to come to room temperature, but it will keep everything fresher, tastier, and safer for longer.

1. Place the sliced eggplant in a bowl and sprinkle with the salt. Toss to coat each piece thoroughly. Then arrange the eggplant slices and garlic in your fermentation vessel, a row at a time, stacking as you go.

2. Add plenty of weight on top to press out the liquid that will become the fermenting brine. There should be enough after 24 hours. If the eggplant is not completely submerged, add a small amount of water until covered.

3. Set your fermentation vessel in a spot where you can keep an eye on it, out of direct sunlight, and let ferment for 7 days. Then taste. The eggplant is done when it develops a wonderful sour flavor. To be sure, check the pH (page 52); it should be below 4.6.

4. When it's ready, transfer the eggplant and all the delicious bits of fermented garlic to a clean towel and pat dry. Place in a bowl and toss with the oregano and chile flakes, if using.

5. Place the bay leaf in the bottom of a quart jar. Stack the eggplant and garlic in layers in the jar. Every two layers, pour a little olive oil over the top. At the end, pour in enough olive oil to completely submerge the vegetables.

6. Put the lid on the jar and tighten. Allow to cure at room temperature for a week, after which the eggplant is ready to eat. Store in the refrigerator, where the eggplant will keep for up to 3 months. To serve, allow it to come to room temperature. Top off with oil as needed to keep remaining eggplant submerged.

IN THE PICKLE JAR
Sour Eggplant

See photo on page 263

yield: about 2 quarts (1.9 l)
technique used: Mastering Brine Pickling (page 101)

This recipe came to Kirsten by way of our friend Darra Goldstein, who mentioned she'd come across sour eggplant in Georgian cuisine. Kirsten raised an eyebrow, as she does when intrigued, and started looking for recipes. She didn't have to look further than our bookshelves; Darra's *The Georgian Feast* had a stuffed eggplant meal and Olia Hercules's *Summer Kitchens* revealed a Ukrainian version of fermented eggplants. Internet searches found a few vinegar-pickled eggplant recipes using the Georgian spicy condiment adzhika (a fermented version of which is in *Fiery Ferments*). We settled on our Fermented Mirepoix/Sofrito Mix (page 224), which is a recipe that stands on its own without the eggplant. You will have leftover stuffing. Ferment it separately for a fermented soup starter, or sauté to begin a dish as you would with a mirepoix or sofrito.

Use any kind of eggplants for this recipe—each has its pros and cons. The slimmer ones fit better in a jar, but the rounder ones are easier to bake and stuff. We also love the small Indian eggplants, sometimes called baby eggplants, for a decidedly fun little pickle on a veggie board.

The unique thing about this recipe is that the eggplants are cooked, which normally would destroy the very microbes we need for fermentation, but no need to worry—the mirepoix mixture contains enough lactic acid bacteria to get the party going. We tried both baking and boiling the eggplants, and time and time again we found that baked was tastier. They are a bit more fragile, but the creamy texture is sublime.

> 3–4 pounds (1.4–1.8 kg) eggplant
> 2 cups (473 ml) Fermented Mirepoix/Sofrito Mix (at right; see note)
> 3 cups (710 ml) Basic Brine (1½ teaspoons/8.4 g unrefined salt per cup unchlorinated water)
> Grape leaves or parchment paper, to top the ferment (optional)

Note: You can stuff the eggplants with fresh mirepoix or fermented mirepoix; it's excellent either way.

1. Preheat the oven to 400°F/200°C.

2. Place the eggplants on a baking sheet, whole. Prick once with a fork. Bake until soft, about 20 minutes for medium eggplants. They are ready when you can easily pierce them with a fork yet there is a small bit of resistance. Remove from the oven and set aside to cool.

3. While the eggplants are baking, prepare the mirepoix.

4. When the eggplants have cooled, cut a slit lengthwise down the middle of each one, leaving the stem end intact; do not cut all the way through. It will be like a clamshell. Open it to stuff each eggplant evenly with as much mirepoix as it will hold and still close.

5. Carefully place the stuffed eggplants in a fermentation vessel that will also be the storage container. We use a half-gallon jar. Small eggplants can go in as is. Larger eggplants should be rolled carefully into a bundle.

6. Pour in enough brine to cover them. Store any leftover brine in the fridge (it will keep for a week; discard thereafter and make a new batch, if needed).

7. Place a grape leaf or piece of parchment paper, if using, over the eggplants to keep them submerged. Follow the instructions for your fermentation vessel. For a jar, if using the burping method (page 44) make sure there is little headspace and seal lid tightly. Burp daily or as needed.

8. Set your fermentation vessel on a plate in a spot where you can keep an eye on it, out of direct sunlight, and let ferment for 9 to 20 days. The brine will get cloudy, and you won't see much change in the color of the carrots; you can taste your ferment as soon as it is sour. It's delicious after about 9 days, and after 20 days it will be fully sour.

9. Keep the eggplants in the container you fermented them in, as they are difficult to move. Top off with brine, if needed, to keep them covered, and store in the refrigerator, where they will keep for 6 months.

VARIATION
Sour Eggplant Dip
You can use this fermented eggplant to make a delicious dip/spread. Combine 1½ cups (355 ml) Sour Eggplant (page 223), with its stuffing, with 1 cup (115 g) walnuts and 2 tablespoons (30 ml) olive oil in a food processor. Process until smooth.

Fermented Mirepoix/ Sofrito Mix

See photo on page 189

yield: about 1 quart (946 ml)
technique used: Relishes/Chutneys/Salsas/Salads (page 74)

This mix originated as a time saver—a classic sauce and soup starter that we kept in the fridge, ready to go when we were on the go. The vegetable combination became one of our favorite stuffings for fermentation.

- 4 **medium carrots (about 1 pound/450 g), grated or finely diced**
- 2 **celery stalks, finely diced**
- 1 **medium onion, diced**
- 1 **tablespoon (17 g) unrefined salt**
- 1 **bunch parsley (about 1 cup/96 g loosely packed), roughly chopped**
- ½ **bunch cilantro (about ½ cup/48 g loosely packed), roughly chopped**
- 1 **whole head garlic, cloves separated and peeled**
  Grape leaves or parchment paper, to top the ferment (optional)

1. Combine the carrots, celery, and onion in a bowl. Add the salt and toss to mix. Combine the parsley, cilantro, and garlic in a food processor and process to a paste. Add the paste to the diced vegetables and mix thoroughly.

2. Pack the mixture into a crock or jar.

3. Place grape leaves or parchment paper and weight, if using, on top. Follow the instructions for your fermentation vessel. For a jar, if using the burping method (page 44) make sure there is little headspace and seal lid tightly. Burp daily or as needed. Alternatively, top the ferment with a quart-size ziplock bag. Press the bag down onto the top of the ferment and then fill it with water and seal.

4. Set your fermentation vessel on a plate in a spot where you can keep an eye on it, out of direct sunlight, and let ferment for 10 to 20 days. As the vegetables ferment, the brine will get cloudy. The vegetables are ready when they are pleasingly sour.

5. To store, transfer to smaller jars, if necessary, and tamp down. Pour in any brine that's left. Tighten the lids, then store in the fridge, where the mirepoix/sofrito will keep for 1 year.

Create Your Own Recipes

» Salt-press cubed eggplant (see page 80), using 1 scant teaspoon (6 g) salt to 1½ pounds (680 g) eggplant, then ferment them with garlic and basil.

» Salt-press cubed eggplant and ferment with your favorite kimchi flavors, or prepare them in a pickling bed (see page 87) using gochu-jang paste and allow to ferment for a week or more.

» Follow the recipe for Fermented Eggplant in Olive Oil, but use curry spices (page 165) or an achar mix similar to what is used in Fermented Carrot Achar (page 275).

» Instead of mirepoix/sofrito, stuff the egg-plants with caponata-style stuffing, with kalamata olives, partially dried tomatoes, fresh garlic, and capers.

RUTABAGA KRAUT, *page 320*

SEA-CHI (a.k.a. Sea Kimchi), *page 186*

GARLIC PASTE, *page 237*

ETHIOPIAN-INSPIRED COLLARD FERMENT, *page 209*

CURRIED GOLDEN BEETS, *page 165*

WINE KRAUT, *page 178*

HABANERO JICAMA, *page 251*

PEAS AND CARROTS, *page 293*

PICKLED SHIITAKE, *page 267*

ESCAROLE

Escarole is a broad-leafed member of the chicory family. The chicories have been an important food crop for centuries; they're native to the East Indies, spreading first to Egypt, then into Greece and the rest of Europe. Escarole makes a wonderful kimchi.

YOUR RAW MATERIAL

A cool-season green, escarole is best from December through April. The young plants are tender and are nice in a fresh salad; the more mature plants are perfect for fermenting. Escarole is also a great base for krauts and kimchis made without members of the cabbage family. When shopping for escarole, make sure the leaves are bright green and fairly uniform in color.

IN THE CROCK
Escarole Kimchi

See photo on page 305

yield: about 3 quarts (2.8 l)
technique used: Mastering Kimchi Basics (page 117)

This brassica-free kimchi has generous amounts of garlic and chile that make it pungent and bold. You can also try different combinations of the chicory greens. We make a medley of escarole, endive, and radicchio we affectionately call "Chic-chi."

 Plan ahead, as this requires a brining period of 6 to 8 hours or overnight.

1 gallon (3.8 l) Soaking Brine (1 cup/269 g unrefined salt per gallon unchlorinated water)
2 large heads escarole
2 large carrots, shredded
6–8 cloves garlic, minced
1 tablespoon (6 g) fresh ginger, grated

3–4 tablespoons (48–64 g) chile pepper flakes or salt-free gochugaru

1. Pour the brine into a large bowl. Rinse the escarole in cold water and remove any wilted or damaged outer leaves; reserve a few unblemished ones. Cut the escarole in half lengthwise. Submerge the escarole and reserved leaves in the brine. Use a plate as a weight to keep them submerged. Set aside, at room temperature, for 6 to 8 hours or overnight.

2. Transfer the escarole to a colander set over a large bowl to drain, reserving the brine. Set aside the brined outer leaves.

3. Meanwhile, combine the carrots, garlic, ginger, and chile flakes in a large bowl and mix.

4. Chop the brined escarole into 1-inch pieces and add to the bowl. Massage the mixture thoroughly, then taste for salt. Usually the brined escarole will provide enough salt, but if it's not to your liking, sprinkle in a small amount, massage, and taste again.

5. Transfer the vegetables into a crock or jar, pressing as you go. Add any liquid left in the bowl, and top off with enough of the reserved brine, if needed, to submerge the vegetables.

6. Cover the kimchi with the brined leaves, or parchment paper and weight if you have one. Follow the instructions for your fermentation vessel. For a jar, if using the burping method (page 44) make sure there is little headspace and seal lid tightly. Burp daily or as needed. Alternatively, top the ferment with a quart-size ziplock bag. Press the bag down onto the top of the ferment and then fill it with water and seal.

7. Set your fermentation vessel on a plate in a spot where you can keep an eye on it, out of direct sunlight, and let ferment for 7 to 14 days. Start taste-testing on day 7. It will be quite mild at this point, like a half-sour pickle. The escarole will have a translucent quality, and the brine will have an orange-red hue. It's done when it reaches your desired sourness level.

8. Place kimchi in the refrigerator, where it will keep for 1 year.

FENNEL

A member of the parsley family (along with caraway, cumin, and dill), fennel is native to southern Europe and grows all over the continent and in the Middle East, India, and China.

According to Anglo-Saxon herbal tradition, fennel is one of the nine sacred herbs and is associated with longevity, courage, and strength—attributes perhaps arising from its powerful and plentiful flavonoid antioxidants. It's also known as a cure for hiccups.

YOUR RAW MATERIAL

The entire plant is edible. Snip the leaves when they're young and add to salads and krauts. The celery-like stems are good when young; when mature, the stalks will become woody. Fennel seed has a slight anise flavor, milder than that of the bulb, and somewhat nuttier.

IN THE CROCK

Fermented Fennel Cranberry Chutney

See photo on page 161

yield: about 2 quarts (1.9 l)
technique used: Relishes/Chutneys/Salsas/Salads (page 74)

This delicious chutney highlights fennel, which has the unique quality of being both sweet and savory. The chutney heads toward that sweeter side. It goes well on sandwiches, in wraps, on a bowl, or as a condiment on a cheese or charcuterie board.

Fennel stalks can finish a bit woody. Slice some very thin and add to the mix, or use in a pickling bed or broth.

WASTE NOT

Make fennel "capers." Slice the fennel stalks crosswise paper-thin. Put in a jar and cover with Basic Brine (page 102). Use the root end of the fennel, if you didn't already, to press down. Seal jar. Ferment and burp jar as needed for 5 days.

10 medium fennel bulbs
2 sweet onions (or whatever type you have), diced
1–2 tablespoons (17–34 g) unrefined salt
1 cup (121 g) dried cranberries
½ cup (80 g) raisins
5 or 6 cloves garlic, minced
Grape leaves or parchment paper, to top the ferment

1. Thinly slice the fennel bulbs. (For a finer texture, chop the slices.) Put the fennel in a bowl with the onions. Sprinkle in 1 tablespoon of the salt, working it in with your hands. Then taste. You should be able to taste the salt without it being overwhelming. Add more salt if needed. You may need to pound this mixture a bit to get the brine; if it's stubborn, let sit, covered, for 30 to 45 minutes.

2. Once you have brine, add the cranberries, raisins, and garlic. Toss and massage again for a few minutes to get everything mixed.

3. Pack the mixture into a crock or jar. Place grape leaves or parchment paper on top, and weight if you have one.

4. Follow the instructions for your fermentation vessel. For a jar, if using the burping method (page 44) make sure there is little headspace and seal lid tightly. Burp daily or as needed. Alternatively, top the ferment with a quart-size ziplock bag. Press the bag down onto the top of the ferment and then fill it with water and seal.

5. Set your fermentation vessel on a plate in a spot where you can keep an eye on it, out of direct sunlight, and let ferment for 7 to 14 days. The ferment is ready when the flavors of the dried fruits have mingled with the delicious sourness of the ferment.

6. To store, transfer to smaller jars, if necessary, and tamp down. Pour in any brine that's left. Tighten the lids, then store in the fridge. This will keep, refrigerated, for 1 year.

Be Good to Your Gut Fennel Chutney

See photo on page 189

yield: 1 pint (473 ml)
technique used: Relishes/Chutneys/Salsas/Salads (page 74)

This tasty chutney doubles as a tasty digestive tonic, with herbs to help balance your digestive system. Enjoy a little of this ferment before or with your meal to help your system perform better. It also has anti-inflammatory and liver-supportive properties.

The ingredients all play a role. Fennel is known for digestive health and reducing gas, and ginger is a warming herb that can settle an upset stomach. The combination of turmeric root and black pepper is an anti-inflammatory powerhouse. The piperine in black pepper also aids in increasing hydrochloric acid secretion. Dandelion root and leaf are amazing for the liver and kidneys, and the root is also rich in inulin, a soluble fiber that works as a prebiotic. The apple slices give this ferment a nice sweet balance and are also rich in inulin.

2 fennel bulbs, sliced finely crosswise
1 tablespoon (2 g) chopped dried dandelion root (see note) or 3 tablespoons (18 g) finely minced fresh dandelion root
1 tablespoon (11 g) finely grated fresh ginger
1 tablespoon (11 g) finely grated fresh turmeric or 1 teaspoon (2 g) ground turmeric
½ teaspoon (1.4 g) freshly ground black pepper
½ teaspoon (1.4 g) freshly ground fennel seeds

1 teaspoon (6 g) unrefined salt
¼ cup (40 g) dried apple slices, cut into
    smaller chunks
Grape leaf or parchment paper, to top the
    ferment

Note: If the dried dandelion root pieces are large, pulse them quickly in a spice grinder or blender to break into smaller pieces.

1. Combine the fennel, dandelion root, ginger, turmeric, black pepper, and fennel seed in a large bowl. Sprinkle in the salt and, using your hands, massage it in to release the juices. Once you have brine, add the dried apple pieces. At this point, you should have a moist mixture.

2. Pack the mixture into your fermentation vessel, pressing down to remove air pockets as you go. You should see some brine on top of the mixture when you press. There will be only a small amount of brine. Don't worry if it "disappears" between pressings. As long as the relish is damp, you have enough. Place a grape leaf or parchment paper on top of the relish and add weight if you have it.

3. Follow the instructions for your fermentation vessel. For a jar, if using the burping method (page 44) make sure there is little headspace and seal lid tightly. Burp daily or as needed. Alternatively, top the ferment with a quart-size ziplock bag. Press the bag down onto the top of the ferment and then fill it with water and seal.

4. Set your fermentation vessel on a plate in a spot where you can keep an eye on it, out of direct sunlight, and let ferment 5 to 14 days. It's ready when you taste that sour of the ferment.

5. To store, transfer to smaller jars, if necessary, and tamp down. Pour in any brine that's left. Tighten the lids, then store in the fridge. This will keep, refrigerated, for 1 year.

Create Your Own Recipes

» Add fennel slices to a mixed-vegetable pickle pot.
» Add thinly sliced fennel bulb to Naked Kraut (page 173); we like a 3:1 ratio of cabbage to fennel.
» Ferment green fennel seeds to capture their unique flavor; use the same method as Pickled Green Coriander (page 203).

FLOWERS

This section invites you to explore buds, petals, or seed pods. Flowers make small bites that are nourishing for joy rather than sustenance. Gathering them will not only diversify your diet but will also expand your worldview. Just the act of picking a handful of petals or leaves that will soon grace your table is rewarding and grounding.

You must study what you are picking to be sure you have the correct plant, and you must think about stewardship (see Harvest Considerations, page 232). This section only scratches the surface of what can be wildcrafted and fermented. For a deeper look at foraging combined with fermentation, we recommend the work of Alexis Nikole Nelson, known online as BlackForager. They can be found @blackforager on Instagram or alexisnikole on TikTok. *Wildcrafted Fermentation* by Pascal Baudar and *The*

Forager Chef's Book of Flora by Alan Bergo are also noteworthy.

Kirsten Writes

❋ When I was young and first living on my own, I started growing things. At first pots in a window, then pots on a tiny patio. As patches of ground became available, I moved to dirt. I was determined to grow useful things, and as far as I was concerned at that time, this meant food. Why waste time with showy flowers? It pains me to remember that mindset because now I experience unmeasurable joy growing flowers. This delight transfers to my fermentation work with edible flowers. Some make things beautiful and others add incredible flavor.

This is a very short list of a few common edible flowers that will hold their flavor, texture, or color in a ferment. Experiment. We found some of our favorite flowers for fermenting into cider, natural sodas, or vinegar have flavors that don't hold up in the strong acidic, saline environment of a lacto-ferment. Any flower with flavor can also be added to a kvass. Use our Rose Kvass recipe on page 234 as a jumping-off point. It uses beets, a classic, but kvass can be made from many other vegetables.

Calendula (*Calendula officinalis*) petals: These honestly don't add a lot of flavor but they have many medicinal qualities. The best part is that when liberally added to any light-colored ferment, the petals give the ferment a confetti-specked appearance.

Chive blossoms and other young allium flowers: You can't go wrong with adding chive blossoms to a ferment for light allium flavor and beautiful color. We add blossoms on the stem to brine ferments and add small flowers to krauts or condiments. Other members of the onion family have delicious flowers but are usually white and much less showy in the final ferment. See also the profile of garlic scapes (page 238), another flower bud.

Hibiscus: This is a common showy garden flower, but we are thinking about the varieties most commonly used for tea: *H. sabdariffa*, *H. acetosella*, and *H. rosa-sinensis*. The tea is easy to find in grocery stores and can be added to a ferment for color and a nice sour flavor. Roselle (*H. sabdariffa*) is extra fun if you can get it fresh.

HARVEST CONSIDERATIONS

Native Plant Society member and wild gardener Barbara Hughey offers harvest considerations:

When we begin to include wild foraged foods in our menus, a few simple things can ensure that gifts from nature are protected from overharvesting. The best way to wild harvest responsibly is to only pick what you need. Collect only where the plants are plentiful and consider how those plants reproduce. If harvesting the whole plant, consider when its seeds are mature so that they may grow again next season. We can gather and scatter the seeds to expand the area where the plants are growing. Doing some commonsense things like this, with plant conservation in mind, can be our way of giving something back each time we take. In this way we can rest assured that those plants will be there to enjoy well into the future.

Fun fact: It is a relative of okra. The calyces make a delicious tart fruit that can take the place of rhubarb or cranberries in fermentation.

Lavender: Culinarily, lavender is tricky. It can have a cool, refreshing flavor, or it can feel like you're eating potpourri if you're too heavy-handed with it. Mellow the floral tones by quickly toasting the buds over a dry skillet before adding them to a ferment. To determine whether you like the fermented flavor before committing to a batch, take 1 cup of Naked Kraut (page 173) and add a pinch of lavender. Mix thoroughly, then press into a jar. Let ferment for a day or two, then taste the developing flavor to decide.

Magnolia: Many common varieties are edible but will have varying degrees of deliciousness. The buds and young petals have a ginger-y or spicy cardamom-like flavor, and when too mature, the petals will turn bitter. The darker the variety, the stronger the flavor. For fermentation, you can brine-pickle them in Basic Brine (page 102) or add them to kraut and condiment ferments. Edible varieties include *Magnolia coco, M. grandiflora, M. denudata, M. hypoleuca, M. kobus, M. mexicana, M. pterocarpan,* and *M. soulangeana.*

Marigold (*Tagetes tenuifolia*): This tiny fragrant flower, sometimes called signet marigold, golden marigold, or lemon marigold, is a species of wild marigold in the daisy family (Asteraceae). We grow the varieties Lemon Gem and Tangerine Gem and put them in our achars, such as Fermented Carrot Achar (page 275), and we dry-ferment like shio-zuke salt-cured blossoms. They will give enough moisture if you press them quite well; if needed, add a small amount of Basic Brine (page 102). The buds can be fermented like very small capers (see Pickled Green Coriander, page 203).

Rose petals: Rose is another one of those flavors that people love or hate. If you want them to stand up to fermentation and their fragrance to carry through, it's best if you can find roses meant for culinary applications, because some roses taste like nothing, and others are quite delicate. We have done a dry-brine fermentation of the petals (using the procedure for whole leaves; see page 78) with success. They make a wonderful addition to your fermented herb larder and hold up well. Once fermented, they could be dried as a flavor powder (see page 142)—we have found the lightly salted rose dust to be quite sublime on creamy things.

CAPERS

Capers are any pickled flower buds (unopened) or seed pods. In fact, pickled artichokes are technically a giant caper. Another over-the-top caper is sunflower buds, which we have used as a statement piece in our summer pickle combinations. To pickle sunflower buds, harvest immature tightly closed heads (make sure you harvest a bit of the stalk—it's tasty). Medium-size, multiheaded varieties work best. We peel the stalk before fermentation, but we wait to trim off the outer leaves until they're fermented and we're ready to eat them because they are pretty in the jar. Follow the recipe for Fermented Artichokes (page 146), except use Basic Brine (page 102) instead of High Brine.

You can also ferment nasturtium flower buds and the young seed pods of other brassicas. Play around with whatever other different edible buds or seed pods you might like. In general, you will want to harvest seed pods early in their development or they will be on their way to woody and will not have a pleasing texture. To test, simply pick and eat; you will know if they are turning fibrous.

Rose Kvass

Makes 1 quart (946 ml)

Any edible flower with tasty flavors can be infused and fermented as part of a kvass. We love this one. The earthiness of the beet complements the rose in flavor and in color—it is a perfect match.

    1   large beet, scrubbed or peeled
½–1   cup fragrant rose petals
    1   teaspoon (6 g) unrefined salt
    1   quart (946 ml) unchlorinated water

1. Chop the beet coarsely into ½-inch (2.5 cm) pieces. (Don't grate them. Grating gives the microbes too much surface area to work with, and they'll break down the sugars too quickly, leading to alcohol production—and not the good kind.)

2. Place the beet and rose petals into a half-gallon jar. Mix in the salt and top with the water. This ferment doesn't need much headspace.

3. Place the jar in a spot where you can keep an eye on it, out of direct sunlight. Cover with a cloth and let ferment for 7 to 21 days, stirring daily. You will see some bubbling. For more effervescence, seal the jar with its lid and use the burping method (page 44).

4. This tonic is meant to be made regularly and consumed quickly; nonetheless, it will keep, refrigerated, for many months. When you've drunk it all, you could add more salt water to the beets remaining in the jar and ferment again; the resulting kvass will be weaker but still worthwhile. After the second ferment, chop the beets and add them to a soup.

Salt-Cured Blossoms (桜 塩漬け Sakura No Shio-zuke)

yield: not much
technique used: Mastering Tsukemono and Pickling Beds (page 85)

Here is another lovely way to preserve flowers for their essence, but especially the color and zhuzh they will add to future meals. Decorate cookies or sprinkle on cakes for that sweet saltiness, or add to pickle plates and boards. Or, bring a sense of occasion to rice with a few blossoms on top. Most important, have fun.

Salted cherry blossoms are a very traditional type of tsukemono. They are typically made with pink Japanese cherry tree (*Yaezakura*) blossoms, but this technique can be used for any cherry or other edible blossom. We have used lilac blossoms (yum), plum blossoms, and edible marigolds. A general rule of thumb is to use a quantity of salt equal to 20 percent of the weight of your blossoms. We use white sea salt, as it is visually beautiful.

Pick blossoms somewhere that you know is not sprayed with chemicals and choose blossoms that are not fully open. It is best to pick in the morning, as soon as the dew has been dried by the sun.

    1   cup (230 g) loosely packed cherry blossoms
    2   tablespoons plus 2 teaspoons (46 g) sea salt
    2   tablespoons (30 ml) umezu, plum wine vinegar, or unseasoned rice vinegar

1. Lay out blossoms on a tray and remove any tree debris you may have picked up. Don't wash the blossoms.

2. Toss the blossoms with 2 tablespoons plus 1 teaspoon salt. Put into a container that you can top with weight (page 45). Let sit overnight.

3. Drain off any liquid that develops and add the vinegar. Replace the weight and allow to sit for 3 more days.

4. After 3 days, again drain off the liquid and spread the blossoms to dry on a tray lined with a clean towel. Allow to dry in a window or outside. They should be dry in about 3 days.

5. Place dry blossoms into an appropriately sized jar. Toss with the remaining 1 teaspoon salt. Seal the lid. They will keep at room temperature for 6 months or refrigerated for 12 months.

GARLIC

There are five elements: earth, air, fire, water, and garlic.

—LOUIS DIAT, CHEF OF NEW YORK CITY'S RITZ-CARLTON, 1940s

Garlic contains allyl sulfide, a compound with strong sterilization power. It gets credit for some of the health magic of kimchi. It also adds great flavor.

When we first started our business, we had to restrain ourselves from adding garlic to every ferment, but restraint became a lot easier when we began to produce commercial-sized batches—when you move from cloves to heads, a few minutes becomes a few hours of peeling. Now that we are making small batches again, garlic has crept its way back into our ferments; for long-term storage, flavor, and getting through winter colds, nothing beats garlic. Garlic can be fermented by itself as a paste or as a small pickle.

Simply peel as many cloves as you are willing to peel, put in a jar, and cover with Basic Brine (page 102), which will thicken over time.

YOUR RAW MATERIAL

The word *garlic* comes from the Old English *gar-leac*, meaning spear leek. It is harvested in mid-summer and hung to dry in barns and sheds. It is available year-round in most markets. Choose heads that are firm to the touch; soft cloves indicate age or spoilage.

There are an estimated 300 varietals but only two types: hard necks and soft necks. The soft necks are longer keepers and are the type you often see braided. Use either type and any variety to make fermented pastes to extend your harvest. Garlic flavors range from mild, nutty elephant garlic (closely related to the leek) to the much spicier porcelain varieties.

IN THE CROCK

Garlic mellows during fermentation. Fermented garlic paste is delicious. It's curious, though: You'll notice that the "sauer" or acidic taste is mild and sweet. The bite, or heat, of raw garlic also disappears, but the flavor is still garlicky. In fact, fermenting garlic is a great way to eat it "raw," because it doesn't linger on the palate the way raw garlic does.

Fermented garlic will darken over time. You may notice it turning to a light caramel color that deepens gradually. This is normal and not a sign of spoilage.

My Pickled Garlic Is Blue!

Blue garlic is safe to eat, tastes normal, and is caused by a chemical reaction of the sulfur-containing amino acids and enzymes in the garlic that can be (but aren't always) activated by acid. We like what Dr. Luke LaBorde of Penn State University's Department of Food Science says: "You're just rearranging some molecules inside the garlic." In northern China, blue-green pickled garlic is made on purpose. It's called Laba garlic and is made on Laba, a traditional Chinese holiday.

WHAT ABOUT BLACK GARLIC?

Black garlic is often referred to as fermented, but it's actually not. It's an understandable mistake, given that it takes a lot of time and patience and the transformation is just as delicious and seemingly miraculous as any fermentation. Black garlic is made using a long, slow cooking process under high humidity. The result is a synergy of different chemical reactions—enzymatic browning, the biochemical process called the Maillard reaction, and another tasty browning we know in the kitchen as caramelization. Enzymatic browning is an enzyme-driven process that we see every time we watch our picked fruit begin to turn brown. The Maillard reaction is not enzymatic, but a browning reaction (think toasting bread) that involves reducing or condensing the sugars (carbohydrates) with proteins or peptides. Caramelization is not an enzyme-driven reaction, either. Caramelization happens when heat breaks down the sugar, oxidizing it into rich brown deliciousness.

Garlic Paste

See photo on page 226

yield: about 1 pint (473 ml)
technique used: Pastes (page 76)

You'll want to have this paste on hand year-round. When you don't feel like peeling and mincing fresh cloves, the paste adds instant garlic flavor to any dish. Fair warning: Plan on peeling time. It's worth the effort, as the paste is invaluable for convenience. We love it mixed with a little fresh parsley and tossed with fresh homemade oven fries just before serving.

6–8 heads garlic, cloves separated and peeled
2 teaspoons (11 g) unrefined salt

1. Process the garlic to a paste consistency in a food processor. This paste has a sticky, thick, gooey consistency (which makes it easier to keep it submerged). Sprinkle in the salt. Not much will change after salting, which makes it difficult to distinguish the brine. Don't worry—the fermentation will work. *Note:* If available, add 1–2 tablespoons of fermented brine. This will add a little juice and jump-start the process. Do *not* add water.

2. Press the paste into a quart jar. More liquid will release as you press, and you should now see a little brine. If using the burping method (page 44), make sure there is little headspace, top with a round of parchment paper, and weight if you have one, then seal the lid tightly. Watch the lid for pressure building up. With this recipe you may never need to burp, or at most just once. Alternatively, top the paste with a quart-size ziplock bag. Press the bag down onto the top of the ferment, then fill it with water and seal.

3. Set the jar in a spot where you can keep an eye on it, out of direct sunlight, and let ferment for 14 to 21 days, or longer. The garlic will turn darker the longer it ferments. It is caramelizing. When fermented, it will be milder than when it was raw and have some acidity.

4. To store, tamp down the paste to make sure it is submerged in its brine, press a fresh round of parchment paper directly on top, and seal the jar with its lid. This paste will keep, refrigerated, for 1 year or more.

Moroccan Garlic Paste

yield: about ½ cup (118 ml)

Use this spicy paste to add bold flavor to just about any dish. It's quite salty, which is good for seasoning meat and coating roasting veggies; just add a bit of olive oil.

2 heads garlic, cloves separated and peeled
2 tablespoons (30 ml) lemon juice
2 teaspoons (6 g) freshly ground black pepper
2 teaspoons (6 g) ground cumin
2 teaspoons (11 g) unrefined salt

Follow the recipe for Garlic Paste at left, processing the garlic to a paste and combining it with the other ingredients before salting.

GARLIC SCAPES

Scapes are the flowering stalks of garlic plants. Growers cut them off to get large bulb development. The flavor of scapes can be a nice substitution for garlic cloves in fermented krauts and kimchis. To ensure a seamless substitution, create a scape paste in a food processor; for nuggets of garlic flavor, slice the scapes. *Note:* Scapes tend to ferment firm, so slice thinly if that is a concern.

YOUR RAW MATERIAL

Garlic scapes arrive at farmers' markets and in CSA boxes in early summer. If you've planted garlic, cut the scapes from your own patch early, when the curls are just poking above the leaves, to ensure tenderness.

Scapes should be firm but still flexible and not turning woody, as they will be too tough to enjoy.

Christopher Writes

One summer, we convinced our eldest son and his fiancée to work in the fermentation kitchen during their break. Because garlic scapes have a natural curl, Kirsten thought they'd look good as pickled ringlets. That's all she shared with the kids before heading out to a market, leaving them with a pile of scapes and five cases of pint jars. When we returned 12 hours later, we found 50 jars of "Celtic knots"—exquisitely coiled and twisted scapes in their jars with rosemary packed in the empty spaces. Fifty jars of artistic beauty, which when you factor in the labor costs was extremely unprofitable, but a joy to display at the markets.

IN THE CROCK

Garlic Scape Paste

yield: about 1 pint (118 ml)
technique used: Pastes (page 76)

This is a concentrated condiment, delicious as instant garlic seasoning or as a spread. It's easy to make, it makes full use of garlic plants, it's a great time-saving condiment, and best of all, no peeling!

- 1 pound (454 g) garlic scapes
- 1 tablespoon (15 ml) lemon juice
- 1 teaspoon (6 g) unrefined salt

1. Cut the triangular tip off the bulbs of the scapes. (The tip is dry and stringy and doesn't purée well.) Cut the scapes into 1-inch pieces. Blend in a food processor to the consistency of pesto. Sprinkle in the lemon juice and salt.

2. Press the paste into a quart jar. More liquid will release as you press, and you might see a little brine. If using the burping method (page 44), make sure there is little headspace, top with a round of parchment paper, and weight if you have one, then seal the lid tightly. Watch the lid for pressure building up. Alternatively, top the paste with a quart-size ziplock bag. Press the bag down onto the top of the ferment, then fill it with water and seal.

3. Set the jar on a counter, out of direct sunlight, and let ferment for 5 to 10 days. Start taste-testing on day 5. It's ready when it's mildly garlicky, with a light sour taste, and the bright green color has faded.

4. To store, tamp down, press a small round of parchment paper directly on top, and seal the jar with its lid. This paste will keep, refrigerated, for 1 year.

Pickled Garlic Scapes
See photo on page 160

Pickle scapes as you would asparagus (page 149), or use them as a flourish in a medley of pickled vegetables.

GINGER

Ginger (*Zingiber officinale*) is a perennial favorite addition to many fermented goodies. Ginger's warm, woodsy flavor is pleasingly hot, with rich, sweet notes. It is a common ingredient in many traditional fermentations. We don't put ginger in everything, but it always comes to mind because it immediately elevates even the simplest ferment. Plus, ginger possesses anti-inflammatory properties and is also beneficial to the probiotic microbes. When ginger is added to ferments, more lactic acid bacteria are produced at the end of the fermentation and throughout the storage time. It seems that the antibacterial properties of the gingerol compounds in ginger protect the good bacteria from the bad.

Cultivated in tropical Asia for more than 3,000 years, ginger is perhaps one of the oldest fundamental spices. Its origin is ambiguous, but it was used extensively in the cuisines and medicines of ancient China and India. (Pots found in New Delhi dating from around 2500 BCE had residues of turmeric, ginger, and garlic.) Because it is easily transported, whether fresh or dried, ginger was a good candidate for early trade and found its way into savory dishes and sweet confections everywhere.

YOUR RAW MATERIAL

Ginger is available year-round, but like all produce, its freshness waxes and wanes due to harvest times, shipping, and storage. The other factor affecting flavor is how long the rhizome was allowed to grow. Ginger is most pungent and fibrous when harvested after 8 to 10 months of growth. This is the ginger you will most likely find in grocery stores. The skin is thick and papery, and the roots do not appear as plump. This older ginger is better for recipes in which the ginger is grated. The flavor is wonderful, but the fibers can get in the way of a pleasing ginger pickle.

For the following recipes, ideally, you will find ginger that is plump, with a thin, moist, almost translucent skin. This young ginger will not need to be peeled.

What about the papery skin, you ask? There is no reason, beside aesthetics, to peel the ginger root. When we are grating the root in with many other ingredients, it is simpler to scrub the skin and to leave it on. Plus, the skin is where our friends the lactic acid bacteria hang out. That said, if you are making the following recipes, you may want to peel your ginger for the aforementioned aesthetics. The following recipes are inspired by the Japanese tradition of tsukemono (see Chapter 6).

Fermented Ginger Pickle

yield: about 1 pint (473 ml)
technique used: Dry Brining (page 73)

In early winter, the produce section is loaded with newly harvested ginger, galangal, and turmeric roots; they are full, succulent, and fresh. This is the time to preserve them. If you are fortunate, you might find varieties beyond the widely available yellow ginger, such as the milder baby ginger—labeled "pink," "young," "new," or "stem" ginger—or the zestier blue Hawaiian.

This recipe can be used for any kind of ginger, turmeric, or galangal, although galangal is more fibrous and better suited for a grated paste. We use these slices throughout the year as tiny sides, to flavor meals, or to put in other ferments when fresh roots are unavailable.

> 1 **pound (454 g) fresh ginger**
> ½ **teaspoon (2.8 g) unrefined salt**

1. Peel the ginger (pro tip: scrape the edge of a spoon over the skin to easily remove the peel with very little waste) and slice as thinly as possible on the bias—think of the pickled ginger strips alongside a plate of sushi. Place these slices in a bowl, then mix in the salt.

2. Pack the mixture tightly into your fermentation vessel, then follow the instructions for that vessel. For a jar, if using the burping method (page 44) make sure there is little headspace and seal lid tightly. Burp daily or as needed. Alternatively, top the ferment with a quart-size ziplock bag. Press the bag down onto the top of the ferment and then fill it with water and seal.

3. Set your fermentation vessel on a plate in a spot where you can keep an eye on it, out of direct sunlight, and let ferment for 7 to 14 days. As the ginger ferments, the color will change slightly. The brine will be milky. You will taste a light acidity.

4. Place the pickled ginger in an appropriately sized jar, with a piece of parchment on top, where it will keep in the refrigerator for 1 year.

Honey-Fermented Ginger

See photo on page 262

yield: about 1½ cups (355 ml)

Honey ferments are fermentation candy. Just plain delicious. The honey is full of all the good microbes but very stable. As soon as you disrupt the balance by adding moisture—in this case, the ginger slices—those microbes will wake up and start fermenting. Substitute turmeric root for a sunny-colored, delicious variation.

> ½ **pound (250 g) ginger**
> **About 1¼ cups (300 ml) raw honey,**
> **enough to cover ginger**

1. Peel the ginger and slice as thinly as possible on the bias. Place in a jar with a tight-fitting lid. Cover with honey. Tighten the lid.

2. Set the jar on a plate on your counter, out of direct sunlight. Every day, flip over the jar. This will keep the ginger below the honey. Burp the jar as needed (page 44) to release pressure. In a few days, the honey will begin to liquefy. Then it will bubble profusely. Keep flipping and burping the jar as needed. It will be ready when active fermentation settles down, 3 to 4 weeks.

3. Store the honey and ginger at room temperature. It will keep indefinitely.

Honey-Fermented Garlic

Both culinary and medicinal, honey-fermented garlic is a simple but powerful ferment that will become a staple in your pantry. For those who have heard that botulism can be a problem with garlic, this is a safe ferment; the botulism spore can't grow in the acidic environment of the fermented honey.

Follow the recipe for Honey-Fermented Ginger, facing page, but use 1¼ cups garlic cloves (about 5 heads) in place of the ginger and use 1½ cups honey. Peel the cloves, then crush lightly with the back of a chef's knife to release some moisture. When adding the honey, be sure to leave about 1½ inches of headspace in the jar. The ferment will be ready when the bubbles settle down, the honey becomes runny and dark, and the garlic mellows.

IN A PICKLING BED
Miso-Fermented Ginger

yield: about ½ cup (118 ml)
technique used: Mastering Tsukemono and Pickling Beds (page 85)

When we wrote our book *Miso, Tempeh, Natto & Other Tasty Ferments*, we ended up with a plethora of miso. Fortunately it doesn't go bad and just gets better as it ages—and it let us make this pickle with every miso from dark to light. Turns out, we needn't have bothered; the flavor is fantastic with any miso, so use your favorite.

This fermented ginger is delicious in grain bowls, alongside sushi, or chopped in a dressing. As with all the ginger recipes, young, fresher roots will yield a more tender product. The ginger juices left behind in the miso pickling bed impart a luscious flavor. Reuse the bed for another vegetable, or use it as is for a delicious gingery-warm sweet cuppa miso (see page 99).

  ½ **pound (227 g) ginger root, julienned**
  ⅓ **cup (92 g) miso**
  1 **tablespoon brown sugar (12 g) or mirin (15 ml)**

1. Peel the ginger, if needed, and slice very thinly on the bias. If your ginger is older, try a julienne cut; we find that does a better job of breaking up the fibers, creating a more pleasing little pickle.

2. Combine the miso and sugar in a small container or jar with a tight-fitting lid. Nest the ginger in miso. Screw on the lid. Set in the fridge to ferment for 2 days to 2 weeks.

3. Store this ferment in the fridge, where it will keep for several months. But you will eat it way before then.

GRAPE LEAVES

A few years ago, in a fermentation class we were leading, a young woman and her mom shared that in their homeland of Armenia, many people preserve grape leaves for *dolmas* (stuffed grape leaves) in plastic water bottles: They pick the leaves, roll them up, put them through the top of the bottle, and use a stick to keep stuffing in more rolled-up leaves until the bottles are tightly packed. Then they seal the bottles and let the leaves ferment for up to 1 or 2 years.

YOUR RAW MATERIAL

When you use grape leaves to top ferments, they do more than keep everything under the brine: They also release tannins, which help keep the veggies crisp. If you preserve the leaves in early summer, you have them on hand for use during winter fermentation.

Those of us with well-established grapevines are in good shape; otherwise, you'll have to make friends with someone who grows grapes organically. The variety of grape doesn't matter; use whatever you can get your hands on—leaves from table grapes, Concord grapes, wine grapes, or whatever.

Early-summer leaves are more tender, but you can harvest any time before their color changes in the fall. If you're picking late in the season, select leaves near growing points; they're the youngest. Choose the largest ones, so that they are big enough to stuff.

IN THE PICKLE JAR
Preserved Grape Leaves

yield: about 1 quart (946 l)
technique used: Mastering Brine Pickling (page 101)

Use whole leaves to make *dolmas* or to top any crock of brine pickles when fresh leaves are unavailable.

2–3 dozen fresh grape leaves
2–3 cups (473–710 ml) Basic Brine
(1½ teaspoons/8 g unrefined salt per cup unchlorinated water)

1. Rinse the leaves in cool water. Put in a bowl, cover with the brine, and let soak for 1 hour. Then remove the leaves, reserving the brine.

2. Stack the leaves in piles of eight or more—you can make one big pile or several smaller ones. Tightly roll each pile from stem end to tip (like cigars).

3. Pack the rolled leaves into a jar, wedging them under the shoulder. Pour in enough of the brine to cover the leaves completely. Store any leftover brine in the fridge (it will keep for 1 week; discard thereafter or dry out and reclaim salt and make a new batch, if needed).

4. The tightly wedged grape leaves usually stay in place on their own, so you won't need to weigh them down. Put on the lid loosely and cover the jar with a towel, or tighten the lid if you intend to release CO_2 with the burping method (see page 44).

5. Set the jar on a plate in a spot where you can keep an eye on it, out of direct sunlight, and let ferment for 1 week. During the fermentation period, monitor the brine level and top off with the reserved brine, if needed, to cover. The leaves are ready when they go from verdant green to dark, dull green and the brine is cloudy.

6. Store in the fridge in the same jar, with the lid screwed on tight. Make sure the leaves are covered in brine. These will keep, refrigerated, for 1 year or longer.

Jessica Alonzo:
Creating and Selling Local Texan Ferments

Jessica Alonzo launched Native Ferments TX, a larder shop that sells ferments local to Jessica's region at a few farmers' markets and online, in 2021. "I do what I do out of respect for the farmers, their hard work, and great produce. I want to highlight their produce through my fermentation processes and make the foods easily accessible to our community," Jessica says. Part of her mission is to teach—to educate people so they know that fermented foods can be easily and safely made in their homes and enjoyed in their everyday cooking. In doing so, Jessica hopes to connect them with their local foodshed.

Jessica's journey with cooking began when she was a child, helping her mom cook for large family gatherings. These warm memories of food were instrumental in her decision to go to culinary school. Her fermentation journey began when she started working at a fine dining restaurant in Dallas that was focused on sourcing local ingredients. That Dallas restaurant had a larder, which opened up a whole new world of culinary flavors to her. Jessica says, "I started learning about fermentation and preservation. I was so amazed with the transformation of ingredients and delicious flavors that occur during fermentation. I quickly started researching, reading books on fermentation, pickling, preservation, and experimenting. Through my fermentation projects, I've learned to adapt various preservation techniques to work on Texas produce and ingredients."

Native Ferments TX is an example of how we can use fermentation to support food systems holistically. Over the past few years, Jessica has built relationships with local farmers because there's a symbiotic relationship between the farmers and restaurants. "For example," she says, "the farmers would have slightly blemished crops or too much of a crop; we would gladly take the produce and find different ways to preserve it, then incorporate it into the menu. Finding new ways to cross-utilize ferments and preserves also helped with food costs at the restaurants while adding new flavors to the seasonal food. This is how whole utilization became such an important part of what I do today." (Whole utilization is the same idea as zero-waste, but more realistic. It's the idea that we can use all of an ingredient by creatively using the bits that may have been thrown away.)

"Finding new ways to cross-utilize ferments and preserves helped with food costs at the restaurants while adding new flavors to the seasonal food."

BEET-CELERY
FERMENTED SALAD
page 166

SUNFLOWER CAPERS,
page 233

BRINE-CURED OLIVES,
page 282

PINK GIARDINIERA,
page 198

FERMENTED ARTICHOKES,
page 146

FERMENTED EGGPLANT IN OLIVE OIL, *page 221*

FERMENTED CILANTRO COCONUT SAUCE, *page 204*

GEORGIAN-STYLE FERMENTED GREEN TOMATOES, *page 334*

PICCALILLI, *page 196*

HERBS

A well-stocked fermentation larder (a shelf or two in the door of your refrigerator), with herbal pastes, rich condiments, and fermented salads, will keep you grabbing these foods for flavor without even thinking about it.

When you ferment fresh herbs (culinary or medicinal), you increase the magic they have to offer. Medicinal herbs pair wonderfully in culinary ferments. Some examples are Be Good to Your Gut Fennel Chutney (page 230) and Nettle Kraut (page 277). Beyond preserving the flavor, you are getting the benefits of consuming fresh herbs and in a sense keeping the herb alive through the live probiotic microbes that are now on board. For herbs and spices that you have to buy dried, rather than fresh, fermenting is a wonderful way to breathe microbial life and enzymatic activity back into them.

To get started with your own herb-based ferments, start with herbs you know well and enjoy. Think about what you might find yourself using. If you like to cook with fresh herbs, you might make an herbal paste with your favorite combination. Fresh parsley, cilantro, oregano, and basil are great bases for making blends with the drier aromatics such as sage, rosemary, and thyme.

Blend your favorite combination of herbs together with some salt (about 1.5 to 2 percent by weight) to make a paste, and ferment as described in Chapter 5 (see page 76). Use this paste to add flavor (and live probiotics) to anything from salad dressing to a hummus dip. A good rule of thumb is to taste your herbal creation raw, as you are making it; if it tastes good raw, chances are it will taste amazing fermented.

For more ideas, see the profiles for basil (page 153), cilantro (page 202), dandelions (page 219), parsley (page 289), and shiso (page 325).

Herbs are also wonderful to incorporate in condiments and pickling beds.

Herbal "Quick Pickling Bed" & Condiment

By Jessica Alonzo

yield: about 1 quart (946 ml)
technique used: Mastering Tsukemono and Pickling Beds (page 85)

This ferment shows you how versatile ferments in your larder can be, meeting your need in the moment. The paste itself can be used as a condiment. I like to use it as a condiment on cooked proteins, for example, steak or grilled chicken—think chimichurri. I use it as a base for salad vinaigrettes and grilled vegetable marinades. Or toss potatoes in the mixture, add butter, and roast . . . super tasty!

I also utilize it as a "quick pickling bed" for other vegetables (see facing page). The recipe calls for whole herbs, but especially when you're planning to use it as a pickling bed, feel free to use herb stems and/or peels instead.

- 2 medium onions (around 1 pound/450 g), roughly chopped
- 1 (2-inch/5 cm) piece fresh ginger, peeled and roughly chopped
- 2 stalks celery, with leaves, roughly chopped
- 15 cloves garlic

1 cup (25 g) chopped cilantro
½ cup (13 g) chopped parsley
3 Anaheim peppers, stemmed, seeded, and
    roughly chopped
1 jalapeño pepper, stemmed, seeded, and
    roughly chopped
1 tablespoon (5 g) toasted coriander seeds
1 tablespoon (8 g) toasted cumin seeds
1½–2 tablespoons (25–34 g) unrefined salt

1. Place the onions, ginger, celery, garlic, cilantro, parsley, Anaheim peppers, jalapeños, coriander, cumin, and salt in a food processor and process to a paste-like consistency. Depending on the size of your processor, you may need to split the ingredients into two batches.

2. Press the paste into an appropriately sized jar. More liquid will release as you press, and you should now see a little brine. If using the burping method (page 44), make sure there is little headspace, top with a round of parchment paper, and seal the lid tightly. Watch the lid for pressure building up. With this recipe you may never need to burp or at most just once. Alternatively, top the paste with a quart-size ziplock bag. Press the bag down onto the top of the ferment, then fill it with water and seal.

3. Set your fermentation vessel on a plate in a spot where you can keep an eye on it, out of direct sunlight, and let ferment for 3 to 4 weeks. The paste is ready when it's pleasingly sour and pickle-y tasting, without the strong acidity of vinegar, and the flavors have mingled.

4. Store in refrigerator. This will keep for 3 months.

To use as a pickling bed: You can submerge any vegetable in this paste, but you want to be mindful of water content. Vegetables with higher water content such as radish, cucumber, and summer squash will need to be salt pressed prior to being placed in the pickling bed so that the excess moisture does not dilute the fermented paste or create the potential for mold growth. Follow pressing methods on page 80.

Typically, a pickling bed made with this paste will cure vegetables in 2 to 4 days. To maintain the paste as a pickling bed, add 1 teaspoon of salt after each use. When the vegetables are pulled out, add the salt, tuck the paste back into a jar—with little headspace—and return to the refrigerator. As a pickling medium, the paste can be used two or three times. Don't throw it away when it's no longer active, though—it still has plenty of flavor and can be used to flavor other dishes.

HORSERADISH

Preparing fresh horseradish comes with pain. If you do not like the nose-burning, eye-watering intensity that could succeed in driving you out of the kitchen, then fresh horseradish may not be for you. If you want a good story of the sacrifices you, the food artist, make to feed people amazing food, then this is the perfect veggie.

Prepared horseradish—the kind you find in most stores—always contains vinegar or citric acid, which is necessary for the stabilization of the volatile oils. As soon as the cells of the root are damaged by grinding or chopping, enzymes begin breaking down these oils. The sooner the introduction of acid, the more the sharp flavor is retained. A pure lacto-fermented horseradish condiment has a mellower flavor than that of typical commercial preparations because we have to wait for the biological activity to change the sugars to acid. This takes more time than adding vinegar.

To get around this, we acidify the horseradish ferment with a little brine from a previous ferment. Although the acid helps to stabilize the heat, this ferment will continue to mellow over time. Make small quantities, more often.

YOUR RAW MATERIAL

In season, you'll find fresh roots in the produce section of the grocery store and at farmers' markets. The outside should be a khaki-earthy color, and a bit gnarled is fine. Look for roots that are firm and free of blemishes. Inside it should be creamy white—the whiter, the fresher. If you have access to leaves, they are flavorful, plus they are a handy size to use as ferment toppers and contain helpful tannins.

Kirsten Writes

I wish I could recall what moved our two oldest boys, at ages 10 and 7, to harvest and grind some of the horseradish root from our garden. They didn't even like horseradish. I do remember the squeals of both agony and delight. I do remember the evacuation. The boys, wearing swimming goggles and bandannas across their faces like bandits, and the Cuisinart full of half-ground roots were escorted out to the porch.

FERMENTISTA'S TIP

Pickle Brine with a Kick
Many traditional Russian pickles call for slices of horseradish root; add them to the brine of a cucumber pickle so their flavor infuses the brine.

IN THE CROCK

Fermented Horseradish

yield: about 1 cup (473 ml)
technique used: Pastes (page 76)

Use this as you would any other prepared horseradish. Or make a horseradish cream sauce: Add the fermented horseradish to a combination of sour cream and mayonnaise. Use a fermented beet brine for beautiful color.

½ pound (227 g) horseradish root
1 teaspoon (6 g) unrefined salt
2–3 tablespoons (30–44 ml) previously fermented brine or lemon juice

1. Peel the horseradish, cut into small pieces, and process to a paste consistency in a food processor. Sprinkle in the salt and add the brine or lemon juice.

2. Press the paste into a pint jar. More liquid will release as you press, and you should now see a little brine. If using the burping method (page 44), make sure there is little headspace, top with a round of parchment paper, and seal the lid tightly. Watch the lid for pressure building up. With this recipe you may never need to burp or at most just once. Alternatively, top the paste with a quart-size ziplock bag. Press the bag down onto the top of the ferment, then fill it with water and seal.

3. Set on the counter, out of direct sunlight, and let ferment for 3 to 7 days. It's ready when it is acidic and tastes like prepared horseradish.

4. To store, tamp down to make sure the ferment is submerged in its brine, press a small round of parchment paper directly on top, and seal the jar with its lid. The horseradish will keep, refrigerated, for 6 months.

FERMENTISTA'S TIP

Horseradish Kraut

Add fresh horseradish to any kraut after the kraut has fermented. This stabilizes the "hot" flavor; if you incorporate it early, the grated root loses its volatile oils and the heat gets lost.

JICAMA

Jicama root has a mild sweetness and a clean, crisp texture that people often enjoy raw. The plant is a long vine native to Mexico. You can generally find it in most supermarkets.

Jicama is a rich source of fiber and prebiotics, so it is great gut food. It also ferments easily, adds crunch to any ferment, and is delicious.

YOUR RAW MATERIAL

Select jicama roots that are firm and feel heavy for their size. Bigger doesn't mean better; the large ones can be woody or tough and contain little moisture, which is an issue if you plan to ferment.

Jicama contributes a nice crisp texture to a variety of pickle combinations. Just peel and cut the roots into spears about the size of French fries, or dice them.

IN THE CROCK

Grated and fermented, jicama retains its crispness and its light sweetness during fermentation. Because of its high starch content, the brine usually ends up thick and milky rather than watery.

Jicama makes a nice base for relishes and chutneys, as its mild flavor lends itself to many herb and spice combinations. To capitalize on the sweetness, add dried fruits. To ferment it alone, follow the directions for Naked Kraut (page 173), substituting grated jicama for the cabbage (see photo on page 304).

Fermented Jicama Green Salsa

yield: about 1½ quarts (1.4 l)
technique used: Relishes/Chutneys/Salsas/Salads (page 74)

This recipe makes a spicy, cool, crispy ferment. Fermented peppers add delicious funk, while the jicama adds crunch and some sweetness. We use it as a chunky side to add a fresh element to the plate and even more food for the gut. It contains inulin—a great prebiotic.

> 2 poblano chiles, stemmed, seeded, and roughly chopped
> 1 large green chile, stemmed, seeded, and roughly chopped
> 3 jalapeños, stemmed, seeded, and roughly chopped
> 1 small onion, roughly chopped
> 3 large cloves garlic
> 1 tablespoon (11 g) finely grated fresh turmeric
> 1 teaspoon (3 g) ground black pepper
> 1¼ tablespoons (21 g) unrefined salt
> 1 medium jicama (about 1½ pounds/680 g), peeled and diced
> 4 or 5 unsweetened dried pineapple rings, torn into small pieces (about ⅓ cup/54 g)

1. Combine the poblanos, green chile, jalapeños, onion, garlic, turmeric, and black pepper in a food processor and process until finely chopped. Transfer to a medium bowl. Sprinkle with the salt. The mixture will become juicy immediately. Add the jicama and dried pineapple pieces and stir well to combine.

2. Pack the mixture into your fermentation vessel, pressing out air pockets as you go.

3. Follow the instructions for your fermentation vessel. For a jar, if using the burping method (page 44) make sure there is little headspace and top with a grape leaf or parchment paper and weight if you have one, then seal lid tightly. Burp daily or as needed. Alternatively, top the ferment with a quart-size ziplock bag. Press the bag down onto the top of the ferment and then fill it with water and seal.

4. Set your fermentation vessel on a plate in a spot where you can keep an eye on it, out of direct sunlight, and let ferment for 7 to 10 days, until it has developed an acidic quality.

5. To store, tamp down to make sure the mixture is submerged in its brine, then tighten the lid. This will keep, refrigerated, for 1 year.

Jicama Kimchi

yield: about 1½ quarts (1.4 l)
technique used: Relishes/Chutneys/Salsas/Salads (page 74)

This kimchi-inspired jicama ferment is chunky, crunchy, and addictive. It never lasts long in our house. Jicama has a high water content, so we make this kimchi as a dry brining ferment, which creates a rich and delicious spicy sauce that envelopes the jicama.

> 1 large jicama (about 2 pounds/900 g)
> 1½–2 tablespoons (25–34 g) unrefined salt
> 8 cloves (25 g) garlic, minced
> ¼ cup (24 g) ginger, minced
> 1 bunch scallions, including the greens, sliced into 1½-inch (4 cm) pieces
> 4 tablespoons (32 g) gochugaru or 1–2 tablespoons (8–16 g) chile pepper flakes

1. Peel the jicama, cut into ½-inch (1.3 cm) cubes, and put in a large bowl. Sprinkle in the salt, working it in with your hands for a minute or two. Place a towel over the bowl and let it rest for 30 minutes or so.

2. Add the garlic, ginger, scallions, and gochugaru to the jicama. Mix well, then taste. You should be able to taste the salt without it being overwhelming. Add more salt if necessary. Massage until you see brine building at the bottom.

3. Pack the mixture into a jar or crock, pressing to release any air pockets. More brine will release at this stage and you should see a juicy sauce throughout the ferment.

4. Follow the instructions for your fermentation vessel. For a jar, if using the burping method (page 44) make sure there is little headspace and top with a grape leaf or parchment paper and weight if you have one, then seal lid tightly. Burp daily or as needed. Alternatively, top the ferment with a quart-size ziplock bag. Press the bag down onto the top of the ferment and then fill it with water and seal.

5. Set your fermentation vessel on a plate in a spot where you can keep an eye on it, out of direct sunlight, and let ferment for 6 to 14 days. You won't see a lot of changes; the jicama keeps its color and the brine stays thick and bright red. Start taste-testing on day 6. The jicama is ready when it is pleasingly sour.

6. To store, transfer to smaller jars, if necessary, and tamp down. Pour in any brine that's left. Tighten the lids, then set in the fridge, where the kimchi will keep for 1 year.

IN THE PICKLE JAR
Habanero Jicama
See photo on page 227
yield: about 1 quart (946 ml)
technique used: Mastering Brine Pickling (page 101)

Sometimes as a market vendor you find yourself in a place that is absolutely wrong for your product. One such time was a Saturday morning market at a winery. People did not want wine so early in the day, and they certainly did not want to try sauerkraut. We only sold one jar of sauerkraut that cold, dreary spring morning, but we were inspired to create something new. A couple came by who had just come home from Mexico, where they had tried a fiery relish of pickled beets, cauliflower, jicama, and habanero peppers. We have no idea what they ate, but Habanero Jicama is what we crafted after hearing their story.

- 1 **large beet, peeled and diced**
- 1 **small cauliflower head, diced**
- 1 **jicama, peeled and diced**
- 2 **tablespoons sweet onion, diced**
- 1–2 **dried habanero peppers (depending on how much heat you want)**
- 3 **cups (710 ml) Basic Brine (1½ teaspoons/ 8 g unrefined salt per cup of unchlorinated water)**
  Grape leaves or parchment paper, to top the ferment (optional)

1. Prepare vegetables and combine in a bowl. Place habanero peppers in the bottom of your fermentation vessel. Pack the vegetables in the vessel and pour in the brine to cover completely. Reserve any leftover brine in the fridge. (It will keep for 1 week; discard thereafter and make a new batch, if needed.)

2. Place grape leaves or parchment paper, if using, on top. Follow instructions for your fermentation vessel. For a jar, if using the burping method (page 44) make sure there is little headspace and seal lid tightly. Burp daily or as needed. Alternatively, top the ferment with a quart-size ziplock bag. Press the bag down onto the top of the ferment and then fill it with water and seal.

3. Set your fermentation vessel on a plate in a spot where you can keep an eye on it, out of direct sunlight, and let ferment for 10 to 20 days. As the vegetables ferment, the brine will get deep red and somewhat cloudy. The vegetables are ready when they are pleasingly sour.

4. To store, transfer to smaller jars, if necessary, and tamp down. Pour in any brine that's left. Tighten the lids, then store in the fridge, where they will keep for 1 year.

KALE

In the first edition of this book, we pretty much said you shouldn't bother fermenting kale. While kale can be a challenging ferment, for reasons we will share, we no longer believe it is a hard no. Kale is cold-hardy and grows in the winter in many northern climates, which makes it a great choice for seasonal eating. Also, just a few plants can produce more than you will know what to do with. For this reason, among others, we knew we had to revisit this green we eat so much of. Although just a couple of years earlier we'd proclaimed, "Don't do it, make kale chips instead," we made friends with fermented kale. We still like kale chips, but now we also love kale in kimchi, krauts, and fermented salads.

YOUR RAW MATERIAL

As with many of the best vegetables for fermentation, kale is a member of the brassica family. Kale is wonderfully rich in vitamins and minerals— calcium, folate, magnesium, iron, vitamins C, A, and K, and antioxidants. It is also a decent source of fiber, which most of us get too little of.

While a cousin to the cabbage, it is a little trickier to ferment all on its own. We use it as part of a larger recipe, in a ratio of four parts other vegetables to one part chopped kale.

With kale in particular, if the top of the ferment is exposed to oxygen, it becomes very foul smelling. In our trials, kale seemed more susceptible to this than cabbage. It is crucial to get everything pressed under the brine and to keep as little headspace as possible. To our palate, kale ferments accentuate the salty flavor. If you are someone who doesn't like things too salty, salt carefully and embellish your kale ferments with other bold, unflinching flavors.

The most surprising insight from the kale fermentation trials is that the green varieties finished brighter and tastier than the purple or red varieties. For example, curly kale, Siberian kale, and lacinato (dinosaur) kale produced clean, pleasing acid flavors, while the Redbor and Scarlet kale ferments had more bitter compounds. We also found that the hardy, textured lacinato kale was not too tough to enjoy postfermentation.

Naked Kale

yield: about 1 quart (473 ml)
technique used: Mastering Sauerkraut (page 61)

The idea behind this recipe is preservation. The resultant fermented kale can be quickly braised, yielding a simple side of greens, presalted and tangy, no need to add vinegar. This kale can also be added to another ferment, tossed into soups and stews, or used any other way you would use cooked (or frozen) kale. In this recipe, we've left out the stems, but if you, in the spirit of less waste, decide to add them, slice them thinly for the best texture. For other stem ideas, see page 142.

In the kale trials, we also wanted to find the best technique for the best result. We dry-salted each variety, we brine-fermented each variety, and we tried blanching first, then salting and fermenting. The clear winner in the side-by-side comparisons was dry brining, which is the technique in this recipe. While the brine fermenting was easiest, in that the kale is chopped, stuffed into a jar, and covered in Basic Brine, the flavors

GUNDRUK AND OTHER TRADITIONAL SUN-DRIED GREEN FERMENTS

In the first edition of this book, we shared that we had been unsuccessful at making gundruk, also spelled gundru, from kale. Gundruk is a traditional fermenting method indigenous to the Nepali living in the Himalayan regions of India, Nepal, and Bhutan. Since then, we have come to a much deeper understanding of Himalayan ferments and the traditional processes used to make them, which often combine dehydration and lactic acid fermentation. Another part of our problem was that gundruk is made from a local variety of mustard, and as you will read in the mustard greens profile, Asian mustards are very different from the mustard greens we have in North America.

Gundruk is made in the fall, when there is produce to preserve in abundance. There are, of course, regional variations to the process, but in all the processes we have researched, there are two stages of dehydration. First, the fresh leaves are wilted for a couple of days, and then they are crushed into earthenware jars or pits to ferment. In some regions, the leaves are shredded—with no water added—while in other regions, they are left whole and water is added.

Second, after the fermentation, the leaves are removed and sun-dried. The dried leaves can then be stored at room temperature. Anybody who has tried to preserve their entire garden with fermentation will understand why this makes a lot of sense. Dried leaves are more stable than other forms of preserved goods, and they take up much less space.

Throughout the world, we see greens preserved in similar ways. These nutritious preserved greens are often used in soups (where they hydrate) with other flavorful ingredients, which is how we experienced this type of ferment in Myanmar.

were dull and the texture tougher. This may be because dry brining requires some good massaging. Interestingly, the blanched fermented well despite no added starter, but the flavors were watery, less acidic, and less appealing.

> 1 pound (450 g) kale
> 1–1½ teaspoons (9 grams) unrefined salt

1. Strip the leaves from the stems, chop the leaves, and put them in a large bowl. Sprinkle with the salt and, using your hands, firmly massage it into the leaves. The salt will feel gritty for a bit, but eventually the leaves will let off enough moisture to create a brine. Don't expect a lot of it; this is almost a dry ferment. Taste it. It should taste salty but still pleasing; if not, add a bit more salt. If you've put in a good effort and don't see much brine in the bowl, let it stand, covered, for 45 minutes, then massage again. If you still have no brine, you can add a bit more salt or a few tablespoons of unchlorinated water.

2. Press the kale into a jar. If using the burping method (page 44) make sure there is little headspace and seal lid tightly. Burp daily or as needed. Alternatively, top the ferment with a quart-size ziplock bag. Press the bag down onto the top of the ferment and then fill it with water and seal.

3. Set the jar on a plate in a spot where you can keep an eye on it, out of direct sunlight, and let ferment for 7 to 14 days. The kale is ready when the green changes, it has a pleasing acidic smell, and it tastes pickle-y.

4. For storage, press a small round of parchment paper directly on top of the kale. For longer-term storage, you might add a small amount of freshly made Basic Brine (page 102) on top to help keep

everything fresh. Screw on the lid and store in the refrigerator, where the kale will keep for 6 months.

Kale Kimchi

yield: 1½ quarts (1.4 l)
technique used: Dry Brining (page 73)

This recipe is kale forward and uses the kale stems, so you won't be throwing them out. We like the texture and flavor of the dried goji berries, but you could use currants or other small dried berries. Instead of salting and waiting, as with most of the kimchi recipes, the greens are prepared more like a sauerkraut.

> 2 bundles (1 pound/450 g) kale greens
> 1 large onion, thinly sliced
> 1 large carrot, grated
> ½ cup (60 g) daikon or other radish, grated
> 2–2½ teaspoons (11–14 g) unrefined salt
> 6 cloves garlic, minced
> 2 jalapeños, minced
> 3 tablespoons (21 g) goji berries
> 2–3 tablespoons (22–33 g) finely grated fresh ginger
> 3–4 tablespoons (24–32 g) gochugaru or 1 tablespoon chile pepper flakes
> Grape leaves or parchment paper, to top the ferment

1. Prepare the kale by separating the leaves from the stems. Slice the stems finely and put in a bowl. Save one leaf to top the ferment, chop the rest into bite-size pieces, and add them to the bowl with the stems. Add the onion, carrot, and daikon. Add 2 teaspoons of the salt, and with your hands, massage it into the leaves. Then taste. You should be able to taste the salt without it being overwhelming. Add more salt if necessary. Continue to massage the vegetables until brine begins developing. The kale won't release much, but the other vegetables will. If you've put in a good effort and don't see much brine in the bowl, let it stand, covered, for 45 minutes, then massage again.

2. Add the garlic, jalapeños, goji berries, ginger, and gochugaru and mix well.

3. Pack the mixture into a crock or jar, pressing to release air pockets as you go.

4. Place grape leaves or parchment paper on top. Follow the instructions for your fermentation vessel. For a jar, if using the burping method (page 44) make sure there is little headspace

and seal lid tightly. Burp daily or as needed. Alternatively, top the ferment with a quart-size ziplock bag. Press the bag down onto the top of the ferment and then fill it with water and seal.

5. Set your fermentation vessel on a plate in a spot where you can keep an eye on it, out of direct sunlight, and let ferment for 5 to 7 days. The kale is ready when the green color becomes muted, it has a pleasing acidic smell, and it tastes pickle-y, perhaps with an effervescent zing.

6. When the kale is ready, transfer to smaller jars, if necessary, and tamp down. Pour in any brine that's left. Tighten the lids, then store in the fridge, where it will keep for 1 year.

KOHLRABI

Although unfermented kohlrabi is sweet, unpretentious, and delicately flavored with hints of broccoli or cabbage, the fermented version is nicely acidic and tastes very similar to its cabbage cousin. Make it plain or dress it up with the same flavors as you would cabbage.

YOUR RAW MATERIAL
Despite its bulbous appearance, kohlrabi is actually a swollen stem. Peak season, when the flavor is sweetest, is spring through early summer, although kohlrabi is available year-round.

Look for deep green leaves with no yellowing. Select small kohlrabi; the skin is still thin and you can use the whole vegetable. Larger ones have an inedible woody layer that you must peel off; use a paring knife, as the skin is too fibrous for a potato peeler. If the globe

is enormous, it will be quite woody inside so don't bother fermenting it.

IN THE CROCK
Kohlrabi Kraut
yield: about 2 quarts (1.9 l)
technique used: Mastering Sauerkraut (page 61)

This is a straightforward sauerkraut à la kohlrabi. Try this recipe plain, or jazz it up with any of the spices that work well in cabbage krauts.

> 3½ pounds (1.6 kg) kohlrabi
> 1–1½ tablespoons (17–25 g) unrefined salt
> Grape leaf or parchment paper, to top the ferment

1. Rinse the kohlrabi in cold water, peel if needed, and grate or slice finely with a mandoline. Transfer to a large bowl.

2. Add 1 tablespoon of the salt and massage it into the kohlrabi. Then taste. You should be able to taste the salt without it being overwhelming. Add more salt if necessary. The kohlrabi will soon look wet and limp, and liquid will pool. If you don't see much brine, let the mixture stand, covered, for 45 minutes, then massage again.

3. Transfer the kohlrabi to a crock or jar, several handfuls at a time, pressing down to remove air pockets. You should see some brine on top of the mixture when you press. Top with a grape leaf or parchment paper and weight if you have one.

4. Follow the instructions for your fermentation vessel. For a jar, if using the burping method (page 44) make sure there is little headspace and seal lid tightly. Burp daily or as needed. Alternatively, top the ferment with a quart-size ziplock bag. Press the bag down onto the top of the ferment and then fill it with water and seal.

5. Set your fermentation vessel on a plate in a spot where you can keep an eye on it, out of direct sunlight, and let ferment for 4 to 14 days. Start taste-testing on day 4. You'll know the kohlrabi is ready when the color has muted and it tastes pleasingly sour.

6. When the kraut is ready, transfer to smaller jars, if necessary, and tamp down. Pour in any brine that's left. Tighten the lids, then store in the fridge. The kraut will keep, refrigerated, for 1 year.

Note: For another kohlrabi kraut, see Sauerrüben III (page 343).

Create Your Own Recipes

We like kohlrabi thinly sliced and fermented with all kinds of additions to create a salad. Try sliced Granny Smith apple, scallions, and chile peppers with a squeeze of lime.

Kirsten Writes

I was in town when my phone rang. Christopher nervously told me to call the deli where I had dropped off a 5-gallon bucket of kraut. "They say something's wrong. The flavor is great but the texture is strange."

I talked with the owner. He didn't want the kraut replaced. He just wanted us to know it was different, and wondered why. I talked about diversity in the local farmers' cabbages; varieties can make a difference, and so on. But the truth is, I really wasn't sure why. He wasn't too concerned, so I never went to look at it.

A few months passed. I wanted to bring something new to market and I knew we had a batch of kohlrabi kraut I'd been holding back. I couldn't find it. I still didn't make the connection. The epiphany came months later—I burst out laughing and said to Christopher, "Remember the strange-textured sauerkraut? It wasn't cabbage at all—it was kohlrabi."

LAMB'S-QUARTERS

A prolific plant, lamb's-quarters (*Chenopodium album*) can be found all through North America. Now cultivars of the foraged plant have been developed and can be found at the farmers' market. A distinguishing feature of this highly nutritious green is a grayish powder found beneath the young leaves that gives the greens a silver patina. This plant is similar to red orach and spinach; if you like these greens, you will probably enjoy lamb's-quarters.

YOUR RAW MATERIAL

As with dandelion, this green can be found in back alleys, empty lots, lawns, and your garden. Choose your harvest site away from roadways and landscapes treated with chemicals. As with many greens, the younger leaves early in the season are the most tender. A good rule of thumb is to harvest from plants that are less than a foot tall.

IN THE CROCK

Thyme for Lamb's-Quarters Kraut

yield: about 3 quarts (2.8 l)
technique used: Mastering Sauerkraut (page 61)

This kraut started out as a little experiment just to see how lamb's-quarters would behave in the crock—inquiring minds (like that of our farmer friend Mary, who had an abundant crop) wanted to know. We made the first batch and took it to market, where it sold out immediately. The next week and the week after, we had so many requests that we filled a crock, this time a big one.

2–3 heads (5–6 pounds/2.3–2.7 kg) cabbage
2–2½ tablespoons (34–43 g) unrefined salt
2 bundles (about 1 pound/454 g) lamb's-quarters, finely chopped
2 or 3 carrots, grated
1 red onion, thinly sliced
1 tablespoon (3 g) dried thyme or 2–3 tablespoons (5–7 g) fresh
1 teaspoon (1 g) dried tarragon or 1 tablespoon (2 g) fresh

1. Remove the coarse outer leaves of the cabbage. Rinse a few unblemished ones and set them aside. Rinse the rest of the cabbage in cold water. Quarter and core the cabbage, thinly slice or shred, and transfer to a large bowl.

2. Add about 2 tablespoons of the salt and, with your hands, massage it into the cabbage. The cabbage should begin weeping a brine. Add the lamb's-quarters, carrots, onion, thyme, and tarragon, and massage again. Then taste. You should be able to taste the salt without it being overwhelming. Add more salt if necessary.

3. Transfer the mixture to a crock or jar, a handful at a time, pressing down to remove air pockets. You should see some brine on top of the mixture when you press. If you don't, return the mixture to the bowl and massage again.

4. Top the mixture with the reserved outer cabbage leaves to keep everything submerged, pressing them down under the brine. Follow the instructions for your fermentation vessel. Add weight if you have it. For a jar, if using the burping method (page 44) make sure there is little headspace and seal lid tightly. Burp daily or as needed. Alternatively, top the ferment with a quart-size ziplock bag. Press the bag down onto the top of the ferment and then fill it with water and seal.

5. Set your fermentation vessel on a plate in a spot where you can keep an eye on it, out of direct sunlight, and let ferment for 4 to 14 days. Check regularly to make sure the kraut is submerged, pressing down, as needed, to bring the brine back to the surface. Start taste-testing on day 7. The kraut is ready when it has a pleasing acidic smell, the onion flavor has softened, and it tastes pickle-y, perhaps with an effervescent zing.

6. When the kraut is ready, transfer to smaller jars, if necessary, and tamp down. Pour in any brine that's left. Tighten the lids, then store in the fridge. The kraut will keep, refrigerated, for 1 year.

LEEKS

Leeks originated in the Mediterranean basin and are one of the oldest cultivated vegetables. Egyptian writings show leeks as a barter currency (along with oxen and beer). Despite their warm, dry beginnings, leeks are a cold-weather crop.

Over the years leeks have become one of our go-to vegetables. They are delicious and versatile and high in inulin. As is the case for other members of the onion tribe, any harsh pungency of the raw flavor is mellowed under fermentation.

YOUR RAW MATERIAL

Leeks available at the market are sizable and well developed, but you can eat them at any stage. The white shaft is more mildly flavored than the green, but both ferment well. The outer leaves are often tough or stringy and won't soften as much during the ferment. We use the greens in pastes or thinly sliced. They are also perfect for a pickling bed, or put in a stock. Use the largest outer leaves as ferment toppers, much in the same way you would use cabbage leaves.

As leeks grow, farmers pile soil around their bases to increase the length of the white part, and as a result soil often gets trapped between their layers. This can pose a challenge when preparing leeks. Remove any coarse outer leaves, and trim and discard the roots. Slice off the very darkest part of the stalk down to the light green portion, which is more tender. Slice the stalk in half lengthwise and rinse the layers of the leek under cold running water to remove the grit, taking care to rinse in between all the leaves.

Kirsten Writes

Several years ago our neighbor Tina and I grew a garden together. We both were determined to feed our families largely from this garden. It was a substantial undertaking, and she and I practically lived in the garden. When we were not tending it, we were in the kitchen preserving. Our jar count, pints and quarts, was already in triple digits halfway through the summer.

At one point, all the leeks needed to be harvested at once. We pushed an overflowing wheelbarrow full of leeks to the kitchen door. The question was, what does one do with so many leeks? We called the university extension service's food preservation hotline; they said jarring low-acid leeks would require cooking for 45 minutes in a pressure canner. That wouldn't do. Finally we sliced them, sautéed them in butter, and froze this "soup base" in usable portions. It ended up being a good use, although our freezers smelled like cooked leeks for months.

If only we had known to ferment them.

IN THE CROCK

Leek Paste

yield: about 1 quart (946 ml)
technique used: Pastes (page 76)

Leeks hold their flavor, so they make a versatile base to enhance soups, sauces, and salads. In fact, use this ferment as you would fresh leeks in any recipe.

> 1½ pounds (680 g) leeks, green parts included, cleaned and cut into 1-inch (2.5 cm) pieces
> 1 teaspoon (6 g) unrefined salt
> Grape leaves or parchment paper, to top the ferment

1. Put the leeks in a food processor and pulse until they are finely chopped. Sprinkle in the salt; the leeks will become juicy immediately. The brine will be thick.

2. Press the paste into an appropriately sized jar. More liquid will release as you press. If using the burping method (page 44), make sure there is little headspace, top with a round of parchment paper, and weight if you have one, then seal the lid tightly. Watch the lid for pressure building

up. With this recipe you may never need to burp or at most just once. Alternatively, top the paste with a quart-size ziplock bag. Press the bag down onto the top of the ferment, then fill it with water and seal.

3. Set your fermentation vessel on a counter, out of direct sunlight, and let ferment for 7 to 10 days. It's ready when the verdant green becomes dull yellow and the taste has softened from pungent to slightly sour.

4. To store, tamp down to make sure the ferment is submerged in its brine, press a small round of parchment paper directly on top, and seal the jar with its lid. This paste will keep, refrigerated, for at least 12 months.

Leek–Cracked Pepper Kraut

See photo on page 322

yield: about 2 quarts (1.9 l)
technique used: Mastering Sauerkraut (page 61)

While this kraut has the same comforting simplicity of plain cabbage sauerkraut, multifaceted layers of flavor bring it to a new level. It was a market favorite. The best part is that it's easy to make and versatile. For a beautiful yellow version, add the turmeric.

> 3 pounds (1.4 kg) green cabbage
> 1 pound (454 g) leeks, white and light green parts
> 1½–2 tablespoons (25–34 g) unrefined salt
> 1 teaspoon (3 g) cracked black pepper
> 1 tablespoon (6 g) fresh turmeric root, grated, or 1 teaspoon (2 g) ground (optional)

1. Remove the coarse outer leaves of the cabbage. Rinse a few unblemished ones and set aside. Rinse the rest of the cabbage in cold water. Quarter and core the cabbage, thinly slice or shred, and transfer to a large bowl. Trim and rinse the leeks, slice thinly, and transfer to the bowl with the cabbage.

2. Add 1½ tablespoons of the salt and, with your hands, massage it into the cabbage and leeks. Then taste. You should be able to taste the salt without it being overwhelming. Add more salt if necessary. The cabbage and leeks will soon look wet and limp, and liquid will pool. However, if you don't see much brine, let the mixture stand, covered, for 45 minutes, then massage again. When the vegetables are ready, add the black pepper and turmeric, if using.

3. Transfer the mixture to your fermentation vessel, a few handfuls at a time, pressing down to remove air pockets. You should see some brine on top of the mixture when you press. If you don't, return the mixture to the bowl and massage again.

4. Top the kraut with the reserved outer cabbage leaves to keep everything submerged, pressing them down under the brine. Add weight if you have it. Follow the instructions for your fermentation vessel. For a jar, if using the burping method (page 44) make sure there is little headspace and seal lid tightly. Burp daily or as needed. Alternatively, top the ferment with a quart-size ziplock bag. Press the bag down onto the top of the ferment and then fill it with water and seal.

5. Set your fermentation vessel on a plate in a spot where you can keep an eye on it, out of direct sunlight, and let ferment for 8 to 16 days.

Check regularly to make sure the kraut is submerged, pressing down, as needed, to bring the brine back to the surface. You'll know the kraut is ready when the colors become muted, the brine becomes cloudy, it has a pleasing acidic smell, and it tastes pickle-y, perhaps with an effervescent zing.

6. When the kraut is ready, transfer to smaller jars, if necessary, and tamp down. Pour in any brine that's left. Tighten the lids, then store in the fridge. The kraut will keep, refrigerated, for 1 year.

Leek-chi

yield: about 1 quart (946 ml)
Technique used: Relishes/Chutneys/Salsas/Salads (page 74)

This ferment, based on the kimchi triad of garlic, ginger, and chile, has a surprisingly mild quality. Its appearance is striking—it develops a remarkable yellow color that is pretty on the plate. Dollop this into a soup right before serving, or inside a grilled cheese sandwich for flavor and pizzazz!

Note: If you prefer a more sour ferment, add a teaspoon of sugar to the mixture before fermenting.

1½ pounds (680 g) leeks, white and light
    green parts
2 teaspoons (11 g) unrefined salt
2 large cloves garlic, minced
1 tablespoon (11 g) ginger, finely grated
1 tablespoon (9 g) sesame seeds, lightly
    toasted
1 teaspoon (1.5 g) dulse flakes
2 teaspoons (5 g) dried chile flakes (or to taste)
    Grape leaves or parchment paper, to top the
    ferment

1. Slice the leeks thinly and place in a large bowl. Sprinkle in the salt, toss to coat, then massage the leeks by hand or press with a tamper for about a minute to begin the brine development. Add the rest of the ingredients and mix in to distribute evenly.

2. Transfer the mixture to your fermentation vessel, a handful at a time, pressing down to remove air pockets as you go.

3. Place grape leaves or parchment paper on top, and weight if you have it. Follow the instructions for your fermentation vessel. For a jar, if using the burping method (page 44) make sure there is little headspace and seal lid tightly. Burp daily or as needed. Alternatively, top the ferment with a quart-size ziplock bag. Press the bag down onto the top of the ferment and then fill it with water and seal.

4. Set your fermentation vessel on a plate in a spot where you can keep an eye on it, out of direct sunlight, and let ferment for 8 to 16 days. The ferment is ready when the leeks change from a verdant green to a yellow-green, their pungency softens, and the flavor becomes slightly sour.

5. To store, transfer to smaller jars, if necessary, and tamp down to make sure the leeks are submerged in the brine. Tighten the lids and set in the refrigerator, where the ferment will keep for 1 year.

LEEK FUN FACT

The tyrannical Roman emperor Nero loved leeks, and he believed they'd improve his singing voice. He ate them in soups and prepared in oil, and was called by some Porophagus, the Leek Eater.

RAMPS

The ramp (*Allium tricoccum*), also called a spring onion or a wild leek, is a forest dweller, its green leaves sprouting from its bulb in spring, before the canopy shades the ground. In the Appalachian Mountains, folk medicine claims ramp's power to ward off winter ills. Ramps, like their cousins in the cultivated onion family, are rich in vitamins and minerals.

Onions are important to culinary traditions worldwide, and they were among the first foods recognized for their medicinal value. The onion's reputation spans continents, cultures, and even classes. In some places and times, it was a food to be worshipped, as in ancient Egypt, while in other places and times it was considered a food for the poor.

Ramps appear early in the spring in eastern North America, from Georgia to Quebec. As one of the first fresh green foods to appear, they are a welcome sign and taste of spring. They are also very popular and should be harvested carefully, as the populations have diminished in recent years. No need to harvest the whole bulb; this can affect the patch long term. It's better to harvest the green tops and to leave the roots in place. This method does not kill the plant and provides delicious flavor and wild nutrients in your ferment.

PRESERVED CITRUS,
page 205

HONEY-FERMENTED GARLIC,
page 241

HONEY-FERMENTED GINGER,
page 240

LEMON KIMCHI,
page 187

BRINE-CURED OLIVES,
page 282

UMEBOSHI, *page 300*

FERMENTED TOMATO KETCHUP, *page 337*

SOUR EGGPLANT, *page 223*

WATERMELON RIND–ZUCCHINI SALSA, *page 344*

CHARRED CABBAGE SAUERKRAUT, *page 174*

MANGO, GREEN AND UNRIPE

It is believed that mangoes originated in India, which is still the largest producer and consumer of this fruit. Unripened mango is used very much like a vegetable in much of Asia, notably India and Southeast Asia. Julienned green mango is used both to add tart flavor to salads and other dishes and to tenderize meat. In India, it is often pickled in wonderful condiments. Not all varieties are tasty green; some have bland flavor, while others are too starchy or too tart.

> ### FERMENTISTA'S TIP
>
> **Temperate Zone, No Green Mangoes?**
> *We have had success fermenting unripe peaches. And unripe white strawberries are fun and delicious to pickle and make condiments with.*

YOUR RAW MATERIAL

Unripe mangoes are higher in both vitamin C and gut-healthy fiber than their ripened counterpart. Depending on where you are, green mangoes may be difficult to find. If you have access to unripe, green mangoes, they ferment beautifully.

For fermenting, you'll want to select very hard, unripe green mangoes. Green in this case is double green—both unripe and of a green variety. Green mangoes have a firm texture and enchanting tart flavor. They are significantly less sweet than other varieties of mango, are available earliest in the season, and maintain their crunch throughout all stages of ripeness. The best ones to use would be the ones that are sweet when green, such as those in the Thai family:

Mamuang Kiew Sa Wei, Falan, Okrung, Thong Dam (a.k.a. Black Gold), or Nam Doc Mai—a sour green mango with good crunch, which makes it an excellent choice.

The downside of using unripe mangoes is that they can be difficult to peel. Once peeled they can be grated, julienned, sliced, or even diced or chunked. This gives you a lot of options to make green mango ferments.

IN THE CROCK

Lemongrass Green Mango Pickles

by Sarah Arrazola, St. Pete Ferments

yield: about 1 quart (946 ml)
technique used: Relishes/Chutneys/Salsas/Salads (page 74)

These pickles are addictive. They maintain so much of their tropical mango deliciousness but with a sour bite. The fresh lemongrass is citrusy and aromatic, perfectly fragrant, and it complements the taste of the sour mango.

Using the unripe varieties of green mangoes, or as close to unripe as possible, minimizes sugar development within the fruit in order to favor lacto-fermentation. If you cannot find a green variety of mango, just look for a very unripe, sour, and crunchy (versus sweet and soft or stringy) one. Haden or Kent varieties work well.

2.2 pounds (1 kg) green mango
1¾ tablespoons (30 g) unrefined sea salt
2 stalks (about 20 g) lemongrass, just the bases

1. Rinse the mangoes and remove any blemishes. With a vegetable peeler or knife, remove the skin from all the fruit.

2. Julienne the fruit. Avoid any parts of the mango that appear too ripe (orange-ish in color), as they will have too much sugar. Place the cut mangoes in a large bowl.

3. Add the salt. (I like at least a 3 percent salinity ratio by weight. The higher salinity keeps better control of the rate of fermentation of this tropical fruit.) Mix the mangoes with the salt. The mixture will create its own brine, much like making sauerkraut.

4. Once the mango pieces release a good amount of brine and the liquid drips easily, press them into your fermentation vessel. Layer in the lemongrass stalks, cut lengthwise, as you go.

5. Place a weight on top of the mangoes, covering all the surfaces, and seal. Follow the instructions for your fermentation vessel. For a jar, if using the burping method (page 44) make sure there is little headspace and seal lid tightly. Burp daily or as needed. Alternatively, top the ferment with a quart-size ziplock bag. Press the bag down onto the top of the ferment and then fill it with water and seal.

6. Ferment this for about 3 days at room temperature (76°F/24°C to 78°F/26°C in Florida), then move it to the fridge and let ferment for another 2 weeks.

7. Store in the refrigerator. The flavor stays consistent for about 6 months.

FERMENTISTA'S TIP

A high salt ratio helps slow fermentation in Sarah's subtropical climate, which makes a big difference in final texture and flavor. Another warm-weather technique is to start the fermentation in a warm environment and then move it to a refrigerator for the rest of the fermentation time.

Create Your Own Recipes

» Condiments such as achar and chutney are traditionally made with green mango. *Usha's Pickle Digest: The Perfect Pickle Recipe Book* by Usha R. Prabakaran will inspire your experiments for days.

» Thai salads that include unripe mango are another place to find inspiration.

» Unripe mango is delicious added to kimchi.

» Don't forget about pickling beds. Bury thick slices or cubes in a miso or nuka pot.

Sarah Arrazola: Creating Floridian Flavors

We love asking people about their fermentation creation story. For some, it was a big moment of rebellion or discovery. For Sarah Arrazola, owner of St. Pete Ferments in St. Petersburg, Florida, it was that kombucha was becoming an expensive habit. She and her mom got a SCOBY and began making their own. The lovely part of Sarah's story is that she didn't see fermentation as something unusual; it was just another culinary preparation. She'd been cooking with her family since she was 7. She never researched her fermentation projects; she just made them. It wasn't until she was staying at an Airbnb and the host said, "Oh, you ferment, too," that Sarah said, "I guess." After that realization, she began to try fermenting everything. She says she is inspired in all that she does by her Latinx heritage, her Southern roots, and the cultural exchanges unique to Florida.

Jackfruit Kimchi
We met Sarah in 2017 at the first Florida Fermentation Festival, an event she cofounded with Jackie Vitale at the then Ground Floor Farm. We were immediately blown away by all the flavors Jackie and Sarah shared with us using the fruit of south Florida. Jackie pulled out a jar of Chocolate Cranberry Mole, a recipe from our *Fiery Ferments* book that she'd made with roselle (*Hibiscus sabdariffa*). We found this particularly exciting, not only for the flavor it produced but also because it was a very real example of how recipes and ideas can and should be adjusted to use the ingredients growing in one's backyard.

We fell in love with Sarah's jackfruit kimchi, one of St. Pete's first ferments. There is always something growing in south Florida, Sarah says, and she thinks it is important to use that local abundance and to support farmers. As a small producer starting out, who was influenced by permaculture, Sarah asked farmers what they grew and couldn't get rid of. The answer: jackfruit! This was the beginning of her uniquely subtropical flavors. Many of the fruits, although not native to Florida, are grown there and do well. "Mangoes are so prolific, they should be on the Florida license plate, not oranges," Sarah says.

Space of Collaboration
Sarah finds it exciting that she's built strong relationships with her customers and the farmers. Sometimes, people's ideas about what can and cannot grow on Florida's Gulf Coast are challenged. Brassicas are a crop that was once thought impossible to grow there due to the heat and humidity. But it can be cultivated successfully with the right variety, the right time of year, and the right (if unconventional) sustainable farming techniques. One example is Tokyo bekana—an Asian cabbage that is like a cross between bok choy, napa cabbage, and lettuce—which can be grown in the warmer climate as both a substitute for lettuce and a great kimchi. It is within this space of collaboration with the farmers, the climate, the fruit, and flavor that St. Pete's delicious krauts, kimchis, and kombuchas grow.

MUSHROOMS

Mushrooms ferment better when dried. Their deep, fragrant, earthy flavor is intensified by dehydration, which helps the aroma stand up to fermentation and helps retain the integrity of the mushroom's texture. Plus, dried mushrooms are readily available year-round. There's no need to rehydrate mushrooms before adding them to a ferment—rehydration happens in the brine and all the flavor will stay put. Adding mushrooms to vegetable ferments builds extra umami, which is especially nice for plant-based eating.

If you are fermenting fresh mushrooms, salt and cook them first in case they are a variety that shouldn't be eaten raw due to mycotoxins, which are denatured by cooking. There is a long and strong mushroom fermentation tradition in Russia and Eastern Europe, yet little is still known about the science behind it. Personally, we cannot wait to learn more. We recommend finding Slavic sources for learning more techniques.

YOUR RAW MATERIAL

The most widely available dried varieties are shiitake, porcini, and chanterelles. If you cannot find shiitakes in your regular market, check an Asian market. Look for shiitakes with thick, ridged caps and white cracks. These are grade-A mushrooms, sometimes called *hana*. They are more flavorful than the thinner, brown-capped shiitakes. Look for chanterelles and porcini in specialty markets. Chanterelles have a gold-apricot color that befits their fruity flavor. Porcinis are large and meaty mushrooms that are generally sliced before they are dried.

Of course, there is always the option of dehydrating your own mushrooms. Whether you stumbled across a seasonal deal at the market or have wildcrafted your own, drying mushrooms ensures that you will have high-quality mushrooms whenever you want them.

WILD MUSHROOMS

There's a lot to learn about the various types of mushrooms, especially when wildcrafting. We recommend taking a class in your local area to learn the particulars—the types available and in which season, and how to make sure you have the right mushroom. Always play it safe and be sure of what you are harvesting.

IN THE PICKLE JAR

Pickled Shiitake

See photo on page 227

yield: about 1 quart (946 ml)
technique used: Mastering Brine Pickling (page 101)

These pickles are made with shiitake mushrooms, but other dried mushrooms can be substituted. For brine pickling, you want whole mushrooms. Sliced, crushed, or shriveled mushrooms work well as additions to other ferments but they don't brine as well on their own. The flavor will deepen over time. Sour cherry, oak, and horseradish leaves are traditional in Eastern European ferments, so while they are great on any pickle, we highlight them here.

2 cups (108 g) dried shiitake mushrooms
1 quart (946 ml) unchlorinated water
1 tablespoon (17 g) unrefined salt
2 or 3 cloves garlic
1 teaspoon (2 g) peppercorns
2 or 3 whole dried red chiles
1 bay leaf
Large leaves (grape, sour cherry, oak, or horseradish) or parchment paper, to top the ferment

1. Place the dried mushrooms in a bowl with the water and set aside for 2 to 3 hours. The mushrooms will plump and the liquid will take on a translucent, earthy amber color. This is the liquid for the pickling brine. Pour the liquid through a fine sieve into a large bowl, reserving the mushrooms. Stir the salt into the liquid to create the brine.

2. Inspect the mushroom stems: Remove any that are woody. Pack the mushrooms, alternating with the garlic, peppercorns, chiles, and bay leaf, into a quart jar. Pour in enough brine to cover.

3. Put any leaves or a piece of parchment paper, if using, on top to keep the mushrooms from bobbing up. *Note:* Because mushrooms are soft, these tannin-rich leaves won't crisp the mushrooms but will help keep them somewhat firm. If using the burping method (page 44) make sure there is little headspace and seal lid tightly. Burp daily or as needed.

4. Set the jar on a plate in a spot where you can keep an eye on it, out of direct sunlight, and let ferment for 7 to 10 days. During the fermentation period, monitor the brine level and top off with the reserved brine, if needed, to cover. You will see the dark brine begin to get cloudy. Start taste-testing on day 7. You'll know it's ready when the brine tastes acidic and the mushrooms taste as if they've been marinated.

5. When they're ready, make sure the mushrooms are submerged in the brine, screw on the lid, and store in the fridge, where they will keep for 3 months.

Kirsten Writes

Ilona was one of the first neighbors we met when we moved to our farm. She shared her time and her culture with unparalleled enthusiasm. Three times a week our two oldest sons, 9 and 6, would traipse across the narrow valley and spend the morning with Ilona learning Russian and cooking Ukrainian meals. In payment, the boys would bring the morning's fresh goat milk, warm and sweet. Sometimes I would arrive later with our two younger children to eat the lunch they'd prepared, and I'd giggle at the sight of my boys with white kerchiefs fastened around their heads and white aprons around their waists—that would never have flown at home.

Ilona gave me a book, *The Art of Russian Cuisine* by Anne Volokh, that is still one of my favorite cookbooks. Ms. Volokh shares a delightful traditional method of fermenting mushrooms by layering them in salt in an oak barrel.

MUSTARD GREENS AND SEEDS

It's thought that people began consuming mustard in the Himalayan region of India some 5,000 years ago. The plant still plays a major role in the regional cuisine, especially in the area of the Punjab. The greens have spread to the cuisines of Italy, China, Japan, and Korea, and in more recent history Africa and the American South. In Italy they're braised with garlic; in Asia they're often pickled; and in the South they're often slow-cooked with ham hocks.

Mustard (*Brassica juncea*) is a root-to-tip food plant; its leaves, stems, seeds, flowers, and roots are edible. There are many types of mustards, in all shapes and sizes. Some have showy leaves, such as curly mustards, giant red, or mizuna. Others have thick petioles (leaf stalks) and look a little like napa cabbage or mustard cabbage (*gai choy*). Head mustard (Cantonese: *dai gai choy*, "big mustard greens") looks something like a big-leaved pak choi and is great for fermenting, while *tsatsai* mustard has a knobby, swollen stem that is used in making Sichuan *zha cai* pickles (see page 270). Stay tuned; cultivars specifically bred for their root are becoming more common.

Mustard seeds are used around the globe for their flavor, but also for their preservative qualities. Early on, our ancestors discovered that foods prepared with mustard seeds lasted longer, and so these seeds have a long history of being added to pickled foods to prolong their storage. Even the Latin name for prepared mustard (the condiment made from mustard seed), *mustum ardens*, "burning fire," originated in a roundabout way with fermentation—in this case, wine. For their mustard, ancient Romans mixed ground mustard seeds with must—the juice, skin, and seeds pressed from grapes that were beginning to ferment as they converted to wine.

Mustard seed on its own is a preservative, so it doesn't need to go through the lactic acid fermentation process in order to be preserved. In fact, many traditional pickles and chutneys contained mustard seed for this reason. However, as we've noted throughout, fermentation imbues our foods with a dynamic live-food quality. Lacto-fermentation transforms mustard seeds, a bit of water, vinegar, and perhaps some vegetables or herbs into a healthy, vital, shelf-stable convenience food. And for those who value beauty, the ugly, plastic yellow squeeze bottle makes way for a beautiful jar of vibrant gold.

Waste Not

When you reach the bottom of a jar of pickles, you will be left with the brine, the seeds and spices, and perhaps a clove or two of mellow garlic. Save the brine (to make Brine Crackers, page 369), and for a quick and tasty condiment, drop the spices and garlic into a blender with a splash of the brine and process to a paste consistency. (Remove any stems and anything else woody first.)

YOUR RAW MATERIAL

You'll find many varieties of mustard greens in the produce section of the supermarket or at a farmers' market. We use them all. Mustard greens have the best flavor and mouthfeel when harvested young—they're plump, crisp, and deep green. They have a stimulating, pepper-like flavor when raw that mellows with fermentation.

You will see mustard seeds categorized in four colors: yellow, white, black, and brown. "Yellow" and "white" seeds are the same and the most common. They are light tan and slightly larger than the other colors. When you bite into them, the preliminary taste is sweetness, which is then followed by pleasant warmth.

Black mustard seed is a bit spicier and less common (as it requires hand harvesting) than brown mustard seed, but these monikers are often used interchangeably despite the difference. When you chew darker seeds, you will first taste bitterness, trailed by an aromatic heat on your tongue. Many recipes for mustard mix dark and light seeds in order to provide complex flavors and to control heat levels.

IN THE PICKLE JAR

Bridal Pickles: Zha cai (榨菜)

In China's Sichuan province, lacto-fermented pickles are an important part of the culture and the cuisine. Traditionally, with the birth of a baby girl, her family put up *zha cai* in an earthen jar and continued every year until she married, when she would receive them as a gift; 12 to 15 pots indicated that the time had come.

Zha cai is a ferment made by salting the swollen green stem of a type of mustard, *Brassica juncea* var. *tsatsai*. The stem is lumpy and knobbed and looks a little like a green Jerusalem artichoke.

To make the ferment, the stem is salted and pressed to remove excess moisture. Then it is rubbed with chile paste and put into an earthen pot to ferment—for years.

Mara Jane King (profile, page 111), whose *pao cai* (fermented vegetable) recipe appears on page 112, explained that in China, fermentation is a kaleidoscope of diversity, with versions and variations both regional and cultural. For example, in northern China, a *suan cai* (soured vegetable) ferment that is very similar to kimchi uses napa cabbage, while Taiwan-born fermentista Pao Yu Liu shared with us a *suan cai* recipe (page 272) that uses mustard greens instead.

Pao Yu Liu: Bringing Ferments from Taiwan to London

Pao Yu Liu and Kirsten began their conversation talking about how the worldwide fermentation community has come into itself since the first edition of this book came out in 2014. "Fermentation has changed," Pao said, "in the way it has become so creative. The creativity amazes me. Someone contacted me to write about 'what do I think about people taking over this type of fermentation?' I said what a wonderful thing it is as a technique for us to discover. There are no cultural boundaries. There is so much that can come out of this technique that is important. That's my opinion and I always feel a part of the community that is so open and genuine."

Just Food

Pao grew up in Taipei and has lived in London since she was 21. Although she grew up with fermented foods, they were just food—never a conversation piece. Pao didn't give *pao cai* (fermented vegetables) much thought other than she loved them. In London, she often bought *suan cai* (pickled cabbage or green mustard that is well loved in Taiwan and Asia), and she noticed that the label said, "Do not eat raw." This made her wonder, first, why, and second, whether she might make these ferments herself. After some research, she did just that: She made her own *suan cai*.

In villages, she knew, farmers would stand on the mustard greens to soften the stems and to break the fibers. "Apparently it makes a massive difference in terms of flavor," Pao said. "I didn't have any boots to do that, but I did make sure to really squeeze them here and there after a couple of days of them being weighed down to break the fibers." She stacked the salted, softened greens in a bucket and heavily weighted it. The next morning, she topped them with some rice-washing water. After a few weeks, the greens turned yellow and the bitterness was gone, but the yummy sourness and crunch remained.

What Feels Right

Pao loved the process and the flavors. She began her business, Pao Pop N Pickles, in London in 2017, selling small batches of fermented products at a local farmers' market. Her curiosity about fermentation abounds, and when she visits Taiwan she looks for people fermenting and begins asking them about their process—to the mortification of her children, she says. In Pao's fermentation practice, she told Kirsten, she makes delicious flavor by knowing the rules and working with what feels right and makes sense. In her business, she plans for ways to use everything: "Food waste, what food waste? Most everything can have another life." But also, she noted, "I do what I can, but I am not going to beat myself up for it." This struck us as an important message, as we all are doing the best that we can, and in that there is hope and beauty.

Three Fermented Greens (Suan Cai, Fu Cai, and Mei Gan Cai)

by Pao Yu Liu of Pao Pop N Pickles

Here we have three variations of the same greens undergoing the same initial fermentation but finishing with wildly different flavors and characteristics. This is a choose-your-own-adventure ferment. The fermentation process begins with hanging the greens until they are soft and become pliable enough to fold without breaking. Then they're rubbed with salt, with special concentration on the hard stems. This recipe calls for rice-washing water (water used to rinse rice before it is cooked) to give the lactic acid bacteria extra starch.

This process can be made with any amount of mustard greens. For every pound (454 g) of mustard greens, you will use 14–18 grams of salt to make a 3 to 4 percent salt ratio. See page 103 to make your own salt calculations.

> Mustard greens (choose the ones with big stems)
> Salt (3–4%)
> Rice-washing water to cover greens

Suan Cai 酸菜

1. Hang the mustard greens for a couple of days to soften the stems.

2. Once softened and partially dehydrated, rub them in the salt.

3. Stack the salted greens in a casserole, bucket, or other vessel for pressing (page 80) and weigh them down with another casserole or bucket and heavy books/stones on top. Let sit for 2 days.

4. Take out the greens and either stand on them with some clean wellie boots, or squeeze the stems to break the fibers.

5. Transfer the greens to a glass jar, press them down as much as you can, and cover with rice water.

6. Follow the instructions for your fermentation vessel. For a jar, if using the burping method (page 44) make sure there is little headspace and seal lid tightly. Burp daily or as needed. Alternatively, top the ferment with a quart-size ziplock bag. Press the bag down onto the top of the ferment and then fill it with water and seal.

7. The fermentation takes 2 to 4 weeks, depending on the climate. The greens will turn yellow, and they will be sour and salty.

8. When the greens are ready, continue further to make Fu Cai. Or, stop here and put them in an airtight container and store in the fridge, where they will keep for 12 months.

Fu Cai 福菜

1. After fermentation, sun-dry the greens for a day or two (turning every now and then) until they are 30 to 50 percent dehydrated. Head to step 2, or continue dehydrating and head to step 1 of Mei Gan Cai.

2. Tear the greens into long strips.

3. Squeeze and roll the greens and press into a clean, dry glass bottle using a chopstick. The bottle should be full.

4. Turn the bottle upside down to store to keep out the air and to prevent it from going moldy. It will keep for years.

Mei Gan Cai 梅乾菜

1. When the greens are around 80 percent dried (mostly dry to the touch but still soft), wrap them together into balls. After drying, the salt crystal can be seen on the green; this looks a little like mold but isn't.

2. Mei gan cai will continue to dry and age as time goes on. To store, keep in an airtight ziplock bag, vacuum sealed bag, or airtight jar. If you minimize air contact, it will last around 2 years.

Dua Cai Chua (Vietnamese Pickled Mustard Greens)

yield: about 2 quarts (1.9 l)
technique used: Mastering Brine Pickling (page 101)

This recipe calls for *gai choy*, an Asian mustard green. However, we rarely have access to *gai choy*, so we use curly mustard or some other member of the mustard gang. And we have to say, we love this ferment with any mustard. After a couple of weeks, the flavors truly become a magical mix of sour and crunch. The sugar contributes to the uniqueness of the sour, so don't leave it out.

- 1 head (2 pounds/907 g) gai choy or other mustard greens
- 2 or 3 large or 6 small shallots, or 1 red onion
- 2½–3 cups (591–710 ml) Basic Brine (1½ teaspoons/9 g unrefined salt per cup unchlorinated water)
- 1 tablespoon (12 g) palm sugar or brown sugar

1. Cut the end off the mustard, rinse the greens, and lay out in the sun to wilt for about an hour or on the counter overnight.

2. Strip the leaves from their stems. Cut the stems into 1-inch (2.5 cm) pieces. Roughly chop the leaves. Thinly slice the shallots.

3. In your fermentation vessel, arrange a layer of the mustard greens and stems, then a thin layer of the shallots, and repeat until the vessel is full. Make Basic Brine (page 102) and add the sugar. Pour in enough brine to cover the vegetables completely. Reserve any leftover brine in the fridge (it will keep for 1 week; discard thereafter).

4. Set your fermentation vessel on a plate in a spot where you can keep an eye on it, out of direct sunlight, and let ferment for 5 to 20 days. As the greens ferment, they begin to turn yellowish and the brine becomes cloudy; this is when you can start to taste-test. They're ready after a few days but continue to become more and more interesting and delicious as they ferment.

5. Store in the refrigerator, where the greens will keep for 6 months.

Sour Mustard Greens, Myanmar-Style

When we were in Myanmar, we saw many variations of fermented mustard greens (*mohn nyin ywet*), both in the markets and on our plates in restaurants. We came across big bowls of fermenting mustard greens in brine yellowed with turmeric and spiced with chile peppers, ginger, or both. We saw salted greens packed into jars, and greens that had been salted, fermented, shaped into little round coils, and left to dry in the sun outside homes in Pindaya, a town in Shan State, where they are called *pak som*. These same coiled bundles appeared in the soups we were served, softening in the broth to add both texture and flavor.

In the markets, we often came across a preserved vegetable medley called *mohn nyin tijn*. The name literally means "sour mustard greens" but is a catchall term that refers to a great number of pickled or fermented vegetables. The most common variety is based on mustard greens and often contains carrots, leeks, radish, ginger, and garlic chives along with glutinous rice, rice wine, and hot chiles.

Bavarian-Style Sweet Mustard

See photo on page 188

yield: about 1½ cups
technique used: Pastes (page 76)

This mild mustard is smooth and refined yet retains a rustic heartiness. This version is not quite as sweet as its commercial counterpart; feel free to add more sugar to suit your palate. The onion mellows with fermentation and is a subtle base. Be sure to allow time for the spices to infuse in the water.

Sugar is added after the initial curing period because otherwise the microbes will convert it to sour lactic acid. The vinegar will help ensure the sugar's sweetness stays, but it must be added after fermentation.

½ teaspoon (1 g) whole cloves
½ teaspoon (1 g) whole allspice
1 cup (237 ml) unchlorinated water
⅜ cup (54 g) white mustard seeds
2 tablespoons (18 g) brown mustard seeds
½ large yellow or sweet onion, chopped
2 teaspoons (11 g) unrefined salt

AFTER FERMENTATION

2 tablespoons (24 g) brown sugar or raw honey
1 teaspoon (5 ml) raw apple cider vinegar, or to taste

1. Place the cloves and allspice in a saucepan with the water. Bring to a boil, then remove from the heat and let cool.

2. When the water is cool, strain out the spices. Pour the spice-infused water into a blender and add the white and brown mustard seeds, onion, and salt. Blend until smooth. As the mustard seeds break down, they act as a thickening agent. The mixture will be creamy at first; keep blending until it becomes a thick paste and the onion is completely incorporated.

3. Ladle the paste into a pint jar, pressing out any air pockets as you go. When it is all in, you may need to work out any remaining air pockets with a butter knife. Place the lid on the jar and tighten.

4. Set the jar on your counter and let ferment for 3 to 4 days.

5. After this curing time, open the lid (it may pop slightly as the CO_2 is released) and stir in the brown sugar and vinegar, if using. It will take a little while for the sugar crystals to melt into the mustard, at which point stir again. Now the mustard is ready to serve.

6. Store the mustard in the refrigerator, where it will keep for 6 months.

Fermented Carrot Achar (Gajar Ka Achar)

See photo on page 188

yield: about 3 cups (710 ml)
technique used: Relishes/Chutneys/Salsas/Salads (page 74)

Achars, originating in the Himalayan pickling tradition, are widespread on the Indian subcontinent and made with innumerable vegetables and fruits. These pickles are very different from the brine-drenched ferments that most folks are familiar with. In fact, they sit in the sun, fermenting in a fairly dry mix of spices, ground mustard, and mustard oil. The sun does what the brine does in briny ferments—makes the environment inhospitable to mold and yeasts, in this case by destroying them with UV light.

Achar fermentation traditionally uses mustard oil, which has wonderful preservative qualities and flavor but is often hard to find. Olive oil is a suitable substitute. In this recipe, the ground spices, sesame, and oil come together with an almost pesto-like consistency, a counterbalance to the carrots' crunch. In summer, we like to add a handful of Lemon Gem marigold flowers for a delightful floral quality.

- 1 pound (450 g) carrots, julienned
- 6 green jalapeño or serrano peppers, julienned
- 1 (2- to 3-inch/5–8 cm/13–20 g) piece fresh ginger, finely grated
- 2 tablespoons (45 g) tamarind pulp, seeds removed
- 1½ teaspoons (9 g) unrefined salt
- 1 tablespoon (9 g) sesame seeds
- 3 tablespoons (27 g) mustard seeds, toasted
- 1 teaspoon (4 g) fenugreek seeds, lightly toasted
- ½ teaspoon (1 g) ground Szechuan pepper
- ½ tablespoon (3 g) whole black peppercorns
- 5 tablespoons (74 ml) olive oil

1. Combine the carrots, jalapeño, ginger, tamarind pulp, and salt in a big bowl. Massage with your hands to mix and disperse the tamarind. Cover the bowl and set aside to rest for 8 hours or overnight. This begins the fermentation.

2. Grind the sesame seeds, mustard seeds, fenugreek seeds, Szechuan pepper, and black peppercorns in a spice grinder. Add to the bowl, along with 2 tablespoons of the oil, and stir well.

3. Pack the mixture into an appropriately sized jar. Pour another 3 tablespoons of the oil over the top of the mixture, then tighten the lid.

4. Set the jar in a sunny window to ferment for 7 to 14 days. If pressure builds under the lid, open briefly to burp. The achar will taste pickle-y and sour when it is ready.

5. Store in the refrigerator, where it will keep for about 1 year.

VARIATION
Key Lime Achar

In our home, this condiment is brought out for special meals. It is pungent, sour, bitter, and all the things—so delicious, but not for the faint of palate.

Follow the recipe for carrot achar, above, but omit the carrots and tamarind and add 1 pound (450 g) of Key limes, deseeded. Trim off the stem and blossom ends and thinly slice the limes crosswise. There's no need to let this one sit overnight—when everything is mixed together, pack it in a jar and ferment as instructed.

Yellow Mustard

yield: about 1 cup (237 ml)
technique used: Pastes (page 76)

Turns out this classic American condiment is relatively new to the family of prepared mustards. It was introduced in 1904 at the St. Louis World's Fair.

This homemade version has more body and depth of flavor than its commercial counterparts because the seeds aren't run through a fine sieve. Interestingly, in our experiments, the addition of fresh turmeric root (vs. powdered) brought it closest to the bottled flavor.

Vinegar should be added only after the fermentation. If introduced too early, it will stunt the development of the lactic acid. Added at the right time, once some fermentation has taken place, it knocks back the lactic acid bacteria and stabilizes the ferment, which is especially key if you want to add sweetener.

Note: To make this mustard milder, use warm or hot water in the blender when grinding. For a fun flavor variation, use any leftover fermented brine in place of the water; leave out the salt, adding it to taste after blending.

¼ cup (36 g) white mustard seeds
¼ cup (36 g) brown mustard seeds
1 tablespoon (11 g) fresh turmeric root, grated or pulsed to a paste
2 teaspoons (11 g) unrefined salt
1 cup (237 ml) unchlorinated water

AFTER FERMENTATION
¼ cup (59 ml) raw apple cider vinegar
Sweetener, such as raw honey, to taste (optional)

1. Combine the white and brown mustard seeds, turmeric, salt, and water in a blender. Blend until the mixture reaches a paste consistency.

2. Ladle your mustard into a pint jar, pressing out any air pockets as you go. When it is all in the jar, you may need to work out any remaining pockets with a butter knife. Place the lid on the jar and tighten.

3. Set the jar on your counter and let ferment for 3 days.

4. After this curing time, open the lid (it may pop slightly as the CO_2 is released) and stir in the vinegar and sweetener, if using. Your mustard is ready to serve.

5. Store the mustard in the refrigerator, where it will keep for 6 months.

NETTLES

Fresh wild nettles can be combined with other vegetables in any ferment. This herb (or green; it's both) is so nutritionally valuable that it's worth using even dried leaves if they're available.

YOUR RAW MATERIAL

If you are wildcrafting nettles for kraut, they are best in the spring before they have begun to flower. It is a natural antihistamine that is available during the season when many of us need it most. Cut the tops early and they will get bushier. Later, leave plenty to produce seeds; work with whatever you can harvest without depleting the supply.

Nettles have a dry rustling quality, like crinoline petticoats, when you are chopping them and then massaging them into kraut. But be sure to wear gloves when working with them; they will sting.

IN THE CROCK
Nettle Kraut

yield: about 2 quarts (1.9 l)
technique used: Mastering Sauerkraut (page 61)

The nettle quantity in the recipe can be variable. Because the leaves reduce in volume so drastically, whether you use 1 cup or 3 cups will not make a big difference in the final quantity of kraut. And whether you use a large or small dose of these healthy greens, the nettles add pleasant flavor that does not overwhelm.

- **1–2 heads (3 pounds/1.4 kg) cabbage**
- **2 cups (more or less; about 60 g) chopped and lightly packed fresh nettles, or ½ cup (10 g) dried**
- **1 sweet onion (or a bundle of spring onions with the greens), thinly sliced**
- **1–1½ tablespoons (17–25 g) unrefined salt**
- **6 cloves garlic, minced**

Follow the recipe for Naked Kraut (page 173), shredding the cabbage and combining it with the chopped nettles, onion, and salt. When the cabbage is glistening and you have a small pool of liquid in the bottom of the bowl, mix in the garlic.

OKAHIJIKI GREENS (SALTWORT)

How could you not order one packet each of saltwort, sneezewort, motherwort, and Saint-John's-wort, plus a sample of mad-dog skullcap, which the text said was once a folk remedy for rabies? At a buck a pop, how could you go wrong?
—KRISTIN KIMBALL, *THE DIRTY LIFE: A MEMOIR OF FARMING, FOOD, AND LOVE*, 2010

This succulent green, a member of the goosefoot family, hails from Japan, where it adapted to soils with high levels of salt, as in salt marshes, and is one of that region's oldest vegetables.

In the spirit of diversifying your diet, here are some reasons to try okahijiki: It's rich in laminin, a protein necessary to the health of virtually every type of cell. It also boasts vitamins A and K, calcium, potassium, and iron.

YOUR RAW MATERIAL
Despite its name, saltwort isn't salty. Its name, *okahijiki*, translates to "land seaweed." Nor is it rubbery, like ocean seaweed, or fibrous and dry, which is how it feels to the touch.

Instead, okahijiki is juicy and crisp, with a flavor that hints of mustard. Although these nutrient-dense greens are popular in Japan, it's possible you've never heard of them. You may have a chance of finding them at an Asian market or farmers' market, but you may have to sweet-talk your favorite farmer into trying a small bed of it. Otherwise, go online and find a company that sells the seeds and then grow them yourself. They grow as easily as (tumble)weeds (see page 278).

IN THE CROCK

Okahijiki Kraut

yield: about 2 quarts (473 ml)
technique used: Mastering Sauerkraut (page 61)

This kraut makes a great salad alongside sushi. Shiso leaves (see page 325) add a depth of flavor, but if you can't find them, this kraut is still delicious.

- 1–2 heads cabbage
- 1–2 cups (50–100 g) chopped okahijiki greens
- 1 cup (116 g) thinly sliced daikon radish
- A handful (3 g) fresh or fermented shiso leaves, chopped
- 1 tablespoon (7 g) dried hijiki seaweed (optional)
- 1–2 tablespoons (17–34 g) unrefined salt

Follow the recipe for Naked Kraut (page 173), shredding the cabbage and combining it with the okahijiki, daikon, shiso, hijiki (if using), and salt.

WHEN THE GOING GETS TOUGH . . . THE TOUGH FERMENT!

Okahijiki is a cousin to tumbleweed, which is, perhaps surprisingly, also edible. In fact, in the Dust Bowl era of the 1930s, when the American prairies were parched beyond imagination, tumbleweeds became a valuable food source. At first tumbleweeds, also called Russian thistle, were fermented in salt simply as silage for animals, but after years of drought, tumbleweed kraut became food for humans. Timothy Egan writes in *The Worst Hard Time* (2006), "Ezra and Goldie Lowery came up with the idea to can thistles in brine . . . they were good for you. High in iron and chlorophyll. Cimarron County declared a Russian Thistle Week, with county officials urging people who were on relief to get out to the fields and help folks harvest tumbleweeds."

OKRA

Okra, a member of the mallow family, has its origins in Ethiopia, Sudan, and the Nile River region. It's popular in the cuisines of western and northern Africa, the Middle East, and India. It came to the Americas along with enslaved Africans and took hold in the warmer climates. You'll find it in a variety of regional Southern stews as a thickener. In much of the English-speaking world, okra is known as lady's fingers.

Christopher Writes

My grandparents lived on a small farm just a few miles outside our town, but it seemed like the boonies to me. Grandpa Shockey had retired from the local Coca-Cola bottling plant after 50 years. That's right, he worked the same job his whole life. When they retired, Grandpa focused on his big garden, which was more than an acre, and grew everything, including okra. For me, okra fell into the category of vegetables that are fine as long as they are breaded and fried within an inch of their lives. I would help Grandpa pick "a mess" of okra and then run it in to Grandma in the late morning so that she could start it soaking in buttermilk from the neighbor. By lunch, the heat and humidity of a Missouri summer would force Grandpa and me inside the small farmhouse, where Grandma would have a pile of fried okra draining on paper towels.

YOUR RAW MATERIAL

Select okra pods that are bright green and hefty—2 to 3 inches long. The fruit becomes fibrous and woody as it ripens (after all, okra belongs to the same family as jute and cotton). Stay away from pods that look dry or have blemishes or black spots. Make your pickles soon after you bring home the okra; even in the fridge, they start to degrade in a day or two.

IN THE PICKLE JAR

Curried Okra Pickles

yield: about 1 quart (946 ml)
technique used: Mastering Brine Pickling (page 101)

The curry powder gives this brine a unique yellow, cloudy quality. When the pickles are all gone, use the leftover brine to make delicious crackers (page 369).

1	**pound (454 g) whole okra pods (or enough to fill a quart jar)**
2	**cloves garlic**
1	**teaspoon (2 g) coriander seeds**
1	**teaspoon (1 g) cumin seeds**
1	**teaspoon (2 g) peppercorns**
4 or 5	**dried tomatoes**
½	**red onion, cut lengthwise into a few wedges**
1–2	**teaspoons (2–4 g) curry powder (for a homemade version, see page 165)**
1	**quart (946 ml) High Brine (3 tablespoons/ 50.4 g unrefined salt per quart unchlorinated water)**
1 or 2	**grape leaves or parchment paper, to top the ferment (optional)**

1. Trim most of the stem off each okra pod, leaving just enough to keep the pod closed. Put garlic, coriander, cumin, and peppercorns in the bottom of a jar, then arrange the okra, dried tomatoes, and onion on top.

2. Stir the curry powder into the brine (this prevents the powder from lumping), then pour it into the jar. Make sure everything is submerged. Store any leftover brine in the fridge (it will keep for 1 week; discard thereafter or dry out and reclaim salt and make a new batch, if needed).

3. Top the jar with grape leaves, if you have them, or a piece of parchment paper and for extra security, you can wedge toothpicks in an X over everything to keep things submerged. If using the burping method (page 44) make sure there is little headspace and seal lid tightly. Burp daily or as needed.

4. Set the jar on a plate in a spot where you can keep an eye on it, out of direct sunlight, and let ferment for 7 to 14 days. During the fermentation period, monitor the brine level and top off with the reserved brine, if needed, to cover. You'll know the okra is ready when the green is muted, the brine is cloudy, the ferment has a pleasing acidic smell, and the okra tastes pickle-y, perhaps with an effervescent zing.

5. When the okra is ready, top off with brine, if needed, screw on the lid, and store in the fridge. The next day, check to be sure the pickles are still submerged, topping off with more brine, if necessary. These will keep, refrigerated, for 6 months.

FERMENTED CARROT STICKS, *page 194*

TOMATILLO SALSA, *page 330*

HOT SMOKY SPROUTS, *page 169*

BURDOCK-CARROT KIMCHI, *page 172*

JUNIPER-ONION KRAUT, *page 176*

CAULIKRAUT, *page 195*

PICKLED CRANBERRIES,
page 214

PRESERVED LIMES,
page 205

GARLIC PICKLE SLICES,
page 217

OLIVES

There is a highway rest area in the remote reaches of northern California olive country that is carved from the orchards that surround it, for it is dotted with old olive trees. While we have never driven there specifically to harvest, forage, or plunder (depending on which family member you ask) olives, we've been through at various points in olive season. The way Kirsten sees it, the olives can be picked and enjoyed or fall on the ground and be wasted. Whomever she is traveling with usually wants to go hide under the car, but despite that, they help pick because they want to get away faster, and secretly will love being olive-rich months later.

Olives can be harvested green and unripe or deep dark purple (nearly black) and ripe, or at any point in between. You are reading this correctly; Kirsten has a long season in which to feel fortunate at her favorite rest area. If you are in the northern hemisphere, in early September you can start looking to order fresh green olives online.

We've also seen olive trees in older city parks in the right climate zones, so pay attention. If you find yourself with fresh olives, cure them soon as they bruise quite easily. If you are picking, leave behind wrinkled or damaged fruit. Fruit with little circular light brown scars should also be left, as the scars are a sign that olive fly larvae are loitering inside.

YOUR RAW MATERIAL

Raw olives contain oleuropein, a compound so astringent that it makes you question how anyone ever figured out that olives are a gift from the gods and not poisonous. If you bite into a raw olive, your tongue and cheeks feel awful and the bitterness tells your mouth to spit it out. Enter curing. Most olives are cured in lye (sodium hydroxide) to rid them of the oleuropein. While the lye bath method has been used for thousands of years, its caustic nature can be off-putting. However, olive curing doesn't have to be complicated or feel dangerous. Let the microbes do the work! Lactic acid fermentation breaks down the oleuropein over time, leaving you with tasty olives—no lye baths required.

IN THE PICKLE JAR

Brine-Cured Olives

See photos on pages 244 and 262

yield: about 1 gallon (3.8 l)

technique used: Mastering Brine Pickling (page 101)

This cure can be used for olives at any stage of ripeness, from green to black. It takes time, and it's worth it. We have had to wait up to a year for the bitterness to go away. With a brine cure, we have found that you can fuss with it (read: change out the brine every month or so) or you can just leave it alone. In the end, the process happens deliciously, with or without much involvement from you. We suggest one change of the brine here, but feel free to experiment. **Important:** Keep this ferment in a cool spot; the olives will begin to soften at temperatures above 75°F/24°C.

One final note: It is not unusual for scum and mold to form at the top of the olives. If mold forms, follow the removal process outlined on page 415, or, if you prefer, just move the whole operation into a new vessel, adding fresh brine as needed to keep everything submerged. Anaerobic is always your friend.

4	pounds (1.8 kg) raw olives, ripe or unripe
1–3	whole heads garlic
4 or 5	sprigs fresh oregano (or rosemary, thyme, tarragon, or a combination)
	Dried red chile peppers (optional)
1	gallon (3.8 l) Soaking Brine (1 cup/ 269 g unrefined salt per gallon unchlorinated water)
	Grape leaves or parchment paper, to top the ferment

1. Rinse the olives in cold water. Cut the tops off the garlic heads to reveal the cloves.

2. Pack the olives and whole garlic heads into your fermentation vessel, dispersing herbs and chiles, if using, as you go. Pour in enough brine to cover the olives completely. Top with grape leaves to keep everything under the brine. If you don't have grape leaves, use any large edible leaf, for example, edible greens or maple leaves. If using a jar, place a piece of parchment paper or wax paper between the lid and the olives to avoid corrosion.

3. Set the crock or jar somewhere cool and out of the way to ferment for about 1 month. Then pour out brine, refill with fresh brine, and top with new grape leaves.

4. Over the next 8 to 11 months, check in periodically to make sure the leaves and all the olives are submerged under the brine. Replace the leaves and add more brine as needed. You can begin to taste-test after 6 months; however, in our experience they get better with time. We never eat them before a year's worth of curing.

5. When the olives are ready, transfer them into smaller jars, top off with fresh brine, and top with a new leaf. Store in the refrigerator, where they will keep for many years.

IN THE CROCK
Dry Salt-Cured Olives
yield: about 3 quarts (2.8 l)
technique used: Salt Pressing (page 80)

This cure produces a full-flavored olive, retaining some of that natural bitterness, but in a pleasing way. It is perhaps the simplest way to cure olives. The caveat is that the olives need to be fully ripe. You will be pressing the olives in quite a bit of salt, so you will want to use a container with a top wide enough that you can weigh them down. We like using straight-sided glass crocks or jars. We've used stoneware crocks with success but also have ruined these types of crocks with heavy salt cures that have caused the glazes to crack, so we generally save them for regular ferments. You can also use large, widemouthed jars, Cambro containers, or food-grade plastic buckets.

Olives bruise easily—handle them carefully.

4 pounds (1.8 kg) fresh black olives

2 pounds (900 g) unrefined salt

AFTER CURING

⅓ cup (79 ml) olive oil

1. Prepare the olives by removing any stems, leaves, and blemished olives. Rinse in cold water.

2. Put a layer of salt about ½ inch (1.3 cm) thick in the bottom of your container.

3. Gently arrange a layer of olives on top of the salt. You can do two layers of olives between salt layers, but no more than that. (We generally take the time to place the olives one at a time to avoid bruising them.)

4. Cover the olives with more salt, then add another layer of olives. Repeat until all the olives are completely covered in salt. As you proceed, lightly agitate the container to encourage the salt to settle between the olives. Add weight that distributes evenly over the entire top of the olives.

5. Cover the container with a clean cloth. This is just to keep out dust while still allowing moisture to evaporate. There will be no active fermentation or CO_2 production.

6. Set the container out of the way, in a spot that is dry and cool or room temperature. Avoid places with high humidity, such as your basement.

7. After the first week, check the olives. They should begin to shrivel as they release their juice, and as this happens, the salt will become a moist paste.

8. Keep monitoring over the next week. If the salt becomes wholly liquid, you may want to drain the liquid carefully, keeping the olives in the container. If it is just pooling a bit at the bottom, it is not necessary to drain. If any olives become exposed at the top of the container, cover them with more salt.

9. After about 3 weeks, begin taste-testing: Pull out an olive, rinse it, and taste. The olives are ready when their flavor has mellowed, with a slightly pleasant bitterness. They will be wrinkly yet still plump.

Note: During your weekly checks, if the olives at the top seem too dry, feel free to stir, mixing the wetter salt and olives at the bottom with the drier ones at the top. If you live in a very dry climate and find that the olives and salt paste at the top are becoming rock hard, mix up the olives, spritz in a little moisture if needed, and put a lid on the container to slow down the drying.

10. When the olives are ready, pour them out into a larger container. Pluck the olives out of the salt, put them into a colander or sieve, and shake off as much salt as possible. Then lay them out on clean towels and let them dry overnight. Use the towel to wipe off any excess salt, if you want to.

11. Transfer the olives to a bowl, drizzle them with the olive oil, and use your hands to work the oil into the olives, until they are well coated. Add more oil if needed.

12. Pack the olives into small jars, filling them to the top. Screw on the lids and store in the fridge, where the olives will keep indefinitely.

ONIONS

Onions are often the "secret" to imparting a certain brightness to sauerkraut. In the crock for a basic cabbage kraut, they add a depth to the overall flavor without being oniony or slimy. Chunks of the bulb are a tangy component of pickled vegetable medleys as well. They look good and taste great. We have no proof but have read accounts of people who cannot eat raw onions at all yet can eat and enjoy fermented onions.

One study we read told us onions lack intrinsic lactic acid bacteria. Combined with other vegetables in the fermentation crock or pickle jar, this is not a problem; the other veggies have plenty of the bacteria to jump-start the process. In onion-only relishes and chutneys, adding a little bit of sauerkraut brine can ensure success, although over the years we have never had onions not ferment on their own, even without brine. (After all, lactic acid bacteria can be found everywhere, even on your hands.)

We have yet to meet a member of the onion clan that does not do a fantastic job in a ferment: red, yellow, white, sweet, shallots, chives, leeks (see page 258), scallions (see page 324), and ramps (see page 261).

We have to put in a kind word for shallots: When we have some, they are a go-to allium for fermentation around here. Any of these simple onion ferments can be made with shallots instead.

YOUR RAW MATERIAL

For the freshest onions, select bulbs that are firm and heavy. Old onions will not only be soft but will also have a potent odor. Onions store well in a cool, dark space, but sweet onions have a shorter storage life—unless you ferment them.

IN THE CROCK

Make relishes and chutneys by slicing or dicing the onions; it depends on the texture you'd like. Slicing makes a more substantial condiment with

An Onion a Day

Most onions, especially the outer rings of the red onion, have a high supply of quercetin, a flavonoid that acts to block cancer cell formation. Some nutritionists recommend including a few ounces of raw onion in your diet regularly to increase cancer protection. Researchers in Canada found that fermentation increased the levels of quercetin in onions (they used red onions), which elevates the antioxidant action. Quercetin also deactivates the growth of estrogen-sensitive cells often found to cause breast cancer. "Quercetin is a prime anticancer weapon," says Terrance Leighton, a professor of biochemistry and molecular biology at the University of California at Berkeley. Leighton claims, "Quercetin is one of the most potent anticancer agents ever discovered. It blocks cancer development and, if cancer is already present, its spread."

a variety of applications; you can use it in sandwiches and wraps, atop pulled pork, or as a side. Dicing produces a softer, saucier texture.

The following recipes make 1 to 2 quarts of each condiment. Don't let that scare you off. Onion chutneys and relishes are excellent to have on hand.

Simple Onion Relish

yield: about 2 quarts (1.9 l)

technique used: Relishes/Chutneys/Salsas/Salads (page 74)

>   5 large onions
> 1–1½ tablespoons (17–25 g) unrefined salt
>   1 tablespoon (9 g) mustard seeds
>   1 teaspoon (3 g) ground cumin
>   Grape leaf or parchment paper, to top the ferment

1. Trim the onions by making shallow, cone-shaped cuts on both ends. Peel away the papery outer layers of skin. With a knife or mandoline, thinly slice the onions crosswise into rings.

2. Transfer the onions to a large bowl and sprinkle in 1 tablespoon of the salt, working it in with your hands. Then taste. You should be able to taste the salt without it being overwhelming. Add more salt as needed. When it's ready, mix in the mustard seeds and cumin.

3. Pack the onions into a crock or jar, pressing as you go.

4. Place a grape leaf or parchment paper on top. Follow the instructions for your fermentation vessel. For a jar, if using the burping method (page 44) make sure there is little headspace and seal lid tightly. Burp daily or as needed.

Alternatively, top the ferment with a quart-size ziplock bag. Press the bag down onto the top of the ferment and then fill it with water and seal.

5. Set your fermentation vessel on a plate in a spot where you can keep an eye on it, out of direct sunlight, and let ferment for 7 to 14 days. Check regularly to make sure the onions are submerged, pressing down as needed to bring the brine to the surface. The onions are done when they are translucent, have lost their sharp bite, and are pickle-y tasting, without the strong acidity of vinegar.

6. To store, transfer to smaller jars, if necessary, and tamp down. Pour in any brine that's left. Tighten the lids, then store in the fridge, where the onions will keep for 18 months.

Onion and Pepper Relish

See photos on pages 160 and 322

yield: about 2 quarts (1.9 l)

technique used: Relishes/Chutneys/Salsas/Salads (page 74)

For this mild relish, use only bell peppers; if you want more heat, mix them with habaneros or jalapeños and add 1 tablespoon chile pepper flakes.

>   5 large onions, sliced
>   5 large red and/or green bell peppers, seeded and thinly sliced
>   1 tablespoon (2 g) whole coriander seeds, slightly cracked
>   ½ teaspoon (1.5 g) ground cumin
> 1–1½ tablespoons (17–25 g) unrefined salt

Follow the recipe for Simple Onion Relish at left, adding the peppers with the onions.

Onion Chutney

yield: about 1 quart (946 ml)
technique used: Relishes/Chutneys/Salsas/Salads (page 74)

- 3 large onions, sliced or diced
- 1 apple, diced
- ½ cup (51 g) raisins
- 1 teaspoon (3 g) ground cumin
- 1 teaspoon (3 g) mustard seeds
- 1–2 teaspoons (6–11 g) unrefined salt
- 1 teaspoon (2 g) curry powder (for a homemade version, see page 165)

Follow the recipe for Simple Onion Relish (page 286), adding the apple and raisins with the onions. *Note:* Mix the curry powder with the kraut brine before adding it; this prevents clumping.

"Onion Soup" Seasoning

yield: about 12 ounces (340 g)

You'll need a dehydrator to make this versatile flavoring powder. Sprinkle it on any dish that could use a little zing, just like you'd use store-bought onion soup mix as a seasoning. Try the classic chip dip by adding this flavoring powder to sour cream (see page 371).

- 1 recipe Simple Onion Relish (page 286)

1. Loosely spread the fermented relish on non-stick or silicone drying sheets. Put into a dehydrator set to 100°F/38°C and dry for 14 hours.

2. Transfer the dehydrated relish to a blender and process to a coarse powder.

3. Store in an airtight container. This seasoning will keep at room temperature for 6 months or in the fridge or freezer for up to 1 year.

Cebollas Encurtidas (Pickled Onions)

See photo on page 305

yield: about 1 quart (946 ml)
technique used: Relishes/Chutneys/Salsas/Salads (page 74)

This recipe for vinegar-pickled onion has its origins in Ecuador. Traditionally it's made with *cebolla paiteña*, a smaller and spicier onion than those we get in North America. Our fermented adaptation is delicious.

- 3 red onions or shallots, sliced
- 1 tablespoon (6 g) lime zest (optional)
  Juice of 3 limes
- 1 teaspoon (6 g) unrefined salt

Follow the recipe for Simple Onion Relish (page 286), using the red onions or shallots in place of the sweet onions and the lime zest and juice in place of the sauerkraut brine.

IN THE PICKLE JAR
Pickle onions in our Basic Brine (page 102). Cut them into thicker slices or wedges so they stay firm and crisp through the fermentation—onions cut thin will become too soft and sort of lifeless. Small onions can be pickled whole. You can prepare onions plain or—much more interesting—as a component of the seasoning for a vegetable medley.

PAK CHOI (BOK CHOY)

This Asian green, a member of the vast cabbage clan, is a staple in kimchi. Whether of the large or "baby" variety, pak choi can be sliced into a kimchi as a replacement for, or supplement to, napa cabbage (page 182). *Note:* The larger variety, with its succulent stalks, can cause the brine to take on a bit of a gelatinous quality. The fermentation process overcomes this with time, so if you find yourself with a gelatinous ferment, just tuck it back in for a little more curing time.

YOUR RAW MATERIAL

The commonly available pak choi has glossy, deep green leaves atop succulent, spoon-shaped white stems. It's compact, with a somewhat vertical habit, similar to that of celery. What's marketed as baby pak choi has short, chunky pale green stalks and is much smaller. It's also more supple and tender and has a milder flavor. Both varieties can be fermented. Choose pak choi that has bright, glossy green leaves, with no yellowing and no bruising in the stalks.

GALANGAL

Used in many Southeast Asian cuisines, galangal root is becoming more widely available in specialty markets. This rhizome looks similar to ginger, but it is plumper and its pale orange-red skin is more translucent. Galangal has a distinctive flavor that lies somewhere between citrus and ginger, with a hint of eucalyptus. It adds wonderful notes to your ferments; use as you would ginger, or make a paste to use year-round (page 76).

IN THE CROCK
Thai-Inspired Baby Pak Choi

See photo on page 339

yield: about 1 quart (946 ml)
technique used: Mastering Kimchi Basics (page 117)

Use the small "baby" variety of pak choi for this recipe. The heads remain whole and the remaining ingredients are made into a paste that is stuffed between the stalks. Serve one head as a side dish.

You'll need to plan ahead for this recipe, as it requires a brining period, 6 to 8 hours or overnight.

- 1 gallon (3.8 l) Soaking Brine (1 cup/ 269 g unrefined salt per gallon unchlorinated water)
- 6 or 7 heads baby pak choi
- 1 daikon radish, shredded
- 1 cup (96 g) Thai basil leaves
- 1 (1-inch/2.5 cm) piece fresh galangal root (if unavailable, use fresh ginger)
- 1 teaspoon (6 g) ground cayenne or chile pepper flakes
- 1 stalk lemongrass, thinly sliced
  Cabbage leaf or parchment paper, to top the ferment

1. Pour the brine into a crock or a large bowl. Rinse the pak choi in cold water and submerge the whole heads in the brine. Use a plate as a weight to keep the pak choi submerged. Set aside, at room temperature, for 6 to 8 hours or overnight.

2. Drain the pak choi for 15 minutes, reserving 1 cup of the soaking liquid.

3. Combine the daikon, basil, galangal, and cayenne in a food processor and pulse to a paste. Keeping the pak choi heads whole, tuck small bits of the paste between the stalks of their leaves.

4. Spread the lemongrass slices across the bottom of your fermentation vessel. Lay the pak choi bundles in your vessel, stacking and pressing as you go. When the bundles are all in place, press until the brine covers them; use the reserved soaking brine, as needed, to submerge the pak choi.

5. Top with a cabbage leaf or parchment paper and weight if you have one. Follow the instructions for your fermentation vessel. For a jar, if using the burping method (page 44) make sure there is little headspace and seal lid tightly. Burp

daily or as needed. Alternatively, top the ferment with a quart-size ziplock bag. Press the bag down onto the top of the ferment and then fill it with water and seal.

6. Set your fermentation vessel on a plate in a spot where you can keep an eye on it, out of direct sunlight, and let ferment for 4 to 5 days. Taste-test once the pak choi is completely wilted and dull colored. It's ready when it has a pleasing acidic smell and tastes pickle-y, perhaps with an effervescent zing.

7. To store, place in a jar and tamp down to make sure pak choi is submerged in its brine. Tighten the lid and place in the refrigerator, where it will keep for 4 months.

PARSLEY

Are you going to Scarborough Fair?
Parsley, sage, rosemary, and thyme.
Remember me to one who lives there,
she once was a true love of mine.
—TRADITIONAL ENGLISH BALLAD

Parsley, another Mediterranean health food, is a good source of vitamins A, C, and K and has folate, iron, and a whole host of volatile oils. This herb was used as a medicine even before it came to be known as a culinary herb. The ancient Greeks thought parsley sacred and, like us, used it as a garnish—for athletic champions and tombs of their departed.

YOUR RAW MATERIAL

While there are many varieties of parsley, the two common types you'll recognize are the curly-leaved and the Italian flat-leaf parsley. The flat-leaf variety is thought to be less bitter and more fragrant. Either is successful in fermentation, so use your favorite. Add minced parsley to any kraut or relish, and use the whole stems with leaves to enhance brine pickles. Parsley is a good addition to pastes made with drier herbs such as sage, rosemary, and thyme; it will bring much-needed moisture while still allowing other herbs to shine.

It should be deep green, with no signs of yellowing.

Chimichurri

See photo on page 338

yield: about 1 pint (473 ml)
technique used: Pastes (page 76)

This is our take on the traditional Argentinian condiment. In the original, the distinctive tang comes from wine vinegar; in our version, it comes from the lactic acid.

2 cups (192 g) packed fresh parsley leaves
¼ cup (14 g) fresh oregano leaves or
    2–3 tablespoons (6–9 g) dried
6 cloves garlic
1 jalapeño or 1 teaspoon (2 g) chile pepper flakes
1 small shallot
    Freshly ground black pepper, to taste
    Juice of 1 lime
1 scant teaspoon (6 g) unrefined salt
    Grape leaf or parchment paper, to top the ferment

AFTER FERMENTATION
½ cup (118 ml) extra-virgin olive oil

1. Put the parsley, oregano, garlic, jalapeño, shallot, pepper, and lime juice in a food processor and blend into a paste. Sprinkle in the salt. The mixture will become juicy immediately.

2. Press the paste into a pint jar. More liquid will release as you press, and you should now see a little brine. If using the burping method (page 44), make sure there is little headspace, top with a round of parchment paper and a weight if you have one, then seal the lid tightly. Watch the lid for pressure building up. Alternatively, top the paste with a quart-size ziplock bag. Press the bag down onto the top of the ferment, then fill it with water and seal.

3. Set the jar on a counter, out of direct sunlight, and let ferment for 7 to 10 days. Taste-test when the colors become muted. The ferment is done when it has a pleasing acidic smell and tastes lightly sour.

4. Stir in the olive oil. Eat immediately, or store in a sealed container in the refrigerator, where the chimichurri will keep for a few weeks. Alternatively, hold off on adding the olive oil until you're ready to eat it. In this case, tamp down to make sure the ferment is submerged in its brine, press a small round of parchment paper directly on top, and seal the jar with its lid. Store in the refrigerator, where it will keep for 1 year.

WE ARE FAMILY: ROOT PARSLEY

Root parsley is a variety of parsley grown for its large taproot instead of its greens. That taproot looks remarkably like a parsnip (that is, like a humble, pale carrot), but despite that resemblance, root parsley and parsnips are not alike. Parsnips are sweet; root parsley is not.

You'll find it under a variety of names, among them parsley root, Hamburg parsley, and Dutch parsley. It adds a mild parsley flavor to ferments and does not oxidize, so the white color is preserved during fermentation. Use it as you might a carrot. Add it to any ferment—kraut, kimchi, condiments, or pickles—sliced or shredded.

PARSNIPS

In Europe, the parsnip was the starch of choice before the introduction of the potato. Parsnips also had an important role in desserts: Before sugar was widely available in Europe, this pale tuber was used to sweeten cakes and puddings.

SCHISANDRA BERRIES

Schisandra berries, native to northern China, grow on a plant called magnolia vine. They are used traditionally in Asia for their tangy flavor as well as in medicinal preparations and tonics. They are sometimes called "five-flavor berries," and if you try one, you'll see why. Bite into a berry and allow the flavors to move through your palate. You will taste sweet, sour, bitter, pungent (spicy), and salty.

This quality makes schisandra uniquely flavorful in a ferment, but the berries can quickly overpower it. Use sparingly. You can find the dried berries at herb shops and online (but be sure to purchase them from a reputable source; see the resources section, page 419). Crush the dried berries lightly to release their flavor in a ferment.

YOUR RAW MATERIAL

Parsnips look like carrots with a creamy complexion. They're a cool-season crop, sweetest after a hard frost. For fermentation, you must take into consideration their high sugar content; you will probably want to combine them with an equal amount of other veggies, or to brine-pickle parsnips in bigger chunks.

Select firm, medium-size roots; large roots often have a woody core. Another tip is that parsnips that have fine-hair rootlets on the main root may have been grown in dry soils and also may be more woody.

IN THE CROCK
Parsnip Kimchi

yield: about 1 gallon (3.8 l)
technique used: Mastering Kimchi Basics (page 117)

Dried schisandra berries impart complex flavors; parsnips contribute sweetness. This ferment has a two-step process that requires a brining time of 6 to 8 hours, and the kimchi spends a little more time curing than most of our ferments.

- 1 gallon (3.8 l) Soaking Brine (1 cup/269 g unrefined salt per gallon unchlorinated water)
- 2 heads napa cabbage
- 1 cup (90 g) packed grated parsnips (3–4 medium)
- ½ cup (45 g) chile pepper flakes or salt-free gochugaru
- ½ cup (60 g) packed grated daikon radish
- ¼ cup (25 g) packed grated carrot (about 1 medium)
- 3 scallions, greens included, sliced
- ½–1 head garlic (to taste), cloves separated and minced
- 1 tablespoon (6 g) minced fresh ginger
- 1 tablespoon (4 g) dried schisandra berries, lightly crushed

1. Pour the brine into a crock or a large bowl. Rinse the cabbages in cold water and remove the coarse outer leaves; set aside a few unblemished ones. Trim off the stalk end and cut each cabbage in half. Submerge the cabbage halves and the reserved outer leaves in the brine. Use a plate as a weight to keep the cabbages submerged. Set aside, at room temperature, for 6 to 8 hours or overnight.

2. Using a colander set over a bowl, drain the cabbage, reserving 1 cup of the brine. Set aside the brined outer leaves.

3. Meanwhile, combine the parsnips, chile flakes, daikon, carrot, scallions, garlic, ginger, and schisandra berries in a large bowl and blend thoroughly.

4. Chop the brined cabbage into bite-size pieces, or larger if you prefer, and add them to the bowl. Massage the mixture thoroughly, then taste for salt. Usually the brined cabbage will provide enough salt, but if it's not to your liking, sprinkle in a small amount, massage, and taste again.

5. Transfer vegetables, a few handfuls at a time, into your fermentation vessel, pressing as you go. Add any liquid left in the bowl, and top off with enough of the reserved brine, if needed, to fully submerge the vegetables.

6. Cover the kimchi with the brined leaves, or parchment paper and weight if you have one. Follow the instructions for your fermentation vessel. For a jar, if using the burping method (page 44) make sure there is little headspace

and seal lid tightly. Burp daily or as needed. Alternatively, top the ferment with a quart-size ziplock bag. Press the bag down onto the top of the ferment and then fill it with water and seal.

7. Set your fermentation vessel on a plate in a spot where you can keep an eye on it, out of direct sunlight, and let ferment for 10 to 25 days. When the color of the kimchi becomes muted and the brine is cloudy, you can start to taste-test. It's ready when it has a pleasing acidic smell and tastes pickle-y, perhaps with an effervescent zing.

8. When it's ready, spoon the kimchi into smaller jars, if needed, making sure the veggies are submerged in brine. Screw on the lids and store in the refrigerator, where the kimchi will keep for 6 months.

Create Your Own Recipes

» Parsnips go well with members of the allium family: leeks, onions, shallots, garlic.
» Pair with aromatic seeds, such as cumin, caraway, or juniper.
» Pickle parsnips, in rounds or spears, the same way you would carrots (see page 194).

PEAS

English peas are the ones in pods that you "unzip" by snapping the top and pulling the string, revealing the treasures: small, round, and sweet. Add these round jewels to any ferment. Save the pods to ferment in Basic Brine (page 102), then enjoy the rich green brine and dehydrate the pods to make a fermented flavor dust (page 142).

Sugar snap peas and snow peas have an edible skin, and we've found that fermentation is

a great way to preserve their crisp freshness far beyond their short growing season. Snow peas are flat, with petite seeds hardly visible through the pods. Sugar snap pods are plump, with noticeable peas. Ferment both, either in a dry brine with other vegetables that will release enough liquid to make a brine, or as a pickle submerged in Basic Brine (page 102). The flavor will have depth, and the peas will stay pleasantly crisp.

YOUR RAW MATERIAL

Choose peas that are emerald green. They should have smooth skin and be firm to the touch, and when bent they should feel rubbery but still snap. Stay away from peas that are much longer than 3 inches, as they are likely overgrown and tough.

Both sugar snap and snow peas have a string. To remove, nip the tip of each pea and pull the string that runs along the edge.

IN THE CROCK

Peas and Carrots

See photo on page 227

yield: about 1 quart (946 ml)
technique used: Relishes/Chutneys/Salsas/Salads (page 74)

Make this ferment as the weather warms and you see pea season coming to an end. It's a tasty way to preserve this spring treat so that you can enjoy peas as a summer condiment. The carrots are added for their ability to create brine, because the peas don't release enough on their own.

    2 cups (128 g) chopped sugar snap or snow
        peas, cut into ½-inch (1.3 cm) pieces
    2 cups (200 g) shredded carrots
    1 scallion, sliced
    2 cloves garlic, minced
    1 tablespoon (15 g) grated fresh ginger
    1 tablespoon (15 g) ground turmeric
 1–1¼ tablespoons (17–21 g) unrefined salt
        Grape leaf or parchment paper, to top the
        ferment

1. Combine the peas, carrots, scallion, garlic, ginger, and turmeric in a large bowl. Add a scant tablespoon of the salt and mix thoroughly with your hands. Then taste. You should be able to

taste the salt without it being overwhelming. Add more salt if needed. Let stand, covered, for 30 minutes. At this point, you should have just enough brine to cover the veggies.

2. Pack the mixture into your fermentation vessel, pressing it down to remove air pockets as you go. More brine will release as you press the veggies; you should see the brine above the mixture.

3. Top with a grape leaf or parchment paper and weight if you have one. Follow the instructions for your fermentation vessel. For a jar, if using the burping method (page 44) make sure there is little headspace and seal lid tightly. Burp daily or as needed. Alternatively, top the ferment with a quart-size ziplock bag. Press the bag down onto the top of the ferment and then fill it with water and seal.

4. Set your fermentation vessel on a plate in a spot where you can keep an eye on it, out of direct sunlight, and let ferment for 5 to 10 days. Start taste-testing the ferment on day 5. When it's ready, the flavor of the carrots and peas will have mingled, and it will be pleasingly sour.

5. When the ferment is ready, transfer to smaller jars, if necessary, and tamp down. Pour in any brine that's left. Tighten the lids, then store in the fridge. It will keep, refrigerated, for 6 months.

Create Your Own Recipes

Toss whole or chopped edible-pod peas in with a napa cabbage kimchi or other ferment.

PEPPERS

Fermented chiles—we think a triumph in the preservation canon! The process not only keeps the integrity of their flavor; it also enhances it. We love them so much we wrote an entire book practically dedicated to them, *Fiery Ferments*, because they are so versatile. While they do soften in fermentation, losing the crisp, clean crunch of fresh peppers, they definitely will not become mush.

With fermentation, you can make peppers into pastes, salsas, sauces, and pickles. A pepper mash just may be the easiest (and most classic) way to ferment peppers and is the first step to many a complex hot sauce. It can also be enjoyed as is, which is how we use it. The beauty is that you can use any kind of pepper, from mild to super hot, to create the heat you prefer. In fact, you can make a mash with bell peppers if you would like.

Ripened peppers can be fermented for much longer than most vegetables. The flavors keep getting more and more complex.

Ferments containing a lot of peppers often develop a bloom of Kahm yeast. Pepper pastes, in particular, are susceptible. For this reason, we tend to ferment our peppers in jars, using the burping method (page 44) to keep oxygen at bay. We shake the jar of peppers after each "burp" session to keep the mash integrated. In an open ferment, stirring regularly is your best bet, as it "drowns" the yeast that is trying to grow.

YOUR RAW MATERIAL

Sweet peppers are not spicy or hot, even though they're botanically the same species (*Capsicum annuum*) as their fiery chile siblings. Sweet peppers carry a recessive gene that prevents development of the capsaicin.

HANDLING HOT CHILES

The compound that makes chiles hot and spicy is capsaicin. All peppers have it, to varying degrees, except the bell pepper. Capsaicin oil is in the white pith and in the tissue around the seeds. It can cause a reaction even when you touch it.

Because capsaicin is an oil, it's not easy to wash off. Before you cut any of the hot chiles, put on a pair of thin protective gloves or rub a small amount of cooking oil on your hands; either acts as a barrier. When you've finished handling the chiles, wash your hands in hot water with dishwashing liquid or an oil-cutting soap. If there's still a problem, rinse your fingers in lemon juice or rubbing alcohol, then rub in a little aloe vera or milk. The casein in milk, and in products made from it—such as buttermilk and yogurt—neutralizes the capsaicin.

The lungs are even more vulnerable. Airborne capsaicin irritates the mucous membranes, and inhaling this compound can cause breathing problems. You'll feel it as a tightening in the lungs, or you'll start to cough. Use caution in seeding, chopping, or grinding raw chiles if you suffer from any breathing problems, particularly asthma; do all this processing in a well-ventilated area. Capsaicin is still active during cleanup, so take care when washing and rinsing your equipment.

The most common sweet peppers are red and green bell peppers, but there is a color out there for everyone—yellow, orange, purple, brown, and even black. Green peppers are the unripe version of their ripened counterparts. They don't have as much sugar and ferment differently but just as deliciously. Purple, brown, or black peppers don't hold their pigment in fermentation. For vivid ferments, use yellow, orange, and red peppers.

Jalapeños and other hot chiles add complexity of flavor and striking color to any ferment. Use a small amount to create depth; use more for eye-watering fire. Hot chiles are an important crayon in the fermentation art box. They are, well, not to use the word lightly, *exquisite* when you ferment them.

Whether or not you remove the seeds is your choice. For the thick-walled peppers such as Fresno or jalapeño, we never remove the seeds; there aren't that many and they provide texture. For more seedy peppers, such as cayenne or small chiles, you may want to remove the seeds for textural reasons. In chiles, the seeds aren't where the heat is. The capsaicin compound lives in the white pith of chiles, not the seeds. They are guilty by association. It is personal preference. The seeds will not harm you or the ferment.

IN THE CROCK

Pepper Paste

See photo on page 304

yield: about 1 quart (946 ml)
technique used: Pastes (page 76)

This paste looks good and tastes great, but the real beauty is its simplicity. We make a gallon of it every year. If the family ate it freely, it would never last, but we save it in small jars and dole it out. The bonus: It gets better over time.

Use whatever type of chile you have. Our favorite is the fire-engine-red Fresno, in part because its color is so appealing. Its heat is similar to a jalapeño, sometimes hotter.

This is our original recipe for 1.5 percent salt. If you are in a warmer climate or want to age the paste for a year or more, increase salt to 1 tablespoon, which is 2.5 percent.

The burping method (page 44) is hands down the simplest way to make a pepper paste that is a gallon or less. It prevents Kahm yeast blooms. BUT you need to keep on top of burping. Pepper pastes can turn a jar into a lava cannon if the carbon dioxide builds up too much, which early in the active ferment can happen overnight.

1½ pounds (680 g) chiles, stemmed and roughly chopped
2 teaspoons (11 g) unrefined salt

1. Put the chiles in a food processor with the salt and pulse until coarsely chopped.

2. Put the paste into an appropriately sized jar.

3. Set the jar on a counter, out of direct sunlight. It will begin to ferment in the first day or two. When you see the lid tighten with pressure and the pepper pulp float to the top of the brine, "burp" the jar, cracking open the lid for just a second to release the built-up gas, then screwing the lid back on tight and shaking the jar to homogenize the brine and pulp. Each day during active fermentation you will need to do this at least one or two times a day. Don't be surprised if it is more.

4. Once the fermentation begins to slow, you will notice that pressure builds up more slowly. Stop burping the jar. You can continue to shake it.

If you stop burping the jar when there is still enough pressure and fermentation that a layer of CO_2 sits in the jar's headspace, you will find that you can let this ferment sit for weeks, months, or years without refrigeration or trouble. Until you open the jar and break the seal, that is.

5. The color of the peppers stays vibrant, so you won't see a color shift, but you will smell the change in acidity when burping the jar. You can eat the paste as soon as it is acidic. This ferment is delicious at 3 weeks, but feel free to ferment it for as long as you like.

6. To store, make sure headspace is minimal and seal the jar. This paste will keep, refrigerated, for 2 years or longer.

Roasted Fermented Pepper Mash

Use this recipe for any thick-walled peppers, from sweet Italians or bells to chiles. Roasting some of the peppers adds dimension to the flavor, while keeping raw peppers in the mash ensures a good amount of live lactic acid bacteria to get the fermentation started. This can be eaten after 2 to 3 weeks, or let it go much longer.

> **1½ pounds (680 g) peppers, sweet or hot**
> **2 teaspoons (11 g) unrefined salt**

1. Preheat your oven's broiler.

2. Broil 1 pound (454 g) of the peppers until blistered, 5 to 10 minutes on each side. When they are blistered on all sides, remove from the oven and place in a paper bag. Fold over the top of the bag to hold in the steam. Let the peppers cool, then peel off the skins and remove the stems and seeds. Place in a food processor.

3. Stem, seed, and roughly chop the remaining ½ pound (225 g) of raw peppers. Place them in the food processor with the roasted peppers. Add the salt. Process to your desired consistency—perhaps a rough, even chop for salsa or a purée for a saucier condiment. The peppers will become juicy immediately.

4. Follow the fermenting instructions for Pepper Paste (page 295).

TAKE IT FURTHER
E-Z Hot Sauce

To make a basic hot sauce, strain any pepper paste through cheesecloth to remove seeds or thicker bits. Splash in a bit of raw apple cider vinegar and *voilà*—hot sauce! The leftover pulp makes a tangy flavoring to add to anything from refried beans to guacamole.

Sambal

yield: about 1 pint (473 ml)
technique used: Pastes (page 76)

Sambal is an Indonesian chile sauce. Traditionally it consists of chile peppers and salt ground with a mortar and pestle. Each region, however, has its variation: Chiles may be cayenne, Thai bird's eye, or Spanish; recipes may call for lime juice or lemongrass, shrimp paste or molasses. What they have in common is that they're always hot!

This recipe comes from Auguste Wattimë, who was born and raised on the Maluku Islands (the Moluccas) of Indonesia, famous for cloves, nutmeg, and mace—hence their nickname, the Spice Islands. The bouillon in the traditional recipe probably reflects the influence of European cultures, from the Portuguese to the Spanish and the Dutch, as it probably replaced the umami-rich local shrimp pastes.

- ½ pound (226 g) fresh hot red chiles
- 1 onion, chopped
- 1 teaspoon (6 g) Garlic Paste (page 237) or 2 or 3 cloves garlic, minced
- 1 bouillon cube or ½–1 teaspoon (2.8–6 g) unrefined salt
- 1 tablespoon (15 ml) lemon juice

Follow the recipe for Pepper Paste (page 295). Combine the chiles with the onion, garlic paste, bouillon cube, and lemon juice in a food processor and process to a paste consistency.

Sweet Pepper Salsa

See photo on page 160

yield: about 2 quarts (1.9 l)

technique used: Relishes/Chutneys/Salsas/Salads (page 74)

We sold this salsa, under the name Pepper Solamente, at farmers' markets. Although it's all peppers, it's a perfect fermented salsa, with all the color and tang of a tomato salsa—just no tomatoes. This salsa is delightful as is, or use it as a salsa starter kit: Before serving, add diced fresh tomatoes and a little minced cilantro to the mixture.

- 3 pounds (1.4 kg) sweet red peppers (the thicker the walls, the better), seeded and roughly chopped
- 1 pound (454 g) jalapeños, seeded and roughly chopped
- 2 medium sweet onions, roughly chopped
- 4 cloves garlic, minced
- 1½–2 tablespoons (17–25 g) unrefined salt

1. Put the bell peppers, jalapeños, and onions in a food processor and pulse to mince. Transfer to a large bowl and add the garlic and 1½ tablespoons of the salt. Mix well, and you'll have enough brine immediately. Then taste. You should be able to taste the salt without it being overwhelming. Add more salt if needed.

2. Pack the mixture into your fermentation vessel, pressing it down to remove air pockets as you go. More brine will release as you press, and you should see brine above the veggies.

3. You will have more brine than usual in this ferment, and the vegetable mass is not very dense, which can cause followers to float and slip around. We find that the burping method (page 44) works best.

4. Set your fermentation vessel on a plate in a spot where you can keep an eye on it, out of direct sunlight, and let ferment for 14 to 21 days. Check daily. It will begin to ferment in the first 1 to 2 days. You will see the lid tighten with pressure and the pepper pulp float above the brine. As pressure builds in the lid, you will twist the lid to release pressure and close again quickly. Then shake contents to homogenize brine and pulp. Each day during active fermentation you will need to do this at least one or two times a day, maybe more.

5. Once the fermentation begins to slow, probably after 14 days, you will notice you don't have to release pressure very often. You can start to taste-test the ferment as soon as it smells acidic when you are burping it. It's ready when it has developed a pleasingly sour acidity, like salsa. It will stay vibrantly colored.

6. When it's ready, spoon the ferment into smaller jars, if necessary, leaving as little headspace as possible. Tighten the lids, then store in the fridge, where the salsa will keep for up to 2 years.

Sebastian Vargo and Taylor Hanna: Making "The People's Pickle"

When the COVID-19 pandemic hit, Sebastian Vargo and Taylor Hanna both found themselves furloughed, with time to cook together at home, experiment with fermentation, and talk and dream about what might be next. They dabbled in a few different business ideas, but their passions brought them back to pickles. They launched Vargo Brother Ferments in the summer of 2020 and started selling their signature "G-Dilla" super-crunchy dill pickle on their Instagram (@vargobrotherferments) account. They have since created myriad flavors and ferments.

The Poor Man's Flavors

Sebastian and Taylor believe that the flavor and the health benefits of fermented foods cannot be separated. They also believe that fermentation can help us make healthy food more accessible to everyone, and to do that we must disrupt what fine dining means. Sebastian says, "We have fallen off of the preservation and probiotic game by design with industrialization. We need to address every layer of fermentation, the cultural aspect and the ease in which to do it. We need to have fermentation accessible to all people."

Taylor agrees: "Umami flavor is accessible to everyone. Not everyone can afford truffles, but fermented food hits all four corners of your mouth the same way truffles do. It is just salt and water and time, and anyone can do that."

"It is the poor man's way of unlocking the greatest flavors in the world," Sebastian adds.

"It's no big deal," Taylor offers. "We will give you a recipe. Sure, buy a jar, but we will tell you how to adjust it to your idea. Fermentation is no big deal—it should be built into our homes. There is no secret information. We don't believe in gatekeeping."

Taylor continues, "Probiotics and having a healthy gut is pretty punk nowadays—one of the last bastions of going against the grain. The food being packaged and sold to us isn't in our best interests. Taking control over the microbes is the starting point. The micro is macro—the starting point to take back your life is through a healthy diet and a healthy gut biome. We are moving toward a space where everyone feels included, and that includes not perpetuating the story that fermentation is elitist."

Taylor says, "Our tote bag reads 'The People's Pickle.'" Sebastian jumps in, laughing: "And the tote bag doesn't lie!"

Layering on Flavor

The people's pickle is undeniably delicious and crisp. Sebastian and Taylor build brine in the same way one builds a good stock—layering on flavor and intention. In the case of the dill pickle, they lay a foundation of tannins with black tea, grape leaves, and bay leaves.

When we spoke to Sebastian and Taylor, they were getting ready to set up a permanent commercial kitchen. Over the next few years, they want to start having their pickles available in locations throughout Chicago. Eventually, they hope to have a pickle shop that serves as a community space with delicious food available to everyone.

IN THE PICKLE JAR

G-Devil (Spicy Pickle Condiment)

by Sebastian Vargo of Vargo Brother Ferments

yield: a little more than 2 quarts (1.9 l)
technique used: Mastering Brine Pickling (page 101)

Sebastian says, "This sauce is 100 percent inspired by our love of pickles and heat and our flagship garlic dill pickle, a.k.a. G-Dilla. I wanted to find a way to incorporate the briny, funky flavors I love into a smooth, vibrant sauce!"

While the cooked hot sauce does not contain live probiotics, the fermentation process has added layers of flavor, acid for preservation, and postbiotics (see page 25).

Sebastian says that you can use the sauce anywhere you want a briny, spicy presence, but G-Devil is "best friends with fried chicken."

- 2 pounds (907 g) serranos, tops removed
- 2 cucumbers
- 2 cups (112 g) fresh dill
- 1 cup (25 g) parsley, stems included
- 4 or 5 grape leaves
- 1 cup (135 g) garlic cloves, peeled and crushed
- 1 tablespoon (9 g) mustard seeds, toasted
- ½ tablespoon (1 g) black peppercorns, toasted
  About 2 quarts (1.9 l) High Brine
    (3 tablespoons/50 g unrefined salt per quart unchlorinated water)
  Grape leaves, to top the ferment (optional)

AFTER FERMENTATION

- 2 tablespoons (30 ml) apple cider vinegar
- ½ tablespoon (6 g) sugar

1. Rinse the vegetables. Roughly chop the serranos, cucumbers, dill, parsley, and grape leaves and transfer to a large bowl. Add the crushed garlic, mustard seeds, and peppercorns and mix thoroughly.

2. Pack the vegetable mixture into your fermentation vessel. Pour in enough brine to cover the vegetables completely.

3. Top with grape leaves, if you have them, or a piece of parchment paper, and for extra security in a jar you can wedge toothpicks in an X over everything to keep things submerged. Follow the instructions for your fermentation vessel. For a jar, if using the burping method (page 44) make sure there is little headspace and seal lid tightly. Burp daily or as needed.

4. Set your fermentation vessel on a plate in a spot where you can keep an eye on it, out of direct sunlight, and let ferment for 7 to 21 days. The vegetables are done whenever they have developed pleasing acidity.

5. When the vegetables are ready, strain them out, saving the brine.

6. Place the vegetables in a nonreactive pot and add just enough brine to cover. Bring to a boil, then reduce the heat and simmer until softened, about 30 minutes.

7. Strain the vegetables if you like a thick sauce; leave them unstrained for the moment if you like your sauce thin. Blend on high while the ferment is still hot (be careful!). Stir in the apple cider vinegar and sugar. Let the mixture cool.

8. If you already blended the vegetables to make a thick sauce, transfer the sauce to clean, sanitized jars and seal. For a thinner sauce, strain now, keeping the solids for another flavorful use. The sauce will keep, refrigerated, for 8 months.

PLUMS

Years ago, we planted six tiny prune plum trees because Kirsten loved and missed her grandmother's *Zwetschgendatschi*, a Bavarian plum cake made with fresh prune plums. The trees grew and grew and now we have hundreds of pounds of plums to process and share every year. Many become a plum paste, long-cooked, lightly fermented, and then canned to preserve it. We have fermented them into wine, but prune wine is not a thing for a reason. Prune plum vinegar is delicious, but how much can you really use? We've harvested some plums when they were tiny and green and cured them like olives, and they are a great analog.

In hopes of fewer plums in the fall, we stripped early flowers off the trees, salting them in the style of *sakura no shio-zuke* (salt-cured cherry blossoms) and using them as delicious wild yeast starters. And yet, we have never tried to make umeboshi (pickled plums) with these plums. That is next. Mara Jane King (page 111) says umeboshi made with prune plums is tasty, but pruny.

Around the same time that we planted the prune plum trees, Kirsten's mom brought an ume plum tree to our little orchard. While called a plum, the ume is more closely related to an apricot. It is naturally acidic—it doesn't become sweet even after fully ripening—and is perhaps best known as the specific type of plum used to make umeboshi. Kirsten's mom made her own umeboshi from ume plums, and when the ume plum tree didn't thrive in our orchard, we tried making umeboshi with the fruits we have available to us. Despite their relationship, apricots don't make a

great substitute, we found. Neither do not-quite-ripe greenish peaches (although they did ferment deliciously in sauerkraut). In the end, we had the most success with the small, tart wild plums that grow in our area.

Umeboshi

from *Japanese Home Cooking*, by Sonoko Sakai (reprinted by permission of Sonoko Sakai and Roost Books)

See photo on page 263

Umeboshi is a quintessential Japanese pickle, mouth-puckeringly sour and salty. As with all pickles, it serves as a palate cleanser and aids digestion, but it is also said to cure colds and hangovers.

Kirsten's grandmother had an ume plum tree in her garden that probably was as old as she was. She and Kirsten would always look to the plums and the nightingales as the first signs of spring. The plum blossoms are very hardy and are known to hold up even in the snow. Kirsten's grandmother preferred them over cherry blossoms, which she said were beautiful but ephemeral. She also was known to say that a woman should have dignity, like a plum blossom.

During the ume pickling season, Kirsten helped her grandmother make umeboshi. They sorted the plums by size, cleaned and rubbed them with sea salt, and placed them in a jar with red shiso (perilla) leaves. About a month later, when the rainy season was over, her grandmother took the plums out of the jars and laid them out in the sun to dry for three days in a row, then returned them back to the jar. She would leave some jars alone for more than 6 months, so Kirsten got to taste different vintages of umeboshi. As a special treat, she would occasionally allow Kirsten a sip of the sweet and fragrant umeshu (plum wine).

Fresh ume plums are available in the late spring between May and June in Japanese and Korean markets.

Yield: about 2 dozen

EQUIPMENT

> **Small spray bottle**
> **Ceramic, enamelware, plastic, or glass container, sterilized**
> **Drop lid, sterilized**
> **50-pound (23 kg) stone (or can) that fits on top**
> **Bamboo mats or baskets**

INGREDIENTS

> **2½ pounds (1.2 kg) ripe but firm, unbruised ume (preferably Kaga ume)**
> **1 to 2 tablespoons shochu (Japanese grain liquor) or clear distilled spirit (35 percent alcohol)**
> **½ cup (134 g) sea salt**
> **½ cup (113 g) cane sugar (optional)**

1. Using a toothpick or the point of a sharp knife, remove the small brown stems from the ume. Rinse the ume and set aside any unripe fruit. Also discard any bruised or blemished ume, as they can start to grow mold.

2. Soak the ume in water overnight to remove bitterness. The next day, drain the ume and pat dry with a towel. Place ume in a large bowl and spray them with shochu, using the small spray bottle. Sprinkle and gently rub the salt over the ume using your hands. Repeat until you use up all the ume. Reserve the remaining salt for the shiso leaves (see note).

3. Place salted ume in the container. Put a sterilized wooden lid or a sterilized plate on top of the ume. Place a sterilized weight directly on the top of the lid. The weight will press the plums and extract the brine. Cover the container with cloth or paper and tie a string around the container to hold the cloth or paper in place. Leave it in a cool, dark place.

4. After a few days, check the container. You should start to see the brine that is being extracted from the ume. The brine (umezu or plum vinegar) should cover the ume. If you don't see any brine, you may need to add 2.5 to 5 percent more salt and 5 pounds more weight. You can also sprinkle sugar on top at this stage for a sweeter umeboshi. Gently turn the ume in the container so they get an even coating of brine, replace the lid and weight, and leave the ume for 4 weeks in a cool place.

5. After 4 weeks, take the ume out of the container and reserve the vinegar in the container. Spread the ume on bamboo mats or baskets and place them in the sun. You can cover with a screen to keep out the bugs. Dry them for 3 days, or until the surface of the fruit turns slightly white. The plum vinegar in the pickling container should also get time in the sun, about the same amount of time as the plums.

6. At the end of each day, place the sun-bathed ume back in the container with sun-bathed plum vinegar, and bring the ume back out the next day. Repeat this for 3 days in a row. Then replace the plums one final time and store the umeboshi and the vinegar in separate containers in a cool, dark place. The plums can be eaten after 10 days or so, but it is good to wait for a few months to a year or longer for better flavor.

Note: You can enhance the color and flavor of umeboshi with red shiso leaves. You will need about 50 shiso leaves. Wash the leaves well and drain in a strainer. Weight the shiso leaves. You will use sea salt to equal 10 percent of the weight of the leaves. For example, if you have 4 ounces (113 g), use 2½ teaspoons (13 g) of sea salt. To remove the bitterness of shiso leaves, rub the salt into the leaves, working it in until a dark purple liquid is extracted. Discard the liquid. Once this dark purple liquid is extracted and discarded, you can add the shiso leaves into the umeboshi container. It will turn the ume brine red. This is the umezu (plum vinegar).

The red shiso makes an excellent *furikake* (seasoning sprinkles) called *yukari* for rice, meat, fish, and vegetables. For making *furikake*, dry the pickled red shiso leaves in the sun with the ume and vinegar. When the leaves are fully dried, finely grind them in a spice grinder or with a mortar and pestle. Store the *furikake* in a container with a tight-fitting lid, where it will keep for up to 3 months.

Sonoko Sakai: Making Umeboshi, The Queen

"Most Japanese people love pickles," Sonoko told us. "In fact, when you go visiting in the countryside, people still bring out some pickles and tea, maybe with some onigiri. When a meal is composed, it is a soup and three side dishes, and like the rice, pickles are not mentioned, they are a given—a digestive aid in a meal that is centered around grains."

We were having a meandering conversation about the variety and breadth of tsukemono, touching on everything from the light, quick pickling that most people still have time for to sushi's pickled history (before refrigeration, fish was pressed between layers of soured rice to preserve it long enough to get it from the coastal areas to the interior villages). We were nearly an hour in when Sonoko said, "We still haven't talked about umeboshi. Umeboshi is the queen and probably the most important tsukemono." She told us that umeboshi is thought to combat aging, and she credited her grandmother's umeboshi practice—not just eating but making umeboshi every year—as an important factor in her great longevity (she lived to be 102). Some of Sonoko's best memories of time spent in the kitchen with her grandmother were of pickling.

When Sonoko was a child, her father's job flung the family far and wide, giving her a true cross-cultural upbringing, which she credits for her own sensibilities in the kitchen. But her deep love for cooking came from her grandmother. At one point, her family lived in Japan in a small annex attached by a corridor to her grandmother's home, and Sonoko remembers well running down daily to cook with her. She shared her grandmother's recipe for umeboshi with us, recalling all the times she made it with her grandmother.

As we talked about umeboshi, Sonoko told us that she still had some of the last umeboshi her grandmother had made. The plums were dark and hardened but still edible. In turn, Kirsten told Sonoko that she also had a jar of umeboshi her own mother had made, which she hadn't been able to eat since her mom's passing. We thought about how these live foods created by our hands can outlive us, in this way becoming touchstones that recall the humans who made them.

Sonoko credits her grandmother's umeboshi practice as an important factor in her great longevity.

DILLY BEANS, *page 157*

PEPPER PASTE,
page 295

JICAMA, *page 249*

RADICCHIO-GARLIC KRAUT,
page 312

**HUNGARIAN-INSPIRED
CELERIAC KRAUT,**
page 200

**CEBOLLAS ENCURTIDAS
(PICKLED ONIONS),**
page 287

ESCAROLE KIMCHI, *page 228*

CELERY "STUFFING,"
page 201

POTATOES, SWEET

Sweet potatoes or yams? Most tubers in North American grocery stores are sweet potatoes, even when labeled yams. True yams (of the yam family, Dioscoreaceae) are grown in Africa and in the Caribbean, and very few ever end up in US grocery stores. If you happen to find true yams, you will know it: They are larger than sweet potatoes, they have rounded ends, their skin is tough—almost bark-like—and the flesh is sticky.

So why all the confusion? It is believed that when orange-fleshed, softer-textured sweet potatoes (of the morning glory family, Convolvulaceae) were introduced in the southern United States, growers wanted to differentiate them from the more traditional white-fleshed types. Enslaved Africans called the Southern sweet potato *nyami*, as it reminded them of the starchy, edible root from the lily family that they knew from their homelands. Eventually that name was shortened to *yam* for sweet potatoes, which incidentally are most likely native to the Americas.

Sweet potatoes are considered the world's seventh most important food crop. A 2006 study in India examined whether lactic acid fermentation of sweet potato would be viable for small-scale industries. The study concluded that sweet potatoes could be pickled as such and that the flavor was pleasing. We are going to say the flavor is more than pleasing—it is amazing.

YOUR RAW MATERIAL

Sweet potatoes are available year-round in most stores; however, as with most crops, they are freshest during harvest season, which is in the fall. Look for sweet potatoes that are firm (not soft or wrinkly) and blemish free.

The most common varieties are the more mealy, pale-fleshed potatoes (colors range from creamy beige to yellow or pink), such as Jersey or the Japanese varieties. The types with deep copper-toned and orange flesh are sweeter, moister varieties, such as Beauregard, Jewel,

GOOD AND GOOD FOR YOU

S. H. Panda, M. Parmanick, and R. C. Ray, the authors of the India study cited above, were interested in the nutritional benefits of sweet potato fermentation and its "hygienic" potential as a safe way to process food. They deemed lactic acid fermentation "an important technology" in developing nations:

> Lactic-acid fermentation also has some other distinct advantages, e.g., the food becomes resistant to microbial spoilage and to development of toxins. . . . Sweet potato, in tropical regions, is consumed in the households of small farmers and poor people. Night blindness is a major physiological disorder among these people due to vitamin A deficiency, which can be alleviated by regular consumption of orange-flesh (ß-carotene-rich) sweet potato either fresh, boiled . . . or as lacto-pickles.

and Garnett. Stokes Purple, a relative newcomer with deep purple-magenta flesh, has a rich, dense texture and a sweet flavor that lies somewhere between that of the pale-fleshed varieties and that of the sweet dark orange ones.

IN THE CROCK

Sweet potatoes are one of those vegetables for which it doesn't pay to skimp on the salt, as they will soften.

West African–Inspired Sweet Potato Ferment

yield: about 3 quarts (2.8 l)
technique used: Relishes/Chutneys/Salsas/Salads (page 74)

This recipe was inspired by West African groundnut stew. The sweet potatoes have to be sliced quite finely, which is best done with the slicer side of a grater, a mandoline, the slicing blade in your food processor, or fantastic knife skills.

 5 **pounds (2.3 kg) sweet potatoes, peeled and thinly sliced**
 1 **green bell pepper, diced**
 1 **medium onion, diced**
 5 **cloves garlic, finely minced**
3 or 4 **dried tomatoes, thinly sliced**
 1 **tablespoon (7 g) whole coriander seeds**
 1 **tablespoon (15 g) grated fresh ginger**
 2 **teaspoons (6 g) ground cayenne pepper**
2½–3 **tablespoons (40–50 g) unrefined salt**
   Grape leaf or parchment paper, to top the ferment

1. Place the sweet potatoes, bell pepper, onion, garlic, dried tomatoes, coriander seeds, ginger, and cayenne in a large bowl and mix well. Add 2½ tablespoons of the salt and with your hands massage it into the mixture. Then taste. You should be able to taste the salt without it being overwhelming. Add more salt as necessary. The sweet potatoes respond well to salting and will quickly begin to develop a brine.

2. Transfer the sweet potato mixture, a few handfuls at a time, to your fermentation vessel, pressing down as you work. Top with a grape leaf or parchment paper and weight if you have one.

3. Follow the instructions for your fermentation vessel. For a jar, if using the burping method (page 44) make sure there is little headspace and seal lid tightly. Burp daily or as needed. Alternatively, top the ferment with a quart-size ziplock bag. Press the bag down onto the top of the ferment and then fill it with water and seal.

4. Set your fermentation vessel on a plate in a spot where you can keep an eye on it, out of direct sunlight, and let ferment for 7 to 21 days. Start taste-testing when the brine becomes cloudy. The ferment is done when it has a pleasing acidic smell and it tastes pickle-y, perhaps with an effervescent zing.

5. To store, transfer to smaller jars, if necessary, and tamp down. Pour in any brine that's left. Tighten the lids, then set in the fridge, where the ferment will keep for 1 year.

POTATOES, WHITE

Let's just get this out of the way: These fermented potatoes are meant to be cooked, not eaten raw like pickles. And potatoes store well, so generally speaking, you won't be fermenting them for the sake of preservation. This is all about enhancing flavors, having fun, and, in theory, breaking down some of the carbohydrates before cooking.

Let's talk about fun first. Fermentation should be fun, and playing with how fermentation can enhance or transform flavors is fun. Fermented French fries, oven fries, hash browns, and chips are fun.

Now let's talk about death—not yours. We are talking about the microbes. It is true the probiotics won't survive whatever heat treatment the chips or fries get. But before you mourn the probiotics, let's remember that even if we are fermenting for health, probiotics are not the only bennies—don't forget the postbiotics (see page 25). And do use your leftover fermented brine in soup stocks.

We spent weeks in what will be forever remembered around here as The Great Fry Experiments, fermenting both sweet and white potatoes, cut in spears or thin crosswise slices, at different rates and salt ratios. There was one week in particular when we had 18 separate quart jars that needed burping at least twice a day. We learned that all types of fermented white and sweet potatoes work well for frying, but some are tastier than others. Hands down, russets were our favorite for classic French fries. Yet red and yellow potatoes yielded crispier, lighter potato chips. We found Basic Brine (page 102) to be the best for potatoes, although a few times tasters blindly picked potatoes fermented in High Brine (page 102) because the resultant fries and chips had that extra bit of salt they wanted in their salty snacks. Lower brines were hit-and-miss, sometimes allowing microbes that smelled horrible to thrive. If this happens, send to the compost pile. As far as added flavors, we tried so many herbs and spices. Potatoes fermented with rosemary and plenty of garlic edged out spicy fries and smoked paprika fries, but not by a lot.

As far as sweet potato fries (we didn't try chips), we found the orange-fleshed variety to have better texture than the lighter-colored flesh. The final texture of the lighter-fleshed variety was too chewy, but the flavor was good. Purple-fleshed varieties were just plain beautiful, and the texture and flavor were appealing as well.

As far as timing, we worked in cooler ambient temperatures. While the sweet potatoes ended up more acidic than the whites when full-sour fermentation had been reached, early on there wasn't a huge difference. We liked the fries best when made with potatoes fermented for 3 to 5 days because sour wasn't their only flavor. Further into fermentation they were quite pickle-like, which is also delicious but definitely its own flavor.

GREEN POTATOES

When exposed to light, especially fluorescent light, potatoes can produce a glycoalkaloid called solanine. It's one of the compounds that gives nightshades their dubious reputation. Solanine is toxic and can cause headaches, diarrhea, nausea, vomiting, and central nervous system paralysis. Fortunately, you will know when potatoes have produced solanine because they take on a green hue, often right under the skin. Peeling the potato can reduce the solanine content. If you have doubts about a greenish potato, don't eat it. Cooking doesn't rid the potato of the toxin, and neither does fermentation.

Fermented French Fries or Potato Chips

yield: about a quart, or pound of fries
technique: Mastering Brine Pickling (page 101)

At its core, this is a quick ferment, but make it a few days ahead to allow the flavor time to develop. Ferment the quantity you will want to eat, and when you want to have more, do it again. These last in their brine, refrigerated, for months. If you love them full sour then you can make and have them ready whenever you need them.

This fermentation is all about making a unique fry. It is a delightful example of how easily you can turn the fermentation dial to whatever kind of flavor you are seeking, from mildly fermented to full-sour salt-and-vinegar chips. We experimented with adding many kinds of seasonings to the fermentation vessel to flavor our soon-to-be-fried potatoes; among the best, in our opinion, were black pepper, garlic, rosemary and other fresh herbs, paprika or smoked paprika, and dried chile peppers.

>   2 **pounds (907 g) potatoes**
>   1 **quart (946 ml) Basic Brine (2 tablespoons/
>   34 g unrefined salt per quart unchlorinated
>   water)**

FOR FRYING

>   **Avocado or peanut oil (a few tablespoons for
>   baking or air-frying, or a few cups for deep
>   frying)**

1. Scrub the potatoes and peel if you'd like (we leave the skins on). For fries, cut the potatoes into thin sticks: Slice each one into ¼-inch-thick slabs, then cut each slab into ¼-inch-thick sticks.

For chips, a mandoline is your best bet; you want slices about ⅛ inch thick. In either case, drop the raw potato slices or sticks into a bowl of cool water as you work. This will keep them from browning as well as remove some of the starch.

2. Arrange the potato chips or sticks in your vessel. Pour enough brine over the potatoes to cover them.

3. Follow the instructions for your fermentation vessel. For a jar, if using the burping method (page 44) make sure there is little headspace and seal lid tightly. Burp daily or as needed.

4. Set your fermentation vessel on a plate in a spot where you can keep an eye on it, out of direct sunlight, and let ferment for 3 days.

5. When you're ready to cook the fries, drain off the brine and blot the potatoes with clean towels to dry them.

6. Now you're ready to cook:

To air-fry, drizzle the potatoes with oil. Air-fry according to the method recommended for your air fryer.

To bake, preheat your oven to 375°F/190°C. Drizzle the potatoes with oil and spread them in a single layer on a baking sheet. Bake for 20 minutes, stir if needed, and then turn up the heat to 425°F/218°C and bake for another 20 minutes, or until brown.

To fry, heat a few inches of oil in a Dutch oven or wok to 300°F/150°C. Carefully place a batch of fries in the hot oil, taking care not to crowd them. Cook for 4 to 5 minutes per batch, agitating occasionally with a slotted spoon. You want them soft at this point, not brown. Remove each batch and drain on paper towels.

When all the potatoes have been fried, turn up the heat under your oil. When the oil reaches 400°F/204°C, begin frying the potatoes in batches again, but now you will cook until the fries are crisp and golden. As they finish, remove the potatoes from the oil and drain on paper towels. Cooked fries can be kept hot and crisp on a wire rack set in a sheet tray in a warm oven while the rest are frying. Serve immediately.

VARIATIONS
Miso Fries or Shio Koji Fries

Prepare potato sticks as described in the recipe on page 309, but instead of brining them, place them in a miso pickling bed (page 93) or a shio koji pickling bed (page 92). Let them marinate in the bed for 1 to 3 days, or longer. The flavors will deepen as time progresses.

When you're ready to cook them, preheat your oven to 375°F/190°C. Remove the potato sticks from the pickling bed, wiping off excess paste as you go. You can leave a little of the paste on for extra flavor, but you will have to monitor the baking carefully to avoid the sugars burning.

Put the potato sticks in a bowl, drizzle on a bit of oil, and toss gently to coat. Spread the potatoes in a single layer on a baking sheet. Bake for 30 to 40 minutes, or until browned nicely on the outside and steamy and cooked on the inside, stirring as needed. Serve immediately.

An air fryer also works well, but we don't recommend deep frying for miso or shio koji fries.

IN THE CROCK
Fermented Hashies

yield: about 1 pint
technique: Dry Brining (page 73)

We love hash browns, so it was natural that we wanted to "see what happens" to shredded potatoes in fermentation, with the goal of frying them up as crispy breakfast comfort food with a twist. All hash-brown lovers in our area approved. They turned out lightly salty, lightly fermented, super tasty, and not starchy-soggy in the middle.

As usual, surface area plays a big role. The large surface area of the shreds gives the microbes more immediate access to the carbs they love, speeding up fermentation and adding to the crisp. We like a 1-day ferment with these; with all that starch, they begin to bubble and acidify quickly but aren't strongly sour after just a day. If you want them more sour, simply ferment them longer. Add your favorite spices or herbs to the fermentation jar and you will find that their flavors deepen.

A little less than 1 pound (454 g) white potatoes
1 generous teaspoon (6 g) unrefined salt

FOR FRYING
Avocado oil
Salt and freshly ground black pepper, to taste

1. Grate the potatoes, place in a bowl, and cover with a generous amount of water. Slosh them around with your fingers. You will see the starch release. Pour this off. Repeat. Getting rid of the extra starch will help minimize any rawness in the center when frying.

2. Pour off the water and lightly squeeze the water from the potatoes. You don't want them drenched, but neither do you want them completely dry. Return the potatoes to the bowl, add the salt, and mix well.

3. Pack the potatoes into a pint jar, pressing to release air pockets as you go. You will see brine form around the potatoes. Put the lid on the jar and tighten.

4. Place the jar on your counter, where you can keep an eye on it, out of direct sunlight. When you see the lid tighten with pressure, "burp" the jar, cracking open the lid for just a second to release the built-up gas, then screwing the lid back on tight (see page 44). Ferment as desired; we find 24 hours is nice, although you could also ferment them until they are fully sour, which takes about 3 days. If the potatoes are ready and you are not, place the jar in the refrigerator to slow the fermentation.

5. When you're ready to fry the hash browns, drain off the brine. Spread the shredded potatoes on a clean kitchen towel, roll it up, and twist to wring out moisture. Make sure the potatoes are dry; this will be the difference between crispy or soggy hash browns.

6. Drizzle enough oil to generously coat the bottom of a cast-iron or nonstick pan over medium-high heat. When the oil is warm, spread the shredded potatoes evenly across the pan.

7. Let the potatoes fry without disturbance, so they get browned and crispy on the bottom. Then flip, in sections if needed. Again, fry without disturbing them so they can brown. You may need to add a little oil to keep the edges sizzling, but take care; too much oil and you are at greasy and soggy.

8. When the hashies are browned and crisp on both sides, sprinkle on some black pepper and enjoy. They should be salty, but feel free to add more to taste.

RADICCHIO

Radicchio, a member of the chicory family, is a beautiful salad green with white-veined maroon leaves, and increasingly with many hues of pink. Even though it's often grown as an annual, it's actually a perennial, which means you can harvest leaves year-round. Radicchio is common in salad mixes, but try it fermented; you're in for a treat. We love it grilled and keep meaning to try a charred radicchio ferment, much like our Charred Cabbage Sauerkraut (page 174).

YOUR RAW MATERIAL

Commonly available is radicchio di Chioggia, which looks like a grapefruit-size head of red cabbage, but the texture is more like that of iceberg lettuce. Radicchio de Treviso is burgundy and bullet shaped.

While in many cases salting will help remove bitterness from vegetables, we have found that radicchio holds on tightly to its delicious bitterness—but we also know that not everyone loves that. If you are looking for a less bitter variety, try radicchio Rosalba. It is pink and fluffy, less bitter, and lightly floral. Sugarloaf radicchio is the mildest of all and is green with a light blush.

One more note: We have found that the top layer of radicchio ferments oxidizes easily. To avoid this, keep extra outer leaves or parchment paper on top, and take extra care in keeping the headspace in a jar to a minimum.

IN THE CROCK

Radicchio-Garlic Kraut

See photo on page 304

yield: about 1 quart (946 ml)

technique used: Mastering Sauerkraut (page 61)

This ferment makes a great simple condiment, or use it to create Radicchio Tapenade (page 372).

> 2 heads (about 2 pounds/907 g) radicchio di Chioggia or other variety
> 8 cloves garlic, finely grated or minced
> 2–2½ teaspoons (11–15 g) unrefined salt
> 5 or 6 sprigs basil, leaves removed and chopped (optional)

1. Rinse the radicchio in cold water. Pull off an outer leaf and set aside to use as a follower. Quarter, core, and thinly slice the rest of the radicchio and put in a large bowl.

2. Mix in the garlic, 1½ teaspoons of the salt, and basil, if using, and massage them into the leaves. Then taste. You should be able to taste the salt without it being overwhelming. Add more salt if necessary. The radicchio will soon look wet and limp, and liquid will pool. However, if you don't see much brine, let the mixture stand, covered, for 45 minutes, then massage again.

3. Transfer the radicchio to your fermentation vessel, a handful at a time, pressing down to remove air pockets. You should see some brine on top of the mixture when you press. If you don't, return the radicchio to the bowl and massage again.

4. Top the mixture with the reserved radicchio leaf to keep everything submerged, pressing it down under the brine. Add a weight if you have one. Follow the instructions for your fermentation vessel. For a jar, if using the burping method (page 44) make sure there is little headspace and seal lid tightly. Burp daily or as needed. Alternatively, top the ferment with a quart-size ziplock bag. Press the bag down onto the top of the ferment and then fill it with water and seal.

5. Set your fermentation vessel on a plate in a spot where you can keep an eye on it, out of direct sunlight, and let ferment for 5 to 10 days. Check regularly to make sure the kraut is submerged, pressing down, as needed, to bring the brine back to the surface. The radicchio won't lose its color but the brine will get cloudy; this is when you can start to taste-test. You'll know it's done when it has a pleasing acidic smell, it tastes pickle-y, and the bitterness of the radicchio has softened slightly.

6. To store, tamp down to make sure the mixture is submerged in its brine and tighten the lid. This will keep, refrigerated, for 9 months.

Radicchio Quince Fermented Salad

See photo on page 188

yield: about 2 quarts (1.9 l)
technique used: Relishes/Chutneys/Salsas/Salads
(page 74)

Bitter and slightly sweet, this fermented salad is a power-punched side dish. Of the radicchio ferments, it is Christopher's favorite. The ferment ages well. It stays crunchy and improves as the flavors mingle.

- 1 large head (about 3 pounds/1.4 kg) radicchio de Trevisano or other variety, cored and chopped
- 3 small-medium quince, peeled, cored, and thinly sliced
- 1 small red onion, thinly sliced
- ⅓ cup (35 g) fresh cranberries, sliced in half
- 1 mandarin orange, peeled, sectioned, and cut into pieces
- 1 (2-inch/5 cm) piece fresh ginger, grated (about 2 tablespoons/22 g)
- 2–2½ tablespoons (34–42 g) unrefined salt

Prepare the ingredients as indicated in ingredients list, mix them together in a bowl, and follow method for Radicchio-Garlic Kraut (facing page). This salad will keep for 4 months, refrigerated.

Radicchio Relish

yield: about 1 quart (946 ml)
technique used: Relishes/Chutneys/Salsas/Salads
(page 74)

In this variation, radicchio becomes a relish that punches the bitter right back with its strong herbal flavors. Kirsten loves this intensity, and given that Christopher's favorite flavor is fruity and sweet, this gives you a peek at the personality of our palates (or our individual resident microbes). We make this with the lighter pink varieties, and it is beautiful.

- 1–2 small heads (about 1 pound/450 g) radicchio, cored and chopped
- 1 small fennel bulb, thinly sliced
- 1 medium red onion, thinly sliced
- 1½ cups (165 g) fresh cranberries, sliced in half
- 2 sprigs fresh rosemary, stemmed and finely chopped
- 2 teaspoons (2 g) whole juniper berries, crushed finely or ground
- 1 teaspoon (2 g) freshly ground black pepper
- 2½–3 teaspoons (14–18 g) unrefined salt

Follow the instructions given for Radicchio-Garlic Kraut (facing page), using these ingredients instead. The relish will keep, refrigerated, for 9 months.

RADISHES

Radishes are extremely versatile, and daikons, in particular, are perfect for experimenting with pickling beds. Japanese tsukemono has many variations of daikon pickles.

Many people equate kimchi with fermented napa cabbage, but the radish is an equally important ingredient in kimchi. We include a recipe for *kkakdugi*, a radish-based kimchi; ours is made with watercress. We don't include many recipes for traditional radish-based Asian ferments in this book because an entire book could be written on fermented radish, and there are so many wonderful recipes available elsewhere (we include a radish achar from the pickling traditions of South Asia in our book *Fiery Ferments*, and Sonoko Sakai has a wonderful recipe for kiriboshi daikon in her book *Japanese Home Cooking*). That said, you will see radishes and daikon used throughout this book.

Radishes were a conventional crop in ancient Greece and the Roman Empire. In Bavaria, the radish is one of the symbols of the city of Munich, where salted radishes are consumed with pretzels and beer. Throughout Europe, grain-based meals often include them. In Japan, a drink made from carrots and daikon radishes is said to cleanse the body. Indeed, radishes contain diastase, an enzyme that helps the body digest starches. They also help clear phlegm from the body and are chock-full of vitamins.

Fermenting radishes can emit a funky aroma. That funk isn't present in the flavor, though, so don't let it scare you away. Radishes also lose their tangy bite when fermented, so if you're wary of their spiciness, fermentation may help you grow to love them. They are one of the most delicious fermented vegetables!

YOUR RAW MATERIAL

The many varieties of radish offer an abundance of potential. They come in many sizes, shapes, and colors. Leave 'em whole, grate 'em, slice 'em, dice 'em. Small varieties such as the common Cherry Belle, Champion, Plum Purple, and French Breakfast are some of the first vegetables to appear in temperate-climate gardens and fields and in the market. They make beautiful spring pickles.

Select radishes that are bright and firm; soft or woody radishes are old and don't ferment well.

Radish Fennel Ferment

yield: about 1 pint (473 ml)
technique used: Mastering Sauerkraut (page 61)

This ferment is light, both in taste and in its pastel color, which complements the light pink and white blossoms of early spring.

In traditional Chinese medicine, radishes are a tonic for the liver and gallbladder. They break up fat and phlegm and regulate bile flow. In a sense, eating radishes gets your juices going—it helps your body come out of winter.

As with radishes, fennel is great for digestion, and its light, aromatic flavor complements the more watery, spicy radish. Fennel is also rich in vitamin K_2, which works in the circulation system by breaking up "debris" in blood vessels.

This ferment is very simple. You can start it today and be eating it in 4 or 5 days. It is tasty sprinkled on a green salad or served alongside protein-rich foods such as hard-boiled eggs.

1 bunch small radishes, such as Cherry Belle or French Breakfast
1 medium fresh fennel bulb
1½ teaspoons (8 g) unrefined salt
Grape leaf or parchment paper, to top the ferment

1. This ferment works best if the radishes and fennel bulb are thinly sliced. Save the fennel stalks for an herbal pickling bed or soup stock, but chop a little of the frond into the mix. Braise the radish leaves as greens, or add them to a ferment.

2. Add most of the salt and with your hands massage it into the vegetables. Then taste. You should be able to taste the salt without it being overwhelming. Add more salt if necessary. The vegetables will begin to look wet and limp and liquid will pool.

3. Transfer the mixture to your fermentation vessel, a handful at a time, pressing down to remove air pockets. You should see some brine on top of the mixture when you press. If you don't, return the mixture to the bowl and massage again.

4. Top the vegetables with a grape leaf or parchment paper and weight, if you have one, to keep everything submerged. Follow the instructions for your fermentation vessel. For a jar, if using the burping method (page 44) make sure there is little headspace and seal lid tightly. Burp daily or as needed. Alternatively, top the ferment with a quart-size ziplock bag. Press the bag down onto the top of the ferment and then fill it with water and seal.

5. Set your fermentation vessel on a plate in a spot where you can keep an eye on it, out of direct sunlight, and let ferment for 4 to 14 days. Check regularly to make sure the kraut is submerged, pressing down, as needed, to bring the brine back to the surface. As the radishes ferment, they begin to lose their vibrant color and the brine will get cloudy; this is when you can start to taste-test. You'll know the ferment is ready when everything is pink and has a crispy crunch, with pleasingly sour notes.

6. When the ferment is ready, make sure it is in an airtight container and store in the fridge. The ferment will keep, refrigerated, for 6 months.

WASTE NOT
Ferment radish leaves as you would mustard greens. They are especially nice in any kraut- or kimchi-style ferment.

IN THE PICKLE JAR
Spring Radish Pickles
yield: 1 quart (946 ml)
technique used: Mastering Brine Pickling (page 101)

The chiles provide additional color and spice in this ferment. They're optional, but they do give the pickles some nice punch.

1 teaspoon (4 g) sugar
1 quart (946 ml) Low-Salt Basic Brine (4 teaspoons/22 g unrefined salt per quart unchlorinated water)
1–2 bunches salad radishes, ends trimmed
5 scallions, whites only, halved lengthwise
3 slices fresh ginger
2 or 3 small dried red chiles or 1–2 tablespoons (16–32 g) chile pepper flakes (optional)

1. Add the sugar to the brine and mix to dissolve.

2. Rinse and prep radishes and scallions. (Keep those scallion greens to chop into another ferment.) Pack them with the ginger and chiles into a jar, wedging them under the shoulder of the jar. Pour in enough brine to cover them. Store any leftover brine in the fridge (it will keep for a week; discard thereafter or dry out and reclaim salt and make a new batch, if needed).

3. If using the burping method (page 44) make sure there is little headspace and seal lid tightly. Burp daily or as needed.

4. Set the jar on a plate in a spot where you can keep an eye on it, out of direct sunlight, and let ferment for 7 to 10 days. During the fermentation period, monitor the brine level and top off with the reserved brine, if needed, to cover. As the radishes and scallions ferment, the brine gets delightfully pink. They're ready when you can smell and taste the acidity.

5. To store, make sure veggies are submerged in the brine, then tighten the lid and put in the refrigerator. After a day, check to be sure the pickles are still submerged, topping off with brine if necessary. These pickles will keep, refrigerated, for 6 months.

Radish Cube Kimchi with Watercress (Kkakdugi)

yield: about 2 quarts (1.9 l)
technique used: Relishes/Chutneys/Salsas/Salads (page 74)

Watercress has the distinction of being the oldest known leaf vegetable to have been consumed by humans. It is both a salad green and a medicinal herb. It is said to promote an appetite, and because of this quality, it finds its way into many traditional kimchi recipes. It should be long, leafy, and fragrant, but it has a very short shelf life. You can check the quality of the plant by breaking a stem; if it is older, a thread will show at the break. The peppery quality of the plant varies, but you can use it whether mild or spicy.

Cayenne will make this kimchi fiery hot. You can substitute gochugaru, if you can find it; it ranges from fiery to mild, depending on the variety, and will make this ferment quite beautiful. Paprika is a heat-free option.

- 3 pounds (1.4 kg) daikon radish, chopped into ½-inch (1.3 cm) cubes
- 1 bunch scallions, sliced into 1-inch (2.5 cm) pieces
- 1 bunch watercress, coarsely chopped (about 1 cup, loosely packed, or 35 g)
- ½ cup (42 g) ground cayenne, salt-free gochugaru, or paprika
- 2 or 3 cloves garlic, minced
- 1 tablespoon (11 g) finely grated fresh ginger
- 1 teaspoon (5 g) sugar
- 2 teaspoons (8 g) dried baby shrimp, crumbled (optional)
- 1½ tablespoons (25 g) unrefined salt
  Grape leaf or parchment paper, to top the ferment

1. Combine the radishes, scallions, watercress, pepper powder of your choice, garlic, ginger, sugar, shrimp, if using, and salt in a large bowl. (You may want to wear gloves if using cayenne.) Massage the mixture well with your hands.

2. Transfer the radish mixture to your fermentation vessel, a few handfuls at a time, pressing down to release air pockets as you work. More brine will release at this stage, and you should see brine above the veggies.

3. Top with a grape leaf or parchment paper and weight if you have one. Follow the instructions for your fermentation vessel. For a jar, if using the burping method (page 44) make sure there is little headspace and seal lid tightly. Burp daily or as needed. Alternatively, top the ferment with a quart-size ziplock bag. Press the bag down onto the top of the ferment and then fill it with water and seal.

4. Set your fermentation vessel on a plate in a spot where you can keep an eye on it, out of direct sunlight, and let ferment for 7 to 14 days. Start taste-testing the kimchi on day 7. It is ready when it reaches the desired sourness.

5. When kimchi is ready, make sure it is in an airtight container and store in the fridge. The ferment will keep, refrigerated, for 6 months.

FERMENTISTA'S TIP

IN THE CROCK

Radishes are a great way to save a dry cabbage. Can't get enough brine from a cabbage? Adding a bit of shredded or julienned daikon will save the process.

Create Your Own Recipes

» Ferment radishes in any pickling bed (see Chapter 6).

» Pickle daikon spears in Basic Brine (page 102) to use in sushi rolls. Add shiso for beautiful color and extra flavor.

RAPINI (BROCCOLI RABE)

Despite the "broccoli" in its common name (the Andy Boy company dubbed it *broccoli rabe* in 1964), rapini is in the turnip clan, as reflected by its name: *Rapini* is Italian for "little turnip." The vegetable is actually the sprouting top of the plant. In recent years, the sprouting tops of many other crucifers—such as collards, kale, and mustards—have been sold as rapini. These are all delicious when fermented; let this recipe get you started.

Rapini Kimchi

yield: about 1 pint (473 ml)
technique used: Mastering Kimchi Basics (page 117)

Rapini tends to be bitter, although the bitterness will vary depending on the particular greens, and the bitter flavor won't dominate when fermented. To remove any bitter flavors more thoroughly, soak longer or overnight.

- 1 **quart (946 ml) Soaking Brine (¼ cup/67 g unrefined salt per quart unchlorinated water)**
- 1–2 **bunches rapini, cut into 1-inch (2.5 cm) pieces**
- ½ **cup (50 g) grated radish or turnip**
- 4 **scallions, chopped**
- 2 **cloves garlic, minced**
- 1½ **teaspoons (7 ml) lemon juice**
- ¼ **teaspoon (1.3 g) chile pepper flakes or salt-free gochugaru**
- 1 **teaspoon (5 g) anchovy paste (optional)**
  Unrefined salt, as needed
  Grape leaf or parchment paper, to top the ferment

1. Pour the brine into a crock or large bowl. Submerge the rapini (buds and all) in the brine for 2 hours. Then drain and gently squeeze out the excess liquid.

2. Chop the rapini and place in a bowl. Mix in the radish, scallions, garlic, lemon juice, chile flakes, and anchovy paste, if using. Then taste. The brining process and anchovy paste are generally enough for proper saltiness, but if you can't taste the salt, sprinkle in a bit more.

3. Transfer the vegetables to your fermentation vessel, pressing down to release air pockets as you work. Add any liquid left in the bowl.

4. Top with a grape leaf or parchment paper and weight if you have one. Follow the instructions for your fermentation vessel. For a jar, if using the burping method (page 44) make sure there is little headspace and seal lid tightly. Burp daily or as needed. Alternatively, top the ferment with a quart-size ziplock bag. Press the bag down onto the top of the ferment and then fill it with water and seal.

5. Set your fermentation vessel on a plate in a spot where you can keep an eye on it, out of direct sunlight, and let ferment for 5 to 7 days. Start to taste-test when you can smell the acidity. It's done when the flavors combine to make a pungent, slightly sour, slightly bitter condiment.

6. To store, transfer to smaller jars, if necessary, and tamp down. Pour in any brine that's left. Tighten the lids, then store in the fridge, where the kimchi will keep for 8 months.

RHUBARB

Rhubarb is complicated. The leaf will kill you, the root is a powerful medicinal, and the stalk lies in the realm of the culinary. Many people don't realize the stalk can be eaten raw. Its flavor, when pickled, is unexpected, with a less sour bite than cooked rhubarb.

YOUR RAW MATERIAL

Many people think of rhubarb as an unusual member of the fruit family, and it is often referred to as "pie plant." It is, however, a vegetable, and it ferments beautifully. We've used it a lot over the years; you can find recipes for Rhubarb Kimchi and Rhubarb Achar in *Fiery Ferments*.

Rhubarb is a cool-season perennial that sends up stalks in the spring; as summer temperatures climb, this plant slows its growth, sometimes to the point of dormancy. Look for long, fleshy, firm stalks in spring and early summer.

Rhubarb Relish

yield: about 1 pint (473 ml)
technique: Relishes/Chutneys/Salsas/Salads (page 74)

In our experiments, rosemary was a surprisingly delightful pairing for rhubarb.

5 or 6 **stalks rhubarb**
1 **heaping tablespoon (7 g) minced fresh rosemary**
1–1¼ **teaspoons (6–7 g) unrefined salt**
½ **cup (61 g) dried cranberries**
½ **cup (56 g) dried golden berries (see sidebar, page 320)**
Parchment paper, to top the ferment

1. Cut the rhubarb stalks lengthwise (or into thirds lengthwise if they are very thick), then slice the sections crosswise. You want 2 cups of thin slices. Put them in a bowl and stir in the rosemary. Sprinkle in 1 teaspoon of the salt and, with your hands, massage it into the rhubarb. Let sit, covered, for 10 minutes, then massage again. Mix in the cranberries and golden berries. Then taste. You should be able to taste the salt without it being overwhelming. Add more salt if necessary.

2. Transfer the rhubarb mixture to a crock or jar, pressing as you go to remove air pockets. You should see some brine on top of the mixture when you press.

3. Top the ferment with parchment paper and weight if you have one. Follow the instructions for your fermentation vessel. For a jar, if using the burping method (page 44) make sure there is little headspace and seal lid tightly. Burp daily or as needed. Alternatively, top the ferment with a quart-size ziplock bag. Press the bag down onto the top of the ferment and then fill it with water and seal.

4. Set your fermentation vessel on a plate in a spot where you can keep an eye on it, out of direct sunlight, and let ferment for 5 to 7 days. The rhubarb is ready when its puckering sourness has mellowed and it is pleasantly acidic, as though you'd added a splash of lemon juice.

5. To store, transfer to smaller jars, if necessary, and tamp down. Pour in any brine that's left. Tighten the lids, then store in the fridge, where it will keep for 9 months.

Fermented Rhubarb Infused with Ginger and Cardamom

yield: about 1 pint (473 ml)
technique used: Relishes/Chutneys/Salsas/Salads (page 74)

- 1 **pound (454 g) rhubarb stalks**
- 1 **tablespoon (15 g) grated fresh ginger**
- ½ **teaspoon (1.2 g) ground cardamom**
- 1 **scant teaspoon (5 g) unrefined salt**

Follow the recipe for Rhubarb Relish (page 319), adding the ginger and cardamom to the rhubarb with the salt.

GOLDEN BERRIES

Golden berries, also called Incan berries, Cape gooseberries, and Peruvian ground cherries, hail from the mountains of Peru, where they were cultivated as far back as the time of the Incan Empire. They grow in a husk and are closely related to the tomatillo. You can find them in many health food stores and online. They are a favorite flavoring in ferments, adding a bit of sweetness and citrus.

RUTABAGA

Somehow or another, once upon a time a wild cabbage and a turnip got together and produced the rutabaga. Perhaps the marriage took place in Sweden, whence the name comes. There are references to it in Europe during the Middle Ages as both animal fodder and people food, which is a hint to its association with poverty. The rutabaga is a nutritional and gut-health powerhouse as an excellent source of fiber, including the prebiotic inulin. Although the two are seemingly similar, rutabagas are not turnips. Turnips have a light radish flavor, whereas when eaten raw, the rutabaga has a crisp, sweet flavor, even when large. Once fermented, rutabaga stands out with a touch of sweetness and a nice pale orange-yellow hue.

YOUR RAW MATERIAL

Rutabagas should be heavy, but not overly large, as that may indicate a woody or pithy core. Sometimes rutabagas come waxed to keep them fresh for longer; peel those.

Rutabaga Kraut

See photo on page 226

Why not rutabaga kraut? Keep it plain, or dress it up with any of the herbs or spices that complement this root, such as rosemary or dried orange zest. Shred the rutabaga, then prepare it as kraut, following the process outlined for for Naked Kraut (page 173). Or see the recipe for Sauerrüben III (page 343), which uses rutabaga.

IN THE CROCK

Rutabaga Grapefruit Fermented Salad

yield: about 1 quart (946 ml)
technique used: Relishes/Chutneys/Salsas/Salads
(page 74)

Crunchy, nicely sour, and a little bitter, this fermented salad is bold and refreshing. We make it in winter, when roots and citrus are in season.

- 1 large rutabaga (about 1 pound/450 g)
- 2 teaspoons (11 g) unrefined salt
- ½ grapefruit, peeled, sectioned, and cut into pieces
- 1 medium shallot, thinly sliced
- Grape leaf or parchment paper, to top the ferment

1. A substantial rutabaga requires a sharp, sturdy knife. Peel the rutabaga, then trim off the ends, cut it into manageable wedges, and slice it as thinly as possible (or use a mandoline).

2. Transfer the rutabaga slices to a large bowl and add the salt. Massage briefly to begin building brine. Add the grapefruit and shallot and mix gently, so as to keep the grapefruit pieces somewhat intact. They will make a nice pop in the salad after fermentation.

3. Transfer the mixture to your vessel, pressing down as you go to remove air pockets. Top with a grape leaf or parchment paper and weight if you have one.

4. Follow the instructions for your fermentation vessel. For a jar, if using the burping method (page 44) make sure there is little headspace and seal lid tightly. Burp daily or as needed. Alternatively, top the ferment with a quart-size ziplock bag. Press the bag down onto the top of the ferment and then fill it with water and seal.

5. Set your fermentation vessel on a plate in a spot where you can keep an eye on it, out of direct sunlight, and let ferment for 3 to 7 days. Start to taste-test the salad on day 4. You'll know it's ready when the flavor has developed a nice sour quality.

6. When the ferment is ready, transfer to smaller jars, if necessary, and tamp down. Pour in any brine that's left. Tighten the lids, then store in the fridge, where the rutabaga will keep for 6 months.

ASPARAGUS PICKLES,
page 149

LEEK-CRACKED PEPPER
KRAUT, *page 259*

TURMERIC PASTE,
page 340

SAUERRÜBEN II (sliced
with black pepper),
page 343

ONION AND PEPPER
RELISH, *page 286*

CURTIDO, *page 176*

KIMCHI, *page 182*

VIETNAMESE-STYLE
PICKLED SCALLIONS,
page 324

SCALLIONS

Scallions, also called green onions, are rich in vitamins A and C (especially in the green tops), and they are a welcome addition in just about any ferment. For fermenting, we generally slice them into 1- to 2-inch pieces. The green part does get soft, though, and if you find that unappealing, slice that part paper thin. You can also use the white bulbs of scallions whole in brined pickle medleys.

IN THE PICKLE JAR

Vietnamese-Style Pickled Scallions

See photo on page 323

yield: 1 pint to 1 quart (473 to 946 ml), depending on the size of the scallions
technique used: Mastering Brine Pickling (page 101)

Feasting is a significant part of the celebration of Tet, the Vietnamese New Year. The rich, meat-centric meals can be hard on digestion, however, and this is why *hanh muoi*, the dish this ferment is based on, is an indispensable part of the menu. The scallions create balance in the meal and aid in digestion.

This recipe can also be used to pickle shallots.

1 **pound (454 g) scallions**
1 **quart (946 ml) Basic Brine (2 tablespoons/ 34 g unrefined salt per quart unchlorinated water)**
  Large vegetable or parchment paper, to top the ferment (optional)

FOR DAY 3 OF FERMENTATION
1–2 **tablespoons (12–24 g) unrefined sugar or raw honey (15–30 ml)**
2 **tablespoons (30 ml) rice vinegar**

1. Rinse the scallions and peel off any dry skin. Cut off the green tops; save them for another use.

2. Pack the trimmed scallions into a 1-quart jar, wedging them under the shoulder of the jar. Pour in enough brine to cover them completely. Store any leftover brine in the fridge (it will keep for a week; discard thereafter or dry out and reclaim salt and make a new batch, if needed).

3. Top the scallions with a large vegetable leaf or a piece of parchment paper, if using, to keep them submerged. If using the burping method (page 44) make sure there is little headspace and seal lid tightly. Burp daily or as needed.

4. Set the jar on a plate in a spot where you can keep an eye on it, out of direct sunlight, and let ferment for 2 days. On day 3, whisk together the sugar and rice vinegar, remove enough brine that you can pour in the vinegar mixture, and add it. Let ferment for 2 days longer.

5. Tighten the lid and store in the fridge. These pickled scallions will keep, refrigerated, for 4 months.

SHISO

Shiso, or perilla (*Perilla frutescens*), is a close relative of basil. Its culinary history in Asia indicates that it is as important in that part of the world as basil is in the Mediterranean basin. In addition to its culinary uses, it's medicinal. It is rich in vitamins and minerals. It's considered a warming herb and has anti-inflammatory properties. It also stimulates the immune system, aids digestion, and perhaps helps kill unwanted bacteria in other foods.

Shiso leaves are added to ume vinegar, which is the salted brine of fermenting ume plums, at the last step of the umeboshi-making process, during which the dry, wrinkled plum transforms into a complex condiment with its brick-red color (see the recipe on page 300).

Traditionally, whole shiso leaves were preserved in salt. They have many uses, including as a substitute for the nori in a sushi hand roll. The concentration of essential oils makes for a strong taste described as anything from fennel to mint to cinnamon, depending on the variety and growing conditions. We love the fermented flavor—our best description is a strong floral perfume—and sometimes use it in our kraut (see Shiso Kraut, page 178).

YOUR RAW MATERIAL

Look for shiso at your farmers' market or grow them yourself in the garden or in pots on a windowsill. Nip off the flower buds as soon as they appear; this promotes bushy growth. Plants come with red leaves or green; both ferment well.

IN THE CROCK
Fermented Shiso Leaves

See photo on page 161

yield: less than 1 pint (473 ml)
technique used: Whole-Leaf Ferments (page 78)

Fermentation brings out a salty sweetness, with floral notes, in shiso. The fermented leaves are wonderful little condiments to put on a cheese plate or in a sandwich.

Note: The shiso leaf stalks can be added to vegetable mixes for brining, or fermented in a pickling bed.

> 3 (12-ounce/340 g) bunches shiso leaves
> ¼ teaspoon (1.4 g) unrefined salt

1. Pluck the leaves from their stems, keeping any tender whorls on top whole. Put the leaves into a bowl and sprinkle with the salt. Gently toss and massage the salt into leaves. Don't expect a lot of brine; this is almost a dry ferment.

2. Press the leaves into a pint jar. Top the ferment with a quart-size ziplock bag. Press the plastic down onto the top of the ferment, then fill it with water and seal.

3. Set the jar on your counter, out of direct sunlight, and let ferment for 10 to 20 days. Start taste-testing the ferment on day 10. The sour will be not as obvious as the salt. Ferment to your desired level of acidity.

4. For storage, press a small round of parchment directly on the surface of the ferment. Screw on the lid and store in the fridge, checking periodically that the ferment is submerged. This will keep, refrigerated, indefinitely.

Shiso Gomashio

yield: ¾ cup (90 g)

Gomashio is a Japanese seasoning powder made of sesame seeds and salt. This version combines roasted sesame seeds with the concentrated salty, floral flavor of fermented shiso. The sesame seeds bring protein and calcium, while shiso is a known digestive aid, and they come together here to make a healthy sprinkle that tastes great. Sprinkle on anything!

¼ cup (6 g) Fermented Shiso Leaves (page 325)
½ cup (24 g) sesame seeds

1. Spread the fermented shiso leaves across the trays of a dehydrator. Dehydrate overnight at 100°F/38°C.

2. In the morning, place the sesame seeds in a dry cast-iron skillet over medium heat. Roast for about 10 minutes, stirring constantly with a wooden spoon, until the seeds turn golden brown.

3. Place the sesame seeds and dried leaves in a mortar and pestle and grind together. The mixture will keep for several months on the shelf and for up to a year in the fridge.

SPINACH

I like to eat only things with well-defined shapes that the intelligence can grasp. I detest spinach because of its utterly amorphous character, so much so that I am firmly convinced, and do not hesitate for a moment to maintain, that the only good, noble and edible thing to be found in that sordid nourishment is the sand.

—SALVADOR DALÍ, *THE SECRET LIFE OF SALVADOR DALÍ*, 1942

We'll be honest: The only reason we tried fermenting spinach was for this book—it is A to Z, after all. We imagined that fermented spinach, much like overcooked spinach, would be nothing more than dark green slimy goo. We looked at our beautiful fresh spinach and thought, *How can we do this to it?* But Kirsten was determined to forge ahead. She thought about all the ways cooked spinach is tasty. Spanakopita came to mind, melding spinach with oregano, lemon, and sweet onions. It became our backup plan: If the texture of the ferment wasn't appetizing, then we could cook it between layers of buttered phyllo with a lot of feta.

That turned out not to be a problem; the spinach was delicious when fermented. The texture was not at all what we expected. It even had some crunch, like a fresh spinach salad. We shouldn't have been surprised. Salt keeps things crispy.

Because we'd imagined the melted feta and flaky pastry, we made spanakopita anyway and the recipe (Kraut-a-kopita) is on page 398.

FERMENTISTA'S TIP

Fermentation and Oxalic Acid

Many dark leafy greens—among them red orach, chard, and parsley—contain oxalic acid, the compound that gives wood sorrel and rhubarb their sour taste and creates that woolly feeling on your teeth after you eat spinach. The good news is that fermentation breaks down this compound, reducing its concentration.

Lemon Spinach

yield: about 1 quart (946 ml)
technique used: Mastering Sauerkraut (page 61)

With cabbage and most other ferments, you manhandle the veggies to release brine. Not so with spinach. Here, use your lightest touch—you want the leaves bruise-free.

1	large sweet onion, quartered and thinly sliced
1½–2	teaspoons (8–11 g) unrefined salt
2	pounds (907 g) spinach leaves, chopped
1	generous tablespoon (5 g) dried oregano, crumbled
2	tablespoons (30 ml) lemon juice
	Grape leaf or parchment paper, to top the ferment

1. Place the onion in a large bowl, add 1½ teaspoons of the salt, and, with your hands, massage it into the onions until they release brine. (Having brine now means you can be gentle with the spinach when you add it.) Add the spinach, oregano, and lemon juice, gently working everything together, then taste. You should be able to taste the salt without it being overwhelming. Add more salt if necessary.

2. Transfer the spinach mixture to your fermentation vessel, a few handfuls at a time, pressing down to remove air pockets.

3. Top with a grape leaf or parchment paper to keep everything submerged, pressing it down under the brine. Add a weight if you have one. Follow the instructions for your fermentation vessel. For a jar, if using the burping method (page 44) make sure there is little headspace and seal lid tightly. Burp daily or as needed. Alternatively, top the ferment with a quart-size ziplock bag. Press the bag down onto the top of the ferment and then fill it with water and seal.

4. Set your fermentation vessel on a plate in a spot where you can keep an eye on it, out of direct sunlight, and let ferment for 4 to 10 days. Check regularly to make sure the spinach mixture is submerged, pressing down, as needed, to bring the brine back to the surface. Start taste-testing on day 4. You'll know it is ready when the color is a yellowish or dull green and the spinach has a surprising light crunch and a slightly sour flavor.

5. Store in an airtight container in the fridge. The spinach will keep, refrigerated, for 6 months.

We Are Family: Orach

Orach, also called mountain spinach and purple passion spinach, belongs to the goosefoot family, whose members include beets, chard, and spinach. It's a common green in Europe, where it's been in cultivation for thousands of years—longer than spinach—in Mediterranean countries. In Italy, it's used to color pastas.

Red orach is a vibrant fuchsia that makes it stand out in the produce section of the supermarket, at the farmers' market, and in your ferment. Use it as you would spinach. You can ferment it on its own, following the recipe for Lemon Spinach above. Or try adding a bundle of chopped red orach to Naked Kraut (page 173). It'll turn the batch a beautiful, soft pink.

SEAWEED PRIMER

Sea vegetables, a.k.a. seaweed, are loaded with bioavailable minerals and sodium, and adding them to fermented vegetables is a good way to maximize their benefits. Dried seaweed is simple to use, while fresh takes practice and finesse to ferment, as it can become gelatinous and slimy.

» Lacking roots, seaweed absorbs its nutrients from seawater; this means it picks up all that blows or washes out from land. So make sure your seaweed comes from a clean source— ask the vendor or distributor if you're unsure.

» Some people with hypothyroid conditions who should avoid the cabbage family can offset its effects by adding seaweed to crucifer-based ferments (see Natural Iodine, page 177).

» If you're unfamiliar with sea vegetables, start small. Add just a tablespoon of chopped dried seaweed or a teaspoon of dulse to a quart-size ferment. This will give you the opportunity to see if you like the flavor and texture in the crock.

» Rather than chop or cut seaweed with a knife, snip with scissors.

DULSE (*Palmaria palmata*) comes from the culinary heritage of northern Europe. It's readily available as a coarse powder and is a favorite to sprinkle into a crock of kraut or kimchi. Dulse is a good gateway seaweed, as it adds pretty purple-red flecks to the ferment and the mild flavor may go unnoticed. See the Sea-Chi recipe, page 186.

HIJIKI (*Sargassum fusiforme*) is a coarse-textured seaweed with a strong ocean flavor, but it presents the opportunity to work with another color in the fermentista's palette. It's a glistening black and provides quite an aesthetic contrast to ferments.

ARAME (*Eisenia bicyclis*) is one of the most popular seaweeds in Japanese cuisine. It's a different variety than hijiki but interacts with a ferment similarly, with a milder flavor.

KOMBU (*Saccharina japonica*) is nice to add to any vegetable pickle brine, like you would a sprig of dill, but kombu contributes its own salt as well as nutrients and iodine. (You may want to cut the added salt in your brine solution by ¼ teaspoon for every few ribbons of dried kombu.) This seaweed will double in size when rehydrated and will change the aroma of your ferment. The enhanced flavor will be that of the ocean's briny essence. Add strips of kombu to any vegetable pickle combination. It's especially good with added garlic, ginger, and chile pepper flakes.

NORI (*Porphyra* spp.) is high in protein and vitamin B_{12}. You may know it in the sheet form for sushi rolls, but in its whole dried state, it's a translucent greenish purple. Slice it into a kraut or kimchi for some subtle beauty. It is a mild-flavored seaweed and will not overwhelm other ingredients.

SEA PALM (*Postelsia palmaeformis*), also called American arame, has a mild flavor and when rehydrated in kimchi or other ferment retains a nice crunch. It is one of our favorites. See the Sea-Chi recipe, page 186.

WAKAME (*Undaria pinnatifida*) is a sweet, mild, and tender seaweed. It's one of the most popular of all the sea vegetables. Its texture is slippery, so cut it into small pieces for a kraut or kimchi. It's not suitable for brine pickling. For a different flavor, carefully toast wakame in a dry skillet and then crumble into a powder to add to a ferment.

SUNCHOKES

These tubers are also known as Jerusalem artichokes, earth apples, *topinambur*, or sun roots. A perennial member of the sunflower clan, indigenous to the eastern United States, sunchokes can be found in the wild, in the supermarket, and in many gardens. They have a sweet, nutty flavor that holds up nicely in fermentation. As with many roots, they are sweeter in fall and winter, which is also when they are freshest.

THE RAW MATERIAL

Sunchokes are best firm and without sprouts. Peeling sunchokes is a matter of personal preference. If you prefer not to peel, scrub them well, paying attention to any grit that might hide in the folds. They are also delicious grated as a kraut or added to other ferments.

Inulin

Many vegetables contain prebiotics (soluble fiber that our microbiome loves) such as inulin. Sunchokes and chicory root are the richest sources of inulin. This means when these vegetables are consumed, they promote increased levels and activity of beneficial gut bacteria. However, all this inulin can cause gastric stress because of the gas created. Fermenting these vegetables can predigest some of the inulin, making them more comfortable to consume. For some people with compromised guts, fermenting high-inulin veggies such as sunchokes, leeks, garlic, and dandelion greens isn't enough to end gastric stress.

The Cultured Pickle Shop's Fennel and Sunchoke Kimchi

yield: about 6 quarts (5.7 l)
technique used: Mastering Sauerkraut (page 61)

- 10 pounds (4.5 kg) sunchokes, peeled
- 5 pounds (2.3 kg) fennel bulbs, including their greens
- Garlic, fresh ginger, and chiles, to taste (see note)
- 5–7 tablespoons (84–118 g) unrefined salt

We Are Family: Scorzonera

Scorzonera hispanica, or black salsify, also a member of the sunflower family, has quite a few folk names; two of the more colorful are viper's grass and goatsbeard. Black salsify roots are black, sticky, usually dirty, and a bit gnarled, and so, as a food, at first glance, unappetizing. When you clean and peel the root, your hands will turn sticky and black. The good news—it easily washes off.

Black salsify stays firm when you handle or cook it. Raw, it's crunchy, with a texture almost like coconut. That same crunch and texture make it an excellent candidate for fermentation. You can make a tasty, pure black salsify ferment, but because of the small size of the roots, it's a lot of work for a small return. Instead, add this root to other ferments as you would burdock (see page 170).

Note: Alex Hozven of The Cultured Pickle Shop is quite generous with the garlic, ginger, and chiles in this recipe. Use your own best judgment for the amounts, or start with 1 head garlic, 3–4 tablespoons (33–44 g) minced ginger, and 2–3 fresh chiles or 1–2 tablespoons (6–13 g) chile pepper flakes.

1. Slice the sunchokes and fennel bulbs quite thinly and transfer to a large bowl. Mince the fennel greens and add to the bowl. Mince the garlic, ginger, and chiles, add to the bowl, and mix well.

2. Add the salt to the bowl and mix well. The salt is 3 percent of the weight of the vegetables and should be the perfect amount to maintain a crisp texture. Cover the bowl and let it sit for a few hours, and when you come back to it, the vegetables will have released quite a lot of moisture.

3. Pack the mixture into your fermentation vessel, add followers and weights, and monitor during the next 4 weeks or so, until it has reached your desired sourness.

TOMATILLOS

Tomatillos were originally cultivated by the Aztecs and are still a staple of Mexican cuisine. While tomatillos are sometimes called husk tomatoes, they should not be confused with them. They are more closely related to ground cherries, which are native to the Americas. These fruits all have a papery husk that grows first. The small fruit develops until it fills the space inside the husk.

YOUR RAW MATERIAL

When shopping for tomatillos, you want the husk and the fruit inside to be bright green. This will ensure your tomatillo has a crisp, tart flavor. As it continues to ripen, the husk turns yellow to brown and the fruit turns a pale yellow. As it yellows, more sugars are developing and the fruit is softening. For a crisp, clean flavor and texture when fermenting, it is best to stick with the brighter green fruit.

Tomatillo skins are often sticky; this coating, soapy with bitter saponins, should be rinsed off.

IN THE CROCK
Tomatillo Salsa

See photo on page 280

yield: about 1 quart (946 ml)
technique used: Relishes/Chutneys/Salsas/Salads (page 74)

"This is hands down my favorite one of your ferments. If they all tasted like this, I would eat more of them," one of our offspring told us. Is that a compliment?

This recipe is delicious as a quick condiment that you ferment over a few days. It is a great summery salsa to eat over the course of winter. We've also used this as an enchilada sauce. For a more developed acidic flavor with a wonderful lemon-vinegar quality, allow this salsa to ferment for 3 or more weeks.

- 1 **pound (454 g) tomatillos**
- 1 **medium onion, diced**
- 1–3 **jalapeños, diced (optional)**
- ½ **bunch cilantro, finely chopped**

2 cloves garlic, minced
Juice of 1 lime (for extra lime flavor, include the zest)
Pinch of cracked pepper
1½–2 teaspoons (8–11 g) unrefined salt
Grape leaf or parchment paper, to top the ferment

1. Remove the husks from the tomatillos; rinse the fruits well in cold water. Dice the tomatillos and put them in a bowl. Add the onion, jalapeños (if using), cilantro, garlic, lime juice, and cracked pepper. Sprinkle in 1½ teaspoons of the salt and, with your hands, massage it into the vegetables. Then taste. You should be able to taste the salt without it being overwhelming. The brine will release quickly.

2. Pack the salsa into a jar or crock, pressing down to release air pockets as you go.

3. Follow the instructions for your fermentation vessel. For a jar, if using the burping method (page 44) make sure there is little headspace and top with a grape leaf or parchment paper and weight if you have one, then seal lid tightly. Burp daily or as needed. **Tip:** If you are using more ripe tomatillos, this may have a thinner consistency and, like pepper sauce, it will work best if given a shake after each burp.

4. Set your fermentation vessel on a plate in a spot where you can keep an eye on it, out of direct sunlight, and let ferment for 5 to 21 days. Check regularly to make sure the salsa is submerged, pressing down, as needed, to bring the brine back to the surface. Start taste-testing on day 5. The salsa is ready when the flavors have mingled, becoming almost lemony-acidic. The onions will retain a fresh crispness while the rest of the vegetables will soften.

5. To store, transfer to smaller jars, if necessary. Tamp down to make sure the mixture is submerged in its brine, tighten the lids, and place in the fridge, where the salsa will keep for 12 months.

TOMATOES

There are only two things that money can't buy, and that's true love and homegrown tomatoes.
—GUY CLARK, "HOMEGROWN TOMATOES"

Is not the homegrown tomato the aspiration of every gardener? From the cheery, sweet cherry tomatoes growing in pots at lofty heights on a city balcony to the small patch of fat tomatoes in Grandpa's garden, gardeners measure their summer calendar by when the first red (or almost red) tomato is brought to the table with great pomp.

As summer progresses, tomatoes are in everything. By late September, fresh pico de gallo, Greek salads, and chilled tomato gazpachos may have lost their charm. Sauces, juices, and ketchup have been canned by the quart, and the lovely red orbs still hang on the vine. The gardener secretly thinks about how nice a surprise killing frost would be.

What else can be done? Ferment them green. A study in Portugal, aiming to reduce green tomato waste in the fields, found that fermented green tomatoes showed a significant improvement in the amount of ascorbic acid and antioxidents present, and while tomatine was still present it posed no risk for human consumption.

Fermenting tomatoes requires a little care, or at least finesse in timing. Red, ripe tomatoes are loaded with sugar and soft to begin with. The microbes love all that sugar. Fermentation gets active quickly, and instead of just lactic acid bacteria, yeasts can get involved, giving the ferment fizzy and funky flavors. Some people love that flavor; others think it tastes like old salsa, long forgotten in the fridge.

You can ferment green tomatoes all day long without an issue because the sugars have hardly developed. Most of our favorite tomato ferments are made with green tomatoes. And harvesting them green not only helps you get a handle on a harvest but also lets you save them from a killing frost. You can then ferment them as green salsas, relishes, or pickles. Next best is to use tomatoes that are not quite ripe, hard, and barely orange. (Which honestly aren't that hard to find, as most commercially grown tomatoes are just that.

You will notice the photo of the Georgian-Style Fermented Green Tomatoes on page 245 is more orange than green because of the timing of the photo shoot. We'd eaten all the ones we'd made so there we were looking for the yellowest ones in the pile.) This in-between state works well for salsa and the Chow-Chow recipe on page 334.

Tomatoes are most difficult to ferment when they are at their peak of red ripeness. Soft and sweet, they are headed quickly to decomposition. Your goal is to catch all the flavor and sugar and less of the funk, and you can do that by reducing their water content. Less water means more concentrated flavor and more fermentation control. One option is to dehydrate the tomatoes entirely and use them as an ingredient in other ferments, like you would any dried fruit. Your ferment will retain much of the flavor and sweetness of the tomato.

Other options are to salt-press them or partially dry them, whether in the sun or in a dehydrator, as discussed in Chapter 6. Sun-drying will require warm days that reach 75 to 85°F (24 to 29°C) with a relative humidity below 60 percent.

Tomato Leaf as an Herb

Tomato leaves can be added to any ferment to infuse the flavor of tomatoes into your creation. Anybody who has brushed up against a tomato plant can attest to the leaves' strong aromatic presence. As with other aromatic herbs, a little will go a long way. We know that, reading this, your eyebrows are raised in doubt. Most of us have heard that tomato leaves are toxic, containing the glycoalkaloid tomatine—a rumor left over, perhaps, from when humans thought the tomato itself was toxic. In fact, a study done by the FDA concludes that all parts of the tomato contain varying amounts of tomatine. The leaves have only slightly more than an unripe green tomato, and an adult would have to eat a whole pound of leaves to get a toxic dose. Some studies show tomatine may actually have some benefits for our immune system, as well as cancer-inhibiting properties. The takeaway is that tomato leaves can be safely used as an herb.

We use a dehydrator set to 135°F (57°C). If you start seeing the tomatoes blacken, turn down the heat; the sugars are burning. Or set your oven to 200°F (90°C), spread the tomatoes on a baking sheet, and watch carefully.

IN THE PICKLE JAR

Cherry Bombs

yield: about 1 gallon (3.8 l)
technique used: Mastering Brine Pickling (page 101)

There's no doubt this food is alive! Fermentation transforms these tomatoes into little effervescent bombs. The recipe has achieved a life of its own—every summer, Kirsten's social media feed blows up with tags of people sharing their cheery cherry bombs.

Choose tomatoes that are not fully mature, any color from yellowish green to red, but firm. For best results, don't use tomatoes that are more than 2½ inches in diameter.

These tomatoes, brine and all, make excellent crackers (page 369). And they're also good made with dill, horseradish, and more parsley instead of basil.

4–5	pounds (1.8–2.3 kg) cherry tomatoes
1	sprig parsley or the leafy tops of celery
5 or 6	leafy stems of basil
1	head garlic, cloves separated
1	teaspoon (2 g) peppercorns
1	teaspoon (2 g) coriander seeds
1	teaspoon (4 g) mustard seeds
	Pinch of chile pepper flakes
1	gallon (3.8 l) High Brine (¾ cup /200 g unrefined salt per gallon unchlorinated water)
	Grape or other tannin-rich leaves or parchment paper, to top the ferment (optional)

1. Arrange the tomatoes in your fermentation vessel, incorporating the parsley, basil, garlic, peppercorns, coriander seeds, mustard seeds, and chile flakes around them. Be gentle when packing; riper tomatoes may split occasionally, and they should be removed from the mix. Pour in enough brine to cover the tomatoes completely. Reserve any leftover brine in the fridge (it will keep for 1 week; discard thereafter or dry out and reclaim salt and make a new batch, if needed).

2. Place grape leaves or parchment paper, if using, over the tomatoes to keep them submerged. Follow the instructions for your fermentation vessel. For a jar, if using the burping method (page 44) make sure there is little headspace and seal lid tightly. Burp daily or as needed.

3. Set your fermentation vessel on a plate in a spot where you can keep an eye on it, out of direct sunlight, and let ferment for 6 to 8 days. During the fermentation period, monitor the brine level and top off with the reserved brine, if needed, to cover. Start taste-testing when the brine becomes cloudy. The tomatoes are ready when they are sour and very soft inside, with a champagne-like effervescence.

4. Transfer the tomatoes to jars and top off with fresh brine, if necessary. Top each jar with a fresh grape leaf, if you have them. Then set the jars in the refrigerator. Let sit for 1 to 2 weeks; then they're ready to eat. They'll keep, refrigerated, for about 6 months. They will continue to gain effervescence, even under refrigeration, although not in the jar but in the tomatoes.

Chow-Chow

See photo on page 189

yield: 1 quart (946 ml)

technique used: Relishes/Chutneys/Salsas/Salads (page 74)

Chow-chow is a North American original and most often associated with Southern cuisine. Where the name comes from is unclear. What is clear is that the ingredients vary widely and it has a bit of an everything-but-the-kitchen-sink reputation, likely coming from the fact that chow-chow was a way to preserve produce at the end of the garden season—hence many versions contain green tomatoes. Connoisseurs distinguish between the Southern-style and Northern-style chow-chow, which is said to be generally sweeter.

This recipe uses green tomatoes. If you don't have any, go get those grocery-store, pale orange hard tomatoes, the ones you would never buy otherwise; in this recipe they are redeemed.

1½	cups (300 g) green tomatoes, diced
¼	pound (113 g) green cabbage, chopped
1	medium onion, diced
1	green bell pepper, diced
1	red bell pepper, diced
2–3	teaspoons (12–17g) unrefined salt
2	teaspoons (4 g) mustard powder
1	teaspoon (3 g) celery seeds
1	teaspoon (2 g) ground turmeric
½	teaspoon (1.5 g) mustard seeds

1. Combine the tomatoes, cabbage, onion, and green and red bell peppers in a large bowl. Sprinkle in the salt and, using your hands, massage everything together. Add the mustard powder, celery seed, turmeric, and mustard seed to the bowl and mix well.

2. Pack the mixture into an appropriately sized jar, pressing to release any air pockets as you go. If using the burping method (page 44), make sure there is little headspace and top with a grape leaf or parchment paper and weight if you have one, then seal lid tightly. Burp daily or as needed. Alternatively, top the ferment with a quart-size ziplock bag. Press the bag down onto the top of the ferment and then fill it with water and seal.

3. Set the jar on a plate in a spot where you can keep an eye on it, out of direct sunlight, and let ferment for 5 to 10 days. It's ready when the color fades to dull green, the brine becomes cloudy, the ferment has a pleasing acidic smell, and it tastes pleasingly sour, perhaps with an effervescent zing.

4. Store the chow-chow in an airtight jar in the fridge, where it will keep for 6 to 8 months.

Georgian-Style Fermented Green Tomatoes

See photo on page 245

yield: around 2 quarts (1.9 l)

technique used: Salt Pressing (page 80)

We absolutely love these fermented tomatoes. They are not only delicious but also quick to make and look gorgeous on a charcuterie board. The recipe derives from a traditional Georgian one— that is, the Republic of Georgia, not the US state. A long time ago, Kirsten was at a class where the instructor said, "I always name the lineage of my teachers," and then proceeded to name the person they learned from as well as the people who had taught their teacher. This recipe, likewise, has a lineage of inspiration we'd like to credit: It comes by way of a blog post by Eva Martínez in which she credits Татьяна Пястолова for sharing the recipe with her. When Kirsten reached out to Eva, she resonated with Eva's thoughts when she said, "It's important to make known the recipes so they don't remain in oblivion."

You can use any green tomatoes, whether small or large, but we have found that using 6 to 9 medium ones is better than just a few large ones, as it is easier to pack them in a jar in a way that holds everything in place.

- 2 **pounds (1 kg) green tomatoes (preferably medium size)**
- 2 **tablespoons (34 g) unrefined salt**
- 1 **bunch (65 g) parsley, roughly chopped**
- 4 **stalks celery, roughly chopped**
- 1–3 **jalapeños, as desired, roughly chopped**
- 4 **tablespoons (12 g) dried dill weed or 1 cup (56 g) fresh dill weed**
- 6–8 **cloves garlic, peeled and chopped**
  Large grape leaves or parchment paper, to top the ferment
- 1–2 **cups (237–473 ml) Basic Brine (1½ teaspoons/8.4 g unrefined salt per cup unchlorinated water)**

1. Rinse the tomatoes. Starting at the top (stem end), cut two slits, forming a cross, down through each tomato, stopping before you reach the bottom. Sprinkle salt in each tomato and place in a small casserole dish, wedging them tightly together if you can, with the crosses facing up.

2. Weight the tomatoes heavily with any of the options mentioned on page 46. Cover the dish and let it sit on your counter for 8 hours or

overnight. This will press out the brine, which you'll use later for the fermentation.

3. When you're ready to stuff the tomatoes, combine the parsley, celery, jalapeños, dill weed, and garlic in a food processor and process to a paste.

4. Fill each tomato with the paste, close the slits as best you can, and tuck them into a crock or widemouthed jar, pressing and wedging as you go. When all the tomatoes are in place, pour in the brine created by the initial pressing.

5. Top with grape leaves, horseradish leaves, or any other aromatic herbs, such as celery leaves. Again add weight to the top of this ferment. Place on the counter and repeat the pressing for 24 hours.

6. After 24 hours, check the ferment. If it has not released enough juice to fully cover the tomatoes and leaves, make a small batch of Basic Brine and pour in enough to submerge them.

7. Follow the instructions for your fermentation vessel. For a jar, if using the burping method (page 44) make sure there is little headspace and seal lid tightly. Burp daily or as needed. Alternatively, top the ferment with a quart-size ziplock bag. Press the bag down onto the top of the ferment and then fill it with water and seal.

8. Let ferment for 10 to 20 days. You will know the tomatoes are ready when their color mutes, the brine becomes cloudy, and the smell and taste are pleasingly acidic.

9. Store in an airtight jar in the fridge, where the tomatoes will keep for 6 to 8 months. After tomatoes have been enjoyed, use any leftover pasty brine as a pickling bed or as a flavoring in a dish.

Oil-Preserved Fermented Tomatoes

yield: around 1 pint (473 ml)
technique used: Salt Pressing (page 80)

You can use green or red tomatoes for this recipe. If choosing red, look for tomatoes at the point of firm and barely ripe, not juicy ripe. This is a saltier ferment to begin with, because without enough salt the tomatoes will not preserve well and will be subject to yeast growth. But juicier red tomatoes will take in the salt so quickly that they could end up too salty to eat. It's a delicate salty dance, truthfully, and while we often advocate trusting your senses, here we suggest a measured amount of salt. If you are scaling this recipe up or down, try to stick to a 4 to 5 percent salt ratio: Weigh your tomatoes in grams and multiply that weight by .05 to get the number of grams of salt you need. For example, 1½ pounds of tomatoes is 680 g × .05 = 34 grams, which is 2 tablespoons of salt.

Tip: If your batch does end up too salty, don't despair. Use the tomatoes in stews and sauces as a salty umami addition.

  1½ pounds (680 g) firm tomatoes (preferably medium size)
   2 tablespoons unrefined salt
5 or 6 cloves garlic, peeled and sliced
         Leaves from 1 sprig fresh rosemary

AFTER FERMENTATION
   1 bay leaf
      Dried herbs and spices, as desired (optional)
1½–2 cups (360–480 ml) olive oil

1. Slice the tomatoes into ½-inch (1.25 cm) rounds. As you cut them, dust the slices with salt and place the rounds in a crock or jar, a row at a time, adding the garlic and rosemary and stacking as you go.

2. Add weight on top to press out the liquid that will become the fermenting brine. Cover the jar or crock, set it on a counter, out of direct sunlight, and let ferment for 2 to 3 days. If the jar is sealed, be sure to burp as needed (page 44). Then taste. The tomatoes are done when they have developed a wonderful sour flavor.

3. When they're ready, transfer the tomatoes and all the delicious bits of garlic to a clean towel and pat dry. (Keep the very salty tomato brine left behind in the refrigerator to use for flavoring dressings or broths.)

4. Place the bay leaf in the bottom of a pint jar. Stack the tomatoes and garlic in layers in the jar, sprinkling in any dried herbs and spices you might be using. Every two layers, pour a little olive oil over the top. At the end, pour in enough oil to completely submerge the tomatoes.

5. Put the lid on the jar and tighten. Let cure at room temperature for a week, after which the tomatoes are ready to eat.

6. Store the tomatoes in the refrigerator, where they will keep for up to 3 months. To serve, allow the tomatoes to come to room temperature. Top off with oil as needed to keep the remaining tomatoes submerged.

Fermented Tomato Ketchup

See photo on page 263

yield: about 1 pint (473 ml)
technique used: Pastes (page 76)

Ketchup has an impressively long history as a fermented condiment. The names of many tasty, dark, fermented sauces throughout Asia—for example, *kecap* in Southeast Asia—derive from the ancient Hokkien Chinese word *kê-tsiap*, meaning a fermented fish sauce. Colonialism and the global quest for flavors brought condiments with the same name but made from a wide variety of ingredients, from anchovies to mushrooms to, you guessed it, tomatoes. Here's our fermented version.

This ketchup can be made with tomato paste, partially dried plum tomatoes, or partially dried paste-type tomatoes of any other kind. This is a short ferment, and the microbes that drive it come from the brine and the raw honey. If you don't have raw honey, be sure to use the brine; if you don't have brine, be sure to use raw honey.

Umami enhancers include a pinch of ground cayenne or a splash of Worcestershire sauce or fish sauce. Add them before or after fermentation, if you like.

- 1 pound (454 g) ripe plum tomatoes, or 1½ cups (340 g) homemade tomato paste, or 2 (6-ounce/170 g) cans tomato paste
- 1 generous teaspoon (7 g) unrefined salt
- ½ teaspoon (1.2 g) onion powder
- ¼ teaspoon (0.5 g) ground allspice
- ¼ teaspoon (0.5 g) ground cinnamon
- ⅛ teaspoon (.025 g) ground cloves
- 2–3 tablespoons (30–44 ml) fermented brine or pepper paste
- 1 tablespoon (15 ml) raw honey

AFTER FERMENTATION

- 1–2 tablespoons (15–30 ml) raw honey
- 2 tablespoons (30 ml) raw apple cider vinegar

1. If you are using tomato paste, skip this step. If you are using fresh tomatoes, you'll need to partially dry them: Preheat the oven to 200°F/93°C. Line a baking sheet with parchment paper. Slice the tomatoes in half and lay them, cut side facing up, on the baking sheet. Bake for 2 to 4 hours, until they are lightly dried but still somewhat juicy. Then let cool.

2. If you are using tomato paste, combine it in a bowl with the salt, onion powder, allspice, cinnamon, cloves, brine, and raw honey. If you are using partially dried tomatoes, combine them with the rest of the ingredients in a food processor and process to a paste.

3. Transfer the paste to a pint jar, pressing out air pockets as you go and leaving a couple of inches of headspace. Top with a round of parchment paper and seal the lid tightly.

4. Set the jar on a counter, out of direct sunlight, and let ferment for 2 to 5 days. Burp the jar daily (see page 44) or as needed. If you want very little sourness, stop the fermentation at 2 days.

5. When the fermentation is done, stir in the honey and vinegar. Press a small round of parchment paper directly on top of the ketchup, seal the jar with its lid, and store in the refrigerator, where it will keep for 6 months.

BLAUKRAUT, *page 190*

TURMERIC PEPPER
KRAUT, *page 341*

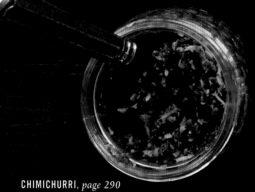

CHIMICHURRI, *page 290*

SHISO KRAUT, *page 178*

CRANBERRY RELISH,
page 213

LEMON-DILL KRAUT,
page 177

THAI-INSPIRED BABY
PAK CHOI, *page 288*

THREE Cs, *page 175*

EDGY VEGGIES, *page 197*

TURMERIC

Each spice has a special day to it. For turmeric it is Sunday, when light drips fat and butter-colored into the bins to be soaked up glowing, when you pray to the nine planets for love and luck.

—CHITRA BANERJEE DIVAKARUNI, *THE MISTRESS OF SPICES*, 1997

Turmeric has a long history of culinary and medicinal use in India, Indonesia, and China. It has received a lot of attention worldwide for its anti-inflammatory and cancer-fighting qualities, and many studies are focusing on turmeric's effect on ailments such as arthritis, Alzheimer's, liver damage, and various digestive issues. Its active compound, curcumin, is a powerful anti-oxidant. Interestingly, when turmeric and black pepper are consumed together, the active ingredient in pepper, piperine, boosts our bodies' ability to take in and use the curcumin.

YOUR RAW MATERIAL

If you want color, this is your ingredient. With varying amounts of fresh or dried turmeric, you will be able to turn your ferments anything from chartreuse yellow to a deep gold.

The recipes here use fresh turmeric root. It is a brown-skinned rhizome, akin to ginger in appearance, but with a deep orange flesh. It has a warm but almost astringent or bitter flavor, sometimes with delicate peppery notes. Some people find the flavor musty or earthy. If you are unfamiliar with it, it is worth exploring in your creations, dried or fresh.

The recipes here can also be made with ginger root. Likewise, you can substitute turmeric for ginger in our Fermented Ginger Pickle (page 240) or Honey Fermented Ginger (page 240), which is absolutely delicious.

IN THE CROCK
Turmeric Paste

See photo on page 322
yield: about ½ pint (237 ml)
technique used: Pastes (page 76)

We use this paste for flavoring anything from scrambled eggs to sauces and steamed or sautéed vegetables. The salt content recommended here is adequate for fermentation, but if you want an all-in-one seasoning paste, with salt and flavor mixed together, you can increase the salt by about one-third. Add other spices to make a paste that is uniquely yours.

> ½ **pound (227 g) fresh turmeric,**
> **roughly chopped**
> ½ **teaspoon (1.4 g) freshly ground black pepper**
> ¼–½ **teaspoon (1.4–2.8 g) unrefined salt**

1. Combine the turmeric, pepper, and salt in a food processor and pulse to a paste consistency.

2. Press the paste into an appropriately sized jar. More liquid will release as you press, and you should now see a little brine. If using the burping method (page 44), make sure there is little headspace, top with a round of parchment paper, and seal the lid tightly. Watch the lid for pressure building up. With this recipe you may never need to burp, or at most just once. Alternatively, top the paste with a quart-size ziplock bag. Press the bag down onto the top of the ferment, then fill it with water and seal.

3. Set on a counter, out of direct sunlight, and let ferment for 7 to 10 days. Start taste-testing on day 7. The paste is ready when it has developed acidity. It will be more salty than sour.

4. To store, tamp down to make sure the ferment is submerged in its brine, press a small round of parchment paper directly on top, and seal the jar with its lid. Store in the refrigerator, where the paste will keep for 1 year.

VARIATION
Ginger (or Other Rhizome) Paste

Follow the same procedures, omitting black pepper.

Turmeric Pepper Kraut

See photo on page 338

yield: about 1 quart (946 ml)
technique used: Mastering Sauerkraut (page 61)

This kraut looks like sunshine in a jar and has a bright flavor to match. If you're looking for a little warmth on a gray morning, try this sunny kraut as a complement to sunny-side-up eggs.

- 1 small head (1½–2 pounds/680–900 g) cabbage
- ½ onion, thinly sliced (optional)
- 1½ tablespoons (16 g) finely grated fresh turmeric
- 1 large clove garlic, grated
- 1–1½ tablespoons (17–25 g) unrefined salt
- ½ teaspoon (1.4 g) freshly ground black pepper

Follow the recipe for Naked Kraut (page 173), shredding the cabbage and combining it with the onion, turmeric, garlic, salt, and pepper.

TURNIPS

As the manuscript of this book neared completion, we realized we had forgotten to complete the turnip section. As our farmer friend Melissa quipped, "That's how it is with turnips. Everybody forgets turnips." While a humble root, turnips are nutritionally power packed. They have high levels of antioxidants, phytonutrients, and glucosinolates (which help the liver process toxins). Among other healthful properties, turnips are anti-inflammatory and support the digestive system and bone health. So remember the turnips!

YOUR RAW MATERIAL

The tastiest turnips are those that are young, small, and sweet, which you can find in springtime or in fall, when a second crop is planted. Young turnips with blemish-free smooth skin do not need to be peeled; older turnips can have tough skin that should be peeled. Don't forget the greens—they are a good source of anti-inflammatory agents, vitamin K, and omega-3 fatty acids. Ferment turnip greens as you would mustard and other greens.

IN THE CROCK

Lesser known than sauerkraut are "soured turnips," or *Sauerrüben*. We have included three variations.

Sauerrüben I (Turnip Kraut)

yield: about 2 quarts (1.9 l)
technique used: Mastering Sauerkraut (page 61)

This kraut, with the turnips grated, is the most traditional style of *Sauerrüben*.

    5 pounds (2.3 kg) turnips
1½–2 tablespoons (25–34 g) unrefined salt

1. Rinse the turnips in water. Young turnips do not need to be peeled. If the skin on your turnips is russeted or coarse, peel them. Grate the turnips, then transfer to a large bowl. Save some of the turnip tops or leaves to use as followers.

2. Add half of the salt and, with your hands, massage it into the turnips. Then taste. You should be able to taste the salt without it being overwhelming. Add more salt if necessary. The turnips should begin to look wet and limp and liquid will pool. However, if you don't see much brine, let the mixture stand, covered, for 45 minutes, then massage again.

PICKLING ROMAN STYLE

In his book *Around the Roman Table: Food and Feasting in Ancient Rome* (1994), Patrick Faas quotes first-century Roman agricultural writer Lucius Junius Moderatus Columella on the pickling of turnips:

Take the roundest turnips you can find and scrape them clean if they are dirty. Peel them with a sharp knife. Then, with an iron sickle, make an incision in the shape of an X, as picklers do, but be careful not to cut all the way through. Then sprinkle the incisions with salt, not especially fine. Place the turnips on a basket or in a trough, with a little extra salt, and allow the moisture to dry out for three days. After three days a piece from the inside of one turnip should be tasted, to tell whether the salt has penetrated through. If it has been absorbed, remove the turnips and wash them in their own moisture. If not enough moisture has been secreted, add some salt liquor and wash them in that.

Then place them in a square wicker basket, not too tightly woven, but strongly made with thick wicker. Then place a board on the turnips that can be pressed down within the opening of the basket if necessary. When the board is in place, put heavy weights on it and leave the turnips to dry overnight. Then place them in a jug treated with resin, or in a glazed pot, and pour vinegar with mustard over it, so they are submerged. You can use them after thirteen days.

3. Transfer the turnips to your fermentation vessel, a few handfuls at a time, pressing down to remove air pockets as you go. You should see some brine on top of the mixture when you press. If you don't, return the mixture to the bowl and massage again.

4. Top the shredded turnips with the reserved turnip tops or leaves to keep everything submerged, pressing them down under the brine. Add a weight if you have one. Follow the instructions for your fermentation vessel. For a jar, if using the burping method (page 44) make sure there is little headspace and seal lid tightly. Burp daily or as needed. Alternatively, top the ferment with a quart-size ziplock bag. Press the bag down onto the top of the ferment and then fill it with water and seal.

5. Set your fermentation vessel on a plate in a spot where you can keep an eye on it, out of direct sunlight, and let ferment for 7 to 21 days. Check regularly to make sure the kraut is submerged, pressing down, as needed, to bring the brine back to the surface. You'll know the kraut is ready when the color is muted, the brine is cloudy, the taste is pleasingly sour, and the texture is slightly softer than that of cabbage sauerkraut. If you used red or pink turnips, this kraut will be pink.

6. When the kraut is ready, transfer to smaller jars, if necessary, and tamp down. Pour in any brine that's left. Tighten the lids, then store in the fridge. The kraut will keep, refrigerated, for 1 year.

Sauerrüben II (Sliced with Black Pepper)

See photo on page 322

yield: about 2 quarts (1.9 l)
technique used: Mastering Sauerkraut (page 61)

In this version, the turnips are sliced, yielding a texture more like salad than kraut. We use a generous amount of black pepper. Feel free to use less.

> 5 pounds (2.3 kg) turnips, very thinly sliced
> 1–2 tablespoons (8–17 g) freshly ground black pepper
> 1½–2 tablespoons (25–34 g) unrefined salt

Follow the recipe for Sauerrüben I (page 342), but thinly slice the turnips instead of grating them, and add the black pepper with the salt.

Sauerrüben III (Turnips, Rutabaga, Kohlrabi)

yield: about 2 quarts (1.9 l)
technique used: Mastering Sauerkraut (page 61)

In this three-roots ferment, turnips are joined by rutabagas and kohlrabi. We slice the roots for this *Sauerrüben*, but feel free to grate them; the process is the same.

> 5 pounds (2.3 kg) total of an equal mix of turnips, rutabaga, and kohlrabi, sliced
> 1½ tablespoons (13 g) caraway seeds
> 1½–2 tablespoons (25–34 g) unrefined salt

Follow the recipe for Sauerrüben I (page 342), using the mixture of sliced turnips, rutabagas, and kohlrabi instead of grated turnips and adding the caraway seeds with the salt.

WATERMELON

We love watermelon rinds for the lovely crunch they give pickles and condiments. They are a blank canvas for flavor. Think of watermelon rinds (peeled, of course) as a sensory addition. Watermelon rind pickles taste exactly like cucumber dill pickles when the same spices are used to ferment them. As the rinds are usually tossed, you have nothing to lose and everything to gain.

We've found that over long-term storage, these pickle spears get soft much sooner. However, we've found rinds cut into chunks stay crispy longer, so while the long spears look fantastic, make those for fresher eating. Make salsa or pickle cubes for longer storage.

Can you ferment whole melons? The gorgeous book *Summer Kitchens* by Olia Hercules has a recipe for fermenting whole watermelons—a traditional Ukrainian ferment. We tried it, using small seedless watermelons, which may have been the wrong choice, and we let them ferment for 4 months, which may have been too long. They fermented perfectly and were quite beautiful, but the interior texture was so soft it was nearly gone. Nevertheless, that experiment inspired us to try fermenting whole cantaloupes and honeydew melons. The honeydew melons were not tasty at all, but we loved the cantaloupes. They were definitely a strange pickle, but the color was incredible—like a sunset—and the flavor was fun. (*Note*: To ferment whole melons, you need a giant vessel. Be sure to prick them so fermentation can happen throughout, and use a 5 to 7 percent brine.)

Watermelon Rind–Zucchini Salsa

See photo on page 263

yield: about 1½ quarts (1.4 l)
techniques used: Salt Pressing (page 80) and Relishes/Chutneys/Salsas/Salads (page 74)

This late-summer ferment takes advantage of overly large zucchini (the baseball bats) and watermelon rinds. (Of course, if you don't have huge zucchini, you can use regular-size ones or any summer squash.) It relies on salt pressing to reduce the moisture in the rinds and zucchini, although you could also partially dehydrate them (see page 83). We usually try to use equal parts watermelon rinds and zucchini, but the ratio is fluid.

- 2 pounds (907 g) watermelon rinds and zucchinis
- 2 tablespoons plus 2 teaspoons (46 g) unrefined salt

FOR SALSA

- 2 small red onions, diced
- 4 jalapeño peppers or 1 large red bell pepper, diced
- 3 tablespoons (11 g) chopped cilantro
- 1 teaspoon (1 g) dried Mexican oregano (or whatever kind you have)
- ½ teaspoon (1 g) ground black pepper
- ½ teaspoon (0.9 g) ground coriander seeds
  Grape leaf or parchment paper, to top the ferment

1. Peel and cube the watermelon rinds. Cut the zucchinis lengthwise, scoop out the seeds, and cube, about ¼ inch square. Combine the cubed rinds and zucchini in a large bowl, add the salt, and mix well.

2. Place the cubed rinds and zucchini in a casserole or other container for pressing, cover if needed, and press for 1 to 2 days.

3. After pressing, drain off the salty brine, squeezing the rinds and zucchini lightly to remove excess moisture.

4. Combine the watermelon and zucchini with the salsa ingredients: red onion, jalapeño, cilantro, oregano, black pepper, and coriander. Mix well.

5. Pack the salsa mixture into your vessel, pressing as you go to release air bubbles. Top with a grape leaf or parchment paper and a weight if you have one.

6. Follow the instructions for your fermentation vessel. For a jar, if using the burping method (page 44) make sure there is little headspace and seal lid tightly. Burp daily or as needed. Alternatively, top the ferment with a quart-size ziplock bag. Press the bag down onto the top of the ferment and then fill it with water and seal.

7. Set your fermentation vessel on a plate in a spot where you can keep an eye on it, out of direct sunlight, and let ferment for 3 to 5 days. You will know the salsa is ready when it has a pleasing acidic smell and taste, perhaps with an effervescent zing.

8. To store, transfer to smaller jars, if necessary, and tamp down. Pour in any brine that's left. Tighten the lids, then store in the fridge, where the salsa will keep for 3 months, and longer if you don't mind softening texture.

VARIATION

Watermelon Rind–Zucchini Kimchi

Prepare the watermelon rind and zucchini as directed in the recipe for Watermelon Rind–Zucchini Salsa (facing page). Then, instead of salsa ingredients, add the following:

1 (2-inch/5 cm) piece fresh ginger, grated (about 2 tablespoons/22 g)
6 cloves garlic, diced
4 scallions, thinly sliced
2 tablespoons (18 g) gochugaru, or chile pepper flakes to taste

Ferment as instructed in the salsa recipe.

Watermelon Rind Pickles

To make watermelon rind pickles, save those rinds, peel off the green skin, and slice them into long spears or cubes. Then follow the recipe for New York Deli-Style Pickles (page 216), replacing the cucumbers with your watermelon rinds. You can, of course, use any pickling spices and flavors, but we always come back to these.

WINTER SQUASH

It is a fact that seventy-five per cent of our make-up is the same as a pumpkin. Although we like to think we are special, our genes bring us down to earth.

—MONISE DURRANI, BBC SCIENCE PRODUCER

We began squash trials not because one of us woke up one morning and thought, *Wow, we need to ferment winter squash*—after all, it stores for months, and why preserve something that is perfectly stable? Nope, it was the buckets and buckets of orange squash chunks inundating our commercial kitchen.

Our neighbors were seed farmers, and to harvest the seeds they had to get to said seeds. This meant laying out huge tarps, lifting the squash overhead, and throwing it to the ground with (hopefully) shattering force. Following a squash-smashing session, there were two piles: buckets with the seeds still tangled in their stringy nest and an imposing stack of squash, perfectly good food that is the by-product.

We can't see food go to waste, so there it was: buckets of squash. This was early in our experimentation. We didn't yet fully understand that all veggies can be fermented. We did extensive searches on the internet. At that time, there were no recipes and no shared experiences, which seems funny now. We thought, *Why not?*

We weren't sure what to expect, or even where to start, so we tried every combination and process we could think of. We didn't love brined chunks, although now, having learned about fermentation techniques using preliminary salt pressing and partial drying to reduce moisture content (see page 80), we know they can be quite tasty. Grated squash came out dense, with minimal brine—perfect for a chutney-like condiment. Thinly sliced squash brined in its own salted juices yielded good texture. Chipotle Squash Kraut (facing page) was the winner, as the cabbage provides a little fresh crunch to the squash.

YOUR RAW MATERIAL

Winter squash encompasses a broad, colorful group of varietals, some of which are considered squash and others pumpkins. Some of the common varieties of the more dense, sweet-meat types of squash that behave best in the crock are acorn, butternut, Hubbard, kabocha, and turban squashes, and for pumpkins we like Cinderella, Rouge Vif d'Etampes, and Red Kuri. For varieties with more water content, look at moisture reduction as a first step.

When hardened off at first frost, winter squash stores well through a better part of winter. If you grow your own squash, ferment them early in the storage cycle, as they will continue to soften in cool, dark storage. If you wait until late winter to ferment them, you may be disappointed in the resulting texture. There's more flexibility when you're using commercial crops, as they're kept under refrigeration.

IN THE CROCK

Chipotle Squash Kraut

See photo on page 161

yield: about 1 gallon (3.8 l)
technique used: Mastering Sauerkraut (page 61)

This recipe produces a mild, sweet-ish kraut. The chipotle powder gives it earthy-smoky spiciness, making it a perfect substitute for fresh tomato salsa during winter. Occasionally we had a person at our market stand boldly proclaim, "I don't like kraut." These same people usually left our booth with a jar of this kraut, smiling and declaring that they were going to put it on fish tacos that night.

> 1–2 medium heads (about 4 pounds/1.8 kg) cabbage
> 4 pounds (1.8 kg) winter squash, halved, seeded, peeled, and grated
> 2½–3½ tablespoons (42–59 g) unrefined salt
> 1–2 teaspoons (3–6 g) chipotle powder (or more, if you like extra-hot and smoky)

Follow the recipe for Naked Kraut (page 173), shredding the cabbage and combining it with the squash, salt, and chipotle powder. You should have about equal amounts of squash and cabbage. Don't skimp on the salt, as it may leave you with a softer ferment. This kraut will keep, refrigerated, for 1 year.

Note: If the chipotle mellows too much for your liking during fermentation, you can toss in a bit more before transferring the kraut into storage jars.

Squash Chutney

yield: about 1 quart (946 ml)
technique used: Relishes/Chutneys/Salsas/Salads
(page 74)

This wonderfully thick condiment is both sweet and sour, and its bright orange hue adds a spark to any plate.

1½	pounds (680 g) winter squash, halved, seeded, peeled, and grated
½	cup (50 g) grated carrot (optional)
1–2	teaspoons (6–11 g) unrefined salt
2	cloves garlic, grated
1	tablespoon (7 g) curry powder (for a homemade version, see page 165)
½	cup (90 g) chopped raisins

1. Place the grated squash and carrot, if using, in a large bowl. Sprinkle in 1½ teaspoons of the salt and, using your hands, massage it in. Then taste. You should be able to taste the salt without it being overwhelming. Add more salt if necessary. Add the garlic, curry powder, and raisins, and toss to mix. Let sit, covered, for 30 to 45 minutes.

2. Transfer the mixture to your fermentation vessel, a handful at a time, pressing down to remove air pockets as you go. You should see some brine rising above the squash when you press.

3. Top with the peels of the squash, if you saved them, or parchment paper and a weight if you have one. Follow the instructions for your fermentation vessel. For a jar, if using the burping method (page 44) make sure there is little headspace and seal lid tightly. Burp daily or as needed. Alternatively, top the ferment with a quart-size ziplock bag. Press the bag down onto the top of the ferment and then fill it with water and seal.

4. Set your fermentation vessel on a plate in a spot where you can keep an eye on it, out of direct sunlight, and let ferment for 7 to 21 days. The ferment is ready when the squash is pleasingly sour, with lingering sweet notes. The color will remain bright orange.

5. When the ferment is ready, make sure it is in an airtight container and store in the fridge. The ferment will keep, refrigerated, for 1 year.

Kirsten Writes

I had this big idea that spaghetti squash would be great fermented. So I cut one open and tried forking out the meat, imagining it falling free in little shreds ready to salt. Turns out that the strings do not freely release until the squash is cooked—raw spaghetti squash is difficult to work with.

Create Your Own Recipes

Winter squash is versatile—have fun with it. Try these blends or make up your own:

» Sliced squash with scallions, ginger, garlic, and hot pepper (a blend inspired by kimchi)
» Sliced squash with thinly sliced apples, caraway seeds, and leeks
» Sliced squash salt-pressed or partially dehydrated and then cured in a pickling bed (see Chapter 6; squash really shines here)
» Thinly sliced squash substituted for sweet potato in West African–Inspired Sweet Potato Ferment (page 307)

ZUCCHINI AND OTHER SUMMER SQUASH

Zucchini's terrific, like bunnies prolific.
—UNKNOWN

Despite the Italian name and its status as a stalwart ingredient of Mediterranean cuisine, zucchini is native to the Americas, as are all variations of summer and winter squashes.

YOUR RAW MATERIAL

Summer squash is different from winter squash only in that the ideal time to harvest and eat it is when it's immature, meaning that the skin has not hardened, nor have the seeds developed. That said, for those that do reach maturity, moisture-reducing fermentation techniques (page 80) are a solution. When choosing squash at the market, make sure the sensitive skin is glossy and undamaged, as most of the nutrients are right under the skin. Avoid peeling.

Whichever variety you have, use the small ones to make whole pickles. For these, choose squash that are less than 1 inch in diameter. They can never be too small; some of our favorite "baby" pickles have come from tiny squash with unopened blossom ends.

If you are a gardener with a plant or two, you will have many opportunities to ferment summer squash of different sizes. At the market, they are generally around 8 inches long. Bigger is not better. If the inside is developing seeds and the center flesh is beginning to have a more spongy quality, it is too large to use as is. See recipes such as Watermelon Rind–Zucchini Salsa (page 344) or our Zucchini Peach Relish (page 350) for uses for these baseball-bat behemoths.

Use summer squashes as soon as you can after they've been picked. They degrade in the refrigerator after about 3 days, and the longer they sit, the shorter their fermented shelf life.

PEACH PEEL POWDER

There are a few home-canned items that we absolutely love and reliably make every year. Canned peach halves is one of them. One year, after the skins had been slipped off and piled up like discarded peach dresses, Kirsten looked at them, thought about all the vitamins, flavor, and the cost per pound of those peaches, and considered her options. After all, the skin tastes good, although a bit fuzzy. We dehydrated the skins and made a fine powder. We use this powder as we might use gochugaru. It gives a thick, rich texture and a sweet, peachy flavor to all kinds of ferments.

IN THE CROCK

Zucchini Peach Relish

yield: about 1 pint (473 ml)
technique used: Dehydration (page 83) and
Relishes/Chutneys/Salsas/Salads (page 74)

This relish is inspired by the traditions of South Asian achars. The zucchini is partially dehydrated at the start, then chopped and fermented, yielding crunchy bite-size treats.

We flavor our version of this relish with Peach Peel Powder, which you can make from peach or nectarine skins. You can, of course, choose different seasonings or flavor dust (page 142).

> 1 or 2 **oversized zucchini (1½ pounds/680 g)**
> 1 **teaspoon (6 g) unrefined salt**
> 3 **tablespoons (18 g) Peach Peel Powder (page 349) or other fermented flavor dust**
> **Juice of 1 lemon**
> **Grape leaf or parchment paper, to top the ferment**

1. Cut the zucchini lengthwise into quarters. Remove the seeds. Partially dehydrate the long pieces by leaving them overnight in a dehydrator at 110°F/43°C or laying them out in the bright summer sun for 2 days. They should reduce in size to 30 to 40 percent of their original volume. They'll be moist on the inside, but not wet; the outer skin will be dry, and they will have a somewhat rubbery consistency. Chop into ¼-inch chunks and place in a bowl.

2. Add the salt and, using your hands, massage it into the zucchini, until well coated. The zucchini may release some moisture, but don't expect a lot. Add the peach powder and lemon juice and mix well.

3. Pack the zucchini into a pint jar, pressing out air pockets as you go. It will be very dry compared to most ferments, but that's okay. Your job is to keep it pressed tight. Top with a grape leaf or parchment paper and weight if you have one.

4. If using the burping method (page 44), make sure there is little headspace and seal lid tightly. Burp daily or as needed. Alternatively, top the ferment with a quart-size ziplock bag. Press the bag down onto the top of the ferment and then fill it with water and seal.

5. Set the jar on a plate in a spot where you can keep an eye on it, out of direct sunlight, and let ferment for 7 to 14 days. The zucchini will develop a bright, citrusy acidity when done.

6. To store, tamp down the relish, tighten the lid, and set in the refrigerator, where it will keep for 9 months.

VARIATION
Spiced Zucchini Relish

Try the relish with this seasoning blend in place of the Peach Peel Powder:

> » 1 (1-inch/2.5 cm) piece ginger, thinly sliced
> » 1½ tablespoons (6 g) grated fresh turmeric
> » 1 teaspoon (3 g) toasted brown mustard seeds
> » ½ teaspoon (1 g) toasted cumin seeds
> » ½ teaspoon (1.8 g) toasted fenugreek seeds

Summer Squash Basil Pickles

yield: about 2 quarts (1.9 l)
technique used: Mastering Brine Pickling (page 101)

Have fun with these whole baby-squash pickles. Use a variety of summer squash, such as zucchini, pattypan, and crookneck. If you truly have an abundance, you can pickle the small ones with their blossoms (if they are unopened or recently bloomed; pluck off any ragged, tired blossoms). The blossoms hold up well to the brining, and the effect is striking and has a taste to match—something to awe your friends, if you are willing to share. Feel free to use your favorite pickling spice (see page 158 for a recipe) instead of basil.

Note: Zucchini can be anywhere from the size of your pinky finger to about 5 inches long and 1 inch in diameter. It's best if all the vegetables in one jar are similarly sized.

½–1 **pound (227–454 g) whole baby zucchini or summer squash**

4–5 **cloves garlic**

2 **sprigs basil**

1–2 **whole dried red chiles, sweet or hot**

2 **quarts (1.9 l) High Brine (3 tablespoons/ 50 g unrefined salt per quart unchlorinated water)**

Grape or other tannin-rich leaves or parchment paper, to top the ferment

1. Arrange the squashes, garlic, basil, and chiles in your fermentation vessel. Pack tightly, but take care not to damage the squashes' skin. Pour in enough brine to cover them completely. Reserve any leftover brine in the fridge. (It will keep for 1 week; discard thereafter or dry out and reclaim salt and make a new batch, if needed.)

2. Place grape leaves or a piece of parchment paper, if using, on top. Wedge toothpicks in an X over everything to keep submerged. Follow the instructions for your fermentation vessel. For a jar, if using the burping method (page 44) make sure there is little headspace and seal lid tightly. Burp daily or as needed.

3. Set your fermentation vessel on a plate in a spot where you can keep an eye on it, out of direct sunlight, and let ferment for 3 to 5 days. During the fermentation period, monitor the brine level and top off with the reserved brine, if needed, to cover. Start taste-testing when the brine becomes cloudy. When they're ready, the squashes' colors will appear dull and they will taste pickle-y with a softer texture.

4. Store in the refrigerator, where they will keep for 4 months.

Part 4

On the Plate

**Incorporating Fermented Foods
into Your Daily Meals**

Sauerkraut is tolerant, for it seems to be a well of contradictions. Not that it would preach a gastronomic neutrality that would endure all heresies. It rejects dogmatism and approves of individual tastes. It forms a marvelous combination with numerous spices: juniper berries, coriander seeds, peppercorns, cranberries, apples, stock, and wine. . . . Its flavor sustains various potato dishes. . . . The variety of meats to which it consents is infinite: sausages of all kinds, hams, bacon, quenelles, pickled and smoked pork, goose, pheasant, etc. It makes excuses for red wine, although it has a weakness for beer. . . . Each stomach may find its own happiness in it.

—JULIEN FREUND (1921–1993), FRENCH SOCIAL SCIENTIST

PHOTO ON PREVIOUS SPREAD:
FERMENT-FORWARD BOARDS, *page 364*

Here you are: You've made or bought some ferments. You know these fermented vegetables are good for you, you know they taste good on your fork straight out of a jar, but that only goes so far. What else can you do with these "sauer" vegetables?

We hope that the recipes in this part of the book not only bring flavor and joy to your table but also help you understand ferments as an ingredient like any other, and that you use these "new" ingredients, tossing them into a dish as readily as any familiar one.

We offer recipes that are both raw and cooked, and we believe the remarkable flavor is worth the cooking. We also include recipes where the ferment is added at the end of the cooking time—this will lightly warm the ferment, but not damage the live probiotics. Keeping the temperature of the ferment less than 110°F (43°C) will preserve the integrity of the digestive enzymes. But as you have learned, our bodies benefit from these fermented foods whether they are completely alive or absolutely cooked.

In general, when cooking significant quantities of fermented vegetables or fermented brine, use nonreactive cookware. Acidity can cause reactive metals to leach into food, resulting in off-flavors and colors. Examples of what not to use include aluminum, copper, and cast-iron pots. For meals using just a splash of brine, which is no different from cooking with a splash of vinegar or lemon juice, leaching is not an issue.

We have tried to balance meals that require time and thought with recipes that are designed to be simple and quick. There are days when you have time to cook and want to make something special, and there are the everyday moments when you don't have much time to get a meal to the table but still want to eat fresh, healthy food. Ferments are perfect for building, or adding to, simple quick meals, exponentially improving health and flavor. To this end, at the start of most chapters you'll find our Quick and Easy section, which offers simple ideas for getting ferments into your meals without digging deep into a recipe.

The thread that binds the recipes is fermented vegetables, not a particular cuisine. We love the foods of many cultures and wish to honor and respect the traditions and places from which inspiration and often fusion came. We hope these recipes will inspire you to fashion your own new family favorites.

CHAPTER 10

Breakfast

CULTURE FOR THE GUTSY

Some people can't imagine kraut in the morning; others couldn't start without it. Once tried, ferments for breakfast become almost an addiction. So many people, ourselves included, have felt our days start brighter with improved digestion. From elaborate weekend breakfasts to simple spreads to top your toast, we hope these ideas enhance your mornings.

Most of the ways we eat our ferments just happen; there are no recipes. Having a ferment on the table with any meal is as natural as the ever-present salt and pepper shakers.

In our home, we have a pantheon of regular flavors—the ferments we know will dress up most meals, blending with the simplest of foods. You'll find your favorites, and before you know it, you will be just adding the ferments and not thinking twice.

RANCHER ENCHILADAS, *page 361*

QUICK AND EASY BREAKFAST IDEAS

Hot Cereal

Make your favorite: buckwheat, mixed grain, or oatmeal (steel-cut or regular, soaked and fermented, or instant). Just be sure to cook it in water, not milk.

Top with a pat of butter or a tablespoon of olive oil, and heap on a healthy dose of your favorite ferment. Or substitute hot rice cereal or buckwheat for oats, add an egg, and top with fermented veggies. We have to say, kimchi on hot cereal is pretty magical.

Fruit and Green Smoothies

Don't forget to add fermented goodies to your smoothies. A tablespoon or two of Cranberry Relish (page 213) or Carrot Kraut (page 192) adds pizzazz to fruit-based smoothies. If you are a savory green smoothie drinker, the field is wide open; pick any kraut or brine to liven it up.

Omelets, Scrambles, Breakfast Burritos, and Eggs

Any egg breakfast lends itself to the addition of a kraut or fermented vegetable. Toss a little kraut into scrambled eggs at the end of cooking. Pour Sweet Pepper Salsa (page 297) on top of over-easy eggs or huevos rancheros. And here are some of the endless omelet possibilities:

- » Lemon-Dill Kraut (page 177), cheese, and sautéed mushrooms
- » Onion and Pepper Relish (page 286)
- » Salmon, sour cream, and Lemon-Dill Kraut (page 177), or whatever kraut you like best
- » Leek-Cracked Pepper Kraut (page 259) with ham
- » Curtido (page 176), chorizo, and cheese
- » Always relishes or salsas such as Watermelon Rind–Zucchini Salsa (page 344)

Schmears

"Schmear" is New York deli slang for a bagel topping. These spreads can be schmeared on anything from a bagel or toast to tortillas or collard leaves. Substitute vegan alternatives for cheese. These spreads will keep, airtight, for 1 week in the refrigerator.

Herb Schmear

8 ounces (227 g) cream cheese, softened
1–2 tablespoons (5.5–11g) fermented herb paste: Chimichurri (page 290), basil (pages 154 and 155), etc.
A few teaspoons (15 ml) fermented brine or lemon juice

Combine the cream cheese and paste in a food processer and blend until well mixed. Add brine as needed to achieve a creamy texture.

Kimcheese

8 ounces (227 g) cream cheese, softened
¼ cup (43 g) Kimchi (page 182)
A few teaspoons (15 ml) fermented kimchi brine or lemon juice

Combine the cream cheese and kimchi in a food processer and blend until well mixed. Add brine as needed to achieve a creamy texture.

Krautcheese

8 ounces (227 g) cream cheese, softened
3 ounces (85 g) feta cheese
¾ cup (177 ml) kraut of choice: Lemon-Dill
    (page 177), Lemon-Mint (page 177), or
    Lemon Spinach (page 327)
A few teaspoons (15 ml) fermented brine or
    lemon juice

Combine the cream cheese, feta, and kraut in a food processor and blend until well mixed. Add brine as needed to achieve a creamy texture.

Cranberry Blue Cheese

8 ounces (227 g) cream cheese, softened
3 ounces (85 g) blue cheese
½ cup (118 g) Pickled Cranberries (page 214)
A few teaspoons (15 ml) cranberry brine or
    lemon juice

Combine the cream cheese, blue cheese, and cranberries in a food processor and blend until well mixed. Add brine as needed to achieve a creamy texture.

Gado Gado Schmear

1 cup (250 g) peanut butter
½ teaspoon (2.5 ml) honey
½ teaspoon (2.5 ml) shoyu or soy sauce
½ cup (118 ml) Kimchi (page 182)

Combine the peanut butter, honey, and shoyu in a bowl. Lightly squeeze the kimchi to drain, saving the brine; chop finely. Add the kimchi to the peanut butter mixture. Stir until smooth, adding brine as needed to achieve a creamy texture.

Sauerkraut Frittata

serves 4

Gluten-Free, Vegetarian

Sauerkraut is a natural with meats and sausage, and it is just as well suited to eggs and cheese. A frittata is essentially a flat omelet that has the stuffing baked into it. It has the flamboyance of a quiche without the work (or gluten) of the crust. And it is ready to be served all at once, with none of the hassle of keeping individual omelets warm.

The beauty of this recipe is that it can be varied easily just by changing the type of kraut or herbs.

1 medium onion, thinly sliced
2 tablespoons (30 ml) olive oil
6 eggs
    Salt and freshly ground black pepper
    Scant ¼ teaspoon (0.5 g) freshly grated
        nutmeg
3 cloves garlic, minced
1½ cups (355 ml) your favorite ferment, drained
2 tablespoons (28 g) butter
2 tablespoons (10 g) Parmesan cheese (optional)

1. Preheat the oven to 350°F (175°C).

2. Sauté the onion slowly in 1 tablespoon of the olive oil until caramelized; set aside.

3. Crack the eggs into a large bowl. Add salt and pepper to taste, nutmeg, the remaining 1 tablespoon oil, and garlic. Beat lightly.

4. Gently squeeze the kraut to remove most of the liquid; it should be moist but not dripping. Stir the kraut and the cooled caramelized onions into the egg mixture.

KRAUTCHEESE,
page 359

HERB SCHMEAR,
page 358

GADO GADO SCHMEAR,
page 359

5. Heat a 10-inch ovenproof sauté pan over medium-low heat. Melt the butter in the pan, then turn off the heat and pour in the egg-kraut mixture. Transfer the pan to the oven.

6. Bake for 20 to 25 minutes, or until set.

7. Remove from the oven and sprinkle with the Parmesan, if using.

Rancher Enchiladas

See photo on page 356

serves 6

Gluten-Free

Years ago, when we were still in college, a friend made a variation of this recipe for us. She told us they were the enchiladas her mom had eaten on the ranch she grew up on in Silver City, New Mexico. We dubbed them Rancher Enchiladas, and the recipe has traveled with us through the years, now updated with the addition of curtido. This Latin American ferment shines here. Prepare these enchiladas for a Sunday morning brunch or for any meal of the day.

This recipe is simple, but it requires a bit of finesse at the end to put it all together and get the six plates to the table. *Note:* The recipe calls for enchilada sauce, but you could use a reduced chile pepper ferment in its place.

FILLING

- 1 onion, diced
- 1 tablespoon (15 ml) olive oil
- 1 pound (454 g) ground grass-fed beef
- 1 tablespoon (6 g) chile powder
- ½ teaspoon (1.3 g) ground cumin
- ½–1 cup (118–237 ml) coconut or other frying oil

- 1 dozen corn tortillas
- 2 cups (473 g) Curtido (page 176)
- 6 eggs
  Butter, for frying the eggs
- 3 cups (710 ml) or 2 (16-ounce) cans red enchilada sauce
- ½ pound (227 g) cheese, cheddar or jack style, shredded

1. Preheat the broiler. Set six ovenproof plates on the counter.

2. Make the filling: Sauté the onion in the olive oil until translucent. Add the beef, sprinkle in the chile powder and cumin, and cook until the beef is browned and cooked through. Keep the filling warm over low heat.

3. Fill the bottom of a small pan with enough coconut oil to cover a tortilla. Heat the oil until it is very hot but not smoking, then fry the tortillas, one at a time, for about 5 seconds each, until softened but not crisp.

4. Using tongs, transfer the tortillas to a paper towel–lined baking sheet to drain.

5. Place one tortilla on each plate. Evenly divide the beef filling among the tortillas. Spoon about ⅓ cup of the curtido over each one and top with another tortilla.

6. Using multiple pans, fry the eggs over-easy in the butter, and place one on top of each tortilla stack.

7. Divide the enchilada sauce evenly over the tortillas, sprinkle on the cheese, and place the plates under the broiler for 5 to 8 minutes to melt the cheese. Serve immediately.

Smoky Kraut Quiche

See photo on facing page

serves 6 to 8

VEGETARIAN

The smoky kraut gives this quiche a rich "meaty" flavor, although it remains vegetarian.

CRUST

- 1⅓ cups (160 g) unbleached all-purpose flour
- 7 tablespoons (98 g) cold butter, cut into small pieces
- 1 egg
  Pinch of salt

FILLING

- 2 cups (473 ml) Smoky Kraut (page 175), with the brine squeezed out
- 8 ounces (227 g) Swiss cheese, shredded
- 3 eggs
- 1 cup (237 ml) half-and-half
- ¼ teaspoon (0.5 g) ground nutmeg

1. Make the crust: Put the flour in a bowl and rub in the butter. Add the egg and the salt, and combine with a fork until the mixture resembles a coarse meal.

2. Transfer the dough to a floured work surface and knead lightly until the mixture holds together. Try not to overwork the dough.

3. Shape the dough into a 4-inch disk, wrap in plastic, and refrigerate for 30 minutes.

4. Meanwhile, prepare the filling: Put the drained kraut in a bowl and toss with the shredded cheese. In another bowl, whisk the eggs with the half-and-half; stir in the nutmeg.

5. Preheat the oven to 400°F (205°C).

6. Remove the dough from the refrigerator and let soften for 5 minutes. Roll out the dough on your work surface, flouring the rolling pin as necessary, to fit a 9-inch pie pan. Fit the crust in the pan and crimp the edge.

7. Spread the kraut/cheese mixture in the crust evenly, then pour the egg mixture over that.

8. Bake the quiche for 30 minutes, until set and nicely browned. Let cool for 5 to 10 minutes before serving.

SMOKY KRAUT QUICHE

FERMENT-FORWARD BOARDS

For Breakfast, Lunch, and Dinner

Kirsten Writes

In studying food patterns in agrarian societies, anthropologist Sidney Mintz identified a concept he termed "Core-Fringe-Legume Hypothesis."[14] Every culture, he noticed, had a culinary tradition where complex carbohydrates take the center of the plate (the core), surrounded by the fringe—all the delicious sides that decorate the bowl, give variety to the palate, and offer nutrients for the gut. We come back to this concept over and over because it makes so much sense as a way to eat lighter on the planet, and it is better for your gut.

In my mind, this core-fringe pattern has always equated to grain-, rice-, or legume-centered meals, or a meze platter, with its hummus and pita and deliciously seasoned vegetables. But recently I had an "aha" moment. At different points in my upbringing, I was fed this way. I knew that is how we ate when we lived in Asia, but it occurred to me that when I lived in Germany with my grandmother as a child, I also ate in a way that was starch-forward. The higher-cost, higher-calorie ingredients were toppings, condiments, and little bites. In the morning, I walked to the baker to bring home fresh, dark whole-grain bread, or to the butcher to get a cured spreadable meat such as Teewurst (a ferment-cured sausage) or liverwurst. When I returned home, my grandmother would lay out the bread and a board with the sausage, some cheese, jam, and butter. The delicious, dark sourdough bread was the core, butter was spread on the bread, and we could choose: The bread got a piece of meat *or* a piece of cheese. We could have as much bread as we wanted, but the rest was to be consumed in moderation. We called this breakfast an *Aufschnitt*, a jam-centered breakfast board with some meat and cheese. An *Aufschnitt* is what the Italians call *salumi*, the French call *charcuterie*, and Americans call deli meats or cold cuts. We always had our biggest hot meal at lunch, and dinner was another *Aufschnitt*, this time with more cuts of many different cured meats, pickles, cheeses, a selection of breads, pretzels, and rolls and butter.

The charcuterie-style meals I grew up eating were humble food, not the high-end boards on today's Instagram food scene, where abundance is piled on boards and then on crackers. Instead, the idea was to consume small portions of delicately sliced meat or cheese. The cured meats had concentrated complex flavors, and we didn't miss a giant slab of meat.

A beautiful board with a diversity of tastes and colors is still my favorite breakfast (and lunch or dinner). As a mom, I felt like as long as everything I put out was good food, the children had agency over their own plate on those days. As an eater, who doesn't love noshing on this or that? As a social creature, I enjoy the slow pace of this type of eating, which allows more time to be in community with my people, not to mention more time to chew and digest.

You can build a charcuterie board with anything you like—with meat or not—but we hope you use it as an opportunity to share and brag about your ferments.

Your base can be a large cutting board or simply a selection of small boards, plates, or bowls. When people are sitting around a table for a meal, the latter is more practical for passing around this-and-that. Use what you have. The food and ferments, with a little planning, will make it lovely.

Think about the architecture and design of your board. With your layout, you can mix and match the heights, shapes, textures, presentation, and spacing of your choices. Offer a variety. Choose a few different cheeses—some hard, some soft and spreadable, some sliced. The same goes for the meats—some smooth (such as sliced ham), some textured (for example, salami), some spreadable (such as pâté).

With the accompaniments, such as pickles, jams, and other condiments, you may want to introduce a rainbow of color, or perhaps you'll want a color theme, or a theme for the season or event. The point is, there are a lot of options to explore. Here are some ideas.

The Core
» Bread: whole-grain, sourdough, and/or gluten-free
» Crackers and crisps: salty, seedy, sweet, briny, or gluten-free
» Grain-free (optional): lettuce leaves for wrapping, cucumber slice "crackers"

Things to Put in Little Bowls
» Mustards
» Herb pastes
» Fruit pastes
» Jams and preserves
» Relishes
» Salsas
» Oil-preserved eggplant or tomatoes
» Butter and/or oils

Things to Slice and Stack
» Pickles (any kind!)
» Fresh cucumber slices (to be used instead of crackers), radishes, and other crisp veggies
» Dolmas (made with your own fermented grape leaves)
» Lettuce leaves (for wrapping)

Things to Pile
» Krauts (try something colorful!)
» Chutneys
» Kimchis
» Fermented salads

Things to Scatter
» Olives
» Pickled veggies and mushrooms
» Dried fruits
» Nuts
» Flower capers
» Edible flowers

CHAPTER 11

Snacks

A PICKLE A DAY KEEPS THE DOCTOR AWAY

Snack time is not just a good time to grab some fermented vegetables. In many ways, it is also a perfect time to incorporate these foods into your routine. The bright flavors are the perfect pick-me-up for any time of year. On a summer day when it feels too hot to eat, the added salt and electrolytes can feel nourishing. We often take ferments with us on hikes or on picnics for this very reason. While there is nothing easier than just grabbing your favorite pickles and munching on them, we have come up with a few more ways to inspire you. This chapter starts with crackers, crisps, and dips and ends with snacks that can also be hors d'oeuvres—ferments sophisticated enough to be paired with wines.

CLOCKWISE FROM TOP LEFT
BLACK BEAN SALSA, *page 371*
BRINE CRACKERS, *page 369*
CHIPOTLE KRAUT DIP, *page 370*
RADICCHIO TAPENADE, *page 372*

Brine Crisps

yield: 1 pound crisps
Gluten-Free, Vegan, Raw

So now that you are a fermentista, your refrigerator contains many colors and flavors of kraut, kimchi, and pickles. You are setting out a fermented favorite with every meal.

But there is something else: a collection of small jars in the back of your refrigerator with leftover brine from the sauerkraut, kimchi, or pickles. As a fermentista you know to save all this wonderful elixir that is left at the bottom of your crock or jar. As purveyors of all things kraut, we ended up with very big jars of leftover brine. That is when we developed these popular crisps (and the crackers on page 369).

These are like chips—unevenly sized and you can't stop putting them in your mouth. You can use either brown or golden flaxseeds. We like to use a mix; the contrast between the duller-looking brown seeds and the shiny golden ones gives the crackers a textured look.

2 cups (300 g) flaxseeds
1½ cups (356 ml) any fermented brine
1 cup (237 ml) spring water

1. Mix the flaxseeds and brine in a container that can hold them plus expansion as the seeds soak up the brine.

2. Cover the container with a lid and let soak for 12 hours, stirring occasionally if convenient (in other words, if you are starting the soak at night to make crackers the next day, no need to get up through the night and stir).

3. Spread your gelatinous flaxseed goo evenly on dehydrator trays equipped with sheets for making fruit leathers. Don't try spreading this on the normal dehydrator screens (like we did our first batch) unless you have great patience for cleaning tiny, ironed-on seeds out of the mesh. The thinner you spread, the thinner the crisps. With practice, you can get the seeds so thinly spread that when they are finished you can break them up with your hands to the size you like. If you decide to leave them a bit thicker, the crisps will work better for dipping into spreads.

4. Dehydrate at or below 103°F (39°C).

5. Check the crisps after 10 to 12 hours. When they are mostly dry, flip them over to finish evenly, about 1 hour longer.

6. When the crisps are completely dry and crispy, break the sheets apart to the desired size. Store in an airtight container. They will keep fresh for several weeks. If you want to re-crisp them, dehydrate them for about an hour.

Brine Crackers

See photo on page 366

yield: 1 pound crackers

Gluten-Free, Vegan, Raw

This versatile recipe can be varied by using different nuts, substituting chia seeds for a portion of the flaxseeds, or adding spices or ground dried veggies. It's a variation of the Brine Crisps recipe on the facing page, but the crackers are sturdier than the wispy crisps. They are cut into small squares and hold up to spreads. The crackers (and the crisps) take on the flavors of whatever fermented brine you use.

- ¾ pound (340 g) flaxseeds
- ¼ pound (113 g) almonds
- 1 quart (946 ml) fermented brine

1. Mix the seeds, nuts, and brine in a bowl or container with a lid and soak for 12 hours, stirring occasionally if convenient.

2. In a food processor, blend the mixture to a uniform consistency. Then spread the mixture evenly on the dehydrator tray with sheets, as described in the Brine Crisps recipe on the facing page.

3. Dehydrate at or below 103°F (39°C).

4. Check the crackers after 10 to 12 hours. When they are mostly dry, flip them over to finish them evenly, another 1 to 2 hours.

5. Transfer to a cutting board and cut to the desired size. Store in an airtight container. The crackers will keep fresh for several weeks.

CRISP AND CRACKER TIPS

» Flip over your crackers or crisps when they are still a little sticky but mostly dried. This way you will get both sides nicely dried.

» Better dehydrators can give you better results in terms of the evenness of the drying and preservation of the raw enzymes. Choose one with a thermostat and timer if possible.

» If using a household blender instead of a food processor, process just a little bit of the cracker mixture at a time and empty it into a large bowl as soon as the blades begin to struggle to blend everything evenly.

» If using a Champion-style juicer instead of a food processor, be sure to use the blank to push everything straight through instead of the juicing screens.

» Your yield will equal the amount of seeds you start with, so 1 pound of seeds, mixed with 1 quart of brine, results in a little more than 1 pound of crackers.

» If you use other nuts in place of the almonds, the crackers may be a little more "oily."

» If you don't have enough brine for the recipe, use what you have and make up the difference with unchlorinated water. The flavor will be much more subtle but still delicious.

Pickled Nuts

yield: 4 cups

Gluten-Free, Vegan, Raw

Soaking nuts in salt water increases their digestibility. Nuts contain enzyme inhibitors and phytic acid; both are broken down by soaking. The salt neutralizes the enzyme inhibitors, allowing our bodies to absorb the nuts properly. So it was a natural for us to use ferment-enhanced salt water, or brine, to soak the nuts.

The best part is the sublime flavor this achieves—crispy, with a hint of salt. Curried brine on cashews, curtido brine on pumpkin seeds . . . let your imagination lead you. The process is the same for whatever nut you choose to soak: almonds, walnuts, pecans, cashews, hazelnuts, pine nuts, and so on. It also works for seeds!

> 4 cups (945 ml) nuts
>
> Enough fermented brine to cover the nuts

1. Soak the nuts in the brine for 12 hours.

2. Spread the nuts out on a dehydrator tray.

3. Dehydrate at 103°F (39°C) or less for a total of 12 to 14 hours.

4. Check the nuts after 10 to 12 hours. When properly dried, they will be lightly crispy; if not, they will be soft and pithy. If the nuts are not dry, dehydrate for another couple of hours. It is important that the nuts be fully dry, or else they could become moldy when stored—that is, assuming they aren't gone as quickly as they are around here.

5. Store in an airtight container. They'll keep fresh for several weeks.

Chipotle Kraut Dip

See photo on page 366

yield: about 1 cup

Gluten-Free, Vegetarian

Chipotle peppers are believed to date back to the Aztec civilization. The presumption is that smoke-drying the jalapeños came about as a way to solve the problem of how to preserve the fleshy-walled, rot-prone chiles. The smoky notes followed by the jalapeño's heat is a winning combination.

As we mentioned earlier in the book, the heat of the pepper comes from the alkaloid capsaicin (page 294). The capsaicin fire is "put out" (or at least mellowed) by the fats in the sour cream or avocado, making the dip a mild snack.

Serve this dip with chips, crackers, or veggie slices such as carrot, celery, and bell peppers.

> ½ cup (118 ml) Chipotle Squash Kraut (page 347)
>
> ½ cup (120 g) sour cream

Simply mix the squash kraut with the sour cream in a bowl.

VARIATION
Vegan Dip

> 2 ripe avocados
>
> ½ cup (118 ml) Chipotle Squash Kraut (page 347)
>
> 1 tablespoon (15 ml) lemon juice

1. Cut the avocados in half and remove the seeds. Scoop the avocado pulp into a bowl. Mash with a fork to a fairly smooth consistency.

2. Add the Chipotle Squash Kraut and the lemon juice. Stir until well mixed.

French Onion Dip

yield: 2 cups

GLUTEN-FREE, VEGETARIAN

This is not your grandmother's onion dip made with powdered soup mix; rather, it's an unprocessed probiotic dip that will satisfy that junk food desire, without the junk.

½ cup (118 g) "Onion Soup" Seasoning (page 287)
1½ cups (360 g) kefir cheese or sour cream
1 teaspoon (2 g) paprika
Juice of 1 small lemon (2 tablespoons/30 ml)
Pinch of salt

1. Put the dehydrated onion seasoning in a blender or food processor and pulse to break it up. Then add the kefir or sour cream, paprika, lemon juice, and salt. Pulse just enough to blend the ingredients.

2. Refrigerate the dip for a few hours to allow the flavors to mingle.

Black Bean Salsa

See photo on page 366

yield: 2 cups

GLUTEN-FREE, VEGAN

When we have tortillas and cheese available, the go-to snack for our teenage children is quesadillas. Tortillas topped with cheese and Black Bean Salsa make a nutritious snack that is robust enough to hold them until dinner. This salsa also works as a dip with corn chips.

1 cup (170 g) cooked black beans
2 large tomatoes, diced
1 avocado, diced
½ bunch cilantro, chopped
½ cup (118 ml) Simple Onion Relish (page 286), chopped, or your favorite fermented onion recipe
1 teaspoon (6 g) Garlic Paste (page 237) or 1 clove garlic, minced
½ cup (118 g) diced Edgy Veggies (page 197) or 1 jalapeño, diced
Juice of 1 lime

1. Combine the beans, tomatoes, avocado, and cilantro in a bowl. Stir in the onions, garlic paste, Edgy Veggies, and lime juice.

2. Allow the salsa to sit, covered, at room temperature for an hour to let the flavors meld.

3. Taste, and refrigerate when the flavors have blended. The salsa will keep for about a week in the fridge.

Radicchio Tapenade

See photo on page 366

yield: 2 cups

GLUTEN-FREE, VEGAN, RAW

If you want to ease into eating bitter vegetables, this recipe is perfect. The bitter element is softened by the strong flavors of the cured olives and capers. Enjoy this as a spread on your favorite substrate, such as crackers, crusty bread, or potatoes.

- 1 cup (237 ml) packed Radicchio-Garlic Kraut (page 312)
- 1 cup (120 g) pitted kalamata olives, drained
- 1 (4-ounce/113 g) jar capers, drained
- 1–2 tablespoons (15–30 ml) olive oil (optional)

Put the kraut, olives, and capers into a food processor. Pulse until nearly smooth. Add the oil, if using, for a creamier texture.

Baba Ganoush

yield: 2 cups

GLUTEN-FREE, VEGAN, RAW

The beauty of this recipe is the speed with which it is prepared. No roasting and scraping hot eggplant, just measuring and blending. Because the fermented eggplant is already acidic, the traditional lemon juice can be omitted. We now use our Sour Eggplant, and it is a fun twist to have the extra flavors added by the mirepoix veggies.

This is good as a dip for pita triangles, chips, or crackers. It can be part of a Middle Eastern meze plate. And if you are looking for a hearty snack, it can also be used as spread on an open-faced sandwich or wrap.

- 2 cups (473 g) Sour Eggplant (page 223)
- ½ cup (120 g) tahini
- 3 cloves garlic or 1 head roasted garlic
- 1–2 tablespoons (3.8–7.6 g) chopped fresh or fermented parsley
- Pinch of salt
- Olive oil
- Smoked paprika

1. Put the eggplant, tahini, garlic, parsley, and salt in a food processor and purée.

2. Serve the dip in a shallow bowl, garnished with a drizzle of olive oil and a sprinkling of smoked paprika.

KRAUT BALLS,
page 374

Kraut Balls

See photo on page 373

yield: 16 balls

Most of us can't resist something deep-fried, and these tangy, creamy balls are no exception. The history of sauerkraut balls lies somewhere in the area of Akron, Ohio. Being on the West Coast, we've never tasted authentic, traditional ones, but our version is tasty. We do not specify which flavor kraut to use, having found that almost any one works well.

Serve as a hot hors d'oeuvre or a decadent side, with mustard sauce for dipping.

  1 cup (142 g) coarsely chopped ham
  1 tablespoon (14 g) butter
  1 small onion, finely diced
  1 cup (120 g) unbleached all-purpose flour
    Pinch of dry mustard or ½ teaspoon (2.5 g)
       prepared mustard
  1 cup (237 ml) milk
  2 cups (473 ml) sauerkraut, drained and finely
       chopped
1–2 tablespoons (3.8–7.6 g) minced parsley
  ½ cup (75 g) potato flour
    Enough coconut oil to deep-fry

MUSTARD SAUCE
  ½ cup (120 g) Dijon or fermented mustard
  ½ cup (120 g) sour cream

1. Put the ham in a food processor and pulse until it is finely chopped.

2. Melt the butter in a skillet and add ham and onion. Sauté until the onion is translucent and lightly browned.

3. Stir in the flour, mustard, and milk. This will thicken quickly; keep stirring until the flour and milk are cooked. It will become a fluffy paste.

4. Take the pan off the heat and let cool. Mix in the sauerkraut and parsley.

5. When it is cool enough to handle, roll the mixture into walnut-size balls. They will be sticky, so roll them in a dish of potato flour, giving them a light coating. (This saves the step of rolling them in beaten egg and breadcrumbs and gives the balls a crisp texture and a hint of French-fry flavor.)

6. To prepare the sauce, mix the mustard and sour cream together.

7. Heat the oil in a deep fryer or saucepan. Drop the balls into the hot oil and fry until brown, about 5 minutes. Serve hot, with mustard dipping sauce on the side.

Beet Kraut on Cucumbers

serves 6

GLUTEN-FREE, VEGETARIAN

This recipe definitely can be dressed up or down. Its fun color, crunchy and creamy texture, and slight sweetness please kids, but it also looks chic served on a wooden tray or beautiful plate as an hors d'oeuvre at a party.

- 4 ounces (113 g) cream cheese or fresh chèvre, at room temperature
- 1 cucumber, sliced into rounds
- ½ cup (118 ml) Simple Beet Kraut (page 163), lightly drained
- Small sprigs of dill (optional)

Spread the cream cheese on the cucumber rounds. Top each one with a dollop of beet kraut and garnish with a sprig of fresh dill, if you have some.

Smoky Dates

serves 6

GLUTEN-FREE, VEGETARIAN

This hors d'oeuvre speaks for itself. Sweet, smoky, tangy! Omit the cheese and it becomes both vegan and raw.

- 6 Medjool dates
- 12 small, thin slices flavorful aged hard cheese (optional)
- ¼ cup (59 ml) Smoky Kraut (page 175) or Naked Kraut (page 173), lightly drained

1. Slice the dates lengthwise. Remove the pits.

2. Stuff the dates with the cheese (if using) and top with kraut; otherwise omit the cheese and tuck a bit of kraut in each date.

Lunch

FERMENTS ON THE GO

There is a proverb that goes "Eat breakfast like a king, lunch like a prince, and dinner like a pauper." Many people believe this means your biggest meals should be enjoyed during the earlier parts of the day. While modern science tells us there is some truth to this old proverb, in many ways our modern lifestyle does not accommodate a rich, nutrient-dense lunch. This chapter will demonstrate simple ways that your midday meals can become nutritional feasts. We'll begin with some quick and easy options for the road (such as sandwich and wrap fillings, hand pastries, and salads) or meals that you can cook up at home without much fuss.

BLAUKRAUT WITH BLUE CHEESE AND WALNUTS, *page 390*
TEMPEH REUBEN, *page 379*

QUICK AND EASY LUNCH IDEAS

Sandwiches

While we've included specific recipes for sandwiches, any sandwich can take some kraut. And don't let "sandwich" hold you back; all the recipes in this chapter can be rolled up into your wrap of choice.

Grilled cheese sandwich variations with kraut could be a whole chapter. Try Leek-Cracked Pepper Kraut (page 259) with sharp cheddar cheese, or Swiss cheese with sliced garlic dill pickles. Or, get the same umami of cheese plus ferment with tsukemono vegetables—especially miso-zuke (page 92).

Many ferments, not just dill pickles, are great chopped and tossed in tuna salad, especially Curtido (page 176), or nukadoko-fermented kale stems. Or make it sardine salad with OlyKraut's Eastern European Sauerkraut (page 181) and mayonnaise.

How about turkey with Fermented Fennel Cranberry Chutney (page 229) and Brie?

Wraps and Flatbreads

Flatbreads, tortillas, pitas, naan, and other wraps and flatbreads are easy vessels for myriad combinations: veggies, cheeses, meats, salads, ferments; anything goes. The kraut, kimchi, relish, or pickles will provide the zing for anything you can think up and wrap up.

There are many gluten-free wraps available. Our favorite is collard leaves. They are sturdy enough to wrap like a burrito. Slice off the thick stem at the base of the leaf, then run a rolling pin quickly down the spine of the leaf to soften it enough to fold or roll. If you want a bit more of a tender wrap, wilt the leaf slightly by laying it quickly on a hot, dry skillet.

Nachos, Quesadillas, Tacos, Burritos

Anything you would put salsa on can take a ferment. Especially suited for this is Curtido (page 176), Tomatillo Salsa (page 330), Chipotle Squash Kraut (page 347), West African–Inspired Sweet Potato Ferment (page 307), or any of the pepper and onion ferments. Using ferments for salsa is particularly appealing in the winter months. They add the much-needed bling to the winter array when the fresh tomatoes are from far away and the pico de gallo is crunchy.

Pizza

Ferments are great in the same tangy or salty way that pineapple and olives are. You'll never look at pizza the same way again if you try chopped Preserved Lemons (page 207) or other citrus as a topping, or mix with olive oil for a unique base or foccacia topping. Either dollop the kraut (or other ferment) on top when the pizza comes out of the oven, or make sure the kraut is under the cheese. When exposed in the oven, shreds of cabbage will burn before the pizza is done.

Sausages and Hot Dogs

Fermented condiments up the culinary ante of any sausage or hot dog (meat or plant-based). Some of our favorite toppings include Pickled Onions (page 287), Yellow Mustard (page 276), Bavarian-Style Sweet Mustard (page 274), Sweet Dill Relish (page 218), Onion and Pepper Relish (page 286), Simple Onion Relish (page 286), Chow-Chow (page 334), Piccalilli (page 196), Pepper Paste (page 295), and sliced Edgy Veggies (page 197).

Tempeh Reuben

See photo on page 376

serves 6
Vegetarian

This open-faced sandwich incorporates a few traditionally fermented ingredients and is definitely a fusion: tempeh from Indonesia, soy sauce from Japan, sauerkraut from the cold climes of Europe, and the concept of the Reuben sandwich from somewhat disputed origins in the early part of the twentieth century in the USA.

- 1 (16-ounce/454 g) package tempeh
- ½ cup (118 ml) water
- ¼ cup (59 ml) soy sauce
- 1–2 tablespoons (15–30 ml) avocado oil
- 1 medium onion, diced
- ½ cup (230 g) mayonnaise, Homemade Sunflower Mayonnaise (page 393), or Almonnaise (page 392)
- 1 tablespoon (15 g) Fermented Horseradish (page 248) or prepared horseradish
- 6 pieces Jewish-style caraway-seeded rye bread
- 2 cups (473 ml) Naked Kraut (page 173) or Simple Beet Kraut (page 163)
- 2 cups (226 g) grated Swiss cheese

1. Preheat the broiler. Set an oven rack in the middle position.

2. Slice the tempeh thinly. Bring the water and soy sauce to a simmer in a skillet and add the tempeh slices. Simmer for 1 to 2 minutes on each side. Remove from the pan and set aside. Rinse the cooking liquid from the pan.

3. Return the pan to the stove and warm the oil over medium heat. Add the tempeh and onion to the pan and sauté until the onions are translucent and the tempeh is lightly browned. Remove from the heat and set aside.

4. Make the sauce by mixing the mayonnaise and horseradish together; slather this on the slices of rye bread.

5. Put the bread, sauce side up, on a baking sheet. Divide the tempeh mixture among the six sandwiches. Top each open-faced sandwich with a generous helping of kraut and Swiss cheese.

6. Broil until the cheese is bubbling, about 5 minutes. Serve hot.

Tempeh Salad

serves 6
Gluten-Free, Vegan

This sandwich filling is quite tasty and gives you a double dose of fermented foods. We use this basic concept for infinite variation depending on the current ferment population in the fridge.

Serve the tempeh salad on crusty bread, in a wrap, on crackers (gluten-free if you wish), or rolled up in collard leaves.

- 1 cup (237 ml) vegan chicken-flavored broth (or chicken broth, if you prefer)
- 1 (16-ounce/454 g) block tempeh
- ½–1 cup (115–230 g) mayonnaise, Homemade Sunflower Mayonnaise (page 393), or Almonnaise (page 392)
- 3–4 tablespoons (42–56g) Celery "Stuffing" (page 201)
- 1 New York Deli-Style Pickle (page 216), diced
- ¼ red onion, diced
- Salt and freshly ground black pepper

1. Bring the broth to a simmer and add the block of tempeh. Simmer for 3 to 5 minutes on each side, allowing the tempeh to soak up the flavors. Watch the pan so that it does not run dry.

2. Remove the tempeh from the pan; let cool to the touch. Dice it into cubes and put them in a bowl with the mayonnaise, celery ferment, pickle, and onion, and add salt and pepper to taste. Mix well.

   Tip: Use ferments to flavor and add crunch to any creamy "salad"-type sandwich filling—chicken salad, egg salad, sardine salad (like tuna but sustainable), tofu, and so on.

Fish Tacos

See photo on facing page

serves 8

Gluten-Free

This recipe suggests four different ferments. Each lends its own mood to the tacos, and each version is delicious.

   4 (6-ounce/170 g) tilapia fillets
      Scant ¼ teaspoon (1.4 g) salt, to rub on fish
   ¼ teaspoon (0.75 g) freshly ground black pepper
   1 tablespoon (14 g) coconut oil
   8 corn tortillas
   2 cups (473 ml) Chipotle Squash Kraut
      (page 347) or Curtido (page 176); or
      1 recipe Cabbage Salsa (page 393); or
      1½ cups Chimichurri (page 290)
   4 jalapeños, thinly sliced
      Lime wedges (optional)

1. Sprinkle the fish with the salt and black pepper and rub them in lightly.

2. Melt the coconut oil in a large skillet over medium-high heat, coating the pan. Lay the fish fillets in the pan and cook for 3 minutes on each side, or until the fish flakes easily.

3. Warm the tortillas on a dry, hot skillet until soft.

4. Divide the fish fillets, your chosen ferment, and the jalapeño slices evenly among tortillas. Serve with lime wedges, if desired.

SUSTAINABLE FISH

Fish can be a confusing food source. Which species are threatened? Which are subject to heavy metal contamination? Which should be wild caught and which should be farmed? Then there are the nets and the dolphins. . . . Some farmed fish are proving to be a good protein choice for feeding an increasing population. Tilapia, tra, and barramundi can be produced sustainably in small-scale operations, feeding local economies. A good discussion about our relationship with the sea and its food can be found in *Four Fish* by Paul Greenberg.

Kimchi Pancake

by Su-In Park (profile on page 184)

serves 2 to 4

This is one of our favorites. It can be an appetizer, banchan (side dish), snack, or light meal. It's easy, quick, crispy, tangy, and spicy. The batter comes together in minutes. The recipe works with basic pantry items and whatever leftover produce in your fridge needs a little attention. It's flavored with aged sour kimchi—and we know that most folks who love kimchi have a long-neglected jar lurking in the back of their fridge and don't know what to do with it. Here's the answer.

FISH TACOS

1 cup (120 g) all-purpose flour
Pinch of salt
Pinch of sugar (optional)
1 cup (237 ml) water or unflavored club soda
½ cup (85 g) chopped kimchi
2 tablespoons (30 ml) kimchi brine
2–3 cups (473–710 ml) vegetables, such as
   carrots (matchstick), onions (thin slices),
   green onions (½" slice), chives (1" slice),
   green cabbage (shredded), spinach
   (chopped), or other favorites
Oil (olive, grapeseed, canola, sunflower, or
   safflower), as needed

1. Combine the flour, salt, and sugar, if using, in a large bowl and whisk to mix.

2. Gently fold the water into the dry mixture. Avoid overmixing; you want to just wet the dry ingredients.

3. Toss in the kimchi, kimchi brine, and vegetables, and gently fold the batter over the vegetables until they are evenly coated. You want to put a light coating on the vegetables. If the batter is too thick, add a bit of water, a tablespoon at a time. If too watery, add extra flour.

4. Let the batter rest for 5 minutes.

5. Heat a cast-iron or nonstick skillet over medium heat. Add a tablespoon of oil, swirling the pan to coat the surface. Spoon the batter into the pan, spreading it thinly and evenly to the size of the pancake you want. Cook until the edges are dry and the surface opaque. Then flip, press down gently with the back of the spatula, and let cook until underneath is lightly browned.

Note: While you're cooking, adjust the temperature as needed. If the pan seems like it needs more oil, lift up one side of the pancake with a spatula, add oil, then set the pancake back down and slide it around to spread the oil underneath. For extra-crispy pancakes, use extra oil.

6. Serve hot, at room temperature, or chilled. If sharing, cut into triangular pie slices or squares; if enjoying individual pancakes, tear apart into bite-size pieces with chopsticks and enjoy.

Freeze any leftover pancakes with parchment paper between each pancake. Reheat frozen or thawed pancakes in a skillet with a little oil.

Gazpacho

serves 6

Gluten-Free, Vegetarian, Raw

This is a quick, healthy summer soup. We can't emphasize the "quick" part enough—this is one of those recipes that makes you happy you have a fermented larder. It's a natural place to include fermented vegetables, herbs, or garlic. Those vegetables can be anything from summer squash to okra—feel free to improvise. For strong, spicy notes, stir in a bit of Pepper Paste (page 295). We like our soup chunky, but you can also purée it.

Serve your gazpacho with crusty bread for a light lunch or with Sauerkraut Frittata (page 359) for brunch.

4 cups (946 ml) tomato juice
1–2 cups (200–400 g) diced fresh tomatoes
2 scallions, thinly sliced
2 tablespoons (30 ml) olive oil
1 teaspoon (5 ml) honey
1½ cups (354 g) diced Edgy Veggies (page 197)
   or a combination of pickled vegetables
3 tablespoons (42 g) Sweet Pepper Salsa
   (page 297)

¼ teaspoon (0.6 g) ground cumin
¼ teaspoon (0.6 g) ground cayenne
   Salt and freshly ground black pepper

1. Combine the tomato juice, tomatoes, scallions, oil, and honey in a large bowl. Stir in the fermented veggies, salsa, cumin, and cayenne, and mix well. Season with salt and pepper to taste.

2. Put the soup in the refrigerator and chill for at least 1 hour before serving.

Fermented Gazpacho

serves 4
Vegetarian

Two gazpachos in one cookbook might sound like too much, but they are very different soups. The gazpacho, on the facing page, is all about using your fermented vegetables; this version is a fermented soup and tastes very different—instead of just using some fermented elements, the whole soup is fermented. The optional stale bread will add additional dimension to texture and flavors. It requires some preplanning but is deliciously worth it.

For a heartier soup, add chopped ham and hard-boiled eggs when serving.

In summer, this will ferment quickly; in cooler weather it may take a little longer.

Note: This soup is thickened with stale bread; feel free to use gluten-free. It calls for canned tomato sauce or juice, but when tomatoes are in season you can use 2 pounds fresh Roma or other tomatoes; scoop out the seeds and any tough white core, then purée the tomatoes.

FIRST FERMENTATION
1 small cucumber, diced (remove the seeds first if they are mature)
½ red or yellow onion, diced
1 green bell pepper, diced
1 small zucchini, diced (optional)
2 cloves garlic
1 teaspoon (6 g) salt
¼ teaspoon (0.6 g) ground cumin

SECOND FERMENTATION
3¼ cups (775 ml) canned tomato sauce or tomato juice

AFTER FERMENTATION
1 (3- to 4-inch/7.5–10 cm) length sourdough baguette or 2–3 slices bread, preferably stale
3–4 tablespoons (45–60 ml) extra-virgin olive oil, plus a drizzle for serving
1–2 tablespoons (15–30 ml) sherry vinegar or red wine vinegar
   Salt and freshly ground black pepper
   Fresh herbs and croutons, for serving

1. Combine the cucumber, onion, bell pepper, zucchini, garlic, salt, and cumin in a bowl and mix thoroughly. As you mix, you will see brine forming.

2. Press the vegetables into the bottom of a half-gallon jar. Weigh down the vegetables, making sure there is little headspace at the top of the jar, then seal the lid tightly.

3. Set the jar on a plate in a corner of your kitchen to ferment. If the lid starts to bubble up, simply open the lid for a moment to "burp" the ferment. Ferment for 1 to 2 days. The vegetables will sour quickly.

4. When the vegetables are fermented to your liking, it's time for the second fermentation: Add enough tomato sauce to nearly fill the jar. Replace the lid, sealing tightly.

5. Let ferment, continuing to burp the jar as needed. The tomatoes have a lot of natural sugar and will ferment quickly. They also have a tendency to get funky because yeast will often move in. Ferment until you like the flavor. This can be as short as a few hours to 1 to 2 days, or longer if you want the soup to be more sour or even bubbly. You can make this decision based on how warm it is and how quickly (or slowly) your veggies achieve sourness.

6. Break up the stale bread into pieces, put in a bowl, and add enough water to cover. Let sit for a minute or two to soften, then squeeze out the excess water and put the bread into a blender. Add the fermented gazpacho, 3 tablespoons olive oil, and 1 tablespoon vinegar. Purée, then taste. Add another tablespoon of olive oil and vinegar, if desired, and season to taste with salt and pepper.

7. Put the soup in the refrigerator and chill for 3 to 4 hours before serving.

8. To serve, drizzle with extra olive oil and sprinkle with fresh herbs and croutons.

Fermented Poutine

serves 2
Gluten-Free, Vegetarian

What is poutine? Delicious, messy, gooey, fried—it has it all—comfort food. Poutine is said to have originated in rural Quebec's dairy region in the 1950s. The fresh cheddar cheese curds of the region were served atop French fries and gravy—a delightfully humble dish. Poutine has been both berated and mocked, but it doesn't matter what anyone thinks. It is fun and sloppy and lends itself perfectly to a fermented riff.

2 cups (330 g) Fermented French Fries
    (page 309), fermented but not yet fried
½ cup (112 g) Brine-Made Cheese Curds (below)
    Greens, such as arugula or spinach, for garnish
1½ cups (1 batch) White Miso Gravy (facing
    page), warmed if desired

1. Bake or fry the Fermented French Fries, following the instructions for that recipe. (You can make the gravy while the fries are cooking.)

2. Put the fries on a large plate. Top with cheese curds, garnish with greens, and drizzle with gravy. Serve immediately.

Brine-Made Cheese Curds

yield: about 10 ounces
Gluten-Free

Once upon a time, we were cheesemakers. We look back on that time now with a mixture of feelings. Christopher often fondly recalls our "cheese cave" with its gallon jars of feta cured in olive oil and ripening wheels. Kirsten misses having all that, yes, but cannot distance that memory from how much work that was every single day of the year, for quite a few years. We miss it and we don't. And we would 100 percent do it again. One son had a couple of cows, the other several goats; it is an understatement to say we had copious amounts of milk. Although Kirsten usually made cheese daily, sometimes we simply didn't have the fridge space or time to process all that milk for cheesemaking, so we would make curds instead.

To make curds, you heat the milk and then add an acid, often lemon juice or vinegar, which causes the milk solids to coagulate, leaving behind the whey. It's a quick conversion, which is why it's a good way to get through a great volume of milk in a short volume of time. We ate the curds as is or made them into queso blanco or paneer, and the whey went to the fruit trees.

In the spirit of using what we have, we experimented with acidifying the milk with the brine from our ferments instead. The results were fantastic. Kimchi, pickles, curtido—it didn't matter, all these preseasoned brines were delicious.

You can use brine-made curds to top a bowl, in a salad, or in poutine. Don't toss the whey—it can be used in many ways, the simplest of which is as the broth in a potato soup or a hearty stew.

½ gallon (1.9 l) whole milk (not ultra-pasteurized)
Scant ¾ cup (177 ml) fermented brine*

***Note:** The more traditional acid for making cheese curds is lemon juice. For ½ gallon of milk, you'd use ¼ cup (59 ml) lemon juice.

1. Put the milk in a heavy-bottomed, nonreactive pot. Heat slowly, stirring occasionally, to the point just before a boil (around 190°F/88°C).

2. Add the brine and stir gently. Remove from the heat. You will see the curds begin to separate. Stir a few more times, then allow the curds to sit for a few minutes.

Sometimes the milk doesn't coagulate (separate) immediately. It may be that the temperature isn't quite warm enough. Keep slowly warming the pot. You may need to add more acid to encourage curd separation, but proceed cautiously, as too much acid will cause the curds to be small, like ricotta, instead of larger curds.

3. Scoop the curds from the whey and place in a fine sieve or a piece of cheesecloth. Let drain (catch the whey in a large bowl or pot) for 15 to 20 minutes.

White Miso Gravy

yield: 1½ cups
Gluten-Free, Vegetarian

This gravy is very flavorful in the salty umami way that gravy should be. And it is super easy—no flour, no lumps, not much in the way of cooking. It takes 10 minutes at the most. Use unsalted butter instead of olive oil for an even creamier version. Enjoy it on biscuits, mashed potatoes, roasts, or anywhere else you love gravy.

3 tablespoons (45 ml) olive oil
½ medium onion, diced
2 cloves garlic, minced
⅓ cup (92 g) white miso
¼ cup (15 g) nutritional yeast
⅔ cup (158 ml) water

1. Heat the olive oil in a small saucepan over medium heat. Add the onion and garlic and sauté until translucent and browning, 10 to 12 minutes. Remove from the heat and let cool.

2. Combine the cooled onion mixture with the miso, nutritional yeast, and water in a blender and blend until creamy. Alternatively, combine these ingredients in a widemouthed jar and use an immersion blender to blend them.

3. Use in all the sloppy, delicious ways you like to use gravy. Feel free to warm it up before using. Store any leftover gravy in the fridge, where it will keep for 2 weeks.

SUSHI-NORIMAKI

Stuffed Portobellos

serves 4
GLUTEN-FREE, VEGETARIAN

When we sold fermented vegetables at farmers' markets, we made recipe cards to give to customers who wanted to know how to use ferments in recipes. These mushrooms were one of the first recipes we came up with to share with our customers. The earthy mushrooms, sharp cheese, and acidic kraut complement one another perfectly.

   To make this dish as an hors d'oeuvre, use cremini mushrooms or baby portobellos instead.

   4 **portobello mushrooms**
   1 **tablespoon (14 g) butter**
   1 **tablespoon (15 ml) olive oil**
   4 **cloves garlic, minced**
   1 **cup (237 ml) drained and packed Lemon-Dill Kraut (page 177) or your favorite kraut**
   4 **ounces (113 g) goat cheddar cheese, grated**
   1 **scallion, finely sliced**

1. Remove the stems from the mushrooms and chop. Set aside the caps, leaving them whole.

2. Heat the butter and oil in a large Dutch oven or other heavy pan with a lid. Add the mushroom stems and garlic and sauté lightly over medium heat.

3. Meanwhile, for the filling, loosely chop the drained sauerkraut and put it in a bowl. Add the cheese and scallion, then add the sautéed stems and garlic and toss together.

4. Leaving the oil in the pan, return it to the stove over low heat. Lay the mushroom caps in the pan, top sides down.

5. Divide the filling mixture into four portions and form it into patties. Place a patty on top of each portobello. Put the lid on the pan and cook over low heat for 10 to 15 minutes.

6. Meanwhile, preheat the broiler.

7. When the cheese has melted and the mushrooms are soft, place them under the broiler set on low to lightly brown the tops. Serve hot.

Variation
Put this filling on rye bread and toast slowly under a low broiler setting.

Sushi-Norimaki

See photo on facing page
serves 4
GLUTEN-FREE, VEGAN

The first sushi was packaging for fermented fish. Cookbook author Madhur Jaffrey explains that records from sixth-century China describe preserving raw fish by wrapping it in boiled rice. Amino acids from the fermenting fish and lactic acids from the fermenting rice preserved the fish for as long as several years. The rice was thrown away when the fish was eaten. The same type of recipe showed up in eighth-century Japan, and eight centuries later the Japanese began eating both fish and rice that had been pickled over a few days. In the nineteenth century, vinegar replaced fermentation in the rice and fresh fish completed the transformation to the sushi we enjoy today.

   Here, fermented vegetables bring the taste of fermentation back to sushi. This simple rolled sushi—norimaki—is made with a sheet of nori seaweed spread with vinegared rice and a line of filling.

VINEGARED RICE (SUMESHI)

1 cup (200 g) sushi rice
3 tablespoons (45 ml) rice vinegar
1 tablespoon (12 g) sugar
1 teaspoon (6 g) salt

FILLING

Any fermented vegetables (whatever you have on hand; tsukemono-influenced flavors, such as umeboshi or vegetables from pickling beds, are especially nice)

ASSEMBLY

4 sheets nori
2 tablespoons (18 g) sesame seeds

FOR SERVING

1–2 tablespoons (14–28 g) pickled ginger (page 240)
1–2 tablespoons (16–32 g) wasabi paste
Shoyu or soy sauce

1. For the vinegared rice, soak the rice in cold water for 10 to 15 minutes, then drain.

2. Transfer the rice to a saucepan and add 1 cup water. Cover and bring to a boil over high heat. Lower the heat and simmer, covered, for about 10 minutes, or until the water has been absorbed. (*Note:* The trick is not to remove the lid and yet know when the water has been absorbed; do your best, removing the lid to check quickly once.)

3. When the rice is cooked, remove the saucepan from the heat and set aside, covered, to rest for 10 minutes.

4. Meanwhile, mix the rice vinegar, sugar, and salt in a bowl until dissolved.

5. Place the rice in a shallow dish. Sprinkle the vinegar solution over the rice, then fold it in.

Allow the rice to cool to tepid before you begin to roll.

6. Prepare your choice of pickled vegetables; you will want ½-inch-long matchstick pieces.

7. To assemble and roll the norimaki: Cut each sheet of nori in half crosswise. Lay a nori sheet on a sushi rolling mat. Place 2 to 3 tablespoons of the rice on the middle of the sheet, spreading it evenly over the surface; leave a ½-inch margin on one side.

8. Sprinkle a thin line of sesame seeds along the center of the rice. Arrange the pickled veggies on top.

9. Pick up the mat, keeping your vegetables centered, then roll the mat over to meet the other side. Press and roll the mat over your roll lightly. The roll will stick together from the moisture in the rice. When the roll is tight, cut it into six even pieces.

10. Repeat the steps to assemble and cut the remaining seven rolls. Arrange all the pieces on a plate and serve with pickled ginger, wasabi paste, and shoyu.

FERMENTISTA'S TIP

Storing Leftover Norimaki

The vinegar, which was added to this evolving recipe in the nineteenth century to replace the fermentation of the rice, does provide a measure of preservation. Rolls should never be put in the refrigerator, as the rice will get hard. Keep them in an airtight container in a cool spot if you don't intend to eat them immediately, for up to 1 day.

Tempura

serves 4 to 6

VEGETARIAN

We make these with any brine-pickled or pickling bed–fermented vegetable. Because the pickled vegetables have a salty tartness on their own, the dipping sauce can simply be shoyu (soy sauce) with a splash of rice vinegar.

BATTER

    2 egg yolks
1½ cups (355 ml) ice water
1¾ cups (210 g) unbleached all-purpose flour
     High-quality high-heat oil, for deep frying
3–4 cups (710–946 ml) pickled vegetables, drained

FOR SERVING

     Hot cooked rice
     Vietnamese Pickled Carrot and Daikon
     (page 193), or your favorite ferments

TEMPURA OIL

Traditionally sesame oil is used in the frying of tempura. Interestingly, at the highbrow tempura establishments in Japan the oil is only used once. It is then sold to the lesser establishments, where it is used a few more times.

1. Put the egg yolks in a bowl. Add the ice water, slowly stirring and blending it well as you go. If you are feeling a need to be authentic, stir with chopsticks.

2. Add the flour all at once and mix lightly; you don't want to wake up the gluten or to warm the batter. The batter should be cold and lumpy.

3. Pour the oil into a small saucepan or deep fryer to a depth of ½ inch and heat over high heat to about 360°F (182°C); you will know the oil is hot enough if a drop of the batter sinks to the bottom, sizzles, and bounces up to the top. (*Note:* The temperature of the oil should be monitored constantly. If it cools too much, the batter will absorb the oil and your tempura will become soggy. To maintain the temperature, fry only a few pieces at a time.)

4. Pat the pickled vegetables dry with a paper towel.

5. Coat the vegetables in batter. Fry for about 1 minute on each side.

6. Serve immediately over a bowl of steamed rice, with a side of pickled carrot and daikon.

Blaukraut with Blue Cheese and Walnuts

See photo on page 376

serves 4 to 6

GLUTEN-FREE, VEGETARIAN

This recipe is almost as simple as serving the kraut straight from the crock. In a few minutes you have dressed it up and created a gourmet salad, worthy of any occasion.

    1 cup (115 g) walnut pieces
    1 tablespoon (15 ml) walnut oil
    1 crisp sweet apple, cored and thinly sliced
    2 cups (473 ml) Blaukraut (page 190)
    ½ cup (85 g) crumbled blue cheese

1. Preheat the oven to 350°F (175°C).

2. Toss the walnut pieces with the oil. Spread them on a baking sheet and toast in the oven. This should take 4 to 5 minutes; watch them carefully to avoid overbrowning.

3. Remove the nuts from the oven and allow them to cool.

4. Toss the apple with the blaukraut. Sprinkle the blue cheese and walnuts over the top and serve.

Celeriac Remoulade

serves 4

GLUTEN-FREE, VEGETARIAN

This is a variation on the French salad of the same name. The acidity comes from the fermented celeriac instead of the traditional lemon juice. This creamy salad can be served alongside any main dish; try roast chicken or poached fish. It also makes a good sandwich filling.

    ¼ cup (58 g) mayonnaise, preferably homemade
       (page 393)
    2 tablespoons (30 g) crème fraîche or
       sour cream
    1 teaspoon (5 g) Dijon mustard
    1¼ cups (296 ml) Naked Celeriac Kraut
       (page 199)
    1 tablespoon (3.8 g) minced fresh parsley
    1 tablespoon (15 g) minced New York Deli-Style
       Pickle (page 216) or other lacto-fermented
       dill pickle
    ½ teaspoon (2.5 g) minced capers
       Pinch of dried tarragon, crumbled
       Salt and freshly ground black pepper

1. In a small bowl, whisk together the mayonnaise, crème fraîche, and mustard to create the dressing.

2. Mix in the celeriac kraut, parsley, pickle, capers, and tarragon. Add salt and pepper to taste.

Beet and Celery Salad

serves 4

GLUTEN-FREE, RAW, VEGAN

This quick, magenta-colored salad fuses the fresh with the fermented deliciously.

- 1 cup (237 ml) Simple Beet Kraut (page 163)
- 4 stalks celery, thinly sliced on the diagonal
- ¼ cup (59 ml) apple juice or cider
- 3 tablespoons (45 ml) sunflower oil (if you can find the cold-pressed oil that tastes like sunflower, all the better)
- 4 scallions, finely sliced
- 2 tablespoons (7.6 g) chopped fresh parsley
- 1 tablespoon (15 ml) apple cider vinegar

Combine the kraut, celery, and juice in a bowl. Add the oil, scallions, parsley, and vinegar. Mix well and let the salad marinate for an hour before serving.

Wilted Spinach Salad with Rhubarb Relish

serves 4 to 6

GLUTEN-FREE, VEGAN OPTION

The rhubarb relish adds a wonderful zing that brightens this classic salad. It can be made with bacon, in which case the hot bacon fat from frying is the first step in making the warm dressing that will wilt the spinach.

For a lighter or vegan variation, omit the bacon (and its grease) and substitute olive oil. If using olive oil, remember to heat it gently; it does not do well with high heat.

- 1 pound (454 g) fresh spinach
- 2–3 slices bacon or 2–3 tablespoons (30–45 ml) olive oil
- 1 red onion, thinly sliced
- 2 tablespoons (30 ml) balsamic vinegar
- ½ cup (130 g) Rhubarb Relish (page 319)
- Salt and freshly ground black pepper

1. Wash and dry the spinach. Place the greens in a salad bowl.

2. If using bacon, fry the slices until crisp, then remove them from the pan, leaving behind the melted fat.

3. Warm the melted bacon fat or the olive oil, then add the onion. Sauté until the onion slices begin to caramelize. Then add the balsamic vinegar and continue to cook until the onions have caramelized completely and the balsamic has reduced and thickened.

4. Pour the hot onions and dressing over the spinach, then toss. Add the rhubarb relish, season with salt and pepper, and toss again.

5. If you used bacon, crumble the slices and sprinkle on top of the salad. Serve warm.

Coleslaw

serves 4

Gluten-Free, Raw, Vegan

The tang of the kraut blends nicely with the sweetness of the fresh carrots in this simple coleslaw.

- 2 cups (473 ml) plain sauerkraut
- 1 cup (100 g) grated carrots
- 1 cup (230 g) Homemade Sunflower Mayonnaise (page 393), Almonnaise (at right), or your favorite store-bought mayo

1. Put the sauerkraut in a sieve and gently squeeze out the liquid. Then put the kraut in a bowl with the shredded carrots.

2. Toss the vegetables together, then mix in the mayonnaise.

Kirsten Writes

As much as I love cooking with fresh whole ingredients, there are days when I don't want to spend much time in the kitchen. Ferments in salads to the rescue!

Salads, where we expect to find tangy flavors, are a natural place to showcase fermented veggies. Adding a few fresh vegetables and some olive oil mellows out the acidity and transforms a kraut into a gourmet salad. Add a little mayo instead of olive oil, and you have a zingy take on traditional coleslaw. I share some of our favorites in this section, but any salad can be dressed up with a last-minute dollop of something fermented.

Almonnaise

yield: about 2 cups

Gluten-Free, Raw, Vegan

We've been making this eggless mayonnaise since our vegetarian days in the early 1990s. Marilyn Diamond wrote the original recipe in *The American Vegetarian Cookbook*.

- ½ cup (72 g) raw almonds
- ½–¾ cup (118–177 ml) water
- 1 generous teaspoon (1.25 g) nutritional yeast
- ½ teaspoon (2.8 g) salt
- 1–1¼ cups (237–296 ml) cold-pressed light oil
- 3 tablespoons (45 ml) lemon juice or fermented brine
- ½ teaspoon (2.5 ml) apple cider vinegar

1. Put the almonds in a food processor, blender, or Vitamix. Grind until they are a fine meal.

2. Add about half of the water, along with the yeast and salt. Blend this first, then slowly add the remaining water until you have a creamy consistency.

3. With the motor running on low speed, drizzle in the oil in a thin, continuous stream until the mixture thickens.

4. With the machine still running, add the lemon juice and vinegar; keep blending for about a minute, until the mayonnaise thickens a bit more.

Homemade Sunflower Mayonnaise

yield: about 1 cup

GLUTEN-FREE, RAW, VEGETARIAN

Homemade mayonnaise is simple to prepare and worth the effort. It has the reputation of being tricky, as it can be sensitive and every once in a while it will fail, separating and looking as though it is curdled. Don't be disheartened if this happens; often adding an extra yolk will help it emulsify.

- 1 whole egg
- 1 egg yolk
- 1 cup (237 ml) cold-pressed sunflower or avocado oil
- 1 tablespoon (15 ml) lemon juice or fermented brine
- Pinch of salt

1. Put the whole egg and egg yolk in a blender or food processor, and blend for a few seconds.

2. With the motor running, begin to drizzle in the oil in a thin stream. When the mixture reaches the desired consistency, stop; you may not need the full cup of oil.

3. With the motor running again, add the lemon juice and salt. As soon as it is blended in and the mixture has thickened, your mayonnaise is ready.

VARIATION
Aioli

Use the same process to make aioli, replacing the sunflower oil with olive oil. The aioli will have a rich color and olive flavor but may not set up quite as thick. After it's blended, mix in about 1 teaspoon Garlic Paste (page 237).

Cabbage Salsa

serves 4 to 6

GLUTEN-FREE, VEGETARIAN, RAW

This coleslaw can be used as a chip dip, a side salad, or a dressing for a sandwich. Or try wrapping it up in a burrito or fish taco.

- 1 cup (70 g) shredded fresh cabbage
- 1 cup (237 ml) Naked Kraut (page 173; there's no need to drain it)
- ½ cup (80 g) finely diced red onion (fresh or fermented)
- 2 tablespoons (20 g) Cilantro Paste (page 203), or chopped fresh cilantro
- 1 tablespoon (15 ml) E-Z Hot Sauce (page 296) or jalapeño brine
- 1 clove garlic, minced
- ¾–1 cup (173–230 g) Homemade Sunflower Mayonnaise (at left), Almonnaise (page 392), or your favorite store-bought mayo
- Freshly ground black pepper

Combine the cabbage, kraut, onion, cilantro, hot sauce, and garlic in a bowl and mix well. Add the mayo, starting with ¾ cup and adding more as needed to reach the desired creaminess. Season with pepper to taste.

FERMENT-FORWARD LATKES, *page 400*

CHAPTER 13

Dinner

BRINE AND DINE

When we first started having many ferments in our refrigerator we felt like we'd discovered a little-known secret—we always had something fresh and flavorful to put out with a meal. This could be to save time or because we didn't have any fresh vegetables to prepare. Either way, a fermented larder makes dinnertime so much easier. The meal always feels nutritious and flavorful, even if it is simple pasta.

At dinnertime we enjoy humble food that is simple to prepare. In the past this was because we were feeding a houseful of kids and large one-pot meals with a pile of sauerkraut were efficient. Now, the pot is smaller but the comfort is the same. We hope the recipes we have chosen will bring you similar comfort. Many are variations of old-world, traditional, unassuming one-pot meals.

QUICK AND EASY DINNER IDEAS

Our family enjoys meals that are based on building your own, which was born out of the desperation that can come with the effort to create a balanced meal during the late-afternoon witching hour with a baby and three young children. Something simple such as baked potatoes with five or six toppings was easy to put together, and for the kids a meal with à la carte toppings gave them a sense of ownership over what was on their plate. The kids could "build" their meal right at the table, and we knew that as long as a few of the toppings were our ferments, we had won the eat-your-veggies battle.

The kids are big, the parents are less tired, but we still have many meals like these.

Baked Potatoes

Kirsten's Aunt Eleanor was visiting to help at our youngest son's birth, and one night she made baked potatoes. After scrubbing and poking the potatoes with a fork, she rubbed a tiny bit of oil and some flaked salt on the skin. We already liked eating the potato skins, but this small step brought them to the next level.

For this meal, we simply prepare the potatoes as described above and bake them. Right before serving, we get out small bowls and fill them with three or four different ferments and a few nonfermented toppings. The ideas here are just to get you started—anything you love or happen to have on hand is probably perfect.

Potato Toppings
- » Any herb pastes, especially Fermented Cilantro Coconut Sauce (page 204), or Chimichurri (page 290)

- » Any ferment you have on hand (we mean it—anything in this book is good on baked potatoes)
- » Chopped Preserved Limes (page 205)
- » Dairy-free or full-dairy shredded cheese or feta crumbles
- » Dairy-free or full-dairy sour cream
- » Steamed or raw vegetables

Chili

If you make chili, bring fermented condiments to the table—you will never eat chili without something fermented again!

Chili (and Refried Bean) Toppings
- » Curtido (page 176)
- » Charred Cabbage Sauerkraut (page 174)
- » Simple Onion Relish (page 286)
- » Chow-Chow (page 334)
- » Chipotle Squash Kraut (page 347)
- » Pepper Paste (page 295)
- » Tomatillo Salsa (page 330)

Noodles, Fried Rice, and Stir-Fries

Top noodle bowls and fried rice with krauts or kimchi. For this, we like Carrot Kraut (page 192), Burdock Kimchi (page 171), Pickled Shiitake (page 267), Vietnamese-Style Pickled Scallions (page 324), or any miso-zuke (page 92), nuka-zuke (page 85), or suan cai or any other fermented mustard greens (page 272).

Whole-leaf ferments like shiso (page 325) or Thai basil (page 155) are wonderful to garnish a stir-fry or fried rice right before serving.

Refried Beans

yield: 12 cups

Gluten-Free, Vegan option

Hands down, our kids would tell you homemade refried beans are their favorite meal. Once soaked and simmered, a big pot of beans becomes a meal and countless snacks; in this recipe the fermented element comes in the soaking liquid, and because kraut is so delicious on beans, especially refried beans, we recommend you try making your own if you never have.

We learned to make refried beans when we were in college in Tucson. At first we made them with lard, as we had been taught. In our vegetarian years, we made them with copious amounts of olive oil. Now we use lard when we have raised our own hog, and when we are out of that we use olive oil. We use a full cup of oil for a large pot of beans; however, you will still have a great pot of beans if you would rather use less.

This recipe is for a big pot of beans that will make two or more meals. Don't forget to soak the beans the day before you want to eat them.

> 4 cups (850 g) pinto, Anasazi, or cranberry beans
> 1–2 tablespoons (15–30 ml) any fermented brine, if available
> 4–5 cloves garlic, minced
> 1 tablespoon (17 g) salt, or to taste
> ½–1 cup (118–237 ml) olive oil or good-quality lard, melted
> Again, any more ferments for topping!

1. Put the beans in a large bowl or pot and cover them generously with water. The beans will double in size as they soak, so use enough water to keep them all submerged. Add the brine, if using. Cover and set aside. After 12 hours, pour off the water and replace with fresh water.

2. When you are ready to cook the beans (ideally after 24 hours of soaking them), pour off the soaking water and rinse the beans.

3. Put the beans in a pot, add enough water to cover them by a few inches, and bring to a boil. Carefully skim off any foam that rises to the top. Reduce the heat and simmer until the beans are soft, about 1½ hours. Check occasionally to make sure there is plenty of water over the beans as they cook.

4. When the beans are soft, remove them from the heat and drain. Put the beans back into the pot with the garlic, salt, and oil. Mash with a potato masher. Add fresh water as needed to achieve a smooth, creamy texture. Homemade refried beans are smoother and softer than canned.

5. When you're ready to eat, warm the beans over medium heat and serve in a bowl, in a burrito, or in a taco with any kraut you choose.

6. Store leftovers in a sealed container in the refrigerator for up to a week. Warm leftovers in a pot, adding water as needed and stirring often.

FERMENTISTA'S TIP

Fermentation and Beans

Adding fermented brine to soaking beans helps break down the complex sugars (raffinose and stachyose) and neutralizes phytic acid, making the beans more digestible.

Kraut-a-kopita (Spanakopita)

serves 6

Vegetarian

Spinach brings to mind Greek spanakopita, redolent with oregano, lemon, and sweet onions. With some misgivings—the family is divided about the texture—we tried to make a ferment with the flavors (page 326), and it's good! The spinach has some crunch, similar to that of a wilted spinach salad. But we've found its highest and best use is in a delicacy we've christened Kraut-a-kopita. This variation of the classic Greek spinach pastry is quick to prepare, as the fermented spinach is one of the main ingredients. We eat this as a hot main dish accompanied by a Greek salad. It makes a nice appetizer, too, alone or as part of a meze platter.

> 1 pound (454 g) frozen phyllo pastry
> ¾–1 cup (1½–2 sticks/168–224 g) butter, or
>   1–1¼ cups olive oil, or a combination

FILLING

> 3–4 cups (710–946 ml) Lemon Spinach
>   (page 327)
> 4 eggs
> 1 pound (454 g) crumbled feta cheese
> 1 tablespoon (7.5 g) unbleached all-purpose
>   flour
> ½ teaspoon (1.5 g) freshly ground black pepper,
>   or to taste

1. Preheat the oven to 375°F (190°C).

2. Defrost the phyllo pastry according to the directions on the package.

3. Melt the butter over low heat. Lightly brush the bottom and sides of a baking dish with a bit of the melted butter. (We use a casserole dish about the size of a chafing dish, but a 9 × 13–inch dish works, too; phyllo sheet sizes vary, so use a pan that fits the sheets you have or trim the phyllo to fit your pan.)

4. Prepare the filling: Put the fermented spinach in a colander for a few minutes to drain slightly. Meanwhile, break the eggs into a bowl and beat lightly. Mix in the feta, then add the drained spinach, flour, and black pepper.

5. Lay out the phyllo sheets and cover them with a slightly dampened, clean tea towel or plastic wrap, as the phyllo tends to dry quickly. Lay the first pastry sheet on the buttered pan; brush it lightly with the melted butter and add another sheet. Continue layering and buttering until you have used 8 to 10 sheets; this should be about half the package.

6. Spread the filling across the entire surface of the phyllo. Now, to form the top crust, repeat the layering process until the sheets are used up. If you are using a smaller pan, roll the edges under and tuck them into the sides; this makes a nice, pie-like effect.

7. Bake for 45 minutes, or until crisp and golden. Let stand for 10 minutes before cutting into squares. Serve warm or at room temperature.

Sauerkraut Strudel

serves 6

VEGETARIAN

Many cuisines wrap fillings, sweet or savory, into layers of dough. The High German word *Strudel* literally means "whirlpool," which is what the wrapped dough looks like, swirling through a soft, warm filling. Serve this sauerkraut version with applesauce and pickled vegetables, such as beets.

> 1 pound (454 g) frozen phyllo pastry
> ¾–1 cup (1½–2 sticks/168–224 g) butter, or
>   1–1¼ cups olive oil, or a combination

FILLING

> 2–3 tablespoons (28–42 g) butter
> 3 cups (480 g) diced onions
> 2 eggs
> 8 ounces (227 g) cream cheese, at room
>   temperature
> 4 cups (946 ml) Naked Kraut (page 173) or
>   any other favorite kraut
> 1 cup (113 g) grated Swiss cheese
> ½ cup (60 g) grated cheddar cheese
> 1 cup (200 g) cooked white or brown rice (this
>   is a great use for leftovers)
> 2 teaspoons (5.7 g) caraway seeds
> 2 teaspoons (2 g) dried dill weed
>   Salt and freshly ground black pepper

1. Preheat the oven to 350°F (175°C).

2. Defrost the phyllo pastry according to the package directions.

3. For the pastry, melt the ¾–1 cup butter over low heat. Lightly brush a baking sheet with a little of the melted butter.

4. For the filling, melt the 2–3 tablespoons butter in a skillet over low heat. Add the onions and sauté until translucent.

5. In a bowl, mix the eggs with the cream cheese until smooth. Add the onions to this mixture, along with the kraut, Swiss and cheddar cheeses, rice, caraway seeds, and dill, and season with salt and pepper. Mix well.

6. Lay out the phyllo sheets and cover with a slightly dampened, clean tea towel or plastic wrap, as the phyllo tends to dry quickly. Lay the first pastry sheet on the prepared baking sheet; brush it lightly with the melted butter and add another sheet. Continue layering and buttering until you have used 12 to 15 sheets.

7. Spread the filling lengthwise along the bottom third of the top sheet, in a 3-inch-wide swath, leaving a 3-inch border along the edge of the pastry. Gently fold the long sides over the filling and, starting with the short side nearest you, carefully roll up the dough until you have formed a log. Tuck the edges under the log and arrange seam side down in the middle of the baking sheet. Brush a little more melted butter over the surface.

8. Bake the strudel for 50 minutes, or until golden crisp on the outside and set on the inside.

Ferment-Forward Latkes

See photo on page 394

serves 2 as a main course, or 4 as a side dish
VEGETARIAN

Thanks to the slight acidity the ferment brings to these potato pancakes, they have a lighter flavor than their all-potato counterpart. As with Su-In Park's Kimchi Pancake (page 380), these latkes are a versatile way to use up a forgotten ferment. They can be a side dish or, with the addition of sauces, carry the meal—they're just as comfortable with sour cream as with an Asian-style peanut or dipping sauce.

- 1 cup (156 g) peeled and shredded potatoes
- 1 cup (170 g) packed drained kimchi, or any cabbage- or greens-based ferment
- 3 tablespoons (22.5 g) unbleached all-purpose flour
- 3 eggs, beaten
  Pinch of salt (optional)
- ½ cup (118 ml) peanut or coconut oil, for frying
  Sour cream or other sauce, for serving

1. Put the grated potatoes in a strainer or colander and squeeze well to remove any extra moisture.

2. Combine the potatoes, kimchi, and flour in a medium bowl and stir together. The goal is to have a nice coating of flour on the potatoes and vegetables. Mix in the eggs and add the salt, if you think it's needed.

3. Heat the oil in a large skillet over medium-high heat until it is hot. Place large spoonfuls of the potato mixture into the hot oil, pressing down on them to form patties ¼ to ½ inch thick. Brown the latkes on one side, then turn and brown the other side.

4. Serve hot, with sour cream or sauce of choice.

Rösti

serves 2 or 3 as a main dish, or 4 to 6 as a side dish
GLUTEN-FREE, VEGAN

Rösti was originally a starch-forward farmer's breakfast in Switzerland. It is generally made of potatoes and egg and fried like a pancake, very much like a latke. There are also röstis made of shredded celeriac, kohlrabi, or a combination. That shredding of the vegetable was our hint to try rösti with fermented vegetables. The flavor is bright and tangy. We often put caraway in our celeriac kraut, which rounds out the flavor.

The rösti can be small, about 3 inches in diameter, or larger pan-size cakes, like a thick crêpe. Serve them with a salad and tomato soup for a lovely dinner. You can also top them with smoked fish and roll them up.

For this recipe, it is not necessary to squeeze the brine from the krauts; it provides the liquid for the batter.

- 1 cup (234 ml) Naked Celeriac Kraut (page 199)
- 1 cup (234 ml) Kohlrabi Kraut (page 255)
- 1 cup (92 g) garbanzo bean flour
- 2 eggs
- 2–3 tablespoons (28–42 g) coconut oil, for frying

1. Combine the krauts, garbanzo flour, and eggs in a medium bowl and stir together.

2. Add enough oil to a large, heavy-bottomed skillet to coat its bottom, and heat the skillet over medium-high heat until the oil is hot. Drop spoonfuls of the rösti mixture into the hot oil, pressing down to form patties about ¼ to ½ inch thick. Brown on one side, then turn and brown the other side.

3. Serve hot.

Burmese-Style Ginger Salad (Gyin Thoke)

serves 2 as a main dish, or 4 as a side dish
Gluten-Free, Vegan option

We traveled to Myanmar in 2017, and we cannot express how impactful that trip was. Everyone we met welcomed us with kindness and love. We went for numerous reasons, one of which was to experience *laphet*—fermented green tea leaves. Myanmar is the only place where the leaves of the tea plant are eaten as greens and not just used for making tea.

Culinary traditions in Myanmar offer many superb salads (or *thoke*, the Burmese word for salad, which in literal translation means "mixed by hand"). But these salads aren't just variations of raw greens with dressing, as they are in the West. Instead, they offer a wide range of flavors and textures that come together beautifully, with a lot of wonderful little crunchy bits, such as fried garlic or shallots, chickpeas, and various roasted seeds and nuts.

We re-created this ginger salad (*gyin thoke*) based on one we enjoyed on our trip. In a way, it is similar to *laphet thoke*, but the flavors come from a more familiar palate than the (delicious) funk of fermented tea leaves, and, not to mention, the ingredients are much easier to source. We have also added more lettuce than would be traditional. This ginger salad is spicy, refreshing, and filling, and it can be enjoyed on its own as a light meal.

Note: Don't let all the prep work scare you off. It is worth it. And the leftovers are good, too, so you can always make more than you need and enjoy it again, without any of the work the second time around. As a variation, you can use any richly flavored ferment in a similar preparation.

¼ cup (36 g) sesame seeds
½ cup (80 g) pumpkin seeds
½ cup (146 g) peanuts
3–4 tablespoons (45–60 ml) peanut or coconut oil, for frying
6–8 cloves garlic, sliced
1 shallot, thinly sliced
Juice of 1 lemon
2 tablespoons (30 ml) fish sauce, or ¼ teaspoon salt and 1 teaspoon dulse
1 teaspoon (5 ml) brine from the fermented ginger (below)
4 or 5 leaves napa cabbage, finely shredded
1 small head red leaf or romaine lettuce, finely chopped
½ cup (120 g) Fermented Ginger Pickle (page 240), finely chopped
1 Roma-type tomato, diced
Chopped cilantro, for garnish

1. The first step is roasting the seeds and peanuts, separately, in a heavy-bottomed skillet. Heat the skillet over medium heat. Add the sesame seeds and toast, shaking or stirring the pan often to ensure they do not scorch. When they are lightly browned and smelling of sesame, which should take just a few minutes, they are ready. Immediately transfer them from the skillet to a small bowl; set aside.

2. Repeat this process to toast the pumpkin seeds; they will take slightly longer to toast. Let them cool, then chop them roughly and set aside in a small bowl.

3. Repeat this process for the peanuts. Again, once they are toasted and cooled, chop them roughly, then set aside in a small bowl.

4. Heat 1½ to 2 tablespoons of the oil in a small pan over medium-high heat. Add the sliced garlic, reduce the heat to medium, and fry until golden, 4 to 5 minutes. Remove the pan from the heat. Use a slotted spoon to remove the garlic from the oil; set aside on a paper towel to blot up any excess oil. Save the garlic-infused oil; it's delicious, can be used in other cooking projects, and will keep in the refrigerator for a few weeks.

5. Repeat this process to fry the sliced shallots, using another 1½ to 2 tablespoons of the oil and stirring frequently as they bubble and brown to prevent them from sticking. They will take from 6 to 10 minutes. Again, once you have removed the shallots, save this oil; it is gold for flavoring and will keep for a few weeks in the refrigerator.

6. Combine the lemon juice, fish sauce, and fermented ginger brine in a good-size salad bowl and stir to mix.

7. Now the fun part—putting it all together. Place the cabbage and the lettuce in the salad bowl and mix with the sauce until evenly coated. Set the toasted sesame seeds, toasted pumpkin seeds, toasted peanuts, fried garlic, fried shallots, chopped pickled ginger, and diced tomato in small piles along the edges, keeping them separate. Sprinkle cilantro over the lettuce mixture.

8. The arrangement makes an impressive presentation. Bring it to the table this way, and mix everything together when you're ready to serve.

MAKING CHICKEN BONE BROTH

Bone broths are truly a flavor foundation for soups, plus they are easy to make and can be frozen for long-term storage. They just require a bit of planning. Here's how we make chicken bone broth.

Put a whole chicken in a stockpot with any "extra bits"—that is, the neck or giblets, if you have them. Cover the chicken with cold water and bring it to a full boil, then turn down the heat immediately. This helps draw the flavor. Skim off any foam that develops, taking care not to remove the fat.

Let simmer for about 1 hour, then remove the whole chicken from the broth. Remove the meat from the bones to use for another dish. Then put all the bits—skin, bones, and cartilage—back in the pot. Add any vegetable scraps you've saved (fresh or frozen): onion ends or greens, celery butts, stems, peelings, and so on. Add a tablespoon of vinegar to draw the minerals from the bones. Bring the pot to a simmer again and cook all day, anywhere from 6 to 12 hours.

Strain and use immediately, or cool and freeze in portion-size amounts.

Polish Pickle Soup

serves 4
GLUTEN-FREE, VEGAN OPTION

It was a glorious spring day, in the way that only May can deliver in southern Oregon. The fields and mountains were green, the apple blossoms sprinkled the ground with petals, and the scent of lilacs wafted through the air. We were at a gathering of neighbors, talking about, well, what else, fermenting vegetables. Pickles, to be exact. Our neighbor shared that his ex-wife was Polish and she grated pickles into soups. Kirsten was intrigued and went home with some concepts, but mostly she wanted to grate a pickle.

- 6 medium potatoes, peeled and cubed
- 2 medium carrots, sliced
- 3 cups (710 ml) chicken bone broth or vegetarian broth
- 2 tablespoons (28 g) butter or sunflower oil
- 6–7 scallions, sliced
- 2 cloves garlic, minced
- ½ teaspoon (1.5 g) mustard seeds
- 1 cup (237 ml) pickle brine
- 2 large New York Deli-Style Pickles (page 216) or other lacto-fermented dill pickles, grated
- 1 teaspoon (1 g) dried dill weed or a couple of sprigs fresh dill, chopped
- Salt and freshly ground black pepper
- Minced fresh chives, for garnish
- Sliced hard-boiled eggs, for garnish (optional)

1. Put the potatoes, carrots, and broth in a medium pot. Bring to a boil, then reduce the heat and simmer until the potatoes are tender. Remove from the heat and set aside.

2. In a nonreactive soup pot, heat the butter or oil over medium heat. Toss in the scallions, garlic, and mustard seeds, and cook, stirring often, until the scallions and garlic are soft, but not browned.

3. Transfer the potatoes, carrots, and broth to the soup pot. Using a potato masher, gently mash the vegetables. You only want to break them up a bit. This will thicken your soup.

4. Add the brine, grated pickles, and dill weed. Bring the soup to a simmer, and let simmer for a few minutes to allow the flavors to meld. If the soup is too thick, you may add a bit more brine or broth.

5. Season to taste with salt and pepper, garnish with the chives and eggs, if using, and serve hot.

Braised Blaukraut

serves 6
GLUTEN-FREE

In Kirsten's childhood, this sweet and sour vegetable side dish was made with fresh cabbage, onions, and tart apples and sprinkled with a little sugar and vinegar. The acid of the added vinegar preserved the red color of the cabbage, which would otherwise turn blue with cooking. Our take on this recipe uses fermented red cabbage, onion, and apples, and the ferment's acidity preserves the beautiful color. It gets its sweetness from thick balsamic vinegar, and the flavor of the dish will be directly affected by the vinegar you use. This warm salad, alongside potatoes, is rich enough to serve as a light dinner.

Note: The quality and types of balsamic vinegars vary greatly, depending on where and how they're made. Some are thin and quite acidic, while others are thick and sweet, almost syrupy. In this recipe we use the longer-aged, thick, sweet type; it is concentrated, so you don't need much.

6 slices bacon
1 medium onion, diced
2 cups (473 ml) Blaukraut (page 190)
2–3 teaspoons (10–15 ml) aged balsamic vinegar
Raw pine nuts, for garnish

1. Fry the bacon in a heavy-bottomed pan until brown and slightly crisp. Remove the bacon from the pan, leaving behind the melted fat. Let the bacon cool, then crumble it and set aside.

2. Add the onion to the pan with the bacon fat and sauté over medium-high heat until translucent.

3. Turn off the heat, add the blaukraut, and braise in the heat remaining in the pan, stirring frequently.

4. When the blaukraut is warm, splash on the balsamic vinegar to taste and toss in the crumbled bacon.

5. Garnish with pine nuts before serving.

Palestinian Lentils and Rice (a recipe from the West Bank)

serves 4 to 6
Gluten-Free, Vegan

The loft of our barn is a one-room, off-the-grid space that has the charm of horses and goats rustling around underneath you as you sleep. Our dear friends Annaliese and Scott asked if they could live in this space after the birth of their son Zeke. They enjoyed the simplicity of the space and were able to spend three months putting all their energy into bonding. We enjoyed having a baby around and sharing meals with Scott and Annaliese, who have traveled extensively and are wonderful cooks.

This dish, made by Annaliese, was our introduction to the Middle Eastern sumac-spice blend za'atar (page 179), which she included in the rice; we have modified her recipe by including Za'atar Kraut (page 179) instead. It is a one-pot meal, although especially wonderful when served with a fresh salad or a vegetable dish. This simple meal has become a staple at our home.

½ cup (118 ml) olive oil
1 onion, diced
2 cloves garlic, minced
1 bay leaf
½ teaspoon (1.3 g) ground cumin
¼ teaspoon (0.5 g) ground turmeric
1½ cups (255 g) uncooked basmati rice
(brown if you have time, white if not)
1½ cups (300 g) uncooked lentils
6 cups (1.4 l) water
2–3 onions, sliced into rounds
½ cup (54 g) slivered almonds
2 cups (473 ml) Za'atar Kraut (page 179)

1. Heat ¼ cup of the olive oil in a heavy-bottomed pot over medium-high heat. Add the diced onion and garlic and sauté until translucent. Add the bay leaf, cumin, and turmeric and sauté for 1 minute longer.

2. Add the rice and lentils and stir until they are coated in oil. Add the water. Bring to a boil, then cover the pot and simmer over low heat until the rice and lentils are tender.

3. Meanwhile, heat the remaining ¼ cup olive oil in a heavy-bottomed skillet over medium heat. Add the sliced onion rounds and let cook, stirring occasionally, until caramelized.

4. Dry-roast the slivered almonds in a small skillet over low heat.

5. When the rice-and-lentil mixture has finished cooking, keep it in the pot or scoop it onto a serving platter. Spread the kraut evenly over the rice and lentils. Then spread the caramelized onions and sprinkle the almonds on top.

Choucroute Garni

serves 8

Gluten-Free

Traditional dishes vary depending on the region they're from and the economics that shaped family recipes. Choucroute garni as a peasant dish is very simple—perhaps just bay leaves, juniper berries, apples, onions, and a little bit of meat in the form of pork knuckles or salt pork. As this meal climbs the economic ladder, it is outfitted with bacon and sometimes many types of sausage, ham, or wild game.

As sauerkraut marched west from Germany and Eastern Europe, it landed in the Alsatian region of France, where this dish got the elegant name "dressed sauerkraut" (*choucroute* is a French modification of the German-Alsatian *Sürkrüt*). With this dressy name, it also took on elements of French cuisine, such as the use of goose or duck fat or the addition of foie gras.

Humble or fancy, this dish is a mound of slowly stewed sauerkraut served on a platter piled high with various meats. The recipe here is what Kirsten grew up eating, in many variations. It is traditionally served with plenty of mustard, whether Dijon or Bavarian (page 274), and is well complemented by crusty bread and boiled potatoes.

4 thick strips bacon

2 medium onions, diced

2 tart apples, sliced

4–6 cups (1–1.4 l) sauerkraut; try Naked (page 173), Juniper-Onion (page 176), or OlyKraut's Eastern European (page 181)

2½ cups (590 ml) Riesling or fresh apple cider, plus a splash for deglazing

1 cup (237 ml) chicken stock

2 teaspoons (4 g) juniper berries

3 or 4 bay leaves

1 teaspoon (2 g) whole peppercorns

A few sprigs parsley and thyme, tied with a cotton string

4 bratwurst sausages

4 bockwurst (or similar) sausages

Mustard, for serving

FERMENTISTA'S TIP

Rinsing Kraut

Traditional recipes call for rinsing the sauerkraut before adding it to the pot in this recipe. If you were using a very salty or canned kraut, you would definitely rinse it, but if you are using your own freshly fermented kraut, there's no need to drain or rinse.

1. Preheat the oven to 250°F (120°C).

2. In a heavy-bottomed, nonreactive pot with a lid, fry the bacon strips until they start to brown and the fat is rendered.

3. Add the onion and apple and sauté in the bacon fat until soft. Remove the bacon and chop into small pieces. Add the sauerkraut to the pot, stirring it into the bacon grease. Return the chopped bacon to the pot. Add the Riesling or apple cider, the chicken stock, and the juniper berries, bay leaves, and peppercorns. Stir everything together and place the bundled parsley or thyme on top.

4. Put the lid on the pot, set in the oven, and let cook for 2 to 3 hours.

5. About 30 minutes before serving, fry the bratwurst and bockwurst in a skillet; when they're browned on all sides, deglaze the pan with a bit more wine or cider. Pull the kraut pot out of the oven, remove and discard the herb bundle, and pour the liquid from deglazing over the kraut. Tuck the bratwurst and bockwurst into the kraut, put the lid back on the pot, and set it back in the oven to cook for another 30 minutes.

6. Serve warm, with plenty of mustard.

VARIATION
On the Stove
Here's a quick stovetop version of this dish: Fry bratwurst (omit the bacon) in a large, nonreactive pan, then remove and set aside. Add the onions and apples to the fat. When the onions and apples are caramelized, deglaze the pan with the wine or apple cider; omit the chicken broth. Add the spices, omitting the herb bundle. Add the bockwurst and simmer until warm. Return the bratwurst to the pan; when everything is warm, remove from heat and add the sauerkraut, stirring gently to warm.

Zuurkoolstamppot

serves 4

Gluten-Free, Vegan option

This Dutch dish is a mash of root vegetables, such as potatoes, carrots, parsnips, or whatever combination is available. The beauty of *stamppot* is its versatility and also that it's warm, hearty, and easy to make. This is a very thick stew, and not as smooth as mashed potatoes. It is often served with sausage as a main dish.

- 3 pounds (1.4 kg) mealy potatoes, such as russets, peeled and cut into ½- to 1-inch cubes
- 2–3 stalks celery, sliced
- 2 carrots, cut into thick slices
- ½ teaspoon (2.8 g) salt
- 2 cups (473 ml) milk, vegetable broth, or chicken broth
- 2–3 cups (473–710 ml) sauerkraut
  Minced fresh parsley or celery leaves, or fermented parsley or celery leaves

1. Put the potatoes, celery, and carrots in a soup pot and cover with water; add the salt. Bring to a boil over medium-high heat, then reduce the heat to low and let simmer until the potatoes and carrots are soft but not falling apart. Drain and mash the vegetables.

2. Return the cooked vegetables to the pot, add the milk or a rich broth and mash lightly; some of the vegetables should retain a chunky texture. Add the sauerkraut and mix everything together. Warm over low heat or in a warm oven.

3. Serve warm, garnished with parsley or celery leaves.

❋ *Stamppot* is one of the first things I think of when I think of Dutch cuisine. My family lived in Rotterdam when I was 16. It was proudly set before me when I was invited to meals with the families of friends. Translated literally, it means "stamped pot," as in mashing the vegetables. It is warm comfort food.

Zwiebelkuchen

serves 4 to 6

We first encountered *Zwiebelkuchen* in the medieval German town of Bacharach, which hugs a strip of land between the Rhine and the steep vineyard-dotted hills lining the valley.

There are a few weeks each year when the young white wine that is not finished fermenting can be bought. Called *Federweiss*, this wine is light and fruity and, we learned, packs a higher alcohol content than usual. It is traditionally paired with *Zwiebelkuchen*, an onion-rich pan pastry. We have improvised here by using fermented onions, which give this pie a bright, tart flavor that pairs nicely with white wine.

DOUGH

  1 (¼-ounce/7 g) package active dry yeast
  1 cup (237 ml) warm milk
1½ cups (180 g) unbleached all-purpose flour
  4 teaspoons (19 g) butter, at room temperature
    Oil, for greasing bowl

FILLING

  4 strips uncured bacon
½ cup (120 g) sour cream
  2 eggs
    Salt and freshly ground black pepper

  1 cup (245 g) packed Simple Onion Relish (page 286), drained

1. Begin by making the dough: In a large bowl, dissolve the yeast in the warm milk (it should feel like a comfortable warm bath to your fingers) and let stand until frothy, about 5 minutes.

2. Incorporate a cup of the flour into the milk, stirring with a wooden spoon. Add the butter and mix with your hands or the spoon to combine fully, then add enough of the remaining ½ cup flour to form a soft dough. Turn out the dough onto a floured work surface and knead it for a couple of minutes; the dough will be on the wet, sticky side.

3. Lightly grease the bowl and return the dough, flipping it over to coat it with oil. Cover the bowl with a damp kitchen towel and place in a warm spot to rise, until it has doubled in size.

4. When the dough has doubled in size, make the filling: Fry the bacon strips until crisp. Drain the bacon, saving the fat, and set aside to cool.

5. In a bowl, whisk the sour cream into the eggs. Season with salt and pepper. Crumble the bacon and add it to this mixture, along with the onion relish. (For an extra-rich pie, you can stir in a tablespoon or two of the bacon fat.)

6. Preheat the oven to 375°F (190°C).

7. Punch down the dough. Then roll it out and place on a baking sheet. Crimp the edges a bit—imagine a galette meets a pizza crust.

8. Spread the filling evenly across the top of the dough.

9. Bake the pie for 30 minutes, or until it is nicely browned and a toothpick inserted in the center comes out clean.

CHAPTER 14

Dessert

REALLY?

This chapter provided a lot of entertainment in the Shockey household during recipe development. There were, without a doubt, more raised eyebrows and eye rolls passed between the children than with any other section of the manuscript.

"Why would you put sauerkraut in a perfectly good cheesecake?" one of them asked Christopher, who, coming off the success of his sauerkraut macaroons, had decided to reproduce Great-Grandma's sacred New York cheesecake—laced with mint sauerkraut. We all agreed that it didn't have a positive mouthfeel, and it may have been the first time in the history of our family that a cheesecake went unfinished.

You can be assured that the recipes we've decided to share are the successes—the critics were vigorous and extremely discerning.

NORTHWEST GINGERED CARROT CAKE, *page 410*

Northwest Gingered Carrot Cake

See photo on page 408

serves 12

VEGETARIAN

One of our traditions is that the birthday person gets to pick the three meals on his or her birthday as well as the "cake," which is in quotes because more than one person in our family is a fan of pie rather than cake. Still, on the cake side of our family, carrot cake rules. When we were brainstorming desserts for this book, we knew we needed to tackle carrot cake.

It wasn't difficult to get to a ginger-carrot ferment for the cake, as the ferment enhances the regular version—it's somehow lighter and richer than the original, which may come from the interaction of the baking soda and the ferment. The basic recipe is from a favorite baking book, *Williams-Sonoma Essentials of Baking*. The cake is incredibly moist and spicy, so you don't need much in the way of frosting. We sometimes frost with just a light spread of sour cream. Otherwise, use your favorite cream cheese frosting.

    Butter, for greasing the pans
 2 cups (240 g) cake flour, plus a dusting
       for the pans
 2 teaspoons (9.2 g) baking powder
 2 teaspoons (9.2 g) baking soda
 ½ teaspoon (2.8 g) salt
 1 teaspoon (3.2 g) ground cinnamon
 ½ teaspoon (0.9 g) ground mace
1½ cups (340 g) sugar
 4 eggs
1¼ cups (280 g) coconut oil, melted and cooled
    Grated zest of 1 orange

 3 cups (710 ml) Carrot Kraut (page 192)
 ½ cup (50 g) walnuts or pecans, lightly toasted
       and chopped
 ½ cup (61 g) dried cranberries or raisins

1. Preheat the oven to 350°F (175°C).

2. Butter and lightly flour either two 10-inch round pans or one 9 × 13–inch rectangular pan.

3. Sift the flour, baking powder, baking soda, salt, cinnamon, and mace into a medium bowl.

4. In a large bowl, whisk together the sugar, eggs, oil, and orange zest. Stir in the carrot kraut.

5. Using a rubber spatula, fold the dry ingredients into the wet ingredients until combined.

6. Finally, add the nuts and dried fruit. Pour the batter into the prepared pans.

7. Bake until a toothpick inserted in the center of the cake comes out clean, usually 30 to 40 minutes. As soon as the middle no longer looks different than the edges and begins to crack a bit, remove the pans from the oven to preserve the moistness of the cake.

Chocolate Sauerkraut Cake with Coconut Kefir Glaze

serves 12

GLUTEN-FREE, VEGETARIAN

This recipe is by Michaela Hayes-Hodge. We interviewed Michaela for the first edition of this book. At the time she ran a small fermentation company in New York City and had a fermentation station at Gramercy Tavern. Michaela told us that she saw fermentation not only as a culinary art but also as a real part of local sustainable food systems. We are happy to report that she has continued to follow her passion and is now a co-owner of Rise & Root Farm, a 5-acre farm owned and run cooperatively by four intergenerational, multiracial, and LGBTQ+ women. They are located in the Black Dirt region of Orange County, New York, in the lower Hudson Valley. The farm is rooted in social justice, and through the healing power of food and farming they work to build a more equitable food system.

Sauerkraut chocolate cakes have bounced around in various iterations arising from the German and Eastern European immigrants to North America. The acidic ferment provides the moisture much in the way that buttermilk does in other baked goods. Michaela's version is deliciously gluten-free. It has a complex nutty flavor from the addition of buckwheat flour. The sauerkraut keeps the cake from drying out and becoming crumbly, which can be a problem for gluten-free foods.

Michaela and Kirsten talked about which krauts, beyond Naked, would work in this recipe. She originally used a turmeric-chile kraut; as we had a turmeric-pepper kraut in the refrigerator, we tried it, although with a bit of trepidation. The

cake was great. The turmeric did not stand out. How about Chipotle Squash Kraut (page 347)? We agreed that many flavors might pair well.

Butter, shortening, or oil of choice, for
  greasing the pan
⅔ cup (80 g) buckwheat flour
⅔ cup (80 g) millet flour
⅔ cup (95 g) white rice flour
⅔ cup (56 g) cocoa powder
1½ teaspoons (6.9 g) baking soda
1¼ cups (296 ml) hot water
½ cup (108 g) Earth Balance shortening or
  butter, melted
1 teaspoon (5 ml) vanilla extract
1⅓ cups (301 g) sugar
1 egg
1 cup (234 ml) Naked Kraut (page 173),
  puréed smooth

GLAZE
3 tablespoons (45 ml) coconut kefir or
  coconut milk
1 cup (114 g) confectioners' sugar, or as needed

1. Preheat the oven to 350°F (175°C).

2. Grease a 12-cup Bundt pan with the fat of your choice.

3. Combine the flours, cocoa, and baking soda in a medium bowl. Whisk together and set aside. (*Note:* Feel free to substitute 2 cups all-purpose flour for the gluten-free mix.)

4. Combine the hot water, melted shortening or butter, and vanilla in a small bowl. Whisk together and set aside.

5. In a large mixing bowl, beat the sugar with the egg until pale yellow and fluffy. Stir in the wet and dry mixtures, alternating between the two, and beginning and ending with the wet mixture.

6. Fold in the sauerkraut, then pour the cake batter into the prepared pan.

7. Bake for 45 to 55 minutes, or until a tester inserted into the center of the cake comes out clean. Let cool in the pan for about 15 minutes, then turn out on a rack.

8. To make the glaze, mix the coconut kefir and sugar together. Drizzle the glaze over the cooled cake.

Note: You can change the consistency of the glaze by using more or less sugar. For a special touch, use a thinner glaze as a base layer, then top with a layer of thicker glaze. This trick gives your glaze more texture. Your cake will look festive, and you will enjoy the more complex quality as it melts in your mouth.

You will probably eat this cake too quickly to notice, but the kefir icing is a live food and will continue to ripen (in other words, get more sour) as it sits.

Sauerkraut Coconut Macaroons

See photo on facing page

yield: 1 dozen

Gluten-Free, Vegetarian

Rinsed and drained sauerkraut has the consistency of flaked coconut in baked goods, so it only seemed natural to give it a try in our favorite gluten-free cookies. We suggest you wait to tell your tasters about the sauerkraut until after they rave.

These are moister than typical macaroons. Baking on parchment paper helps with removal of the warm macaroons to a cooling rack or straight to mouth.

   1 cup (237 ml) Naked Kraut (page 173)
   4 large egg whites
   ¾ cup (170 g) sugar
   ¼ cup (28 g) tapioca flour
  1½ teaspoons (7 ml) vanilla extract
   ¼ teaspoon (1 ml) almond extract
   2 cups (120 g) unsweetened shredded coconut

1. Preheat the oven to 325°F (160°C). Line a large baking sheet with parchment paper.

2. Rinse and drain the sauerkraut in a colander. Squeeze to remove all the moisture you can. Chop the sauerkraut to roughly the same size as your coconut to aid in the visual deception.

3. In a large bowl, combine the egg whites, sugar, tapioca flour, and vanilla and almond extracts. Add the sauerkraut and coconut and mix until well combined.

4. Drop by rounded tablespoons, about 2 inches apart, on the prepared baking sheet. Bake until lightly golden brown.

5. Let the macaroons cool on the baking sheet for 1 minute, then transfer to a wire rack to cool completely, if you can leave them alone that long.

VARIATION
Chocolate-Beet Coconut Macaroons

Use Simple Beet Kraut (page 163) in place of Naked Kraut, and add some chocolate chips—or better yet, chunks—to the mix before forming the macaroons. These will bake up to be a nice toasted pink, with the chocolate soft and gooey.

Rhubarb Fool

serves 4 to 6

GLUTEN-FREE, VEGETARIAN

Kirsten fermented rhubarb with cardamom specifically with a lacto-fermented variation of this iconic dessert in mind. Our daughter walked into the kitchen and saw the fresh strawberries and whipped cream on the counter next to where Kirsten was working. Her finger was headed for the cream when, mid-dip, she noticed the jar of fermented rhubarb. "Oh no, really?" she asked.

It turned out to be a hit and not nearly as heavy as its syrupy, cooked counterpart.

- 1 cup (260 g) Fermented Rhubarb Infused with Ginger and Cardamom (page 320)
- 2 cups (284 g) fresh strawberries
- 3 tablespoons (36 g) sugar
  Zest of 1 lemon
- 1 pint (473 ml) whipping cream
  A few drops of vanilla extract

1. Combine the fermented rhubarb, strawberries, sugar, and lemon zest in a food processor and blend together.

2. Combine the whipping cream and vanilla in a large bowl and whip until stiff. (*Note:* We don't add any sugar. Feel free to make the cream to your taste.)

3. To serve as a fool, fold the rhubarb-strawberry sauce into the whipped cream. Or, for more of a spectacle, layer the sauce and cream in tall parfait glasses.

SAUERKRAUT COCONUT MACAROONS

Scum

THE GOOD, THE BAD, AND THE UGLY

Let's demystify scum, a.k.a. the stuff on top of the brine that shouldn't be there. What follows is a gallery of images to help you assess the characters growing on your ferment.

Foam Is Harmless

The first thing that might appear on the surface is foam. It doesn't need removing unless the amount becomes thick and unwieldy. We normally leave foam undisturbed until the ferment is finished, as it tends to settle down. The less you touch your brine, the less likely you are to contaminate it.

Remove foam if it's excessive. Otherwise, leave it alone. A thick brine layer is important, and every time you dip into the crock, the brine level falls. When the active fermentation is finished, you can remove all the foam and other scum and enjoy the beautiful ferment underneath.

A Kahm-mon Problem

Kahm yeast is a harmless surface yeast. Because it is oxygen-loving, it will show up on any exposed surface of a ferment over time when given the chance. On brine, when touched, a film of Kahm yeast breaks apart into tiny floating flecks and can take a long time and a lot of patience to remove. And the next day it is back with a vengeance. If it is just a thin film, it is better to stir it under daily and to wipe off the sides of your vessel with a clean cloth. Doing this daily will drown it.

A thick, frothy layer of Kahm yeast should be removed. Over the long term, an excessive amount of yeast will cause the ferment to lose acidity, which can leave it open to contamination by other microbes and potentially make it not safe to eat. If your brine-based ferment has a healthy surface layer of yeast and has been at room temperature for a longer time, be sure to check that the ferment is still acidic before consuming it. A properly acidic ferment smells and tastes acidic, or pickle-y. The surest confirmation is to test the brine with a pH meter or pH strip; the pH should be 4.6 or below.

Interestingly, the formation of Kahm yeast is much less likely to happen in a dry-brine packed ferment such as sauerkraut, a relish, or a whole-leaf ferment. In this case, a thick layer of yeast can be a sign that your ferment—or at least its top layer—has not been maintaining an anaerobic environment. Once the offending yeast is removed, and possibly also the top layer of your ferment, you will reach the deeper layers of ferment that were not exposed to oxygen, and the protective acidity here will be intact.

Over the years we have found a few tricks to help control Kahm.

» **When preparing your ferment,** plan to use the burping method (page 44) or other system that keeps oxygen out of the ferment.

» **In an active fermentation,** if you see thick or copious amounts of yeast, remove as much of it as you can (this is a meditation for sure). If your ferment is brine-based, top it off with more brine to keep everything submerged and to lessen the headspace in the fermentation vessel. For any ferment, you can use a spritz to help keep the yeast at bay.

» **If your ferment is finished,** remove the yeast and make sure there is as little headspace as possible in your storage container; transfer the ferment to a smaller jar if necessary. Tighten the lid and store in the fridge. It is unlikely to return.

Remove Surface Mold

You will easily recognize the bluish furry stuff or sometimes spots of a brownish-orange gelatinous substance. Mold is no good, but as long as it stays on top of the brine, your veggies are safe and anaerobic. Simply spoon it off as it develops.

Remove the mold by carefully ladling it out; then wipe down the sides of your fermentation vessel with a clean paper towel. You can also use the leaf topper, or whatever primary follower you have in place, to capture the mold; then toss the leaf, wipe the sides, and replace with a new leaf. If the brine level in this jar is now a little low, top off with fresh brine solution. Then replace the cloth or lid that is covering your fermentation vessel with a clean one.

Keep Things Anaerobic

If fermenting or fermented vegetables become exposed to oxygen for a period of time, the exposed portion could become rotten and not safe to eat. It will appear discolored, soft, even a bit slimy, and sometimes dry with a white film or mold. With oxygen exposure, yeasts, slime organisms, and mold have been given a chance to move in. In general, though, your whole batch is not lost.

DRY-BRINED FERMENTS

For a dry-brined ferment, remove any followers and unappetizing top layers until you reach the level where the brine or tight packing is keeping things anaerobic. At this level, the ferment should be crispy and vibrantly colored. Remove just a little more of the ferment here to make sure you got out all the contamination, especially in the presence of mold.

Carefully wipe the sides of the crock or jar, so that later the good ferment won't be tainted as you pull it out.

BRINE-PICKLED FERMENTS

For brine-pickled vegetables, the whole vegetable will be lost if part of it pokes out of the brine. Here's how to handle that situation.

Early in the fermentation process, just poke the pickle back under the brine and add more brine if necessary.

Often, if you remove the brazen floaters, the rest of the vegetables still submerged under the brine will be fine. Use a clean, nonreactive utensil to check. Add brine if the level is low.

If you don't catch exposed pickles early or they become exposed during the storage period, veggies can become so soft they will almost disintegrate.

Sometimes an entire batch of brine-pickled vegetables is unsafe to eat and should be tossed. Look out for these signs:

» If pickled vegetables are unnaturally light pink, it could mean that the lactic acid bacteria were unable to thrive and got overwhelmed by yeast. (*But note:* Some salts can cause pinkish brine, and some veggies bleed pink into the ferment, including beets, red onions, pink turnips, pink or red radishes, red cabbage, radicchio, and shiso leaves.)

» If pickled vegetables are soft or slimy, they are also unsafe. This texture issue is usually related to insufficient acidity caused by one of the following:
   • fermenting temperature too high
   • not enough salt to overwhelm the slime-producing organisms
   • uneven salt distribution

Toss unsafe batches of brine-pickled vegetables and begin again. You want only crispy, bright-tasting pickles.

Watch your brine levels. The kraut on the left came out of the brine; the kraut on the right is still safe and tasty.

Here, we see a thin layer of Kahm yeast. See A Kahm-mon Problem, page 414.

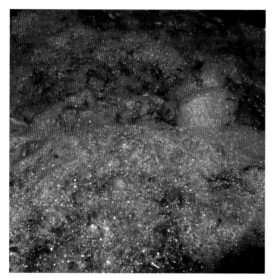

This is the same batch of kraut as seen in the photo at top left, but 3 days later. You should remove this foamy scum if you can do so without exposing the kraut.

This is an extreme example of why using a grape leaf or parchment paper helps keep your ferment safe (the likelihood you'll see this increases with a lot of oxygen and neglect). Carefully remove the leaf and its colony and clean the sides of the container.

This brain-like pattern is a thick layer of Kahm yeast on raspberries that were not kept under the brine (as we preach), so all those berries also had to be removed. See page 414 for information on removing Kahm yeast.

Small flecks of mold have formed on bits of escaped vegetables in this brine. You should remove them when you see them.

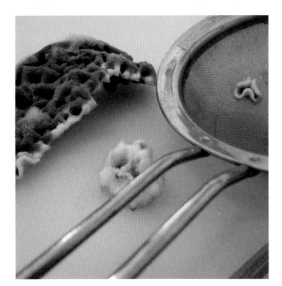

Remove surface mold with a strainer.

These beets continued to ferment in storage. When the lid was removed, they "climbed" out of the jar as the CO_2 was released. They are safe to eat.

Resources

For any fermenting supplies, check your local kitchen and cooking stores first. Thanks to the popularity of the fermenting arts, most of these shops carry a wide variety of supplies. You might just find everything you need.

We also encourage you to look around in your community. So many folks are making and doing these days; look local to find your tribe.

Crocks and Accessories

For new stoneware crocks, check your local hardware store. This will probably be your most cost-effective source, as shipping heavy stoneware can be expensive. Also, your local potters may be making crocks, both straight-sided or with a water seal. The parts to make your own airlock and jar systems, complete airlock jar systems, and pH indicators are available at brewing supply retailers.

There are countless online retailers of gizmos for fermentation. Here are some we have interacted with.

ADAM FIELD POTTERY
https://adamfieldpottery.com
Traditional onggi pots and a fun time-lapse video of the pot-making process

ChouAmi—The Little Fermenter
https://chouami.com
Fermentation kits for both Le Parfait jars or mason jars; high-quality stainless steel airlock systems

INFERMENT
Hadar Iron
https://inferment.com
A clay worker and passionate fermenter whose work is beautiful and website very informative

LEHMAN'S
https://lehmans.com
A great place for many hard-to-find homesteading goodies. They have a nice selection of fermenting supplies.

MUDSLIDE STONEWARE
Colin Dyck
www.mudslidestoneware.com
Beautiful handmade crocks with water seals

PRESERVED
Elizabeth Vecchiarelli
https://preservedgoods.com
A wonderful brick-and-mortar in Oakland, a little fermentation toy store with all the incredible selection of goodies available online

ROOTS & HARVEST

https://rootsandharvest.com

Large selection of fermentation equipment as well as other homesteading tools

THE SAUSAGE MAKER

https://sausagemaker.com

Polish-style fermenting crocks, split-style stone-weighted followers, and a few hand-cranked cabbage shredders

Vegetables, Herbs, and Spices

HAITAI SEEDS (AGROHAITAI LTD.)

https://agrohaitai.com

Stem mustard as well as other Asian vegetable seeds

BURLAP & BARREL

https://burlapandbarrel.com

High-quality, well-sourced herbs and spices

MOUNTAIN ROSE HERBS

https://mountainroseherbs.com

High-quality, certified-organic herbs and spices from a source with sustainable agricultural practices. A good place to find schisandra berries if you can't get them locally.

Informational and Educational Websites

THE FERMENTATION SCHOOL

https://fermentationschool.com

Collective of women throughout the world teaching fermentation

FERMENT NERDS LETTER

https://fermentnerds.substack.com

Kirsten's free subscription newsletter where we head down fermentation rabbit holes. Paid subcribers support her work and get more recipes.

FERMENT WORKS

https://ferment.works

Our own website, with recipes and years of posts

WILD FERMENTATION

https://wildfermentation.com

Sandor Katz's website

Plants Database

NATURAL RESOURCES CONSERVATION SERVICE

https://plants.usda.gov

Fresh Olives for Sale

FAIRVIEW ORCHARDS

https://fairvieworchards.com

Endnotes

[1]Chan, Miin, et al., "Microorganisms in Whole Botanical Fermented Foods Survive Processing and Simulated Digestion to Affect Gut Microbiota Composition," *Frontiers in Microbiology* 12 (2021).

[2]Zhou, Xin-Wei, Hong-Fang Liu, and Xin-Huai Zhao, "The Potencies of Three Microorganisms to Dissipate Four Organophosphorus Pesticides in Three Food Materials During Traditional Fermentation," *Journal of Food Science and Technology* 52, no. 11 (2015): 7353–7360.

[3]Scheers, Nathalie, et al., "Increased Iron Bioavailability from Lactic-Fermented Vegetables Is Likely an Effect of Promoting the Formation of Ferric Iron (Fe(3+))," *European Journal of Nutrition* 55, no. 1 (2016): 373–382.

[4]Hunaefi, Dase, Divine Nkonyam Akumo, and Iryna Smetanska, "Effect of Fermentation on Antioxidant Properties of Red Cabbage," *Food Biotechnology* 27, no. 1 (2013): 66–85.

[5]O'Mahony, Liam, Mübeccel Akdis, and Cezmi A. Akdis, "Regulation of the Immune Response and Inflammation by Histamine and Histamine Receptors," *Journal of Allergy and Clinical Immunology* 128, no. 6 (2011): 1153–1162.

[6]Ekici, Kamil, and Hayri Coskun, "Histamine Content of Some Commercial Vegetable Pickles," *Pakistan Journal of Nutrition* 3, no. 3 (2004): 197–198.

[7]Karami, Ali, et al., "The Presence of Microplastics in Commercial Salts from Different Countries," *Scientific Reports* 7 no. 1 (2017): 1–11.

[8]Al-Hotti, S. and B. S. Kamel, "Utilization of Sea Water in Vegetable Fermentation," *Enzyme and Microbial Technology* 3, no. 4 (1981): 353–356. https://www.sciencedirect.com/science/article/abs/pii/0141022981900132

[9]Bae, Joon-Yong, et al., "Effects of *Lactobacillus plantarum* and *Leuconostoc mensenteroides* Probiotics on Human Seasonal and Avian Influenze Viruses," *Journal of Microbiology and Biotechnology* 28, no. 6 (2018): 893–901.

[10]Dhar, D., and A. Mohanty, "Gut Microbiota and Covid-19: Possible Link and Implications," *Virus Research*, 285, no. 198018, (2020): 1–5.

[11]Kim, H. S. "Do an Altered Gut Microbiota and an Associated Leaky Gut Affect COVID-19 Severity?" *mBio*, 12, no.1 (2021): 1–9.

[12]Yeoh, Y. K., et al., "Gut Microbiota Composition Reflects Disease Severity and Dysfunctional Immune Responses in Patients with COVID-19," *Gut*, 70, no. 4 (2021): 698–706.

[13]Paramithiotis, Spiros, et al., "Evolution of the Microbial Community During Traditional Fermentation of Globe Artichoke Immature Inflorescence." *International Journal of Clinical & Medical Microbiology* 1 (2016). https://doi.org/10.15344/2456-4028/2016/117.

[14]Mintz, Sidney W., and Daniela Schlettwein-Gsell. "Food Patterns in Agrarian Societies: The 'Core-Fringe-Legume Hypothesis' A Dialogue." *Gastronomica* 1, no. 3 (2001): 40–52., https://doi.org/10.1525/gfc.2001.1.3.40.

Bibliography

Allen, Zel, and Reuben Allen. "Onion Aficionados Weep." *Vegetarians in Paradise.* https://vegparadise.com /highestperch312.html.

Atkinson, Catherine, and Trish Davies. *East European Kitchen.* New York: Hermes House, 2001.

Bae, Joon-Yong, Jin Il Kim, Sehee Park, Kirim Yoo, In-Ho Kim, Wooha Joo, Byng Hee Ryu, Mee Sook Park, Ilseob Lee, and Man-Seong Park. "Effects of *Lactobacillus plantarum* and *Leuconostoc mesenteroides* Probiotics on Human Sesonal and Avian Influenza Viruses." *Journal of Microbiology and Biotechnology* 28, no. 6 (2018): 893–901.

Barrangou, Rodolphe, Sung-Sik Yoon, Frederick Breidt Jr., Henry P. Fleming, and Todd R. Klaenhammer. "Characterization of Six *Leuconostoc fallax* Bacteriophages Isolated from an Industrial Sauerkraut Fermentation." *Applied and Environmental Microbiology* 68, no. 11 (2002): 5452–58.

Barrett, Francis. "Pepper and Peppers." *Iberia Nature.* https://iberianature.com/material/peppers.html.

Battcock, Mike, and Sue Azam-Ali. *Fermented Fruits and Vegetables: A Global Perspective.* FAO Agricultural Services Bulletin no. 134. FAO, 1998. https://fao.org /3/x0560e/x0560e00.htm.

Baudar, Pascal. *Wildcrafted Fermentation: Exploring, Transforming, and Preserving the Wild Flavors of Your Local Terroir.* White River Junction: Chelsea Green, 2020.

Belleme, John, and Jan Belleme. *Japanese Foods That Heal: Using Traditional Japanese Ingredients to Promote Health, Longevity & Well-Being.* North Clarendon: Tuttle, 2007.

Bergqvist, Sharon W., Ann-Sofie Sandberg, Nils-Gunnar Carlsson, and Thomas Andlid. "Improved Iron Solubility in Carrot Juice Fermented by Homo- and Hetero-Fermentative Lactic Acid Bacteria." *Food Microbiology* 22, no. 1 (2005): 53–61.

Bisakowski, Barbara, Avtar S. Atwal, Nancy Gardner, and Claude P. Champagne. "Effect of Lactic Acid Fermentation of Onions (*Allium cepa*) on the Composition of Flavonol Glucosides." *International Journal of Food Science and Technology* 42, no. 7 (2007): 783–89.

Bitterman, Mark. *Salted: A Manifesto on the World's Most Essential Mineral, with Recipes.* Berkeley: Ten Speed, 2010.

Body Ecology. "5 Unusual Leafy Green Vegetables You Should Know (and Eat!)." July 23, 2008. https://bodyecology.com/articles/5_unusual_leafy _green_vegetables_you_should_know-php.

Braverman, Lewis E., and David S. Cooper, eds. *Werner & Ingbar's The Thyroid: A Fundamental and Clinical Text.* 10th ed. Philadelphia: Lippincott Williams & Wilkins, 2013.

Bremness, Lesley, and Jill Norman. *The Complete Book of Herbs & Spices.* New York: Viking Penguin, 1995.

Burns, Cortney. *Nourish Me Home: 125 Soul-Sustaining, Elemental Recipes.* San Francisco: Chronicle Books, 2020.

Caruso, Frank L., Peter R. Bristow, and Peter V. Oudemans. "Cranberries: The Most Intriguing Native North American Fruit." *APSnet.* https://apsnet.org /edcenter/apsnetfeatures/pages/cranberries.aspx.

Chan, Miin, Di Liu, Yingying Wu, Fan Yang, and Kate Howell. "Microorganisms in Whole Botanical Fermented Foods Survive Processing and Simulated Digestion to Affect Gut Microbiota Composition." *Frontiers in Microbiology* 12 (2021).

Cohen, H. W., S. M. Hailpern, J. Fang, and M. H. Alderman. "Sodium Intake and Mortality in the NHANES II Follow-up Study." *American Journal of Medicine* 119, no. 3 (2006): 7–14.

Comas-Basté, Oriol, Sònia Sánchez-Pérez, Maria Teresa Veciana-Nogués, Mariluz Latorre-Moratalla, and María del Carmen Vidal-Carou. "Histamine Intolerance: The Current State of the Art." *Biomolecules* 10, no. 8: 1181. 14 Aug. 2020.

Davis, Jeanine M., and Jacqulyn Greenfield. "Cultivating Ramps: Wild Leeks of Appalachia." In *Trends in New Crops and New Uses*, edited by J. Janick and A. Whipkey, 449–52. ASHS Press, 2002. https://hort.purdue.edu /newcrop/ ncnu02/v5-449.html.

Dhar, D., and A. Mohanty, "Gut Microbiota and Covid-19: Possible Link and Implications." *Virus Research* 285, no. 198018 (2020): 1–5.

Dworkin, Martin, Stanley Falkow, Eugene Rosenberg, Karl-Heinz Schleifer, and Erko Stackebrandt, eds. *The Prokaryotes: A Handbook on the Biology of Bacteria: Proteobacteria: Alpha and Beta Subclasses*. 3rd ed. Vol. 5. New York: Springer, 2006.

Ekici, K., and H. Coskun. "Histamine Contents of Some Commercial Vegetable Pickles." *Pakistan Journal of Nutrition* 3, no. 3 (2004): 197–98.

Emory University. "Beneficial Bacteria Help Repair Intestinal Injury by Inducing Reactive Oxygen Species." (2011): *ScienceDaily*. https://sciencedaily.com /releases/2011/05/110510151219.htm.

Espsäter, Anna Maria. "Slow Food in South Korea: An Introduction to Traditional Korean Cuisine— From Kimchi to Bibimbap." *Transitions Abroad*. https://transitionsabroad.com/listings/travel /travel_to_eat/slow_food_in_korea.shtml.

Fallon, Sally, and Mary G. Enig. *Nourishing Traditions: The Cookbook that Challenges Politically Correct Nutrition and Diet Dictocrats*. 2nd ed. New Trends, 2001.

Fleming, H. P., M. A. Daeschel, R. F. McFeeters, and M. D. Pierson. "Butyric Acid Spoilage of Fermented Cucumbers." *Journal of Food Science* 54, no. 3 (1989).

Floyd, Keith. *Floyd's Thai Food*. London: HarperCollins, 2006.

Goldstein, Darra. *Beyond the North Wind: Russia in Recipes and Lore*. Berkeley: Ten Speed, 2020.

Halász, Anna. "Lactic Acid Bacteria," in *Food Quality and Standards*, ed. Radomir Lasztity, 70–82. Vol. 3, *Encyclopedia of Life Support Systems*. Oxford: Eolss, 2009.

Henderson, Judy, Rose Massey, Carrie Thompson, and Lillie Tunstall. "Pickle and Pickle Product Problems." FCSW-497-05. North Carolina Cooperative Extension, 2001.

Hercules, Olia. *Summer Kitchens: Recipes and Reminiscences from Every Corner of Ukraine*. Richmond, CA: Weldon Owen, 2020.

Hui, Y. H., Sue Ghazala, Dee M. Graham, K. D. Murrell, and Wai-Kit Nip, eds. *Handbook of Vegetable Preservation and Processing*. New York: Marcel Dekker, 2004.

Hunaefi, Dase, Divine Nkonyam Akumo, and Iryna Smetanska. "Effect of Fermentation on Antioxidant Properties of Red Cabbages." *Food Biotechnology* 27, no. 1 (2013): 66–85.

Jaffrey, Madhur. *A Taste of the Far East*. New York: Carol Southern Books 1993.

Janiszewska-Turak E., K. Rybak, K. Pobiega, A. Nikodem, and A. Gramza-Michałowska. "Sustainable Production and Characteristics of Dried Fermented Vegetables." *Fermentation* 8, no. 11 (2022): 659. https://doi.org/10.3390/fermentation8110659

Kallas, John. "Making Dandelions Palatable." *Backwoods Home Magazine*, July/August 2003. https:// backwoodshome.com/articles2/kallas82.html.

Karami, Ali, Abolfazl Golieskardi, Cheng Keong Choo, Vincent Larat, Tamara S. Galloway, and Babak Salamatinia. "The Presence of Microplastics in Commercial Salts from Different Countries." *Scientific Reports* 7, no.1 (2017): 1–11.

Katz, Sandor Ellix. *Wild Fermentation: The Flavor, Nutrition, and Craft of Live-Culture Foods*. White River Junction: Chelsea Green, 2003.

Kim, H. S. "Do an Altered Gut Microbiota and an Associated Leaky Gut Affect COVID-19 Severity?" *mBio* 12, no. 1, (2021): 1–9.

"Kimchi." *Magazine F*, no. 12 (2021): 1–151.

Kurlansky, Mark. *Salt: A World History*. New York: Penguin, 2003.

Lewin, Alex. *Real Food Fermentation: Preserving Whole Fresh Food with Live Cultures in Your Home Kitchen*. Beverly, MA: Quarry Books, 2012.

Manay, N. Shakuntala, and M. Shadaksharaswamy. *Foods: Facts and Principles.* 2nd ed. Delhi: New Age International, 2001.

Manjoo, Farhad. "Tipping the Balance for Kitchen Scales." *New York Times,* September 13, 2011.

Martin, Geoffrey. *Industrial and Manufacturing Chemistry: A Practical Treatise.* 6th ed. Philosophical Library, 1955. First published 1913 by Appleton.

Merritt, Marlene. "Your Patients Are Malnourished . . . And So Are You." *Acupuncture Today* 12, no. 9 (September 2011).

Miller, Greg. "Mind-Altering Bugs." *Science.* August 29, 2011. https://science.org/content/article/mind-altering-bugs

Mintz, Sidney W., and Daniela Schlettwein-Gsell. "Food Patterns in Agrarian Societies: The 'Core-Fringe-Legume Hypothesis' A Dialogue." *Gastronomica* 1, no. 3 (2001): 40–52. https://doi.org/10.1525/gfc.2001.1.3.40.

Mollison, Bill. *The Permaculture Book of Ferment and Human Nutrition.* Tagari Publications, 1993.

Mouritsen, Ole G., and Klavs Styrbaek. *Tsukemono: Decoding the Art and Science of Japanese Pickling.* Cham, Switzerland: Springer International, 2021.

Mueller, Kristen, Caroline Ash, Elizabeth Pennisi, and Orla Smith. "The Gut Microbiota." *Science* 336, no. 6086 (June 2012): 1245.

Nicholson, Jeremy K., Elaine Holmes, James Kinross, Remy Burcelin, Glenn Gibson, Wei Jia, and Sven Pettersson. "Host-Gut Microbiota Metabolic Interactions." *Science* 336, no. 6086 (June 2012): 1262–67.

O'Mahony, Liam, Mübeccel Akdis, and Cezmi A. Akdis. "Regulation of the Immune Response and Inflammation by Histamine and Histamine Receptors." *Journal of Allergy and Clinical Immunology* 128, no. 6 (2011): 1153–62.

Panda, Smita H., Mousumi Parmanick, and Ramesh C. Ray. "Lactic Acid Fermentation of Sweet Potato (*Ipomoea batatas* L.) into Pickles." *Journal of Food Processing and Preservation* 31, no. 1 (February 2007): 83–101.

Paramithiotis, Spiros, Agapi Doulgeraki, Alexandra Vrelli, George-John E. Nychas, and Eleftherios H. Drosinos. "Evolution of the Microbial Community During Traditional Fermentation of Globe Artichoke Immature Inflorescence." *International Journal of Clinical & Medical Microbiology.* (2016): 1. https://doi.org/10.15344/2456-4028/2016/117

Pederson, Carl S., and Margaret N. Albury. *The Sauerkraut Fermentation.* Bulletin 824. New York State Agricultural Experiment Station, 1969.

Pennisi, Elizabeth. "Do Gut Bugs Practice Mind Control?" *Science.* January 31, 2011. https://www.science.org/content/article/do-gut-bugs-practice-mind-control.

Pérez-Díaz, Ilenys M., Fred Breidt Jr, Ronald W. Buescher, Francisco N. Arroyo-López, Rufino Jiménez-Díaz, Antonio Garrido-Fernández, Joaquín Bautista-Gallego, Sung-Sik Yoon, and Suzanne D. Johanningsmeier. "Fermented and Acidified Vegetables" in *Compendium of Methods for the Microbiological Examination of Foods.* American Public Health Association: 2015. https://doi.org/10.2105/MBEF.0222.056.

Plengvidhya, Vethachai, Fredrick Breidt Jr., Zhongjing Lu, and Henry P. Fleming. "DNA Fingerprinting of Lactic Acid Bacteria in Sauerkraut Fermentations." *Applied and Environmental Microbiology* 73, no. 23 (2007): 7697–702.

Prabakaran, Usha R. *Usha's Pickle Digest: The Perfect Pickle Recipe Book,* Chennai: Pebble Green, 1998.

Price, R. H. *Sweet Potato Culture for Profit: A Full Account of the Origin, History and Botanical Characteristics of the Sweet Potato.* Texas Farm and Ranch, 1896.

Roberts, J. S., and D. R. Kidd. "Lactic Acid Fermentation of Onions." *LWT—Food Science and Technology* 38, no. 2 (March 2005): 185–90.

Sakai, Sonoko. *Japanese Home Cooking: Simple Meals, Authentic Flavors.* Boulder: Roost Books, 2019.

"Sauerkraut: Problems and Solutions." Oregon State University Extension Service, March 2013.

Scheers, Nathalie, Lena Roassander-Hulthen, Inga Torsdottir, and Ann-Sofie Sandberg. "Increased Iron Bioavailability from Lactic-Fermented Vegetables Is Likely an Effect of Promoting the Formation of Ferric Iron (Fe(3+))." *European Journal of Nutrition* 55, no. 1 (2016): 373–82.

Shibamoto, Takayuki, and Leonard F. Bjeldanes. *Introduction to Food Toxicology*. San Diego: Academic Press, 1993.

Shockey, Kirsten K., and Christopher Shockey. *Fiery Ferments: 70 Stimulating Recipes for Hot Sauces, Spicy Chutneys, Kimchis with Kick, and Other Blazing Fermented Condiments*. North Adams: Storey, 2017.

Stein, Rob. "Microbes May Play Crucial Role in Human Health, Researchers Discovering." *Washington Post*, October 9, 2011.

Stern, Jane, and Michael Stern. *The Lexicon of Real American Food*. Guilford, CT: Lyons, 2011.

Tateno, Machiko. *Japanese Pickled Vegetables: 130 Homestyle Recipes for Traditional Brined, Vinegared and Fermented Pickles*. Tokyo: Tuttle, 2019.

Tezla, Albert, ed. *Ocean at the Window: Hungarian Prose and Poetry since 1945*. University of Minnesota Press, 1980.

Trail, A. C., H. P. Fleming, C. T. Young, and R. F. McFeeters. "Chemical and Sensory Characterization of Commercial Sauerkraut." *Journal of Food Quality* 19, no. 1 (1996): 15–30.

"Virtuous White Produce" in "Health & Science." *The Week*, October 7, 2011: 22. https://theweek.com/articles/481444/health--science.

Volokh, Anne, and Mavis Manus. *The Art of Russian Cuisine*. New York: Macmillan, 1983.

Vorbeck, Marie L., Leonard R. Mattick, Frank A. Lee, and Carl S. Pederson. "Volatile Flavor of Sauerkraut. Gas Chromatographic Identification of a Volatile Acidic Off-Odor." *Journal of Food Science* 26, no. 6 (November 1961): 569–72.

Wood, B. J. B., and W. H. Holzapfel, eds. *The Genera of Lactic Acid Bacteria*. Vol. 2. Springer Science+Business Media, 1995.

Yeoh, Y. K., et al., "Gut Microbiota Composition Reflects Disease Severity and Dysfunctional Immune Responses in Patients with COVID-19," *Gut* 70, no. 4 (2021): 698–706.

Yoon, Sook-ja. *Good Morning, Kimchi! Forty Different Kinds of Traditional & Fusion Kimchi Recipes*. Elizabeth, NJ: Hollym International, 2005.

Zhou, Xin-Wei, Hong-Fang Liu, and Xin-Huai Zhao. "The Potencies of Three Microorganisms to Dissipate Four Organophosphorous Pesticides in Three Food Materials During Traditional Fermentation." *Journal of Food Science and Technology* 52, no. 11 (2015): 7353–60.

Metric Conversion Charts

Unless you have finely calibrated measuring equipment, conversions between US and metric measurements will be somewhat inexact. It's important to convert the measurements for all the ingredients in a recipe to maintain the same proportions as the original.

GENERAL FORMULAS	
Ounces to grams	multiply ounces by 28.35
Grams to ounces	multiply grams by 0.035
Pounds to grams	multiply pounds by 453.5
Pounds to kilograms	multiply pounds by 0.45
Cups to liters	multiply cups by 0.24
Fahrenheit to Celsius	subtract 32 from Fahrenheit temperature, multiply by 5, then divide by 9
Celsius to Fahrenheit	multiply Celsius temperature by 9, divide by 5, then add 32

APPROXIMATE EQUIVALENTS BY WEIGHT	
US	**Metric**
¼ ounce	7 grams
½ ounce	14 grams
1 ounce	28 grams
1¼ ounces	35 grams
1½ ounces	40 grams
2½ ounces	70 grams
4 ounces	112 grams
5 ounces	140 grams
8 ounces	228 grams
10 ounces	280 grams
15 ounces	425 grams
16 ounces (1 pound)	454 grams
0.035 ounces	1 gram
1.75 ounces	50 grams
3.5 ounces	100 grams
8.75 ounces	250 grams
1.1 pounds	500 grams
2.2 pounds	1 kilogram

APPROXIMATE EQUIVALENTS BY VOLUME	
US	**Metric**
1 teaspoon	5 milliliters
1 tablespoon	15 milliliters
¼ cup	60 milliliters
½ cup	120 milliliters
1 cup	230 milliliters
1¼ cups	300 milliliters
1½ cups	360 milliliters
2 cups	460 milliliters
2½ cups	600 milliliters
3 cups	700 milliliters
4 cups (1 quart)	0.95 liter
1.06 quarts	1 liter
4 quarts (1 gallon)	3.8 liters

Acknowledgments

We acknowledge all the makers and traditions throughout time and all places that have done the work; we only hope to spread the magic of working with microbes. We also feel incredibly honored to be part of the current worldwide fermentation community. We can't begin to express our gratitude for all the readers of the first edition of this book. Your interest took the book and us to places and on journeys we'd never imagined. Thank you.

We thank all those who came to our farmers' market booth and book signings, tasted our creations, and told us their stories. We thank our students—at demonstrations, in-person classes, and online—who have continued to teach and inspire us.

There comes the point when you think you can't possibly ask your friends to hear one more word about sauerkraut or fermentation. Yet they continued to read and reread our words and are still our friends. It's because of their patience and time that the orginal book came into existence.

We're fortunate to have gotten to know amazing and humble fermenters throughout the world. These pioneers of nouveau vegetable fermentation are passionate about sustainable food systems and in their approaches to the art and the cause. We wish we could name all the hundreds we have met throughout these years; we certainly would not be working on this second edition without you. We feel deep gratitude for the support of Kathryn Lukas, Sash Sunday, Alex Hozven, Kevin Farley, Addie Rose Holland, Jennifer Sauter-Sargent, Tiffani Beckman McNeil, Michaela Hayes, Mary Alionis, and Helen Bartels, who took part in the first edition, and for Jessica Alonzo, Sarah Arrazola, Taylor Hanna, Mara Jane King, Meredith Leigh, Soirée-Leone, Pao Yu Liu, Su-In Park, Nao Sadewic, Sonoko Sakai, and Sebastian Vargo, who had a hand in the second edition. *Fermented Vegetables* is richer for your stories and recipes.

And then we found Storey Publishing and all the great folks who brought the first edition of this book to a tangible reality. We are deeply grateful to everyone on Team Storey whom we worked with directly or indirectly throughout every step. So many on the team have been behind this book's success since its publication.

Notes

Index

Continue Your Fermentation Adventure

with More Books from Kirsten and Christopher Shockey

Expert guidance and step-by-step photographs provide all the knowledge you need to craft the perfect batch of homemade cider. Sparkling or still, dry or sweet, clear or cloudy, funky or mellow—prepare to explore the wild and wonderful world of cidermaking.

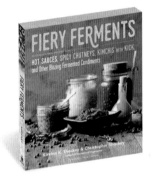

Expand your fermented repertoire with more than 70 recipes for spicy sauces, mustards, chutneys, and relishes from around the globe. An additional 40 recipes for breakfast foods, snacks, entrées, and beverages highlight many uses for the hot ferments.

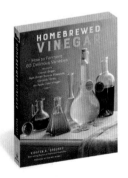

With recipes for 60 delicious varieties of vinegar, this in-depth guide also covers the science of vinegar and the basics of equipment, brewing, bottling, and aging, along with insights into vinegar-making traditions around the world.

Turn humble beans and grains into umami-rich, probiotic-packed superfoods. Master the fundamentals of fermenting soybeans and rice, then go beyond the customary ingredients with creative alternatives including quinoa, lentils, oats, and more.

JOIN THE CONVERSATION. Share your experience with this book, learn more about Storey Publishing's authors, and read original essays and book excerpts at storey.com. Look for our books wherever quality books are sold or call 800-441-5700.